Urban Life and Urban Landscape Series

Welcome to Heights High

The Crippling Politics of Restructuring America's Public Schools

DIANA TITTLE

Ohio State University Press
Columbus

Library of Congress Cataloging-in-Publication Data

Tittle, Diana, 1950–
    Welcome to Heights High :   the crippling politics of restructuring America's public schools /
Diana Tittle.
        p.   cm.   —   (Urban life and urban landscape series)
    Includes bibliographical references and index.
    ISBN 0-8142-0682-4 (alk. paper).   —   ISBN 0-8142-0683-2 (pbk.   :   alk. paper)
    1. High schools—Ohio—Cleveland Heights—Administration—Case studies.   2. Cleveland
Heights High School (Cleveland Heights, Ohio).   3. Educational change—Ohio—Cleveland
Heights—Case studies.   4. School improvement programs—Ohio—Cleveland Heights—Case
studies.   I. Title.   II. Series.
LB2822.25.O3T58   1995
373.12'009771'32—dc20   95-21275
                                                                                                         CIP

Text and jacket designed by Nighthawk Design.
Type set in Bembo.
Printed by Braun–Brumfield, Inc., Ann Arbor, Michigan.

9 8 7 6 5 4 3 2 1

To Calvin Vance,
my high school French teacher,
for lighting the way

Contents

Preface

Although the inadequacies of American public education are hardly news, the publication of Jonathan Kozol's *Savage Inequalities* in 1991 attracted notice. A heart-wrenching exposé of the disgraceful condition of the country's urban school systems, *Savage Inequalities* revealed that poor and minority children are still being denied the quality of education enjoyed by affluent whites nearly forty years after the Supreme Court ruled that segregated schools are inherently unequal. "We now have two completely separate and unequal schooling systems," Kozol discovered. "One educates those who will govern and employ. The other trains, if they're lucky, those who will be governed and may sometimes be employed."

Kozol's book gave dramatic impetus to a growing national consensus that America's system of public education must be radically restructured. Even before the book's publication, concerned parents, lawmakers, and business leaders from around the country had joined university-affiliated educational theorists in calling for systemic reform. For some, the need to push for "excellence in education"—as the restructuring movement has come to be called—was a matter of racial justice; others feared irreversible damage to America's economic competitiveness should great numbers of future workers be undereducated.

Whatever its cause, the pressure on public school educators to effect significant improvements has been increasing in ferocity ever since the publication of the U.S. Department of Education–commissioned report *A Nation at Risk* first raised alarm over the public schools' woefully inadequate performance ten years ago. Today there are at least a dozen major national networks promoting education reform. They range from the New American Schools Development Corporation, a business-supported effort aimed at raising $200 million to finance the design of "break the mold" public schools, to the National Alliance for Restructuring Education, one of nine design teams funded by the New American Schools venture to date. A university-business partnership at work in five states and four urban school districts, the National Alliance provides assistance to school systems wishing to nurture a spirit of innovation. At the same time lawmakers from Texas to

Kentucky have attempted to coerce change by issuing mandates that tighten educational standards. The result is that thousands of individual schools and districts have been prompted to experiment with restructuring in some form. "Schools within a school," year-round classes, all-male academies, parental choice, for-profit administration, community-led management councils—all are being explored as solutions to the current crisis in education.

Given this whirlwind of activity, it is hard for some to understand why the level of national SAT scores, used as a measure of the scholarship and aptitude of high school juniors and seniors, continues to stagnate or decline. Especially among concerned parents and their political representatives, expectations about results now approach a level of urgency best described by the popular phrase: "Just do it." Unfortunately, the inherent difficulties—if not outright impossibility—of reinventing our system of public education have largely been obscured by the clamor for change.

In saying this I do not mean to denigrate the vigorous leadership of such proponents of reform as Ernest Boyer, the late Ronald Edmonds, John Goodlad, and Theodore Sizer. Thanks to their research and writings, we now have a clearer understanding of the nature of the change that must occur if public schools are to ensure that every American child becomes a fulfilled, productive adult and a responsible citizen. However, the glacial progress of the excellence in education movement suggests that educational leaders have paid too little attention to the question of how to bring about the reforms they have proposed. Theories of school improvement have been embraced as if they were self-actualizing and specific recommendations for reform seized without taking into account a basic, if largely ignored, political reality.

The American system of public education, like, so it appears, the AIDS virus, is shockingly resistant to curative measures.

As *Welcome to Heights High: The Crippling Politics of Restructuring America's Public Schools* demonstrates, it is not possible to "just do it." A work of investigative journalism cast in the form of a cautionary tale, *Welcome to Heights High* describes what happens when those theories of reform now being advanced as the best possible hope for salvaging our public education system are introduced into a real-life setting. In laying bare the destructive organizational, political, social, and racial tensions inherent in the way public schools are presently organized and operated, this book seeks to take stock of the obstacles that stand in the way of successful school restructuring.

Welcome to Heights High begins by zeroing in on one troubled high school with a problem common to many: the persistent failure of its minority students. The story opens with the arrival of a new principal, whose deeply held conviction that *all* children can learn prompts him to take on a challenge that has eluded generations of American educators: he is determined to transform the uneasily integrated high school of which he is (nominally) in charge into an excellent learning environment for all students.

The disappointing and, in many cases, abysmal academic performance of black students at Cleveland Heights High School may come as a surprise to some for the simple reason that Heights High is not located in a northern ghetto or the rural South. Instead it serves an integrated, progressive, middle-class suburb of Cleveland, Ohio. Twice named an "All-America City" during the 1970s by the National Municipal League because of its success in coping with the integration of its neighborhoods, the suburb of Cleveland Heights remains nearly two-thirds white today. But its public school system has watched student demographics change from all white to more than 60 percent black in the space of fifteen years.

Heights High School once enjoyed a national reputation for academic excellence, and it is still widely perceived to be a model of successful school integration, thanks to the periodic visits of well-respected journalists such as National Public Radio's Scott Simon, who last year praised the school's "remarkable human assortment" on air. However, by the mid-1980s, this large, suburban institution found itself plagued by unacceptably high failure rates, poor student morale and discipline, gang rivalries, teen pregnancies, and chemical abuse—problems all too familiar to those who read the newspapers.

The process by which Heights High School attempted to pursue reform in the late 1980s, on the other hand, was largely unproven, even though it was widely discussed and heralded in educational circles. With the support of the superintendent of schools, the principal empowered the *teachers* of Heights High to set about creating an ideal school. He encouraged them to throw out all the givens of secondary education and to rethink completely Heights High's form and function.

This strategic planning process, which was awarded $250,000 in grant monies by a local foundation, was called the Model School Project. One of the earliest restructuring attempts spawned by the excellence in education movement, the project was prompted by the principal's belief that the quality of education one received at Heights High depended, it is sad to say, on the color of one's skin. True, the school still had an enviable track record of producing at least a dozen National Merit Scholarship semifinalists each year. But the principal, a relative newcomer to the district, challenged the high school faculty to create an educational environment that allowed every student, not merely affluent whites in upper-level tracks, to achieve academic success. The stakes were high. Can democracy long survive in a country that fails to ensure that all its citizens are equipped to meet the challenges of life in a postindustrial society?

The Model School Project's significance as a bellwether was heightened by its use of teacher empowerment as a vehicle for educational reform. During the 1980s education reformers ranging from American Federation of Teachers union president Albert Shanker to former president George Bush called for increased autonomy for teachers. The reasoning was that self-managing teachers would find more satisfaction in their work and thus be more effective. Yet the majority of public school systems have not rushed to embrace this theory. Most still operate as top-down bureaucracies, a style of management that only increases teachers' resistance to administrative initiatives.

In seeking to train teachers to be agents of innovation, the Model School Project was in the vanguard of the educational reform movement. The design for a model high school that it eventually proposed was also farsighted; it incorporated the most promising theories about how to improve academic achievement that America's leading educational thinkers have to offer.

Among the sweeping changes advocated by the principal and a small band of like-minded teachers who led the restructuring project was the recommendation that the operation of Heights High School be left totally in the hands of a "site-based" management council of teachers, building administrators, and possibly parents. This new governing body would be ceded complete authority over the high school's budget and autonomy from what was perceived to be the inflexible policies, red tape, and second-guessing of the system's central administration. Yet, in advancing the theory that decentralization would result in more effective decision making, the Model School Project leaders did not seek power merely for its own sake. Once site-based management was gained, they planned to restructure their comprehensive high school into smaller families of teachers and students. Theory held that these "schools within a school" would allow for a kind of learning experience new to public (although not private) education: one that was warm, personal, and focused exclusively on the students' acquisition of critical-thinking skills.

Just as important, the new structure would permit the high school to do away with ability grouping, a widespread educational practice whose employment by the Cleveland Heights school district the principal, especially, regarded as an egregious example of institutional racism. At Heights High, the majority of students assigned to low-ability tracks were African Americans, whose misbehavior and poor academic performance, the principal was convinced, sprang from their teachers' low expectations of them.

In the principal's view, the board of education perpetuated ability grouping in order to stem white flight from the district: if white students were given an oasis in an increasingly black high school, perhaps they would feel less need to flee. The leaders of the Model School Project were determined to put a stop to this practice, which seemed to them to be a subversion of the ideal of quality, integrated education to which the district claimed allegiance. If, they asked themselves, integrated education could not be made a reality in Cleveland Heights, one of the few suburbs in America in which blacks and whites chose to live together as neighbors, in what other locale would Martin Luther King's dream of equal opportunity and justice for all Americans be realized?

Yet despite its estimable goals, ample funding, and grassroots leadership by the teaching staff, the Model School Project did not succeed in winning educational equity for Heights High's African-American students, nor did it bring about the desired restructuring of the school. Given the inconclusive academic results of other contemporaneous experiments with teacher empowerment in districts such as Rochester, New York, and Dade County, Florida, it is not clear that the Model School Project would have produced improvements in student achievement, even if its proposals had been fully implemented. But the Model School Project died before a redesign could be effected. In an ironic turn of events, the teacher-led campaign to reinvent Heights High was mortally wounded by the long-simmering frustrations of the very constituency it sought to better serve.

That the Model School Project failed was also due in large part to the fact that its leaders, like all pioneers, ventured into unknown territory without the benefit of a map of the dangers that lay ahead. *Welcome to Heights High,* the product of countless hours of firsthand observation at Cleveland Heights High School and more than one hundred formal interviews with members of the Cleveland Heights public school community, charts those hazards for others with an interest in school restructuring. If the book is not exactly a "how to," it certainly can serve as a vivid example of "how not to." Indeed, readers may wish to make mental notes of points in the narrative at which decisions might have been made differently or other actions might have been taken, for the decision to cast *Welcome to Heights High* as a narrative was purposely made to facilitate such understandings. It is my hope that the graphic portrayal of real-life events can illustrate the intricacies of school restructuring more vividly than would a purely theoretical discussion.

Acknowledgments

Welcome to Heights High could not have been written without the trust and goodwill of the hardworking, dedicated teachers and administrators of Cleveland Heights High School. I have tried to live up to the faith they placed in me by taking no sides in the events herein described, representing as accurately as possible their conflicting views about the school's problems, and resisting the temptations of sarcasm and sensationalism.

I can, however, never repay a special debt of gratitude to Irv Moskowitz and Hugh Burkett. It was their idea that the progress of the Model School Project be documented by an independent observer so that other public schools interested in restructuring might be able to learn from this pioneering experiment—a challenge I volunteered to undertake. Although they were not party to the decision to allow me unprecedented access to the workings of Heights High School, Moskowitz's and Burkett's successors, Lauree P. Gearity and Charles M. Shaddow, selflessly permitted the documentation to continue. The participants in the Model School Project—an ever changing group of Heights High staff members—could also have decided to veto my continuing attendance at Model School meetings at several points during the four years I was an independent observer at Heights High. I heartily thank these individuals for agreeing at each juncture that I could continue my observation.

An even greater courtesy was extended to me by the Model School Project coordinators: Cathleen McBride, William Thomas, Frances Walter, and Steven Young. They tolerated my scribbling presence at their daily planning sessions for nearly two years. Never once did they request that I leave the room, not even during moments of crisis or heated debate, although they recognized that speaking frankly in front of me might not always redound to their credit. Hugh Burkett and Frank Walter also appreciated the risks of being candid with me, yet consented nonetheless to be interviewed at length. To these six talented and visionary educators, who courageously opened their professional lives to intense scrutiny in the hopes of advancing knowledge in and of their field, my sincerest thanks.

In addition, many other members of the Heights High faculty, as well as representatives of the student body, district administration, and the community of Cleveland Heights, graciously granted me interviews. Without the benefit of the information and insights they provided, my understanding of the sociopolitical dynamics of public school systems would have been immeasurably poorer. I would like to thank each of these individuals for his or her assistance, while singling out for special mention the late Lauree Gearity, Daniel MacDonald, Timothy Mitchell, Robert Quail, Cal Rose, Mary Watson, Mark Wessels, and Allan Wolf—all of whom were especially generous with their time.

Cleveland *Plain Dealer* newspaper executives Thomas Vail and William Barnard eased my research into the history of the Cleveland Heights schools by granting me access to the invaluable *PD* morgue. Similarly, Heights High's librarians, especially Barbara Reynolds Schmunk, extended me every professional courtesy. I am also grateful to Bethany Aram, a former editor of the high school's newspaper, who shared her confidential reporter's notes on several pertinent subjects.

At various points in the book's evolution I called upon fellow writers Dennis Dooley, Gary Engle, Mark Gottlieb, Art Klein, and Bill Rudman to read sections of the manuscript. Each of these good friends was unfailingly cheerful in shouldering this chore and immensely helpful in suggesting improvements to the narrative. Ohio State University Press assistant editor Ellen Satrom demonstrated great skill in smoothing the manuscript's rough edges. Special mention should also be made of the contributions of Henry D. Shapiro and Zane L. Miller, Ohio State University Press's Urban Life and Urban Landscape Series editors, and Jeffrey Mirel, associate professor of the Department of Leadership and Educational Policy Studies of Northern Illinois University. Their astute comments helped me to sharpen the book's theme and conclusions. I, however, am solely responsible for any factual or analytical shortcomings that remain.

Enthusiasm for one's work lags from time to time during a book project of this duration. Yet my husband, Tom Hinson, never lost faith in me or my work, and his words of encouragement were a continual source of sustenance to me. I would also like to recognize the efforts of Charlotte Dihoff, acquisitions editor of Ohio State University Press, who extended herself to speed the manuscript's way toward publication.

My thanks to the following publishers for permission to reprint material in this book:

Chapter 1 epigraph from *A Place Called School: Prospects for the Future* by John I. Goodlad. Copyright © 1984. Reprinted by permission of McGraw-Hill, Inc.

Chapter 3 epigraph and afterword quotation from *Dark Ghetto: Dilemmas of Social Power* by Kenneth B. Clark. Copyright © 1965 by Kenneth B. Clark. Copyright renewed 1993 by Kenneth B. Clark. Reprinted by permission of HarperCollins Publishers, Inc.

Chapter 4 epigraph from *Keeping Track: How Schools Structure Inequality* by Jeannie Oakes. Copyright © 1985. Reprinted by permission of Yale University Press.

Chapter 5 epigraph from *Schoolteacher: A Sociological Study* by Dan C. Lortie. Copyright © 1975 by University of Chicago Press. Reprinted by permission.

Chapters 6, 8, 11, and 18 epigraphs from *The Dynamics of Educational Change: Toward Responsive Schools* by John I. Goodlad. Copyright © 1975. Reprinted by permission of McGraw-Hill, Inc.

Chapter 7 and part 3 epigraphs from *The Culture of the School and the Problem of Change* by Seymour B. Sarason. Copyright © 1982 by Allyn and Bacon. Reprinted by permission.

Part 2 epigraph from *The Empowerment of Teachers: Overcoming the Crisis of Confidence* by Gene I. Maeroff. Copyright © 1988. Reprinted by permission of Teachers College Press.

Chapters 9 and 10 epigraphs from *The Quality School: Managing Students without Coercion* by William Glasser. Copyright © 1990 by William Glasser, Inc., Joseph Paul Glasser, Alice Joan Glasser, and Martin Howard Glasser. Reprinted by permission of HarperCollins Publishers, Inc.

Chapter 12 epigraph from *How Children Fail* by John Holt. Copyright © 1964, 1982 by John Holt. Used by permission of Delacorte Press/Seymour Lawrence, a division of Bantam Doubleday Dell Publishing Group, Inc.

Chapter 13 epigraph from *Crisis in the Classroom: The Remaking of American*

Mise-en-Scène

Cleveland Heights High School serves the suburb of Cleveland Heights, Ohio, which is located directly to the east of Cleveland on the escarpment of a shale and sandstone plateau formed some 320 million years ago. Erosion and a glacier—the one that gouged out Lake Erie just a few miles to the north—later smoothed this Paleozoic upthrust into a landscape of rolling hills, which over time came to be covered with broad hardwood forests. The forests were eventually inhabited by tribes of American Indians, who retained stewardship of the land until the early 1800s, when their hunting grounds gave way to the farms of newly arrived white settlers from the East. Later, the farms were divided and subdivided as wealthy Clevelanders, seeking to escape the noise, dirt, and crowds of their industrial city, rushed to the nearby highlands to buy sprawling Tudor homes in a mock-English village with streets named Berkshire, Lancashire, and Coventry. The prestige of the new address was considerably enhanced by its proximity to the seven-hundred-acre summer estate of the petroleum king John D. Rockefeller.

Until the turn of the century, a grade school was sufficient to satisfy the educational requirements of the village's inhabitants, who were men and women largely of Anglo-Saxon stock. In the first decade of the twentieth century, however, the residents became interested in having their own high school, which was subsequently set up in the village schoolhouse. The first freshman class, which chose black and gold as its colors, matriculated in 1908.

In 1926 a three-story, red-brick Elizabethan building—complete with battlements and a clock tower, in keeping with the architectural pretensions of the residents—was erected as a more appropriate home for the high school. The building faced the busy intersection of Cedar and Lee Roads, giving the high school a prominent location in the heart of Cleveland Heights. Four years later a matching wing was built on the western side of the main building to accommodate the school's rapidly growing enrollment.

The newcomers were the offspring of some of Cleveland's Jewish immigrants, who had prospered in their adopted city and could by then afford to pursue the dream of a new home and a good education for their children. They helped to establish Cleveland Heights as a solidly middle-class suburb, and their increasing numbers were the impetus for the founding of a neighboring suburb, University Heights, which joined Cleveland Heights in creating a consolidated school district after World War II.

In time, some of the non-Jewish students at Heights High came to feel a little outnumbered and overshadowed, prompting them to joke that one could hold a meeting of all the school's Gentiles in a phone booth. A stronger strain of anti-Semitism contributed to the failure of a bond issue that was proposed in 1957 to pay for a second public high school to house the overflow of newcomers. Despite these unresolved divisions within the community, residents took great pride in Heights High's growing reputation for academic excellence. No one was particularly surprised (judging by the offhand coverage the story received in the school newspaper) when the National Academy of Sciences announced in 1964 that the high school ranked first in Ohio, and twenty-first in the country, in terms of the number of graduates who went on to earn doctoral degrees. Everybody knew that Heights High graduates were going places.

Well satisfied with the school's academic performance, the community steadfastly supported its physical improvement. A football stadium was built in 1948 and an eastern wing the following year, thus fulfilling the original design's intention that the school building should form the letter H. And, in the early 1960s, soon after the Soviet Union overtook the United States in the race to launch the first earth-orbiting rocket, raising widespread national concern about the soundness of math and science education in America, a low-slung addition of red brick and cast concrete went up along Cedar Road to house new classrooms and administrative offices. The new wing blocked what had formerly been an imposing view of the high school and turned an expansive front lawn into a small concrete courtyard, but it testified to the community's bedrock belief in the value of public education at a time when the Russian Sputnik scare had shaken others' faith in its effectiveness.

The suburb's commitment to its public schools was reaffirmed in the early 1970s, despite the turmoil that had been occasioned in the district by the student rights movement and in the community by the influx of a handful of black families from Cleveland into Cleveland Heights. Investing in a future whose exact nature few could then have discerned, the residents voted in 1972 to tax themselves nearly $20 million in order to renovate Heights High and the district's eleven elementary and four junior high school buildings.

Soon, working- and middle-class blacks who aspired to a better life for themselves and their children began flowing from Cleveland into Cleveland Heights in large numbers, attracted by its plentiful stock of affordable starter homes, well-regarded educational system, and newfound reputation for progressiveness. (Once a bastion of conservatism—a single Republican mayor controlled city hall from 1914 to 1946, a total of seventeen straight terms—the suburb had begun after the war to experience the liberalizing influence of its Jewish population and its proximity to several nearby universities. This gradual shift in its politics was now to stand Cleveland Heights in good stead.) Instead of panicking, the suburb's political, civic, and religious leaders moved aggressively to contain white flight and maintain integration. When the 1980 census showed that the population of Cleveland Heights remained more than three-quarters white, they pronounced their efforts a success.

Yet the effects of racial prejudice could be detected in the demographics of the schools, which had slowly but inexorably changed once again as many white residents moved away or opted for private education when their children reached elementary or high school age. By 1980, students of African-American descent made up more than 45 percent of the district's total enrollment of nine thousand. That year, for only the third time in the district's history, the voters declined to pass an operating levy for the schools. It was the beginning of an uncomfortable new era of uncertainty.

If demographic trends continued, it looked as if the Cleveland Heights schools would in time become largely black.[1] When the day came that black students were in the majority in Cleveland Heights, would the district have the will to maintain its tradition of academic excellence? Or would standards and expectations be allowed to slip? Would the future performance of the Cleveland Heights schools confirm an awful truth: that the quality of education Americans receive depends to a great extent upon the happenstance of their race and class? Or would the community once again rise to the occasion, demanding a solution to this profoundly undemocratic rule?

Part 1
The Culture of Inertia

It is because modern education is so seldom inspired by a great hope that it so seldom achieves a great result. The wish to preserve the past rather than the hope of creating the future dominates the minds of those who control the teaching of the young.

—BERTRAND RUSSELL,
Principles of Social Reconstruction, 1916

1

A Simple Remodeling Job

If we are to improve schooling, we must improve individual schools.

—JOHN I. GOODLAD,
A Place Called School, 1984

From the street there were few signs of Cleveland Heights High School's decline. True, the clock tower atop the main building no longer kept time, and someone who did not share the community's high regard for education had plastered a portrait of Mickey Mouse over one of the clock's four faces. But casual passers-by needed sharp eyes to detect this expression of adolescent humor.

Inside the sprawling suburban school, however, things were obviously a shambles. When, from time to time, students punched gaping holes into the plaster in the main hallways, the damage went unrepaired for months. Stairwells were decorated with graffiti and, occasionally, the crimson residue of cafeteria french fries that had been hurled against the walls. And no matter how often the floors were cleaned and mopped, they soon wore another coat of litter and dirt.

In winter the teachers hung wet paper towels over the thermostats in their rooms to trick the heaters into working. In summer they sweltered because their windows refused to open. Old-timers comforted themselves with the thought that these were but minor inconveniences when weighed against their association with a school of national stature. They could

7

remember the good old days, when all Heights students seemed as brilliant as Donald Glaser, who went on to win the 1960 Nobel Prize in physics. But mathematics teacher Carol Shiles was relatively new to the faculty, and she had yet to become inured to such small indignities as the outlandish color scheme of her classroom.

It was during the last remodeling of the high school, in the mid-1970s, that someone had decided the hallways and classrooms should be emblazoned with orange and yellow supergraphics. This attempt to help make education "relevant" to the students had backfired, however, when the palette became passé. Despite the fact that the supergraphics now grated on the eyes, most of the classrooms in the building had never been repainted, including room 116, home base for Shiles for the 1989–90 school year. Even after several seasons of occupancy, Shiles found her room unpleasant, but she did not see a way to make it better. She knew that "District"—the school system's central administration—would eventually get around to repainting room 116. In the meantime there was nothing a teacher could do to hurry District along.

After thirteen years of teaching, Shiles had come to believe that she could not do much about her students' lack of motivation either. When she joined the Heights faculty in 1985–86, she was required to teach classes that colleagues with more seniority considered undesirable, such as "standard" math courses, offered for students believed to be of low ability. It had been a frustrating nine months. In subsequent years, as she began to receive her share of "expanded" courses, she discovered that students considered of average ability were turned off by math, too. Even college-bound "advanced placement" students did not work very hard, in her estimation. They figured that they would surely get into college somewhere, and only then would they need to start studying.

Shiles had tried everything to capture her students' interest. She had them graph algebraic formulas on computers and fold paper into three-dimensional shapes in order to help them envision geometry. Eventually, she concluded that the kids were probably right: it *was* hard to see how such mathematical concepts would be useful to them in real life. For a time after this unhappy epiphany she considered leaving the profession. Then she decided to attend the first in a series of teachers' retreats sponsored by a new group at the high school called the Model School Project. The retreat was scheduled for the second weekend in August, before the start of the 1989–90 school year, and Shiles decided to sacrifice a part of her summer vacation in hopes of picking up a few motivational tips that she could use in her classroom.

But the organizers of the Model School Project had far larger ambitions for Carol Shiles and her 160 colleagues. In the spring of 1988 they had obtained funding from a Cleveland-based foundation to enable the Heights High faculty to develop a plan for restructuring the high school's operation. What the project's organizers were proposing was radical: to throw out all the givens of secondary school curriculum, class organization, instruction, and building administration. They wanted to encourage the teachers to rethink the form and function of the high school from the floorboards up. Tradition be damned. Heights High's new organizational structure was to be based on the most promising new theories about how to improve secondary education that America's leading educational thinkers had to offer.

Despite their reformative intentions, the project's proponents did not consider Heights High School a complete catastrophe, especially not when it came to serving the needs and aspirations of the highly motivated. Every year without fail for decades, a dozen or more Heights seniors distinguished themselves as National Merit Scholarship semifinalists—a record few high schools in the country could match. The chess team was beginning to display the promise that would bring Heights High a national championship in 1991. The school was also well known for the excellence of its music department. And it had recently become one of only four secondary institutions in the state to offer the demanding international baccalaureate degree for those interested in a curriculum enriched by a global focus. Yet the proposers of the Model School Project believed that nothing less than revolutionary change was needed.

One did not have to search far for justification. In the 1970s the National Municipal League had twice pronounced Cleveland Heights an "All-America City" because of its success with integration. Whether the community continued to maintain its exceptional record as one of a handful of suburbs in the nation in which blacks and whites chose to live as neighbors, or eventually segregated, was thought to depend in large measure on the quality of its public schools. Middle-class families, black and white, could opt *not* to live in a city with ailing schools, and the health of Heights High School was widely perceived as precarious. Many outsiders and residents alike believed that to attend Heights was to risk bodily harm.

While these fears were greatly exaggerated (and, in some cases, racially inspired), it was hard to dispute the fact that Heights High in some ways resembled a large inner-city school, its suburban location notwithstanding. Problems with alcohol and drug abuse, fighting, gangs, racial and personal conflicts, teen pregnancy, and truancy filled the administrators' days, and those who ran afoul of the school's strict disciplinary policies were disproportionately African-American. Many of these students came from single-parent households or from lower-middle-class families in which both parents worked long hours in order to stay abreast of mortgage payments. Others depended on welfare to survive; nearly 10 percent of the city's residents lived on incomes at or below the poverty level, grim demographics that civic leaders did not care to broadcast.

Heights High shared another trouble common to big-city school systems: the persistent underachievement of its students. In days gone by as many as 95 percent of all Heights seniors reportedly went on to college; now the official count stood at approximately 60 percent, and no less an authority than the assistant principal of curriculum privately believed that the number of Heights graduates who completed four additional years of schooling was closer to 20 percent. Low aspirations and weak academic performance were particularly noticeable among the African-American students, who, despite their standing as the school's predominate clientele,[1] were overrepresented in standard, remedial, and vocational classes, as well as among the total number of students failing one or more of their courses.

The disparity between the high-quality education Heights High congratulated itself on delivering and the watered-down courses and punitive treatment many black students received posed an invisible threat to the suburb's hard-won harmony. Yet for the coproposers of the Model School Project, there were more basic matters at stake than a desire to protect property values in Cleveland Heights or to help maintain integration. They called them "equity" issues, by which they meant that the school had a duty to provide every single student with the skills and knowledge needed for a fair start in life. As America's system of public education was founded on this democratic principle, the district's top officials were troubled by their perception that Heights seemed unable to develop the intellectual capabilities of its minority students (and, indeed, its non-college-bound white students) with the same consistency that its girls' track team would soon show in winning three state championships in a row.

Over the years the school system had attempted to address the needs of failing and problem students by offering them a menu of Afrocentric courses, alternative programs, and specialized services. Now the high school principal and the superintendent of schools were advocating that the issue of underachievement be addressed systematically. If the two administrators— both relative newcomers to the district—harbored doubts about the school system's willingness and ability to embrace all-encompassing change, or if they understood the countervailing forces that would have to be overcome in order to achieve educational equity for black children in a predominately white suburb (and society), they betrayed no such lack of confidence to the Cleveland Foundation, the local philanthropy from which they sought a grant to underwrite a strategic planning process. In their grant proposal superintendent Irving Moskowitz and principal Hugh Burkett suggested that the model high school that the faculty would design after a year's research and discussion could serve to close "the gap between the academic 'haves' and 'have-nots.'"

In this objective the Model School Project mirrored the concerns of the latest education reform movement to preoccupy the country. The "excellence in education" movement had been launched in 1983 with the publication of *A Nation at Risk: The Imperative for Educational Reform*. Commissioned by the U.S. Department of Education, the report sounded the alarm that America's declining economic competitiveness could be traced in part to an undereducated citizenry, ill prepared for work or life. As proof it presented a long list of disturbing statistics, including the fact that one in ten of all seventeen year olds was functionally illiterate and six in ten could not solve a mathematics problem requiring several steps. The fear that *A Nation at Risk* articulated—America is falling behind!—inspired a host of would-be reformers to encourage, prod, and goad the country's public schools to rise to a level of excellence they had never before achieved.

Nor were they designed to. Scientific efficiency—the new ideal sweeping industrial America in the early twentieth century—dictated that the country's burgeoning public schools sort children in terms of their perceived fitness for carrying out different kinds of work and educate them accordingly. In a manufacturing-based economy, only a managerial elite need be college educated; the immigrant masses were readied for citizenship and a lifetime of manual labor. Indeed, America's factories could not have thrived without a steady stream of semi-skilled and low-skilled workers. With lack of education no impediment to gainful employment, even as recently as 1950 a majority of public school students did not graduate high school. But the civil rights movement, a prospering country's heightened expectations for its children, the gradual shift to an information-based economy, and the concomitant demand for a better-educated workforce all were to have a salutary impact on the national dropout rate. By the 1980s three-quarters of the country's youth were earning secondary school diplomas, and attention shifted to the challenge of improving the caliber of the high school degree.

Spokespeople from universities, the ranks of business and industry, and state legislatures began calling upon the nation's high schools to provide all students with the rigorous academic training long afforded only the privileged and the talented. These advocates recognized that by the turn of the century one of every three Americans entering the workforce would be nonwhite—the constituency traditionally served least well by public education—and they appreciated the disastrous social and economic consequences that would accrue if these future workers lacked mastery of the three Rs, to say nothing of the ability to think critically.

The forty-first president of the United States joined those determined to promote what he called "tradition-shattering reform." In late September 1989, shortly after the start of the new school year, George Bush summoned the nation's governors to an unprecedented education summit. Convened in Charlottesville, Virginia, the summit produced close to a national political consensus that the system of public education in all fifty states should be "restructured."

As a first step, the summiteers decided to set up a task force to articulate and build broad-based agreement on a set of national educational goals.[2] This approach to restructuring followed a formula that had already proved popular with many state legislators. Seeking to improve the organizational efficiency of public schools through tighter regulation, lawmakers from Texas to Kentucky had issued statewide mandates calling for teacher and student testing and universal curriculum standards. Unfortunately, the strategy the summiteers chose to emulate seemed unlikely to inspire sweeping reform, as it anticipated only the replacement of one group of educational policies and practices with another. If restructuring were ever to become more than a buzzword, its proponents might have done better to adopt the objective that motivated the creation of the Model School Project and pursue changes in the fundamental nature and content of student-teacher interactions.

Finding themselves in the vanguard of educational reform did not displease or dismay superintendent Irv Moskowitz and principal Hugh Burkett, both educators who read widely in their field and who enjoyed the stimulation of new ideas. Should the Model School Project produce marked improvements in academic performance, Heights High School might soon be hailed as a national exemplar of quality integrated education, prompting other troubled urban schools across the country to embrace the concept of restructuring.

But the Model School millennium that the two administrators envisioned did not stop with pedagogy. Moskowitz and Burkett recognized that to alter

Heights High's system of instruction without changing the professional climate at the high school would be merely to tinker. They also saw the Model School Project as a staff development tool, a means of reshaping the beliefs, values, and skills of the faculty. In fact, the two administrators believed that, should the project succeed, it could help to reinvent the profession of teaching.

In their own model school the teachers would be trained for leadership—a far cry from the situation in most school districts, in which faculty members received little encouragement to problem solve and govern. On the contrary, administrators from state boards of education on down routinely made decisions for teachers as if they were irresponsible children. The trouble was that such top-down management flew in the face of political reality. Unlike the workings of, say, a medieval court (which the average public school district otherwise resembled in its taste for gossip, intrigue, and palace revolts), a measure of real power in the schools was concentrated at the bottom. The ability of the principal, the superintendent, or even state or federal government to impose innovation ended when a teacher walked into her classroom and shut the door. She and she alone would decide how the business of education was transacted there. No wonder external pressure on the schools to improve had produced so little real reform over the years.

The Model School Project, on the other hand, was based on a new awareness of the close relationship between autonomy and accountability. If teachers were ever to accept full responsibility for their performance—the hallmark of true professionals—they must be empowered to make their own decisions. In such a brave new world, teachers would slough off their comfortable passivity and rise to the challenge of self-governance, while administrators would cast aside their status as bosses to become the facilitators and implementers of decisions made in consultation with the teachers. In truth, Moskowitz and Burkett, having worked exclusively in top-down bureaucracies, were no better prepared professionally or emotionally than the teachers to accept this unsettling role reversal. Yet the concept of teacher empowerment held considerable intellectual appeal for the two Cleveland Heights administrators, as it did for many others who aspired to reform the public schools.

Teacher empowerment had moved onto the national educational agenda with the 1986 publication of *A Nation Prepared: Teachers for the Twenty-first Century*. A task force report of the Carnegie Forum on Education and the Economy, *A Nation Prepared* posited that the key to vastly improved student achievement lay in creating a "profession equal to the task." The report called for higher entrance requirements, more competitive salaries, and greater autonomy for teachers. The argument that self-managing teachers would take more responsibility for—and find more satisfaction in—their work and thus be more effective made sense to some of those interested in educational reform.

Advocates of teacher empowerment began to push for the transfer of authority for every aspect of a school's operation from central-office administrators to the school's teachers and principal, who would share decision-making responsibilities. Although many reformers argued that such decentralization would unleash the creative powers and problem-solving abilities of those most intimate with the current crisis in the classroom, the new concept of school administration did not win immediate and widespread acceptance. Within the field, the belief in a centralized bureaucracy—with rigidly assigned roles, responsibilities, and lines of authority and accountability—as the only viable model of school organization was too fundamental to be easily reconsidered. Only a few dozen school systems in the country had officially adopted site-based management (although thousands of districts were reportedly experimenting with shared decision making in some form), and fewer still had empowered their faculties to rethink the entire operation of their schools. For this reason Heights High's Model School Project promised to be a singularly important test of the viability of teacher empowerment as a strategy for effecting educational reform.

Largely unsuspecting of their starring roles in a nationally significant experiment, Carol Shiles and fourteen other members of the Heights High faculty and administration participated in the August 1989 Model School retreat. For three days they discussed their perceptions of problems at the high school and brainstormed possible solutions for later use in the design of a model school. Before adjourning they also considered a number of small projects that could be undertaken immediately to get the school-improvement process rolling. Someone tossed out the idea of holding breakfasts each payday to ease the social isolation of an oversized faculty. Another participant suggested that every teacher should "adopt" a student, because she believed that the kids, too, often felt anonymous and lonely in such a large school. And someone else came up with a novel way to deal with the maintenance problems at the high school: the retreat participants should host an all-day cleanup party for their colleagues sometime before the start of the school year.

Although the latter proposal was abandoned as unlikely to attract much enthusiasm, it planted a seed in Carol Shiles. The weekend retreat was the first opportunity she had had in more than a decade of teaching to exchange views on important educational issues with her peers, and the experience re-charged and excited her. Normally a mild-mannered, almost diffident person, she decided to assert herself. She would repaint her classroom!

When Shiles informed Hugh Burkett of her plan, the forty-five-year-old principal betrayed no signs of the impatience with which he privately greeted such indications of how far faculty members needed to be stretched before they would be ready to address the school's most acute problems. Joining into the spirit of Shiles's project, Burkett volunteered to see that a painting crew was deployed to prep the walls of her room. Perhaps Shiles's success in effecting a small change would prompt her colleagues to tackle more significant improvements.

Unfortunately, the principal's gesture of support did not produce the intended results. Whether inspired by Shiles's burst of energy or perhaps concerned about protecting their jobs, the crew members decided to paint room 116 themselves. Shiles was left with only the task of stripping and staining her wooden classroom door. The redecoration of room 116 pleased her nonetheless, for it symbolized a renewed belief in her own ability to make a difference. As she stood near her door greeting the students entering her room on September 6, 1989, the opening day of school, the gleaming surroundings testified to her optimism that it *was* possible to start anew.

The next day a photograph of Carol Shiles, standing on a ladder with paintbrush in hand, appeared in a suburban newspaper. The picture was accompanied by a caption reporting on the unusual initiative the math teacher had shown in refurbishing her own classroom. Shiles had not sought the publicity, however, and she was chagrined to learn that the photo's caption had angered the painting crew, whose members believed that she was taking credit for work they had done. Shiles immediately went down to the custodian's office to apologize for the misunderstanding, but the needless brouhaha left her wounded. Before long she came to regret that she was ever inspired to repaint her room.

This setback, although minor, warned of the substantial challenges proponents of the Model School Project faced. Enterprise was not always cheered and rewarded at Heights High after all. Too often the desire to effect change was met with suspicion, hurt feelings, or outright resistance. In fact, the culture of inertia that so pervaded the school had long since crystallized in a celebrated catchphrase, a standard answer to anyone with the temerity to inquire why a certain practice or procedure could not be altered or improved. The phrase, delivered in a tone weighted with irony, was simply, "Welcome to Heights High."

2

A New Principle

We can, whenever and wherever we choose, successfully teach all children whose schooling is of interest to us. We already know more than we need to do that. Whether or not we do it must finally depend on how we feel about the fact that we haven't so far.

—RONALD EDMONDS,
*A Discussion of the Literature and Issues
Related to Effective Schooling,* 1979

The seeds of the Model School Project were planted by an event Hugh Burkett witnessed the morning he took over as principal of Cleveland Heights High School. On that sunny summer day of August 1, 1984, Burkett was driving to his new job when he noticed a traffic jam ahead. Passage on both sides of Cedar Road had been reduced to a single lane, and as he inched along, Burkett wondered what was causing the holdup. He had been out of action for more than a year while he completed his doctorate in education administration and research at the University of Mississippi, and he was eager to get back to work.

As he approached Heights High School, Burkett saw that a large crowd had gathered in the middle of the street directly in front of the building; driving nearer, he observed that the crowd was composed of teenagers, who were watching something of great interest. When he reached the high school, Burkett was finally able to determine what had attracted the attention of this mass of kids, some of whom were hooting, laughing, and gesticulating. In the center of the crowd, a young black man lay cowering on the pavement as another young black man pounded him about the shoulders, chest, and legs with a bicycle.

Because there was a line of cars behind him, Burkett had no choice but to continue on his way to the parking lot at the rear of the school. Later he learned that the kids out front were summer school students and that the beating was one of those fights that sometimes took place when classes let out for the day. Burkett was shocked by what he had witnessed, especially since district officials had made such a point of assuring him during job interviews that Heights was a great high school. To be fair, they had also informed him that the school suffered from a lack of discipline; but he had not been given to believe that the students were so out of control that their misbehavior could interrupt the normal conduct of business in a city of fifty-six thousand. Oh well, he thought, welcome to Heights High.

Burkett, a rural North Carolinian by birth, had worked throughout the country and seen his share of public schools. In 1967 he began his career in education in an upper-middle-class suburb of Flint, Michigan, as a football coach and social studies teacher (his speciality: the Civil War). Seeking a larger sphere of influence, he left the classroom after his third year of teaching to become principal of a junior high school in Wisconsin. Before going on to earn his Ph.D., he served as principal of high schools in South Carolina and Wyoming. While the assault on Cedar Road had appalled him, it had not unnerved him: he had encountered schools with discipline problems before.

In fact, Burkett regarded himself as a professional troubleshooter. He took pride in the fact that he never lingered at a school longer than it took to solve its problems, noting that "once you got it fixed, it seemed like it wasn't as much fun anymore." Resolving the tensions that accompanied the merger of two high schools, one black and the other white, had preoccupied his tenure in Columbia, South Carolina. In Jackson Hole, Wyoming, he had supervised the funding, design, and construction of a new high school building. Given his wide-ranging experience, Burkett was certain that he could take care of fighting at Heights High.

But the summer of 1984 was to hold yet more surprises about the dimensions of the problems that would later prompt the creation of the Model School Project. As one of his first acts as principal, Burkett arranged to confer that summer with various civic and educational leaders; he wanted to increase his understanding of the issues facing the school and the community.

For the most part, the citizens with whom he spoke reaffirmed the concerns first articulated by his recruiters about the need to maintain the school's reputation for academic excellence and to restore discipline.

Heights High had once been run as strictly as a private school. Even well into the 1960s, administrators would stop female students in the halls and ask them to kneel down; if their skirt hems did not touch the floor, they were sent home to change. But by the end of the decade, the spirit of rebellion against the social and political status quo that was afoot in America had spread to Cleveland Heights.[1] Backed by their parents and sometimes their attorneys, Heights student activists demanded and won the right to peaceful assembly and the abolishment of such perceived infringements on their civil rights as the school's rigid dress code and mandatory study halls.

The new freedom to come and go whenever they were not scheduled to attend class had given birth in the late 1960s to a disciplinary free-for-all. Veteran teachers remembered when it was virtually impossible to make one's way from one end of the building to the other, as students engaged in various forms of relaxation—eating, socializing, playing the guitar—clogged the hallways and stairwells during "study" periods. Heights principals had been struggling to regain control of the building ever since, a challenge that took on a greater urgency when the flow of inner-city black families into the suburb sped up during the 1970s, and incidents of theft, vandalism, drug dealing, weapon carrying, and assault began to make the halls unsafe.

Burkett's immediate predecessor had succeeded in forging a consensus among students and parents for the restoration of mandatory study halls, but he had not dared to tamper with the school's open-campus policy, a student privilege that dated back to the 1940s. Because they were still free to come and go during their lunch hours, which were staggered over several periods, high school students congregated in a municipal parking lot directly across Cedar Road from the high school for a good part of the school day. From what Burkett gathered during the course of his summer rounds, the goings-on in lot 5 were a particular irritant, especially for the Lee Road merchants whose retail district the parking lot served. No one knew for sure what the students did over there, because many of them hung out in locked vans, but everyone suspected the parking lot to be a den of iniquity, where kids drank and smoked dope. Occasionally fights erupted, and these commotions, along with the fact that most of the students seen coming and going from the lot were young African-American men, made some residents leery of shopping in the neighborhood.

When Burkett discovered that high school officials were also reluctant to venture across the street, abdicating to the police responsibility for dealing with lot 5, it was his first inkling that perhaps racial prejudice had not been conquered at Cleveland Heights High School, despite the district's boasts of integration. In time he would come to be absolutely convinced that some of the school's discipline problems could be traced to a reluctance on the part of many teachers and administrators to confront African-American students who were misbehaving, a lapse of authority that he attributed to a fear of black males.

Burkett would display no such reticence during his six-year tenure as principal; having grown up among African Americans in a rural farming community in North Carolina, he did not see them as mysterious others. His childhood playmates had included the offspring of black sharecroppers who helped his father raise tobacco on the Burketts' tenant farm, and he had spent time in their homes. As a result, Burkett believed that he understood quite a bit about black culture, which is exactly what he said to an African American on the search committee interviewing candidates for the principalship in Columbia, South Carolina. When she questioned whether a white person could be sensitive to the needs of the black students, Burkett had responded, "If your principal needs to be black, then I'm not the person you need to be talking to. But if you're looking for someone who cares about black kids and can take care of their needs, then I can do that for you."

Taking care of black students, in Burkett's view, meant treating them no differently than white students, whose inappropriate behavior teachers did not hesitate to challenge. Although the strict disciplinary policies he subsequently instituted at Heights and his zealous enforcement of school rules were eventually to ignite a firestorm of controversy in the community that would scorch the Model School Project and result in Burkett himself being branded a racist, he never stopped regarding himself as a champion of minority students.

Burkett also conferred during the dog days of summer with teachers' union president Glenn Altschuld, a meeting that shed additional light on the mores of his new high school. Altschuld, a Heights High social studies teacher nearing the end of his career, had been head of American Federation of Teachers Local 795 since the early 1970s. A former high school dropout who served with the marines in Korea and completed his G.E.D. and college degree at night upon his return, Altschuld had entered teaching on the advice of his mother, who pointed out to this child of the depression the advantages of choosing steady work. Local 795 was clearly Altschuld's first love, however. For nearly fifteen years as its president he had devoted himself to the task of providing vigorous and, if necessary, adversarial representation of the teachers' rights to competitive pay and improved working conditions.

Altschuld's militancy had placed him at odds not only with a procession of Cleveland Heights superintendents but also with the excellence in education movement. The unswerving devotion of teachers' unions to issues of the pocketbook was becoming increasingly troubling to those interested in school reform, including even Albert Shanker, national president of the American Federation of Teachers and a pioneer in the struggle to win for teachers the right to collective bargaining. An early convert to the cause of public school improvement, Shanker would in the mid-1980s begin crisscrossing the nation, exhorting AFT locals to move beyond their success with collective bargaining and use their influence to seek improvements in teaching as a profession; otherwise—and here was where Shanker's instincts for self-preservation came to the fore—the union risked being swept aside as irrelevant by the growing wave of support for change.

Cynics saw Shanker's call for reform as a ploy to broaden the power base of the teachers' union by embracing "professional" issues. However, if encouraging a new grab for power was indeed Shanker's intent, the majority of the AFT's two thousand local affiliates had failed to take the hint. In Cleveland Heights, as in most other school districts, Shanker's proselytizing barely pierced Glenn Altschuld's complacency. The union president's single-minded pursuit of wage and benefit increases had met only with the approval and gratitude of the rank and file, who had watched a veteran teacher's maximum salary rise from less than $15,000 to more than $35,000 since 1971, when AFT Local 795 wrested the right to act as the teachers' collective bargaining agent away from the local chapter of the National Education Association in an upset election. Given his record of accomplishments, which included various contract provisions limiting the authority of administrators (such as the stipulation that any desired changes in working conditions had to be negotiated with the union), Altschuld had little reason to question his adversarial tactics or narrow focus.[2]

Besides, the union president did not see the need for reform. He believed that America's teachers were doing a decent job, despite what one read in the papers. "So what if the Cleveland public schools graduated only 50 percent of their high school students?" Altschuld asked. He defended that as a pretty good record, given that public schools were now expected to educate 100 percent of the population—"the lame, the halt, the blind, and the handicapped" included. In fact, he believed that the other 50 percent should be *encouraged* to drop out, as all these ne'er-do-wells did in school was to create trouble and scare the good students.

"If something has been the same for thirty years," Altschuld liked to say, "think twice about changing it, because it's probably working." This axiom was a reworking of a favorite motto of the first principal with whom the social studies teacher had worked: "If something has been the same for thirty years, it's probably time to make a change." When the future union leader shared his own version of the motto with the principal, it had driven the poor man crazy. The memory of that moment made Altschuld smile.

Not even during his courtesy call on Hugh Burkett had Altschuld let down his guard against administrative wiliness. He took pains to point out that he had come in his capacity as union president, informing Burkett that a principal had no contractual right to command the time of a teacher during the summer. Having arrived in Cleveland Heights only eighteen months after the community experienced the anguish of its first lengthy teachers' strike, Burkett had already deduced that one of the biggest challenges he faced was establishing a working relationship with the eight union stewards elected by the high school faculty to represent AFT Local 795's interests at the building level. Altschuld's hard-line stance gave the new principal his first real sense of the potential difficulty of that task, however.

The union president also came away from the meeting having taken a measure of his fellow educator. When later one of the high school stewards asked Altschuld if he thought that Burkett was a "hired gun" brought to town specifically to break the power of Local 795, Altschuld shook his head. "But I will tell you this about Burkett," the steward remembered him as saying. "He's a country boy and as slick as they come, so keep your hands in your pockets."

The third week in August, Burkett met for the first time with the six members of his administrative staff, a get-together that provided him with another glimpse of the disdain that teachers and principals in his new school seemed to display toward one another as a matter of course. Commanding the top slot on the agenda was the need to redesign the school's final-examination schedule, the state board of education having decided over the course of the summer to prohibit schools from releasing students early, as soon as they finished their scheduled exams. (This was a longstanding practice at Heights.)

After explaining the situation, Burkett suggested to his administrative staff that they ask the teachers for their thoughts on the best way to restructure the exam schedule before proceeding with the redesign. The puzzlement of some of his assistants about the wisdom of soliciting the advice of teachers on administrative matters was palpable. "There was no need to involve the teachers," they informed Burkett, who decided that he was wasting his breath and abruptly brought the meeting to an end. (Among the new principal's weaknesses was an inability to suffer ignorance or ineptitude gladly.) When he cooled down, Burkett realized that he would simply have to put together a new administrative team whose management philosophy and style were more in tune with his own.

Burkett was hit with another revelation when school began. Having accepted at face value the description proffered during his job interviews of Heights High as successfully integrated, the new principal was shocked to discover the degree to which life at the school was segregated. Yes, it was true that the mood of open racial hostility that marked the 1970s, when the number of black students at Heights High grew from fewer than one hundred to nearly one thousand, seemed to have subsided. Gone for the most part were the days of interracial fistfights and racially inspired brawls and ugly incidents (such as the time Burkett's predecessor witnessed a group of black students label another black kid known to have white friends as an Oreo by pouring a bag of flour over his head in the cafeteria).

Yet now, as then, black and white students seldom socialized. Each race, Burkett noticed almost immediately, kept to its own turf at lunchtime. White students "owned" the cafeteria and the courtyard, while black students congregated in front of the high school or across the street in lot 5.[3] Burkett soon learned that participation on Heights High's sports teams was also a function of race, as well as of interest and ability. Football, basketball, and track, for example, were known to be "black" sports, meaning that white students, observing an unwritten code, seldom tried out for those teams. Soccer, swimming, baseball, hockey, and golf, on the other hand, were recognized by most black students as the exclusive province of whites.

It was not difficult to puzzle out the reason why students of different races seldom mingled outside class. The school system's decision to group students by perceived academic ability meant that blacks and whites to a large extent were not commingled *in* class. Ability grouping limited the opportunities for black and white students at Heights to become friends.

The development of the students' social skills was not the only learning experience that ability grouping affected adversely, in Burkett's opinion.

While grouping seemed to have a negligible impact on high achievers, the principal knew of a growing body of research indicating that consigning students to low-ability groups (no matter how innocently named) was likely to wound their self-esteem, destroy their motivation, and prompt their misbehavior.[4] Burkett had also witnessed firsthand the damaging impact of grouping on student achievement.

Although ability grouping is an organizational given at nearly every public secondary school in the country, Burkett had never questioned the practice until he attended the University of Mississippi, where, as one of the duties of his graduate assistantship, he was put in charge of supervising the sophomore-year practicum for the university's education department. This responsibility required him to place and observe student teachers in classrooms throughout a forty-mile area surrounding Oxford. As he made his rounds, he was struck by the differences in the quality of instruction between low- and high-ability classes, a disparity made all the more stark by the fact that in Mississippi the students assigned to lower-track classes were usually black. The main order of business in those classrooms seemed to be "to get through the period and keep the kids quiet," he observed. "You saw a lot of worksheets, a lot of reading, a lot of answer-the-questions, a lot of movies." Burkett saw very little, however, of the discussion and debate that typified instruction afforded white students in upper-level classes.

The experience forced the Ph.D. candidate to confront, for the first time in his career, his own beliefs about whether African-American children had the same capacity to learn as Caucasians. Burkett, who attended segregated schools throughout his youth, knew that he was not totally free of racial prejudice. How else to explain an incident that had occurred at a Howard Johnson's at which he had stopped on a trip during his first year as a teacher? "I got up and left the restaurant because black people sat at the table next to me," he remembered vividly. Did his atavistic prejudice mean that he was prepared to accept the premise that some children were inherently unteachable, the unspoken assumption on which ability grouping was based? The idea stuck in his throat.

Burkett himself had been a miserable student. He had hated school— what little he saw of it, that is. Having grown up on a hardscrabble tobacco farm, the fifth of six children, Burkett spent summers and a good part of each fall harvesting and curing tobacco, a pattern of existence that continued until the eighth grade, when his parents divorced. The living the family eked out from sharecropping was so minimal that they had to do without such creature comforts as indoor plumbing and interior drywall; and when young Hugh awoke in the morning, he dressed himself in dungarees and boots outgrown by his older sisters.

Farming had taught the boy the value of hard work. Even so, he was unable to put his mind to any undertaking connected with school except football. After Burkett's graduation from high school, his mother literally pushed him onto a bus and sent him off to a small denominational college in Missouri, where a psychology professor befriended him. The professor succeeded in disabusing the ambitionless young man of his conviction that he was dumb, and now he was but a few months away from earning his doctorate. If *he* could learn to learn, Burkett concluded, "then, shit, *anybody* could."

Burkett had arrived, by independent and less than scientific means, at the same conclusion that a Harvard University Graduate School of Education research associate by the name of Ronald Edmonds had reached in the late 1970s. A few years earlier Edmonds set out to locate urban schools successful in providing effective instruction for the poor and disadvantaged. He began by reexamining the data contained in the so-called "Coleman report," an influential national survey of public schools conducted in the mid-1960s that found that academic achievement was more a function of a student's family background and the racial composition of his or her school than of any statistical or financial measurement of the school's quality.[5] Edmonds located at least fifty-five schools in the northeastern United States that met his definition of effectiveness.[6] He then proceeded to analyze their characteristics.

His findings, dubbed the "effective school correlates," were to influence the direction of the subsequent excellence in education movement, for they countered the basic premise of the Coleman report, which seemed to relieve educators of accountability for their performance. In time Burkett would also become familiar with Edmonds's thesis that successful schools were characterized by strong administrative leadership, staff consensus on objectives, high expectations for all students, an orderly atmosphere, a heightened emphasis on academics, and the continual monitoring of every student's progress. First and foremost, Edmonds's research had determined, "effective schools share . . . a climate in which it is incumbent on all personnel to be instructionally effective for all pupils." This unmet challenge, Edmonds believed, was at the heart of the crisis in public education. "Until public schools are held responsible for responding to children rather than the other way around," he stated, "no test of public instruction will have occurred."

Burkett carried an appreciation for the effective schools correlates with him to Cleveland Heights High School; he was committed to making Edmonds's message of hope that "all children can learn" (albeit at varying rates of speed) the guiding light of Heights High. Although national achievement scores showed that fully one-fourth of the students at Heights read at a level below eighth-grade competency, it soon became obvious to Burkett that their teachers, while dedicated and well intentioned, did not feel the need for his instructional leadership. In subtle and not so subtle ways he felt they made it clear to him that his job was "to keep the halls clean and leave us alone."

Burkett had never before encountered a faculty as arrogant and defiant as this one. (Most of the faculty members did not possess Carol Shiles's mild-mannered personality.) Almost all the veteran teachers held master's degrees and a few had earned doctorates, and they acted as if they believed that there was nothing they could learn from anyone.

The teachers' smug attitude was also fostered by the revolving-door nature of public school administration. Five principals had come and gone from Heights High over the previous two decades, their contributions seemingly interchangeable in the eyes of the tenured teachers, who had devoted their lives to the institution. The fact that these men had shouldered no teaching responsibilities and worked in air-conditioned splendor in an office located outside the main building in the Cedar Road addition, where, one faculty member noted, "you don't even hear the bells," contributed to their lack of credibility with the teachers. Whether the Heights High faculty was indeed smarter than the many principals with whom its members had previously worked, Burkett could not say, but he perceived that "they sure as hell thought they were."

There was a teacher who made a different first impression, however. Sometime during the final days of the summer of 1984, Francis X. Walter, one of the younger members of the high school's English department, dropped by the new principal's office to introduce himself. Walter was also the high school's chief union steward. Walter and Burkett were pleasantly surprised to discover both their instant rapport and their shared interest in discussing educational issues and innovations. Feeling himself in the company of a "kindred spirit," Walter proffered his opinion that a school was only as strong as its principal, and he volunteered to do everything within his power to assist Burkett. He hoped to convey the message that the teachers were looking to Burkett to set a new direction for the school and that the union was prepared to assist Burkett in determining that direction. (In saying so, Walter was following his own lead, a course that had already established him as Glenn Altschuld's philosophical opposite and political rival.) Burkett, in turn, recognized Walter as a person with a commitment to effective schooling, a can-do attitude, and a wealth of information about the inner workings of the high school. That fall he invited the English teacher to become his assistant.

Although it pained him to abandon the classroom, Walter reluctantly accepted the offer as the only possibility for career advancement open to him. Sadly, in Cleveland Heights as in most other school districts, the only way for a teacher to increase his influence and compensation was to leave the profession and become either an administrator or a paid executive officer of the union. Walter figured that he had gone as far as he could in the union hierarchy. Even though he had a record of loyal service to the union both as a steward and as a strike captain during the eight-day walkout in 1983, he was not a particular favorite of Glenn Altschuld's.

The appointment proved to be controversial. District officials deemed it unwise because of Walter's strong ties to the union, while some union members interpreted it as a sly attempt on Burkett's part to sap the strength of Local 795.

3

Discipline First

[African-American students] are not being taught; and not being taught, they fail. They have a sense of personal humiliation and unworthiness. They react negatively and hostilely and aggressively to the educational process. They hate teachers, they hate schools, they hate anything that seems to impose upon them this denigration, because they are not being respected as human beings, because they are sacrificed in a machinery of efficiency and expendability, because their dignity and potential as human beings are being obscured and ignored in terms of educationally irrelevant factors—their manners, their speech, their dress, or their apparent disinterest.

—KENNETH B. CLARK
Dark Ghetto, 1965

If Local 795 had lost a progressive leader, Hugh Burkett had gained an invaluable ally, mentor, and right-hand man. In the absence of a formal plan of attack on Heights High's myriad problems, such as would later be afforded by the Model School Project, the principal and his new assistant for staff and student concerns served as a two-person MASH unit. Working intently to treat the school's most obvious distress—the deterioration of its disciplinary system—they became close partners and good friends. As luck would have it, their strengths turned out to be complementary.

Although both men were bright, Hugh Burkett favored action over words, while Frank Walter tended to be the more articulate and reflective of

27

the duo. Burkett made friends and enemies instantly, depending on how one took to his blunt demeanor. His was a critical and challenging frame of mind. A bear of a man with an Amish farmer's beard, bald pate, and the angry, red slash of a scar on his left cheek, he could also be physically quite intimidating. Indeed, one member of the Cleveland Heights–University Heights Board of Education who had voted to approve Burkett's hiring believed that among the prospective principal's qualifications for the job was the fact that he *looked* mean enough to bring a wayward high school under control.

Walter was harder to figure. Only thirty-five years old, reed thin, with neatly trimmed black hair and mustache, he excelled at diplomacy. Although Burkett's junior by five years, it was he who was usually able to smooth the feathers that the principal ruffled, with soothing words and sincere concern. A native Clevelander and the son of a university mathematics professor, Walter enjoyed plays and books. In his off-hours, Burkett retired to a sheep farm that he had purchased a few years into his tenure in an adjacent rural county, working it himself with the help of a hired hand. During his time at the high school, the father of three would marry and divorce his second wife.

Walter, a committed Catholic and the father of two sons, had wed his college sweetheart right after graduation. He and his wife, Frances, Heights High's head librarian, had lived in Cleveland Heights ever since. Like many of the suburb's residents, the Walters were liberal in their social and political views and considered their residency to be an act of conscience, a means of bearing witness to their commitment to integration. They felt similarly about teaching at Heights High.

Burkett, on the other hand, never totally warmed to the unique character of the community. Having grown up in a society whose attitudes toward race were open and unambiguous, he found the residents of Cleveland Heights to be a little hypocritical. They liked to espouse the benefits of living in an integrated community, but he had attended few private parties there "where there was any racial mix."

The unfamiliarity of whites with blacks and vice versa, Burkett quickly recognized, was contributing to the discipline problem at Heights High School. As one of his earliest acts as principal, he began what he envisioned as a long-range professional development program aimed at providing the largely white staff with information and strategies that would ease subconscious fears of confronting young black men. Frank Walter was assigned the task of making arrangements to bring Dr. Jawanza Kunjufu, an educational consultant specializing in black culture and mores, to Cleveland Heights to conduct workshops for students, teachers, and parents on the subject of developing self-esteem and self-discipline in African-American children.

Kunjufu visited the high school in November 1984 and again in late January 1985, proving himself a versatile and popular speaker. He instructed the faculty on the predominate learning styles of African-American children and the importance of providing them with a curriculum and educational materials informed by a multicultural point of view.[1] Then he turned around and lectured an audience of black parents on the need to maintain a family dinner hour, limit television viewing, and engage their children in nightly conversations about the subjects that they were learning in school—a litany of middle-class values that would have offended the audience, Walter believed, had it come from the mouth of a white person.

Kunjufu's residency was followed in April 1985 by that of Charles E. King's. An African-American motivational consultant and an old friend of Burkett's who specialized in building self-confidence in students through vocal expression, King conducted a number of music workshops and an all-school concert in the gym. The students sitting in the bleachers were encouraged to sing along with the school's vocal music groups in the performance of various tunes, and, at the end of the assembly, King led a rousing rendition of "We Are the World." "Even the teachers, who were standing together at one end of the gym, locked arms and joined in the singing," Walter remembered. When he looked back over his career several years later, he decided that the assembly had been his most moving experience in the district.

The mood of goodwill and harmony engendered by King's residency was shared by the students. But the euphoria lasted, according to a Heights High graduate who was a sophomore at the time, "only about a week." An orderly and secure environment for learning could not be acquired for a song, not when unchartered groups with their colors, secret signs, and fierce rivalries had proliferated on campus like weeds on an untended lawn. Not when "drug thugs" (as Walter described the school's in-house pot dealers and pill pushers) held "open court" in the cafeteria every day, their impunity the result of the high school's open-campus policy, which made it impossible for the administration to monitor the comings and goings of more than two thousand adolescents.

Having an open campus also contributed to the more mundane problem of class cutting—students who left at lunchtime for a burger or, just as likely, a beer often did not bother to return—giving Heights High an attendance rate that ranked lower than that of 592 other school systems in the state. (Only twenty-three districts, most of them in Ohio's largest cities, reported worse attendance figures at the time.) Faced with a truancy problem of epidemic proportions, Burkett could have found it easy to forbid students to leave campus, but the new principal opted to wait a year before making a final assessment in the hopes of finding some way of preserving this student privilege.

To buy himself time with the disgruntled merchants nearby, Burkett posted one of the school's security monitors (an innovation of a previous administration) at a McDonald's on Lee Road that students liked to patronize during lunch. Then he set about the task of visiting every history and government class in the school to discuss the changes in student behavior that would have to come about in order for the campus to remain open. He also began the process of computerizing the high school's record keeping because he regarded instant access to truants' names and attendance records as the first step in bringing the problem of class cutting under control.

At the time, attendance and discipline statistics, grades, transcripts, and student and staff schedules were all recorded manually. (Nor were there any computers available in the building for educational purposes.) These primitive working conditions made for chaos each September and again at the beginning of the second semester in late January, when lines of students seeking to make class changes spilled out of the guidance office and down the hallway. Often a month elapsed before all of the students could be scheduled into their new courses, instructional time they lost forever.

Within a year of his arrival, Burkett had supervised the computerization of both attendance records and class scheduling—the automation of student transcripts, grades, and discipline records was to follow—and he had also begun pushing for the resources that would eventually allow for the desktop publishing of the student newspaper and yearbook, the outfitting of a large computer lab with more than a dozen computers for students' academic and personal use, and the purchase of mobile computer units equipped with overhead projectors for classroom instruction. Under Burkett's leadership Heights became the first public school in the country to join a library network, giving students electronic access to the card catalogues of public libraries throughout northern Ohio, their combined collections totaling nearly four million titles.

For his efforts, Burkett won a reputation for aloofness. He was more interested, some teachers said, in hiding in his office and playing with his personal computer than in serving as a stabilizing influence by making the rounds. Even the students, normally preoccupied with their own interests, noted his low profile. "I can't understand why our new principal . . . has not yet had an assembly to introduce himself," a young woman complained in a letter to the editor published in the student newspaper, the *Black and Gold*. "Until he casually introduced himself at the Homecoming assembly, few students recognized him." The latter observation remained a persistent complaint, even after Burkett attempted to raise his visibility by hosting an open "lunch with the principal" to discuss student concerns. Discouragingly, only six young people attended.

It was true that Burkett usually preferred management by objective to management by walking around, a tactic he dismissively described as "hall beating." Maintaining and monitoring up-to-date attendance records, for example, gave his administration the means to enforce a policy of withdrawing a truant from a course after six unexcused absences, an action that resulted in the truant's earning a failing grade. Such a consequence, it was hoped, would provide students with a good reason not to cut class. Another seemingly powerful incentive was put into action when the school began placing computerized telephone calls to the homes of students marked absent from class without an excuse.

The new procedure, which went into effect the second semester of the 1984–85 school year, soon became the butt of students' jokes, as it was not without glitches, such as the muffled quality of the recorded message informing parents of their children's truancy, the calls placed by mistake or at odd hours, and the mysterious disappearance of the attendance slips teachers posted on their classroom doors. "Things will be back to normal soon," a columnist for the *Black and Gold* assured his fellow students, adding facetiously, "Even parents will learn when . . . to be home in order that they, rather than their children, receive the phone call."

As the columnist predicted, some students continued to cut class recklessly, resulting in the withdrawal of pupils from more than two thousand classes during Burkett's first year as principal. The failure of his new tardy policy contributed to his decision to close the campus the following year. (It was not until the 1989–90 school year, when Burkett decided to invest the time and energy of his assistant principals in placing calls themselves to the parents of absent students, that the high school's problems with truancy, tardiness, and class cutting were temporarily brought under control.)

If the snafu with the computerized phone calls created doubts that Burkett meant business, an assembly he called shortly after spring break in 1985 dispelled that notion. There Burkett summarily announced revisions to ten disciplinary rules. Whereas previously the consequences for certain inappropriate behavior had ranged from parent-teacher conferences to detention to suspension, now those actions would automatically be punished with suspension: of three days' duration for loitering in unauthorized areas, of five days' duration for verbal abuse of teachers or failure to follow their directives, and of ten days' duration for fighting, to cite a few examples of the new rules. And anyone found possessing or using a weapon would be recommended for expulsion.

Contrasting sharply in tone with the more flexible and reasoned approach to discipline that marked his first eighteen months on the job, Burkett's get-tough policy was prompted by a terrifying wave of violence that had hit the high school earlier in the winter. In February a sixteen-year-old youth was raped by another youth in a bathroom. In March a seventeen-year-old pupil was stabbed during a fight. The following day a sixteen-year-old student grabbed an administrator by the throat and threatened her life. Given the severity of these incidents, the Burkett administration felt that it had no other recourse than to stiffen the school's disciplinary policies. This decision was officially approved by the superintendent and the board of education, and reinforced in a formal statement to the community by the board that warned, "Let there be no mistake. No one will be allowed to disrupt the learning process."

Even so, students greeted the announcement of the new school rules with "anger and hostility," as most of them never caused serious trouble. Students were especially displeased by the undiplomatic way in which the announcement was made, the *Black and Gold* explained in its traditionally feisty manner:

> Students were herded a thousand at a time into a hot auditorium and talked at for twenty-five minutes. In the voice of a drill sergeant, Mr. Burkett called off the rules one by one, straight through, without once stopping to let the audience catch its breath. . . . Burkett warned the students not to mess up, "because if you do, we're going to get you!" This was immediately followed by the displaying of the document [explaining the new rules] on every classroom door. . . .
>
> A simple notice in the [daily school] bulletin would have quite adequately told the students all they needed to know.

While the students no doubt heard Burkett's message, not all of them decided to pay attention to it. After nine fights took place inside the building in

January 1986 and eight in March, Burkett felt compelled to tighten the rules once again, instituting a policy of emergency removal that allowed the administration to send disruptive or violent students home without the benefit of an official suspension hearing. And in a "state of the school" address made in early March 1986, shortly after two security monitors suffered cuts to their hands when attempting to disarm a knife-wielding student who had been involved in an altercation in the cafeteria, he announced his intention of expelling students who persisted in fighting at school. The ten-day suspension meted out as a penalty for such unacceptable behavior had apparently failed as a deterrent. Now any student caught fighting would automatically be dismissed from school for the duration of the semester, a forced exile that could last up to eighty days, depending on when during the school year the fight occurred.

Much of the violent behavior at Heights High, Burkett was starting to realize, stemmed from rivalries among the school's underground fraternities, sororities, and social groups. The oldest of these was the B.A.T. fraternity, formed at the high school nearly sixty years before. Even in the halcyon 1950s, the B.A.T.s were rowdies who liked to intimidate and harass nonmembers, and they had even been known to crash the private parties of their schoolmates and break up the furniture. Although many of their alumni went on to become prominent Cleveland citizens, the B.A.T.s and their imitators had never shed their interest in picking fights. They remained, in Frank Walter's eyes, "gangs with college aspirations."

Because these pseudo-Greek fraternities and sororities were closed to African Americans when Heights High began to undergo integration in the 1970s, they had spawned a number of parallel black social organizations, most notably, a group called the Brothers, which required its members to be school athletes and maintain a certain grade point average. In the 1980s black students who could not pass muster with the Brothers formed a rival group called the Home Boys, whose only apparent agenda, as far as the Burkett administration was concerned, was to prove their masculinity. (The Home Boys tattooed themselves with their club's insignia and required wanna-bes to jump a Brother as part of their induction ritual.) Young men who found themselves excluded from the Home Boys formed their own cliques, and in this manner the number of unchartered groups at the high school expanded rapidly. The instability of its social scene would in time make Heights High an attractive recruiting ground for full-fledged gangs in neighboring Cleveland or East Cleveland that were looking to start new "sets."

Recognizing that past attempts to outlaw unchartered groups had failed—in the 1950s the district had threatened to suspend fraternity members who refused to sign official "death warrants" putting their groups out of business, only to watch the organizations move their social activities underground—Burkett decided to try a different approach. During the troubled winter of 1986, he asked Walter to establish the Non-Chartered Organization Council as a way of monitoring and rechanneling the activities of the warring groups. In exchange for providing the administration with a complete list of their members and promising to observe the school's disciplinary rules, the unchartered groups were given the right to wear their colors, insignia, and paraphernalia to school. As it turned out, these advertisements only served to escalate tensions among the various groups. ("It created a de facto intimidation factor," Walter discovered. "When five guys in purple T-shirts walked up to you, they might have just wanted to know what homeroom you were in, but it didn't look or feel like that.") After only eighteen months of existence, the council was disbanded as ineffective in curbing gang fighting. Henceforth, the Burkett administration made clear, unchartered groups had no place on campus.

Even as Walter attempted to work with Heights High's groups and gangs, Burkett warned the community that the problem of youth violence could not be solved by the high school alone. When interviewed in the spring of 1986 by the discipline and safety subcommittee of the School Consensus Project (a community-led investigation of the problems facing the Cleveland Heights–University Heights system), he mentioned a coalition consisting of the public schools, city government, police, social service agencies, churches, the juvenile courts, parents, and legal organizations that had been put together in Chicago to deal with gang problems, and Burkett encouraged the School Consensus Project to start such an organization in the district.

At the principal's behest, the school district later invited a representative of the California-based National School Safety Center to come help the community develop a comprehensive plan of action against youth violence. A series of organizational meetings was subsequently held, with diminishing results. In Walter's view, the comments of most of the other participants revealed a "What? Me worry?" attitude toward the problem. Even after superintendent Irv Moskowitz appeared before a joint meeting of the school board and city council to present a bag full of confiscated weapons—including such novel items as handcuffs and a chair leg with nails protruding from it—civic leaders refused to acknowledge the reality of the gang threat, according to a school board member who was present. With no hope of outside reinforcements, the Burkett administration began to take on a siege mentality.

To put muscle into the enforcement of his new disciplinary rules, Burkett had already upped the number of security monitors stationed in the building in the fall of 1985 from ten to eighteen. (Even after budgetary restrictions reduced its ranks to thirteen, the Heights High security force was by far the most heavily staffed of any school in the vicinity.) That same fall he also established the post of chief of security, to which he appointed an African American who had spent the previous two decades working in the Cleveland Public Schools as a district supervisor of safety and security. In addition to planning for the closing of the campus, the new security chief instituted a training program for the monitors and outfitted them with walkie-talkies on which they were taught to communicate using police radio codes.[2]

In the fall of 1986, as part of his multipronged attack on the school's discipline problems, Burkett entrusted Walter with a critical new job, naming him principal of Lee House, the administrative office that handled disciplinary matters involving ninth and tenth graders. (Juniors and seniors came under the supervision of Cedar House.) This was a logical promotion. Walter had supervised all the preparations for the transfer of the ninth grade from junior high school into the high school, a move that had taken place the previous year as part of a districtwide reorganization plan aimed at cutting costs by closing underutilized buildings and reshuffling students. The reorganization, which propelled the high school's enrollment to three thousand students and added twenty-nine teachers to its staff, created as many problems as it solved.

Already among the largest secondary schools in the country, Heights must have seemed to the newcomers a truly impersonal place.[3] They may not have encountered the dehumanizing system of "up" and "down" staircases that was instituted during the 1950s (when enrollment was beginning its climb to a peak of thirty-six hundred) to smooth the passage of the baby-boom generation in the hallways between classes. But they soon discovered that there were not enough lockers, food stations in the cafeteria, or caring adults to go around.

Frequently too immature to handle the freedoms and responsibilities of high school life, ninth graders proved themselves in short order to be the school's most volatile and vulnerable youth. While the board of education continued to report that the system's dropout rate was 1 or 2 percent, more than 25 percent of the students who now entered Heights High as ninth graders would not go on to graduate with their class. Although district officials were less than forthcoming about this phenomenon, the high school's guidance counselors were all too aware of the fact that problem students who did not drop out often spent five or six years accumulating sufficient credits to graduate.

Ninth and tenth graders also began to constitute the preponderance of those suspended or expelled, and dealing with these disciplinary cases kept Walter's hands full. While the number of students suspended from the high school had hovered between three hundred and four hundred a year since the late 1970s, the number of expulsions had increased dramatically since Burkett's arrival. Before 1984 no one had been expelled, Walter guessed, in two or three years. In 1986–87, the first year Walter ran Lee House, seventy-five ninth and tenth graders were recommended for expulsion, along with thirty juniors and seniors.

The 1986–87 school year was also Irv Moskowitz's first as superintendent, and at one point he remarked to the Lee House principal that the high school's suspension and expulsion figures seemed high. "It's more than we ever did in Denver," said Moskowitz, who had previously served as assistant superintendent of the Denver public schools.

The superintendent's remarks echoed a national debate on the question of whether such exclusionary measures violated a student's Fourteenth Amendment rights, particularly in light of the fact that minorities were disproportionately represented among those kicked out of school. In fact, black students were twice as likely as whites to be suspended, a national trend that held true at Heights.[4] But the implicit criticism did not particularly faze Walter. "I didn't think Denver was a very good school system," he explained. And at the time, community sentiment seemed to support the Burkett administration's hard-nosed approach. In a 1986 phone survey conducted by a professional research firm on behalf of the School Consensus Project, a random sampling of residents in the district was asked to tick off concerns about the local schools: discipline was mentioned by the greatest number of respondents. (In this respect, Heights residents were no different from their fellow Americans, who consistently cited lack of discipline as a top concern when asked by national pollsters for their opinions on public education.)

Even as it came down hard on persistent troublemakers (who constituted only about 10 percent of the student body, Burkett guessed), the high school administration displayed some interest in preventive measures. It instituted a number of innovations, such as the "time out" area created in the Lee and Cedar House offices to which students committing minor offenses—talking back to a teacher, say, or wearing a hat indoors—could be sent for informal counseling before their behavior deteriorated further. In-school detention, a strictly monitored, all-day study hall—to which students who had committed more serious offenses such as excessive truancy or tardiness could be sent to work independently instead of being thrown out on the streets—was set up during Burkett's third year at Heights.

The school even instituted group therapy sessions for persistent rule breakers, which were led by a black male social worker. Within a few years these informal rap sessions evolved into a full-blown conflict-mediation program—the latest addition to an array of in-house services aimed at treating the academic, social, and medical problems of students.[5]

If Burkett did little during his first three-year contract to address the troubling question raised by the need for all these special programs—that is, to what extent were they bandages applied to wounds inflicted by inequities inherent in the school system itself?—it may have been due to the amount of time he devoted to the challenge of restoring order.[6] Without a peaceful learning environment for students, Burkett felt he could not turn his attention to meaningful academic reform. That kind of initiative would have to await the return of a modicum of order, which came about during Burkett's second three-year term.[7]

Burkett's vigilance may have been driven as much by the personal as by the pragmatic, though. As a two-year-old child he had nearly lost his life because of a moment of careless behavior on his nine-year-old brother's part. Swinging a brush-clearing implement too close to the toddler, Burkett's brother had slashed the child in the face, a wound so deep Hugh almost bled to death. Grateful for his survival, his mother pronounced the boy her "miracle baby"; but he and his brother, unable to resolve their feelings about what had happened, never spoke of the accident, a silence that erected an invisible barrier between them. The accident left Burkett with a long red scar on his left cheek, as well as a lasting intolerance for the indifference of the young to the potentially dangerous consequences of their thoughtless or angry behavior.

The visceral nature of the principal's commitment to restoring order at the high school revealed itself early on in his willingness to roll up his sleeves and play the enforcer. Maintaining public safety after sporting events or dances was always a problem, as throngs of youths lingered in the streets surrounding the high school, looking to pick a fight or witness one. Over the years a number of young men had been stabbed after school events, and one of the victims had died from his wounds. Nonetheless, Frank Walter was astounded to see Burkett wade into the crowd after the very first home football game of his tenure, single-handedly breaking up the shoving matches and fistfights that inevitably followed these interschool competitions. Burkett never dispensed with this postevent intervention, although later he was accompanied by Walter and another assistant principal whom he had recruited. He and Walter also began to patrol lot 5 during the students' lunch hour, seeking to curb misbehavior and encourage students to return to the school.

Burkett's hands-on supervision of his students' after-hours and off-campus activities caught the eye of the Cleveland Heights police, who were not accustomed to seeing high school officials take an active interest in such matters. The police had come to expect that they would receive little or no cooperation from high school authorities, thanks to an incident of alleged police brutality that took place at Heights High during what the media termed a "race riot" involving some two hundred students in the mid-1970s.[8]

Ever since that day, Burkett discovered, high school authorities had operated according to an unofficial rule: no cops on campus. However, because cooperation with the police had been an accepted practice at the schools at which Burkett had previously worked, he put an end to that longstanding taboo. He did not go so far as to sit down regularly with the police department, a custom at one of his former schools, where the police conferred with the principals every Monday morning, passing along the names of students arrested over the weekend, in case they might pose a hazard to their fellows. Nor, depending on the seriousness of the incident, did Burkett feel compelled to report every on-campus assault or fight to the police, as board of education policy dictated.

However, at some point the Burkett administration began to perform small courtesies for the Cleveland Heights police. Were an administrator to come across a flyer advertising an upcoming house party in the suburb, suspecting that juveniles would be present at the bash, where alcohol and adrenaline were likely to flow, the Burkett administration would turn the flyer over to the beat cops, alerting the police department to a potential trouble spot in the community. Or, if the police showed up with a picture of a young person who had passed a bad check at a business where sales transactions were videotaped, school officials would assist, if possible, in identifying the suspect. In return, patrolmen and officers began sharing information with the Burkett administration about high school students who had run seriously afoul of the law.

By the end of Burkett's second year in Cleveland Heights, the persistent attention to disciplinary matters had begun to show a modest payoff. Average daily attendance for the third quarter of the year stood at higher than 92 percent—still nothing to crow about, but an improvement over third-quarter 1985 figures of 89.5 percent. The number of failures due to unexcused absences declined from 9.1 percent of all grades to 5.4 percent during the same period, while the school's grade point average inched upward from 1.69, a D, to 1.92, a D+.

After the news of these trends was published in the *Black and Gold,* the high school's chief union steward challenged the truthfulness of the administration's data. If attendance and grades were up, it was only because there were now more students in the building, he informed a reporter for the student newspaper, referring to the influx of ninth graders. The *Black and Gold* dutifully printed the steward's illogical objection, as well as his related complaint that administrators were allowing parents to phone in substanceless excuses for their children's absences weeks after they occurred, ignoring a previously established forty-eight-hour deadline. It was this lapse in protocol, the steward claimed, that actually accounted for the reduction in the number of failing grades due to unexcused absences: Students withdrawn from classes and given Fs because of persistent truancy were now being reenrolled as a result of parental fibbing.

If the steward discounted the formidable influence parents wielded over the school, neither did his superiors seem too concerned about the fact that their caving in to such transparent pressure tactics disrupted the smooth operation of the teachers' classrooms. In the next issue of the *Black and Gold,* Burkett coolly pointed out the steward's error in logic: "Contrary to some teachers' claims that the improvement [in grades and attendance] is due to the addition of the 9th graders to Heights, Dr. Burkett said the improvement cannot be attributed to the increase in students because the data is presented by percentage of students in the school."

Perceptions to the contrary, some of the school's most nagging discipline problems were showing signs of melioration, and the time seemed ripe to free Frank Walter for less procedural work. When the high school's long-time assistant principal in charge of curriculum and instruction retired in 1988, Burkett named Walter to replace her. Now Burkett had an enthusiastic second-in-command for another important campaign, this one centering on the professional development of the Heights High faculty.

Unlike other principals who found themselves overburdened by the demands of maintaining a safe and orderly school, Burkett was not willing to enter into a devil's bargain with the teachers. He did not buy into the terms of the unspoken agreement by which many schools across the country operated: that as long as the teachers kept their classes under control and did not unduly add to the administrative workload by sending a steady stream of misbehavers to the principal's office, they were free to teach (or not teach) as they saw fit. Burkett wanted more than peaceful coexistence with the Heights High faculty. His aspirations were deceptively simple. As Walter later described it in a farewell speech to his mentor and friend, Burkett sought to challenge the teachers *to think.*

4
Time for Reflection

In our search for the solution to the problems of educational inequality our focus was almost exclusively on the characteristics of the children themselves. We looked for sources of educational failure in their homes, their neighborhoods, their language, their cultures, even in their genes. In all our searching we almost entirely overlooked the possibility that what happens within *schools might contribute to unequal educational opportunities and outcomes. We neglected to examine the content and processes of schooling itself for the ways they might contribute to school failure.*

—JEANNIE OAKES,
Keeping Track: How Schools Structure Inequality, 1985

With the arrival of Irv Moskowitz, who was named superintendent of the Cleveland Heights–University Heights schools in the summer of 1986, Burkett acquired an even more powerful ally in his endeavor to provide the high school faculty with instructional leadership. In fact, it was Moskowitz who would be the catalyst for the Model School Project.

Tall, slender, and youthful, Moskowitz had come to northern Ohio from a position as assistant commissioner of education for the State of Colorado, eager at age fifty-one to make a personal difference in the education of disadvantaged children. This objective seemed to him more achievable in a small school system. Although they shared a similar philosophy of education, Burkett never totally warmed to Moskowitz; he found the superintendent a

trifle glib. However, Burkett enjoyed talking with Moskowitz, who was a
font of ideas about secondary education, and usually accepted the superintendent's invitation whenever Moskowitz called to suggest lunch.

The two men liked to purchase sausage sandwiches and black olives from
an Italian grocery near district headquarters and picnic in Purvis Park in University Heights when the weather permitted. They would sit in the bleachers at the baseball diamond and kick around the subject of secondary
education. As far as Moskowitz was concerned, the American high school
was an archaic institution. The list of its antiquated features was endless, beginning with a physical plant based on an outmoded assembly-line model;
teacher-centered instruction that fostered memorization at the expense of
developing critical-thinking skills; and a curriculum whose content was basically unchanged from that of nearly a century before. At Heights High
these intrinsic flaws were exacerbated, in Moskowitz's opinion, by the problems attendant to an oversized student body and a declining inner-ring
suburban location. All of these factors combined to create an academic experience for some students that Moskowitz characterized as "custodial." How
many kids, the superintendent wondered, was the high school merely ware-
housing?

In contrast to Moskowitz's abstract musings, Burkett held extremely
heated opinions about the source of Heights High's problems with student
achievement. He agreed with the superintendent's contention that too many
children were being allowed to "limp through" their four years at the high
school, but he attributed that phenomenon to a malaise far more insidious
than institutional ossification. Burkett believed that it was the color of one's
skin, pure and simple, that determined the quality of education one received
at Heights High School.

How else to explain why more than 80 percent of those students allowed
to sign up for "gifted and talented" English were Caucasians, while 80 percent of those channeled into standard, or low-ability, English were African
Americans? This lopsided pattern of enrollment was repeated in social studies, math, and science courses as well. African Americans represented close to
80 percent of those students enrolled in the standard-level courses of the
school's four main academic subjects, even though by the mid-1980s they
constituted a little less than 60 percent of the total student body. They were
also overrepresented among those pursuing general or vocational diplomas
rather than academic degrees.

Despite periodic pressure to do so, the school district had circumvented
all demands that it abolish ability grouping, a program first set up in the early

1960s to provide honors students with an enriched curriculum. After the board of education formally approved the practice of grouping in 1970, the program evolved into a structure so elaborate and entrenched that it had resulted in the absurdity of the high school's offering both standard and gifted and talented physics. In 1979 an internal curriculum committee called upon the school system to put an end to ability grouping, a demand repeated the following year by the Urban League of Greater Cleveland. The civil rights organization released to the newspapers an impassioned report detailing how "tracking goes beyond earlier attempts to meet the needs of the so-called 'gifted and talented' and has begun to foster . . . a dual instructional system characterized by race and class." In response to the unfavorable publicity, then-superintendent Albert Abramovitz decided that ability grouping should not be abandoned, but rather improved.[1]

With 40 percent of the student body still enrolled in low-track classes as of 1985–86, the School Consensus Project (SCP) again sounded the alarm that "students are not being equally challenged to learn and to achieve." Yet SCP's curriculum subcommittee was unable to recommend a remedy, its members having found ability grouping too emotional and divisive an issue to deal with on a rational basis. Instead SCP leaders kicked the issue back to the school district, urging the board of education to reexamine its grouping practices.

Abramovitz's successor, Irv Moskowitz, responded with a written promise to conduct a study. A teachers' committee was subsequently convened at the high school to discuss grouping, but it met only a few times before losing steam. If Moskowitz's promised reexamination was halfhearted, it may have been because SCP's own research showed that fully three-quarters of the parents of students attending district schools supported ability grouping. They accepted the traditional rationale that achievers would be "dragged down" if required to be part of heterogenous classes, while the less motivated or quick would not be able to keep pace with the "bright" kids. The welfare of children other than their own offspring was not a matter of parental concern.

Although he did not share his exact sentiments with superintendent Moskowitz at their lunchtime get-togethers, Hugh Burkett suspected that there was an unspoken reason for the district's intransigence on the issue. He believed that the school system maintained ability grouping at the high school primarily as a means of combating white flight, fearing that the eighty-year-old institution would otherwise become an all-black island surrounded by an indifferent sea of white taxpayers.

That whites were abandoning the school system was indisputable. Between 1975 and 1981, when enrollment in the system declined by 18 percent overall, the number of white students dropped a precipitous 43 percent. Some observers were quick to explain away the significance of the statistics by pointing to the fact that Cleveland Heights and University Heights were home to large populations of Orthodox Jews and Catholics, who often preferred to give their children a religious education. Others made reference to new homeowner statistics showing that white newcomers to the community had substantially fewer children than black home buyers and that the latter made disproportionate use of the public schools.

While these observations were true, it was also true that the percentage of white children who lived in the district but attended private or religious schools had increased from 29 to 39 percent between 1975 and 1981, during which time the number of public school students of African-American descent nearly doubled. When asked whether they thought that parents were transferring their children out of the Heights system because of concern about the increasing number of nonwhites in attendance, a majority of respondents to the School Consensus Project's 1986 research survey said yes.

As Burkett saw it, district officials hoped to slow the loss of Caucasian students from the high school by relegating most African-American students to standard or average-ability expanded tracks, thus creating an oasis for white students in the school's upper-level classes. In the principal's eyes this quiet accommodation to white prejudice and fear amounted to "institutional racism." Burkett regarded the district's case of the disease as especially virulent, given the preponderance of evidence about the harmful effects of ability grouping, and he privately vowed to end, or at least diminish, the use of ability grouping at the high school.[2]

Unlike their principal, however, most members of the faculty supported the high school's reliance on ability grouping. Some did so for reasons of convenience, believing it easier to teach students who were presorted into homogenous groups. Others insisted that the system was acting with the best interests of the slower or problem student at heart. It was unfair, they argued, to expect children who were culturally disadvantaged or at risk because of family or personal problems to compete in the same classes with those who were better prepared academically or more highly motivated.

If there were those who believed that African Americans, who constituted the majority of standard-track students, could not be expected to do well academically because they were inferior to whites, they were careful not to express those sentiments out loud. Yet the staff's attitude toward standard classes spoke volumes. When Burkett came to Cleveland Heights, only select teachers who had an "in" with the administration were allowed to teach gifted and talented courses, which were considered plum assignments because the students were a pleasure to teach. On the other hand, teachers who were in the doghouse with the administration or thought to be incompetent were consigned to teaching standard courses, the educational equivalent of Siberia.

Burkett was convinced that the staff's poor image of standard classes amounted to a self-fulfilling prophesy. He believed that low expectations bred poor performance. For evidence one need look no further than standard-level students' grades, whose distribution did not follow, as one would expect, a normal bell curve. Standard students were more likely to flunk than their fellows in other tracks, even though standard courses employed less challenging textbooks, were taught at a slower pace, and covered less material than their more demanding counterparts—concessions presumably aimed at leveling the playing field for the less "gifted" student. During the first semester of the 1986–87 school year, for example, standard-track kids received 90 percent of all failing grades.

Just as troubling to Burkett, more than one-fifth of all grades meted out that semester had been Fs. (Half of the failing grades were due to poor performance and half due to poor attendance.) The high number of failures seemed to Burkett proof that, on the whole, the faculty accepted the notion that some students were simply unable to learn. Rather than taking a student's failure as a warning sign that they needed to modify their teaching methods, teachers preferred to blame poor performance on the student's lack of motivation or readiness. "Don't judge me" seemed to him to be the prevailing attitude. "I have this program, and it's the *kids* who won't go along."

In their search for scapegoats, the teachers embraced the myth that the vast majority of the kids experiencing academic troubles at the high school were "new" to the district, meaning that these students were the poorly prepared products of the Cleveland public schools they attended before moving to Cleveland Heights. While Burkett's records showed that newcomers to the school were indeed the cause of most of its disciplinary problems, a 1987 survey of ninth graders ordered by superintendent Moskowitz uncovered a different, more uncomfortable reality. Heights High's failing students were not "border jumpers"—kids who claimed to live in the suburb while residing in the inner city—another common myth. The study revealed that more than 65 percent of the school's freshmen had moved into the district no later than their third-grade year. By and large, Heights High's African-American students were Cleveland Heights kids!

Indeed, Burkett sensed that the biggest problem at the high school was the faculty's inability and, in some cases, refusal to respond to the school's changing demographics. Many of the veteran white teachers seemed unwilling or unable to come to grips with the fact that their beloved institution was now predominately black. The transformation of Shaw High School in neighboring East Cleveland from all white to all black in the space of a decade (that suburb having lacked the civic will to combat white flight) was often discussed in tones suggesting that some Heights teachers feared a similar fate for their school. While many white teachers professed to value working in an integrated environment—and their continuing employment at Heights lent some credence to their claims—some of their African-American colleagues privately suspected that this preference was based at least in part on the assumption that an all-black school was an inferior school.

But no matter their race, Heights High faculty members were alike in approaching their students from a middle-class perspective. Most lacked the frame of reference, to say nothing of the special education and training, needed to cope more easily with the readiness, motivation, and values of children whose parents were only a few years removed from the inner city. Lacking the time, predisposition, or skills to do otherwise, the faculty in the main clung to the tried-and-true pedagogy learned in college, despite its unsatisfactory results.

Some teachers defended their decision to maintain traditional methodology and accustomed curriculum as a "refusal to lower standards." Burkett dismissed this characterization. To him the faculty's ability to tolerate a high degree of student failure was nothing less than shameful. By insisting that some youngsters were incapable of academic work, teachers neatly absolved themselves of accountability for student performance. Only when teachers stopped blaming others for Heights High's problems and faced up squarely to their personal responsibility for helping to solve those problems, Burkett insisted, could the high school begin to be turned around.

The lunchtime discussions of Moskowitz and Burkett would inevitably turn to the question of what could be done to remove the faculty's blinders. Out of these brainstorming sessions, sometime in 1987, emerged the concept of the Model School Project.

The idea of asking the faculty to restructure the high school appealed to Moskowitz for a number of reasons, not the least of which was the issue of finances. In Moskowitz's opinion, the healthy raise Glenn Altschuld had negotiated for the teachers immediately before Moskowitz's arrival had squeezed the district's resources to the point that there was now no money for extras, such as hiring consultants to help the high school solve its problems. If Heights High were to be reformed, the answers would have to come from within.

The concept of involving the teachers in a strategic planning process also fit with Moskowitz's desire to do something about the faculty's lack of vision and drive, a perception formed when he toured the building shortly after coming to Cleveland Heights. Shocked by the high school's rundown and gloomy appearance, Moskowitz had asked himself: If the teachers can accept such shabby working conditions, what other, more serious problems are they able to live with? What has happened to their ability to dream?

As a result of his tour, Moskowitz decided to have the high school repainted—a job that had been halted, after most of the first floor was finished, when a number of teachers protested that they had not been consulted about the choice of a color scheme. After it was discovered that the district would end 1986–87 with a multimillion-dollar deficit, the paint job was never completed, with the result that the building's interior thereafter remained a mixture of colors even uglier than before.

Another Moskowitz initiative would have a more transforming effect in that it revitalized the district's interest in providing staff with professional development programming—of which the Model School Project would become a major component. When he discovered that previous superintendents, in attempting to economize, had allowed the budget for the district's human resources department to dwindle to practically nothing, Moskowitz pushed the board of education to allocate resources for staff workshops and training and to create a new central-office position: director of staff development. Moskowitz recognized that skimping on the provision of professional development activities for teachers was a measure of false economy, especially given the unfamiliar demands being placed on them by the system's new clientele.

Although the concept of the Model School Project appealed to Burkett primarily as a means to improved student achievement, he also shared the superintendent's interest in providing teachers with opportunities for professional growth. Both administrators expected that the project would lead to site-based management of the high school. Moskowitz, however, envisioned the transfer of power to be a glacial process involving years of teacher training and "practice" governance, while Burkett had already proved his determination to share decision-making authority with Heights High's faculty, whether the teachers were prepared or not.

Several years before it became a national buzzword, Burkett was promoting the concept of teacher empowerment at Heights High. Even a chief union steward who would later characterize Burkett as an "artful dodger—he'd say one thing to one group, another thing to the next group, and then do a third thing!"—admitted that his first impression of the administrator had been favorable: Here, incredibly, was a teacher-oriented principal. When Burkett mentioned one day that he would prefer to see the faculty run Heights High, the steward was taken aback. "This guy is never going to last," he said to himself. "The board of education will never go for that."

True to his word, Burkett had taken several steps to involve the faculty in the high school's governance, such as reinstating a teacher as chairperson of each of the school's eleven academic departments. The position, which Burkett renamed department "liaison," had been dropped during the previous administration. (The precipitating event: a rebellion by half of the English teachers against what they perceived to be the arbitrary and punitive behavior of the previous administration's appointed chairperson. Seceding from the department, the rebels had elected their own departmental leader. Burkett's predecessor deemed it best to abolish the position of department chairperson altogether rather than try to put down this mutiny.)

Although Burkett had initially appointed the liaison for each department, as was traditional, he soon turned over to the departments the power to select their own leaders, to whom he eventually delegated certain curricular responsibilities. For example, he gave the liaisons the authority to determine, in consultation with their colleagues, their department's course offerings and the power to establish teaching assignments and schedules. Each department also received a modest discretionary budget; in short, their autonomy was far greater than had been the case previously. During the tenure of Burkett's immediate predecessors, teachers could not even give a multiple-choice test without the permission of the assistant principal for curriculum and instruction, who parceled out the standardized Scantron response forms only after she had approved the test's content and format. Burkett remembered that when he arrived at Heights High, the Scantron budget for the entire school was $800. Now that teachers no longer had to grovel to get the forms, which were designed to make grading multiple-choice tests much easier and quicker, the budget had soared to $9,000.

Despite Burkett's instinctive desire to operate the high school on principles others were later to recognize and applaud as shared decision making
and site-based management, he was slow to take action on his conversation with Moskowitz about reforming Heights High. After working for
Moskowitz for nearly a year, Burkett realized that if he tried to follow
through on every one of the superintendent's "what-ifs," he would be
spending all his time "leaping tall buildings." He had a high school to run,
after all, and in the press of more immediate business, the task of getting faculty members excited about restructuring their school slipped to the bottom
of Burkett's list of things to do. Burkett's hesitation may also have had to do
with the relative failure of his attempts to work a similar alchemy with the
building's union stewards.

Burkett had never before been obliged to work with a militant teachers'
union. His only previous experience with organized labor occurred during
college, when he obtained summer employment in a couple of factories.
Accustomed to the backbreaking labor of tobacco farming, he was soon
outproducing his fellow hourly workers at a well-known soup manufacturer
where he had landed a job. His industriousness won him a transfer into paid
piecework. At a can company at which he subsequently worked, the union
had a different tactic for dealing with overproducers. There Burkett was
threatened with physical harm if his output continued to exceed daily quo-
tas. These confrontations left him with an unfavorable impression of labor
unions that his experiences with AFT Local 795 did little to mitigate.

At the monthly meetings that protocol required him to hold with the
faculty's elected representatives, Burkett often tried to steer the discussion to
issues of school program or structure. But ("Welcome to Heights High")
Burkett found that the stewards were interested only in presenting the latest
list of complaints brought to their attention by teachers. These ranged from
recurring gripes about inadequate supplies of toilet paper and soap in the
restrooms and the irritating length of the daily public-address announcements to laments about oversized classes and the lack of needed materials. It
was the stewards' expectation that Burkett or Frank Walter, who was also
present at the sessions, would immediately attend to these problems.

Burkett had tried again and again to develop a collaborative working relationship with the stewards, one that he wished to see characterized not only
by union-management cooperation in identifying problems—a skill at
which he judged the stewards to be excellent—but also by the union's participation in solving them. The stewards had trouble accepting the latter

proposition because of the belief—deeply inculcated in teachers and princi-pals alike by a century of mutual work history—that administrators alone bore responsibility for the efficient running of schools.

In Burkett's view, the stewards pooh-poohed participatory management because they wanted no part of making what might prove to be unpopular decisions, especially those involving the evaluation of their peers. No, the stewards preferred to play a reactive role: informing administrators just how and where their decisions had gone wrong. Some of the stewards, on the other hand, interpreted Burkett's interest in shared decision making as a management ploy to shove more responsibility on teachers, whom they re-garded as already underpaid and overworked. This attitude had led the union to demand and win a provision in its contract prohibiting the district from requiring teachers to participate in professional development activities after working hours. Even if teachers voluntarily chose to take advantage of staff workshops and training, they must be compensated for their participa-tion at an agreed-upon hourly rate. Lacking the resources to pay the teachers for their involvement in designing a model school, Burkett had little chance of getting a restructuring project off the ground.

Perhaps hoping to give Burkett a nudge, Irv Moskowitz mentioned the idea of a teacher-led restructuring project to Larry Peacock, his new director of staff development. On the job for less than a year and eager to build the clout and resources of his department, Peacock rushed to put together a concrete plan. In consultation with a focus group of teachers at the high school, Peacock wrote a first draft of a proposal for the Model School Project, complete with rationale, modus operandi, organizational chart, budget, and timeline. After seeing Peacock's work, Burkett began to believe that what had seemed a speculative conversation with Moskowitz might ac-tually come to fruition. He and the superintendent polished the draft and presented it to the Cleveland Foundation, which agreed in March 1988 to award the requested amount. The school district received $72,000 for the project's first year, a sum that would be swelled by additional Cleveland Foundation grants totalling $177,000.[3] The monies were to be used to pur-chase a precious commodity: teachers' time.

Perhaps because their day was so regimented, Heights teachers seemed to be continually pressed. Feeling themselves too rushed to think things through and do things right, they had become accustomed to operating on the fly. The school system's structure encouraged slapdash work in another way. Although administrators throughout the district were not shy about asking faculty members to serve on ad hoc committees formed to address this or that problem, the teachers' contract, revealingly, made no real provision for meetings.

Whether it was because the district was only going through the motions of involving teachers in planning efforts, or because the union had resisted attempts to lengthen the contractual day, teachers were available for meetings only for fifteen minutes before the beginning of first period and for forty-five minutes after classes ended. These interludes were neither sufficient time to engage in serious planning nor the hours most conducive to producing quality work. (Further evidence that district officials paid lip service only to the concept of participatory management could be seen in the absence of a formal conference room at Heights High. Committee meetings often took place in someone's classroom, with teachers scrunched into students' desks pulled into a ragged circle, as if for storytelling hour.) The Cleveland Foundation grant would allow the Model School Project to proceed on a more professional basis. Grant monies could be used to hire substitutes so that teachers could be released from their classes to conduct research on operational, instructional, and curricular innovations that were proving successful in improving student achievement at the secondary level elsewhere, a knowledge base on which they could then draw in their endeavor to redesign Heights High.

Funds were also available to pay the salary of a part-time project manager, and it was in making a decision about who should be entrusted with this complicated coordinating job that things began to go awry.

5

The Dilemma of Leadership

There is a certain ambivalence . . . in the teacher's sentiments. He yearns for more independence, greater resources, and, just possibly, more control over key resources. But he accepts the hegemony of the school system on which he is economically and functionally dependent. . . . He is poised between the impulse to control his work life and the necessity to accept its vagaries; perhaps he holds back partly because he is at heart uncertain that he can produce predictable results.

—DAN C. LORTIE
Schoolteacher: A Sociological Study, 1975

The job of Model School project manager called for a special person indeed, although at the time no one appreciated the breadth of talents required. The ideal candidate would have possessed the mind of a military strategist, the organizational skills of a presidential campaign manager, the charisma and vision of a great political leader, and the diplomacy of a peace negotiator. Had a job description been written, it might have stated: Articulate a rationale for reform; persuade the faculty of the benefits of change; create study teams to research various components of a model school; inspire teachers to join the study teams; motivate the study teams to carry out a thorough study of the literature of education reform; plan site visits to innovative schools; bring in inspirational speakers and national experts to lecture and consult; respond to serendipitous developments, snags, and crises. Call that phase 1.

In phase 2: Seek input from other staff members and students; help study teams analyze their research findings and shape them into coherent structures, programs, or procedures; assess the strengths and weaknesses of the emerging model; resolve disputes about the philosophy or content of the model; produce agreement on a new direction for the school; devise a way to bring nonparticipating teachers into the fold; keep the principal and superintendent informed and invested in the project; sell the board of education and the community on the final model. Oh, and by the way, continue to teach two classes a day.

Even at a smaller, more homogenous high school, none of these consensus-building tasks would have been easy. At Heights, where the faculty was extremely large and diverse, it was difficult to obtain general agreement on the day's date. (So freethinking was this staff that one teacher invariably objected to the secular performance of hymns or gospel music at student concerts as an unconstitutional blending of church and state.) A bureaucratic system that ceded teachers control only over the life of their classrooms encouraged them to be fiercely protective of their individual and departmental turf.

At the same time, their confinement within the four walls of their rooms pushed them to seek camaraderie and a sense of identity and self-worth offered by affiliation with one of the school's various in-groups. These inevitable fealties furthered the disunity of the Heights staff, an obstacle to consensus that the Model School Project would have to surmount.

The most prominent in-group at the high school was the union, for obvious reasons. The individual teacher was isolated and weak, lacking even the power to command a private office space or a phone of her own. (If she possessed any leverage at all, it lay in her ability to complain, sidestep, and resist. The Heights High faculty had a term for this passive-aggressive behavior: it was called "throwing your body in front of" an unpopular administrative decision.) Yet when teachers came together and spoke with one voice, they possessed the clout to assert their rights. The attractiveness of union affiliation could be witnessed each spring, when a goodly number of the five hundred or so members of AFT Local 795 turned out to pay homage to the union's power at the annual union banquet, an evening of drinking, dining, dancing, and speechifying. At dinner's end it was traditional for everyone to rise and join master of ceremonies Glenn Altschuld in a spirited rendition of a classic labor anthem. "Solidarity forever," they would sing, "for the Union makes us strong."

Not every teacher on the staff was an avowed unionist, of course. There were those who believed it more seemly to promote the interests of their academic departments than to give their professional allegiance to an affiliate of the AFL-CIO. They preferred the warm glow that came from basking in the quiet prestige and small victories of their departments to the beery sociability of the "attitude-adjustment" hours that the union sponsored periodically throughout the year as its answer to classroom stress and burnout.

However, when the interests of their department were threatened or another department favored over theirs, these teachers mentally traded in their white gloves for brass knuckles. (For example, a suggestion that English teachers' teaching loads be reduced by one class per day to compensate them for the extra time they spent after school grading written essays was floated early in Burkett's tenure, but this trial balloon was punctured by shrill howls of protest from all the other academic departments.) Frank Walter often thought that the "ferocious departmentalization" of Heights High reflected the teachers' frustrated desire to have some area of decision making that they could call their own.

Standing up for one's academic department was a trickier business for the African-American teachers, who constituted only about 20 percent of the Heights High faculty. Because many were the sole blacks in their departments, they often felt voiceless in departmental affairs, and some found it necessary to join a caucus called Heights Alliance of Black School Educators in order to bring to the forefront educational and professional issues of concern to them. Still other teachers found validation in cliques, which were often as not formed along the divisions of gender, religion—the faculty had a strong Jewish presence—or outside interests.

While personally rewarding, these narrow professional and social alliances served to cement the "us versus them" perspective that began to be institutionalized in the district with the election of Local 795 as the teachers' collective bargaining agent in the early 1970s. In such an adversarial atmosphere even small differences often became magnified. Battle lines had been drawn at Heights High, for example, over the rights to the teachers' lounge on the third floor. In the nonsmokers' version of the story, the smokers had driven them from room 305 not only because of the offensiveness of their habit, but also because of their propensity to belittle their colleagues and complain about working conditions.

Melding all these factions into a unified team would be one of the biggest challenges facing the Model School project manager. In Irv Moskowitz's opinion, the job called for an experienced central-office administrator.

Hugh Burkett countered with a proposal that the responsibility be placed in the hands of Frank Walter, who had helped him polish the project's grant proposal. Moskowitz then suggested that the position be given to Dr. Allan Wolf, a high school social studies teacher with whom the superintendent periodically jogged.

In most school districts teachers and superintendents do not regularly interact. Wolf's unlikely friendship with Moskowitz came about when a fellow member of Cleveland's Jewish community, a woman who served on the Cleveland Heights–University Heights Board of Education, encouraged Wolf to befriend the new superintendent, who was also Jewish. Moskowitz also enjoyed the company of a good friend of Wolf's, an unsuccessful candidate for the board of education named Saul Isler, who shared the superintendent's passion for fishing. The year after Moskowitz's arrival, Isler decided to make another run for the board, and Wolf served as his campaign manager—a development that had tightened the latter's relationship with the superintendent, even though Isler lost again.

In suggesting Wolf for the job of project manager, Moskowitz was undoubtedly looking to secure a line of communication into the Model School Project (which had also been Burkett's motivation in advancing Walter's name). Yet the high school principal had to agree that having a faculty member lead the project seemed to jibe with the objectives of teacher empowerment. The fact that Wolf was a high school steward, Moskowitz believed, was also a plus, as this affiliation might come in handy when it came time to win the union's approval of whatever changes in teachers' working conditions the implemention of a model school would entail. Neither Moskowitz nor Burkett had tried to secure Local 795's blessing of the Model School Project in advance, feeling it either unnecessary or impossible. This tactical error would come back to haunt the project.

Still, Moskowitz's choice did not sit extremely well with Burkett, who harbored some doubts about Allan Wolf's organizational abilities. A product of the 1960s, the social studies teacher had a pierced ear, a wreath of curly, gray hair, an easygoing manner, and a lively intellect, but he was not exactly noted for his follow-through. (Like Burkett, Wolf preferred the excitement of intellectual discourse to the tedium of translating ideas into practice.) Nonetheless, Burkett bowed to Moskowitz's higher ranking and agreed to Wolf's appointment as project manager. After Wolf decided to accept the half-time job—an agreement the superintendent and high school teacher had cemented during a weekend stroll in mid-April 1988—Burkett could not resist informing Wolf that he had not been his top choice for project manager. Later Wolf was to interpret the unsettling remark as an indication that Burkett wanted him to fail.

As it turned out, the start-up of the Model School Project did not proceed according to plan. Most of the 1988–89 school year was consumed by the process of getting organized. The project was dubiously inaugurated at the high school's April 1988 faculty meeting. The only times during the year that the high school administration was afforded the opportunity to speak face-to-face with the entire staff, faculty meetings were held in the school library the third Wednesday of every month between 3:00 and 3:45 P.M. Usually they were hurried affairs devoted to mundane announcements to which teachers seldom gave their full attention. The inauspiciousness of this forum guaranteed that the explanation of the project's organizational structure, rationale, and objectives would barely register with most of the teachers present. Others with more sensitive antennae interpreted the announcement as a sign that Burkett wished to leave Heights High (a persistent rumor) and was looking for a résumé enhancer that would land him a better job elsewhere.

A few days later the science department requested a private meeting with Allan Wolf, a summons that turned out to be the most excitement generated by news of the project's creation. The science teachers informed Wolf that they objected to the announced plan for the creation of a Model School steering committee to which the project manager would report. Although Moskowitz and Burkett had conceived of this faculty oversight committee as a decision-making body that would establish the study teams, review their work-in-progress, and approve the final model on behalf of all the teachers, the two administrators saw nothing incongruous in reserving for themselves the right to appoint its members. The science department made clear to Wolf its preference that the steering committee be elected by the faculty, but Burkett and Moskowitz were reluctant to see the formation of such a critical entity turned into a popularity contest.

In early May the two administrators proceeded to name thirteen faculty members to serve on the committee, after consulting with Wolf and two teachers from Larry Peacock's original focus group about choices. Because they had selected the committee members with an eye to gender, race, and departmental affiliation, Moskowitz and Burkett were counting on the faculty's eventual acceptance of their appointees as representative. This presumption did not prove fatal, as the steering committee never fulfilled its decision-making responsibilities. It withered away during the project's first year from lack of meaningful work to do, leaving some of its members permanently estranged from the project.

The steering committee did accomplish one important task. In late May it determined the nature of the needed study teams, suggesting that topics to be investigated include curriculum, community and family relations, high expectations, learning styles, professional development, race relations, school structure, site-based management, and student life. If the teams could be formed by the end of the school year, Moskowitz and Burkett had reasoned, then the literature search could be conducted during the summer by one or two members of each team, and the analysis of the research findings could begin immediately upon the resumption of classes in the fall.

The project's one-year timetable, which called for a preliminary model design to be completed by December 1988 and the final model to be presented to the board of education the following March for implementation in the fall of 1989, was another example of administrative shortsightedness. In addition to underestimating the amount of time required to conceive, achieve a mandate for, and implement a redesign of the high school, it ignored the fact that most Heights High teachers regarded their summers as inviolable, time to be used exclusively to recuperate or hold a second job. The teachers' distinct lack of interest in thinking about matters pertaining to education between mid-June and Labor Day undoubtedly explained why Wolf rushed to assure the members of the steering committee at their first meeting that they would not have to do much over the course of the summer— maybe come to his house once or twice for kosher hot dogs and informal discussions.

When less than 15 percent of the 160-member faculty volunteered to participate in the Model School Project after sign-up sheets were circulated in early June 1988, the possibility that the steering committee could immediately mobilize any, let alone all, of the twelve suggested study teams evaporated. Once the project fell behind, its leaders never regained control of the schedule, and the research effort lurched along without benefit of new deadlines for most of the following school year. Sixteen of the initial twenty-three Model School recruits wanted to join the race relations study team, but in the rush to close down shop for the summer, this warning about the teachers' growing frustrations with their uneasily integrated work environment slipped by unnoticed.

When classes resumed in the fall, Wolf and the steering committee redoubled their recruitment efforts, but succeeded in adding only another twenty-five or so teachers to the study teams' rosters. The recruitment effort was hurt by widespread disbelief that the district would approve and implement a *teacher*-designed model school. The usual disgruntlement about committee work, and more than a modicum of apathy, also contributed to the lack of enthusiasm for the endeavor. When finally assembled, the study teams themselves suffered from low energy, in part because Wolf allowed them to fall into the unproductive habit of meeting for a few hurried moments before and after school twice a month. Although monies had been purposely made available to buy the participants' release from class, few study teams were aware of that fact. Even if that information had been communicated, it probably would not have been acted upon.

As it turned out, the organizational structure of the Model School Project arose from Moskowitz and Burkett's erroneous assumption that teachers would jump at the opportunity to put together unencumbered blocks of planning time during work hours instead of being asked to confer, as was usually the case, at the end of an exhausting school day. Most Heights faculty members, however, felt it unfair to their students to miss class on a regular basis, no matter how important the reason. They were not being altogether altruistic; no one welcomed the extra burden of preparing a written lesson plan for the substitute teacher.[1] Nor did the teachers relish the thought of having to listen to their students complain about the sub's misdeeds upon their return.

Uncertainty about their missions also hampered the study teams' effectiveness. Given the odd hours of their meetings, Wolf (who held down a second job teaching a night course at a local university) seldom attended them, and the steering committee representatives who were assigned to serve on different teams and guide their efforts had no clearer sense of what needed to be done than the team members. Moskowitz and Burkett were the only ones with a global understanding of the project. However, in order to encourage the participants to seize the reins of leadership, the two administrators purposely did not attend the steering committee's infrequent meetings. They left it up to Wolf to communicate the project's objectives. Their misreading of the dynamics of teacher empowerment, a process of leadership development that requires the strong backing and intimate involvement of administrators for its energy and direction, would have unfortunate consequences. As Wolf's management style tended to be more inspirational than instructive, the steering committee and the study teams were left to find their own way.

Many of the latter never progressed beyond holding bull or gripe sessions. Others found their jobs impossible to fulfill. Upon discovering that few, if any, of the recommendations to improve building maintenance contained in two previous accreditation studies of Heights High had ever been enacted, the facilities subcommittee of the school structure team decided that a further investment of labor on its part would likely be fruitless as well, and it abruptly disbanded. Still other study teams suffered from indecision. Unable to reach any conclusions about the causes of, and remedies for, their students' unwillingness to invest time and energy in their own educations, the high expectations team decided to survey the teachers and students about their opinions on the subject.

The survey elicited a thin and, at times, acerbic response. In answer to the committee's first question, "Why do students choose academic success?" one teacher wrote: "It's the easy thing to do, just like asking open-ended questions is the easy way for a so-called committee to answer its charge." Undeterred by their colleague's sarcasm about the vacuity of their research instrument, several members of the study team prevailed upon their students to complete the questionnaire. Responding to the question "What does academic failure mean?" one pupil scribbled: "failure in school," while another elucidated: "to give up, person doesn't care." Faced with the challenge of interpreting this feedback, many of the team members began skipping scheduled meetings.

Some teams did become sufficiently well organized to ask the school librarians to conduct a computer search of the reform literature in their subject area, only to be presented with daunting lists containing dozens of citations, which most of the members showed a disinclination to digest. And the handful of teams that went on to order copies of pertinent articles found they had little time to read them. In the end, few of the participants seemed willing to accept responsibility for the quality and completeness of the study teams' work, a dumbfounding lack of professional pride that was only partially explained by the fact that the team members technically could not be held accountable for volunteer work.

Watching these inauspicious developments from the sidelines, Burkett let the summer and early fall of 1988 drift by. Whether for reasons of principle, preoccupation,[2] or a desire to see Allan Wolf become an embarrassment to Moskowitz, he had decided that the direct involvement of administrators in the Model School Project was inappropriate. After obtaining the services of an organizational development consultant to assist Wolf with planning and to act as a group facilitator at steering committee meetings, he exited from the day-to-day life of the project. Or so he wanted it to seem. Actually, Burkett kept his hand lightly on the tiller by making suggestions about next steps to various participants, counting on their natural inclination to repeat the principal's ideas or concerns in discussions later with peers. Still the study teams floundered.

At last despairing of the project's lack of progress and the teachers' limited interest in it—problems that he attributed (somewhat unfairly and naively) to Allan Wolf's shortcomings as a leader—Burkett decided to intervene. He finessed Wolf's disengagement from the project early in 1989 by naming four additional coordinators, whose duties were to "assist" Wolf. Three of the coordinators were drawn from the ranks of study team activists. The fourth was Frances Walter, the librarian who had handled the arrangements for the study teams' literature searches. A former private school teacher, Frances Walter shared Burkett's determination that the model school be derived from scientific research rather than from pooled ignorance (as was too often the case, they both believed, when educators sat down to design new programs).

With the exception of Fran Walter, whose allegiances were suspect in the eyes of some teachers because of her marital ties to administrator Frank Walter, Burkett chose the coordinators not only for their leadership abilities, but also because they were not likely to be perceived as administrative lackeys. English teacher Cathleen McBride and music teacher William Thomas were powers in their own right. McBride was liaison of the twenty-six-member English department, the largest academic department in the high school, and Thomas directed Heights Singers, a coed chorus with perhaps the school's most active booster's club. And the fourth coordinator, English department member Steven Young, who taught American literature and an elective course on satire, enjoyed a reputation as a confirmed cynic. Young held such a low opinion of the trustworthiness of administrators that he immediately fingered fellow coordinator Fran Walter for Hugh Burkett's mole. (It was true that the librarian and the principal were friends and confidants whose idea of a good time was to bat around ideas for the Model School Project over a glass of scotch, but Walter made no secret of that fact.)

Burkett's strategizing about the appointment of coordinators extended to considerations of race. Like Moskowitz, who had delegated the Model School Project's conceptualization to his African-American director of staff development, the high school principal recognized the need for minority participation at the highest level of the project's organizational structure and had seen to it that several black teachers were invited to join the Model School steering committee. However, he had reached the conclusion that none of the two or three African-American teachers who had been active members of the study teams possessed the ability to be effective coordinators. Because Burkett did not want to thrust an outsider into the project's inner circle simply for public relations reasons, he had ended up appointing four Caucasian coordinators.

This was an insensitive decision, at best, given Heights High's status as a school in which two of every three students and one of every five teachers were black. To make matters worse from the perspective of the more militant members of the African-American faculty, three of the four coordinators enjoyed little credibility as advocates for black students, as they were veteran teachers whose seniority or specialization had earned them assignment to predominately white classes.

However, in spite of the undercurrent of racial tension at Heights High, the appointments elicited no public reaction at the time of their announcement. Because of their small numbers, black teachers felt spread thin when it came to taking on volunteer assignments, of which there was always an overabundance at committee-crazy Heights High School. Nobody was going register a complaint about being denied an opportunity to lead an activity heading nowhere.

6

Less Is More

Prepare for college; . . . keep an age bracket out of a job market; pro-
duce a labor force; instill a competitive drive; maintain a certain ho-
mogeneity of values; curb juvenile crime. Those are not stated as
explicit aims or goals. . . . But they are more pervasive in the conduct
of schooling than any list of lofty aims. . . . Schools are overly faithful
to the surrounding society in which the many are exploited for and by
the few. We must get back to basic educational aims . . . and away from
schools serving the dominant class. . . . Clearly, this is a task the
schools cannot do alone. Conceivably, this may be a task that cannot
be done at all.

—JOHN I. GOODLAD
The Dynamics of Educational Change, 1975

Even before he was displaced as the Model School Project's ostensible
leader, Allan Wolf had reached a different conclusion about who was actually in charge. Although Heights High's principal had displayed little interest
in the quotidian workings of the project, the social studies teacher had come
to believe that Hugh Burkett fully intended to dictate its outcome. "Sizer,"
Burkett had instructed Wolf early on during one of their private planning
sessions. "That's where we need to end up. I don't care how we get there."

The "Sizer" to whom Burkett referred was Theodore R. Sizer, a one-
time Phillips Academy headmaster and the former dean of Harvard's Graduate School of Education. In 1984 Sizer had authored *Horace's Compromise*, a
detailed prescription for the improvement of America's secondary schools
that had greatly influenced the excellence in education movement.[1]

Sizer's recommendations could be codified as "less is more." In addition to favoring site-based management and shared decision making, he espoused that public schools should focus exclusively on teaching students to use their minds well and leave vocational, physical, and even driver's education to others. The schools' sole mission should be to produce young adults who had the ability to analyze, criticize, solve problems, and create. (If schools took on any additional responsibility, it should be to help the young become not only good thinkers, but "thoughtful" adults: i.e., fair, caring, and tolerant.)

Just as Sizer advocated the simplification of the high school curriculum into four departments—inquiry and expression, mathematics and science, literature and the arts, and philosophy and history—so he suggested that teachers within those departments cover fewer topics more deeply. He also believed that teachers should act less as lecturers or entertainers and more as coaches, encouraging students to learn by conducting their own inquiries (a concept that came to be known as "the student as worker"). And he recommended that students should demonstrate mastery of subjects through essays, projects, and portfolios, rather than being graded on their ability to pick the right answers to multiple-choice tests.

Sizer was essentially repackaging the moral education of the early American common school with the liberal arts orientation of the academy (the nineteenth-century precursor of the high school), a combination he believed necessary to prepare the young to live and compete in an information-based, postindustrial, global economy. "Can graduates of this high school teach themselves?" Sizer asked in *Horace's Compromise*. "Are they decent people? Can they effectively use the principal ways of looking at the world, ways represented by the major and traditional academic disciplines?" If a school could answer those questions in the affirmative, then in Sizer's opinion it had been successfully restructured.[2]

Allan Wolf had decided that, in the likely event that the teachers were unable to come up with much of a plan on their own, Burkett was betting that he would be able to introduce Sizer's prescriptions to fill the void. (Burkett, in turn, suspected that Irv Moskowitz envisioned making a similar eleventh-hour rescue.) But Wolf was one of only a handful of faculty members, most of them fellow stewards, who sized up the principal's laissez-faire attitude toward the Model School Project as a Machiavellian ruse. Burkett's seeming uninvolvement was generally accepted, and the unrealistic impression that the teachers and the teachers alone controlled the content of the model became cemented among the project participants.

Larry Peacock's conception of the Model School Project had envisioned the creation of an advisory committee of students, parents, and community leaders—a glimmering of recognition that schools are not isolated entities that can be changed independently of the larger and more complex systems of relationships of which they are a part. But Burkett had very little patience for the involvement of noneducators in school affairs, having found in his dealings with the predominately white Heights High parent-teacher association that too often mothers and fathers used their PTA membership as leverage to force administrators to except their children from rules established for the common good. The high school principal had become quite adept at turning down flat all such entreaties, including the standard year-end pleas from parents desperate to gain a child half a credit away from graduation dispensation to walk across the stage and receive a (blank) diploma with the rest of the class. (Even when one supplicant's family informed Burkett that the grandmother of the senior in question was terminally ill and wanted to see her grandchild graduate as her final wish, the principal stood firm.)

With Burkett so little concerned about ensuring his popular standing in the community, it was not surprising that the Model School advisory committee never materialized. As a result, the base of support for the project never expanded much beyond the educators in the building.

Neither was the central administration brought into the proceedings. Burkett had succeeded in extracting a concession from Moskowitz not to intervene directly in the project's operation, but some of the superintendent's central-office colleagues bristled with resentment when it became clear that the study teams had no intention of inviting district administrators to participate in their deliberations. The exclusion of the central-office staff members represented a missed opportunity to give them a firsthand understanding of site-based management and shared decision making and left them with no role to play but that which the participating teachers so devoutly hoped to avoid: critic of the eventual product.

Burkett himself waited in vain for a response to the broad hint he dropped at a faculty meeting in October 1988 about his interest in discussing Model School issues. Declaring that he realized that the project was foundering—a statement Allan Wolf, who was then still project manager, regarded as a deliberate attempt to undermine his leadership—Burkett announced that he had no intention of stepping in to save it. While there were some things he wished to say to the study teams, the principal continued, he would not speak to any of them until he was invited.

When no summons came, Burkett prevailed upon the project's organizational development consultant to raise the issue of "stakeholders" with the steering committee, whose deliberations the consultant helped to facilitate. Although the suggestion that the principal had a right to share his conception of a model school met with resistance from some steering committee members, who feared that his input might be inhibiting—in that the teachers had not yet had a chance to clarify their own ideas—the steering committee reluctantly agreed to invite Burkett to its next meeting. When the committee reconvened in mid-November, Burkett presented its members with his vision of a model school in the form of a memorandum outlining five guiding principles that he said would bring a much needed focus to the work of the study teams.

Sure enough, each of the enumerated principles echoed the writings of Ted Sizer. For example, Burkett suggested that a model school should offer a purely academic curriculum that all students would master; actively engage students in their own learning; and attempt to personalize instruction by shrinking each teacher's class roster to no more than eighty-five students. As most Heights teachers were responsible for instructing somewhere between 125 and 150 students over the course of five class periods, the revised workload would also serve to free up the faculty to confer, pursue professional development opportunities, and participate in the school's governance.

The prospect of teaching smaller classes generated some enthusiasm among the steering committee members, tempered by skepticism about its likelihood, given the district's straitened circumstances.[3] But the thought of a lightened workload possessed sufficient appeal to prompt the curriculum study team to consider and incorporate these Sizerean concepts into its own list of recommendations. The group added, however, an interesting twist, suggesting that the core academic curriculum be taught by interdisciplinary teams of teachers, each team working exclusively with the same small group of students.

By presenting his five guiding principles, Burkett set the direction and tone for the Model School Project's subsequent deliberations. Yet none of the participants seemed to recognize that the course the project was now charting led away from the familiar terrain of the comprehensive high school and headed straight into a countervailing sociopolitical wind.

Even if it was not the product of the kind of systematic and thoughtful deliberation that Sizer had prescribed, there was a compelling rationale for the comprehensive curriculum offered by most public schools in America. At Heights High (as elsewhere), a comprehensive curriculum had evolved to accommodate the diversity and clash of views in America about what constituted a proper secondary education. That no single view predominated was a stasis dictated by the public school's reliance on property taxes: the more wide-ranging a school's mission, the broader its offerings and activities, the better its chances of maintaining widespread taxpayer support.

Like their counterparts across the country, Heights High students were allowed to choose among several "majors"—in this case, college-prep, general, and vocational. To complete the requirements for their chosen degree, they could pick from among 250 mandatory courses or electives, a bounteous curriculum that satisfied the teachers' desire to teach their favorite subjects at the same time that it seemed to fulfill the school's obligation to serve the educational needs of all children. In addition, students looking to fill their after-school hours could choose from an array of fifty clubs and extracurricular activities, including nineteen varsity sports.

Ironically, such a wealth of options could work to the disadvantage of the less sophisticated or unmotivated students, who were often ill equipped to make informed choices about which activities and courses of study would open their minds to the richness and possibilities of life, as well as gain them access to the best jobs and colleges. For them, a comprehensive curriculum that placed no greater premium on calculus than consumer math in satisfying graduation requirements represented a forest of lost academic opportunities in which they could wander aimlessly for years.[4]

Burkett's model school would require educators, parents, and taxpayers to lay aside their differing pedagogical beliefs and come to the unprecedented agreement that all students should receive the same education, a common body of knowledge, and skills that would equip them "to live and work in the 21st century," as the curriculum study team put it. Exactly which skills and knowledge constituted the best possible preparation for life in the third millennium was a question left, for the moment, unaddressed, as was the issue of how the local citizenry—to say nothing of the state board of education, with its dozens and dozens of curricular mandates and regulations —would be brought into the fold.

Even winning the faculty's approval of a purely academic curriculum would be difficult, because such a change meant that vocational and business courses of study must be abandoned, a prospect that introduced the fear that the teachers of these subjects might lose their jobs. If that calamity could likely be avoided by means of retraining or reassignment, there was no getting around the fact that all teachers would be required to give up their sacred freedom to determine course content and conduct according to their own lights. Instead they would have to concentrate on teaching a few important concepts and developing their students' critical-thinking skills.

Approval of Burkett's model school would test the teachers' professionalism in other ways. Instead of grading on the curve, they would have to strive for a uniformly high standard of achievement and mastery. And they would be required to interact more intimately with their students and collaborate more closely with their peers. This final change might prove especially difficult to sell. One of the unadvertised benefits of the job lay in the fact that strict limits were placed on a teacher's interaction with her students and colleagues by the assembly-line model around which public schools are organized. Educators who were working parents, moonlighters, or had grown accustomed to having banker's hours might not welcome an intensification of their on-the-job relationships.

Perhaps because he, too, did not fully appreciate the dimensions of the change he was proposing, Burkett gave no hint of the radical nature of his guiding principles. Nor did the clichéd language in which they were expressed suggest their revolutionary intentions. These omissions made Burkett's vision less threatening to the Model School participants. In due course, the high school principal received invitations to attend meetings of the professional development and site-based management teams, whose members had come, by means of enlightened self-interest, to share his thinking about those topics.

In an interim report laying out the guiding philosophical principles on which each study team had been able to agree, which Allan Wolf had compiled in December 1988 as one of his last acts as project manager, the professional development study team stated that time for teachers to engage in opportunities for "renewal, change, growth, stress management and peer support" should not be left to chance but must be built into the school year. Business and industry may have embraced the concept of workers as "human resources," but the teachers' assertion that the school system should recognize and accommodate their personal and professional needs posed a direct challenge to their status as cogs in the educational bureaucracy.

In the same report the site-based management team went on record as professing a belief in shared decision making. "The school should be run by consensus," the team declared. "The people who should be making the decisions are those who . . . will be living with the decisions." Although seemingly commonsensical, the statement envisioned a change in governance as radical as that proposed by the Declaration of Independence.

The final cornerstone of the model school's foundation was laid by the race relations study team, one of whose guiding philosophical principles stated forcefully, "Racism in any form cannot be tolerated, and that message must be clearly conveyed to all members of this school community." The team's agenda did not end there. Not only did the team seek improvements in personal behavior and institutional practices, it aspired to transform hearts and minds as well. "We must all educate ourselves about racism," another guiding principle declared. "We must acknowledge that racism exists and that all of us, black and white, have been conditioned to some extent by a racist society. We cannot plead ignorance or innocence; the first step in combating racism is recognizing it and clarifying our own perceptions, assumptions, and values."

Despite his private convictions that the district was guilty of institutional racism, Burkett had not been the driving force behind these pronouncements. The study team's passion and a large part of its mission came from its chairperson, Phyllis Fowlkes, one of only two African Americans who had volunteered to lead a Model School subcommittee. A member of the Heights faculty since 1977 and for many years the sole African American in the school's fourteen-person social studies department, Fowlkes held a master's degree in black studies from Ohio State University. She taught a semester-long elective in modern African-American history and, whenever there was sufficient student demand, a semester of early African-American history.[5]

Even so, Fowlkes felt that the high school did not take full advantage of the leadership abilities of the black faculty as a whole or, for that matter, her particular expertise in the area of multicultural curriculum. As proof, she liked to cite the example of her departmental colleagues' allergic reaction to her periodic suggestions that every Heights High student should be required to take an African-American history course. At present Heights students were required to take only American and modern world history and U.S. government in order to graduate.

Fowlkes believed that once knowledge of the many contributions of blacks to world civilization was widespread, it would improve the self-esteem of the high school's African-American students, who, she claimed, had swallowed the Eurocentrism of their textbooks and labored under the cruelly distorted impression that slavery was the high point of black history. She was also convinced that making African-American history compulsory would help to combat the prejudices of the white students, who rarely signed up for the school's Afrocentric electives when left to their own devices.

The other members of the social studies department refused, however, to recommend the measure—not (Fowlkes felt) because of honest disagreement with her point of view, even though an argument could be made that such particularism was divisive and not conducive to understanding that the United States has a history that is multicultural. Fowlkes privately suspected that her colleagues were afraid that they would lose their jobs to persons better qualified to teach African-American history—namely, African Americans. It was a conclusion that did not square with the efforts of the social studies teacher who spent his summer vacation visiting six cities in the South so that he could lecture more vividly on the civil rights movement or the other teachers in the department who did take pains to incorporate Afrocentric materials into their history lessons. Taking her case for mandatory African-American history to building and central-office administrators had not worked, either. Fowlkes attributed her lack of success to the fact that the black staff districtwide lacked the numbers necessary to command acceptance of such minority viewpoints.

Like Fowlkes, many other African-American teachers and administrators in Cleveland Heights had come to feel unappreciated and underutilized, a frustration that was especially grating as theirs was a district in search of ideas about how to better serve black students. Worse yet, certain of their white colleagues—and sometimes even white students and their parents—acted as if they doubted a black person could possess the qualifications to teach at Heights High. While some of her fellow African Americans had learned to swallow their resentment at being so easily dismissed, Fowlkes, a tall, elegant woman with chiseled features and an equally sharp tongue, never stopped fighting for her beliefs. She was always on the attack, expressing acrimonious opinions and espousing extreme positions on issues of legitimate concern.

Seeing a need for more black male teachers and administrators to serve as role models at the high school, Fowlkes couched her argument in accusatory terms, arguing that such a presence would illustrate that African-American men could perform jobs other than sweeping the floors and monitoring the hallways. Regarding the need to improve the district's record of minority hiring in general, Fowlkes was of the opinion that all retiring teachers should be replaced by African Americans. When white teachers passed black teachers in the hallway without saying hello or gossiped about them after they left the teachers' lounge, Fowlkes attributed their impoliteness to racism. "If they act that way toward us who were educated at the same institutions [as they] and live in the same neighborhoods [as they], what are they doing to our students?" she asked at an early meeting of the race relations study team. The question was not meant rhetorically.

Fowlkes did not consider herself a militant; after all, she did not go around "burning buildings or shooting anyone." But her vehemence, as well as her desire to see the race relations study team document the scope and depth of racism at the high school and recommend ways to eradicate it, may have contributed to the thinning of the team's ranks. Both black and white teachers were among the discomfited dropouts. Several of the remaining seven team members—an interracial group consisting of four whites and three blacks—argued in favor of a different mission, that of addressing the question of how to improve race relations at the school.[6]

The subtle difference in the two agendas could be seen in the preliminary projects the race relations study team undertook during the first semester of the 1988–89 school year. Early in the fall the team members hosted a Friday afternoon mixer in the hopes of bridging the separate social lives of the black and white teachers. It attracted a crowd of fifty or so people and was considered a success. Shortly thereafter, the team members previewed a short film entitled *Prejudice* that they were thinking about showing to the faculty. The film featured comedian Bill Cosby, in whiteface, running through a long list of Americans he did not like. The lineup included every known ethnic group and race, as well as women, young people, old people, and even Easterners and Midwesterners. "What this country needs is a good flushing out," Cosby concluded at the end of his litany. "And that's why I'm proud to be what I am—a bigot. And there ain't but two of us left. And I don't like *him.*"

Fearful such pointed humor would unleash emotions—either sullen silence or an outburst of anger—that they were not trained to handle, the study team members dropped the idea of a faculty screening. Even so, the experience proved fruitful in that it revealed the trickiness of consciousness raising and the value of less-threatening interaction—a blending of purpose that would be reflected in the study team's lengthy mission statement. "The fostering of positive race relations and education against racism," the team ultimately decided, "must be an ongoing and organized part of the agenda of the high school, for both staff and students."

Hugh Burkett attended the race relations social. ("Imagine that," a teacher commented on hearing a report of his presence, for in the past the principal had seldom put in appearances at faculty gatherings.) But he did not seek out an opportunity to speak directly with its sponsors. Burkett had long before despaired of bringing the black and white teachers together as a team.

Not that he had not tried. Hoping that, as their numbers grew, African Americans would come to feel a more integral part of the staff, Burkett paid some attention to minority recruitment. During his tenure, he succeeded in increasing the total percentage of black teachers, administrators, and counselors working at the high school from the low to mid teens to the high teens, only to witness little improvement in staff dynamics. For the most part, teachers still preferred to socialize with colleagues of the same race, and, with the exception of Black History Month in February, when black faculty members took responsibility for helping the administration organize a series of in-school assemblies, lectures, and performances celebrating black culture and contributions, Burkett perceived African Americans still to be reluctant to shoulder committee work or leadership roles.

While it was true that most of the black teachers had not rushed to embrace the Model School Project, for example, in that regard they were no different from the majority of their white colleagues, who had also shunned this opportunity to become the masters of their own destiny. The only difference in attitude between the two groups was, perhaps, the degree of their disaffection. That some members of the black staff felt extremely alienated had become clear during Burkett's second year at the high school, when a small group of African-American teachers and administrators requested a private meeting with him. This ad hoc group of activists had discovered during the time they worked together on Black History Month activities that they shared many complaints about the apparent second-class citizenship of African-American students and teachers at Heights High School, and they now sought to apprise the new principal of their concerns.

After hearing the group out, Burkett responded that it would be more appropriate for such issues to be discussed and resolved with the entire staff. But he did not shut the door on the group members' request for additional conferences with him, even though he came away with the impression that their talk about the need for more black role models at the high school masked an irreversible distrust of the white teachers' ability to work effectively with African-American students. Following that line of reasoning, he wondered, would one then arrive at the conclusion that black teachers could not relate to white students? It seemed an unproductive approach. Burkett preferred to frame educational questions in terms of what was best for *all* children.

What a stubborn mule! thought one of the few whites who had joined with the ad hoc group in petitioning Burkett. Why would someone who was working hard to address so many of the issues of concern to the black faculty stoutly refuse to describe his initiatives in language that the black teachers could "hear?" "Man, they didn't want to hear about what's good for all students," the white petitioner remembered. "They wanted to hear about what are you doing for black kids." Burkett's pigheadedness was going to "kill" him yet.

Later the high school principal learned that certain white teachers were outraged that he had conferred privately with the group, complaining that such an action would have been condemned as racist by the black faculty had the situation been reversed. Finding himself in a no-win situation however he proceeded, Burkett deemed it best not to meet again with the African-American activists, who decided to continue gathering quietly on their own. Until dramatic events in the district prompted them to take more concrete action, these meetings served as an informal forum to which all members of the African-American faculty could bring their concerns as they felt the need. Having this kind of an escape valve helped to keep the frustrations of the black staff from building to a head for several years, at which time Phyllis Fowlkes and her Model School study team succeeded in moving the issue of race relations again to the forefront of attention.

7

Solidarity Forever

When people are asked or required to change, a part of them will resist changing, and if such resistance is then reacted to as incomprehensible human perversity, the level of hostility increases.

—SEYMOUR B. SARASON
The Culture of the School and the Problem of Change, 1982

When second semester began in late January 1989, the structure of the model high school remained blurry, although its philosophical foundation had been laid. While attaining even this degree of consensus represented a significant achievement, much work remained to be done. The better-organized study teams needed to turn their guiding principles into workable programs, while the weaker teams had to be encouraged to regroup and start anew. And the teachers who had to date declined to participate in the project—well over two-thirds of the faculty—had somehow to be persuaded to become involved.

To allow them to accomplish these objectives, the project's new coordinators were released from teaching the first-period class of each day. Meeting together daily to discuss next steps—an intellectual exercise that served to cement their commitment to the Model School Project—the four coordinators soon agreed that each of them would attempt to supervise the work of three study teams. Their primary objective would be to encourage each team to prepare a written report recommending how its guiding principles should be put into action. The coordinators also decided to request a summit meeting with the high school stewards in order to sound out the union's thinking on the Model School Project.

Almost a year before, former project manager Allan Wolf had attempted to engage the official interest of Local 795 in the project with no success. The idea of approaching the union came to him after he talked with Philip A. Cusick, a nationally respected professor of education at Michigan State University. "You can't pull this off without the union," Cusick warned Wolf, referring to organized labor's ability to block or impede management-imposed initiatives with which it disagreed. It was not lost on Cusick that in Rochester, New York, and Dade County, Florida—the public school districts that had reportedly made the most progress in empowering teachers—the impetus for change had come from the teachers' union.[1]

Even though Wolf doubted that Local 795 would similarly be interested in promoting education reform, he arranged to meet with Glenn Altschuld during the summer of 1988. Unbeknownst to Burkett and Moskowitz, he had decided to ask the union president to become involved in the project. Altschuld declined the invitation, expressing his opinion that the two administrators were using Wolf to advance their own ends. "Committees formed by superintendents and principals, always, and I mean always, deliver the results that are identical to the desires of the administrator who formed the committee," Altschuld later wrote in a position paper on the issue of volunteer committee work. "The administrator always wins, and the rest of us, even the committee members, seldom knew there was a contest."

In the case of the Model School Project, Altschuld was not sure exactly what mischief Moskowitz and Burkett were up to; he suspected that they themselves did not know. Both administrators, in his opinion, were "educationally stupid," by which Altschuld meant that both believed the lessons they had been taught in college education courses. The union president discounted their dismissive talk about the factory model of public education. If Moskowitz or Burkett had troubled to ask him what constituted a model school, Altschuld would have pointed to the high school he had attended in Cleveland.

Public schools were far superior in his youth, Altschuld believed. For one thing, "they nailed down the desks," which gave every student a sense of security, of having his own safe place. Parents and teachers did not have conferences to discuss how Johnny was doing. As he remembered it, "you received your grades, and you either passed or you flunked." Furthermore, teachers did not have to call parents to let them know that Johnny did not do his homework. If Johnny did not do his homework, Altschuld recalled, Johnny lost points; it was that simple. And if students got into trouble, the schools saw it as their responsibility to discipline them. Schools today did not discipline students, he had observed; they just called the parents. Altschuld doubted that the Model School Project would rectify any of these short-comings.

Despite his misgivings, Altschuld gave steward Allan Wolf his blessing to be involved with the project. Then the union president proffered a piece of advice. "Let some people boycott this project if they want," Wolf recalled Altschuld's saying. "That's union democracy." As the Model School Project progressed, Altschuld's definition of union democracy would become clear: Local 795 operated on the principle that the majority ruled only when the majority agreed with him.

After Wolf was squeezed out of his position as project manager in the winter of 1989, the union's stance of studied neutrality toward restructuring disappeared. When the Model School coordinators sat down in early spring with the high school stewards and some members of the site-based manage-ment study team, who were working on a proposal to create a governing body of teachers and administrators, the stewards' uneasiness with the project surfaced.

To be an advocate or even supporter of education reform was an unfamil-iar and frightening role. Albert Shanker's injunctions to the contrary, the union representatives were obviously more comfortable with the job de-scription contained in the last paragraph of the steward's handbook: "Every-thing . . . said in the preceding pages can be summarized in the words: 'Police the contract.'" True to form, chief steward Ed Esch indicated during the discussion that should any of the innovations the Model School Project pro-posed threaten to undermine the union contract, the union intended to shut it down.

Frank Walter, who attended the session, came away with the impression that the stewards felt a moral obligation to oppose the project, although he could not figure out whether the union leaders were suspicious of it because they regarded it as Burkett's baby, or whether they were calling the project Burkett's baby to justify being suspicious of it. Whatever the case, it was ap-parent that if a model school were ever to be implemented, the teachers' union's attitude would first have to be refocused in a positive direction—a feat that even the iron-willed Burkett had yet to accomplish.

The high school principal had been careful his first few years on the job to solicit Frank Walter's advice about dealing with the union. Even so, conflict with the stewards had arisen early in Burkett's tenure. The principal's first serious problem with the union occurred over an issue of discipline. When Burkett declined to suspend a student whom a teacher accused of threatening to assault her, his action outraged the stewards. Unaware that the teacher had since retracted her claim in discussions with Burkett, Louis Salvator, the high school's chief union steward, sent an open letter to the faculty suggesting that Burkett's lax disciplinary practices would result in increased misconduct as soon as students realized that they could escape punishment for misbehavior.

Burkett responded with his own open letter, in which he accused the stewards of running around wrongly predicting the end of the world like "Chicken Littles." Adding insult to injury, he also denounced them as "kid killers." While Burkett's comments were ill advised, it was true that ensuring strict discipline and teachers' safety was one of the few nonfinancial issues in which Local 795 took an active interest.[2] This reminder of the union's limited perspective, perhaps as much as anything, had caused Burkett's frustrated outburst.

The stewards' agitation with Burkett's disciplinary policies increased when the principal announced the closing of the tardy room. The tardy room was a holding space, supervised by the school's security staff, to which students arriving late to class could be sent to spend the remainder of the period. Even though the procedure resulted in latecomers falling further behind in their lessons, most teachers supported the concept because it removed from their shoulders the disruptive and unpleasant task of disciplining defiant students midclass. For weeks after the tardy room closed, the union stewards pressed Burkett to reconsider his decision, which a few of them suspected had been forced on him by the then-superintendent. The high school's new chief of security came from the same school system as the assistant superintendent, and some of the stewards believed that the security chief had persuaded central administrators that "babysitting" should not be part of his job.

When it became clear that Burkett was not going to revoke the closing, the stewards called a special faculty meeting, attended by perhaps one-fourth of the staff, to discuss options. They then issued an ultimatum. If the tardy room did not reopen within a week, they informed Burkett, teachers would start locking their classroom doors at the bell, leaving late students free to roam the halls—a situation that spelled chaos for the school. According to union lore, the tardy room reopened that same day.

Yet these were mere skirmishes compared to the full-pitched war that erupted over the principal's plan to move from an eight-period to a seven-period day. Burkett had what he believed to be solid academic reasons for wanting to reduce the number of classes per day, which would increase the length of each period from forty to fifty minutes, a seemingly simple change. First, it would allow for the elimination of study halls, time that most students frittered away, if they deigned to show up in the first place. (As study halls were held in such large rooms as the school's thousand-seat auditorium, attendance was virtually impossible to monitor.) The students would benefit in that, lacking the escape route provided by officially sanctioned downtime, they would be forced to take six courses a day instead of a customary minimum of four and maximum of five.

Burkett also regarded the beefing up of course loads as a boon to the cause of student achievement and equity, since it was invariably the standard-track students who signed up for two or three study halls—an undemanding schedule serving only to dilute further the content of their school day and to increase their boredom with it. Yet, surprisingly, the proposed change was opposed by some of the African-American teachers. They were concerned that requiring attendance of six classes a day (to say nothing of the concomitant increase in homework) would pose an undue burden on the majority of African-American students, who were already struggling to keep up because of personal disadvantages, problems at home, or the need to supplement the family's income by working after school. Burkett dismissed these arguments out of hand. When black teachers revealed their own low expectations of black students, it especially infuriated him.

But the major opposition to the change came from the science teachers. They were accustomed to teaching a forty-minute lab following their regular classes two times a week, a combination that would be impossible when study halls were no longer available to pad out science students' schedules the remaining three days a week. Instead they would have to slot lab work into their slightly expanded class periods—a disadvantage Burkett believed was far outweighed by the astonishing amount of additional instruction the typical student would gain over the course of a four-year high school career.

Burkett's attempts to open the science teachers' eyes to "the big picture," as he liked to term the welfare of the entire school, met with little success, perhaps because there was a hidden benefit for them in maintaining an eight-period day. Because they taught two double periods each day, science teachers had only four classes per semester, while their colleagues taught five. It pleased the administration that the proposed new schedule would also remedy this inequity. Equally important, the switch to a seven-period day would eliminate a "duty" period from the schedules of most of the staff. Under the new regimen, a teacher's day would consist of five classes, a lunch period, and a planning period. In other words, the faculty would now be paid strictly to teach, not to also supervise study halls or patrol the cafeteria or hallways one period a day.

Burkett had lobbied to end study halls from his first year on the job, when he realized that their abolition would immediately solve some of the school's discipline problems. (Three study halls a day and lunch provided those students inclined to goof off or slip away from campus with too many opportunities to do so.) By the 1987–88 school year, believing he had won over a sufficient number of teachers, Burkett began what the building stewards took to be formal negotiations aimed at winning their approval of the proposed schedule change.[3]

In the midst of his discussions with the stewards, which chief union steward, Ed Esch, had informed the faculty were taking place, Burkett did something that left the union representatives feeling baffled and betrayed. Late that winter he presented the case for a seven-period day to the Cleveland Heights–University Heights Board of Education, which formally approved the change. Burkett later told Esch that the timing of the presentation had been dictated by Irv Moskowitz. In retrospect Esch concluded that the superintendent's interruption of the negotiations was an early warning sign of Moskowitz's hostility toward the union and the collective bargaining process. But Frank Walter, for one, believed that Burkett decided of his own volition to jettison the attempt to involve the stewards in the decision when he grew impatient with the slow progress of their joint deliberations.

At the time, the high school administration was under considerable pressure to implement the proposed schedule change. In November 1987 and again in February 1988, school tax levies had failed, and principals throughout the district were being forced to cut staff. Only by making better use of the remaining teachers' time could the high school hope to get along with a smaller faculty. As part of his push for greater efficiency, Burkett also decided to eliminate homeroom as a purposeless intrusion on the instructional day.[4] (Pep rallies had earlier been discarded for the same reason. They were now held after school and, as a consequence, were poorly attended.)

Presented with this fait accompli, Local 795 filed two complaints of unfair labor practice with the State Employment Relations Board (SERB), charging that the school district had failed to negotiate a proposed change in working conditions, as mandated by the union contract; and the high school stewards began planning a job action that they hoped would prompt the administration to resume discussion of the issue. The stewards settled upon the idea of confiscating student schedules for the upcoming school year—a job action to which many of their colleagues objected. The stewards nonetheless decided to proceed, oblivious of the fact that by so doing they were guilty of the very sin of unilateral decision making they were protesting.

In spite of the undercurrent of staff opposition, the job action was successfully mounted. When homeroom teachers received the students' schedules from the administration to distribute, more than three-fourths turned the printouts over to the stewards, who locked them in a safe. In the end, the teachers had either been loathe to undermine the union's power, or they had feared the consequences of noncompliance with union directives.[5]

Frank Walter found the union's job action somewhat amusing. Had Hugh Burkett not encouraged the stewards to take a more active role in the school's governance, Walter mused, their response to being excluded from the decision-making process in this instance would probably have been much less aggressive. But Walter's superiors did not share his philosophical attitude toward the disruption, which ended the day after it began when the stewards, having made their point, returned the students' schedules to the homeroom teachers for distribution. The central administration immediately announced that it was placing written reprimands in the personnel files of all teachers who had participated.

The administration's action set off an explosive chain reaction. Local 795 leveled another charge of unfair labor practices with SERB against the school system, which prompted the board of education to file its own claim with the government arbitrator, protesting that what the union was terming a "silent protest" was in fact an illegal job action. Needless to say, the question of the kind of instructional day best for Heights High students was swept away in the blast of recriminations.

Even summer break provided no relief from the wrangling. At midsummer steward Lou Salvator learned he was being transferred to the district's Monticello Middle School, otherwise known as the "Penalty Box" because of its cynical use by various superintendents as a destination for fractious or incompetent high school staff members. Given the timing of the decision, which was announced shortly before 1988–89 contract negotiations began, Salvator concluded that Moskowitz was attempting to send an intimidating message about the superintendent's power over those teachers who represented the union's interests too enthusiastically.

Some of Salvator's colleagues, however, placed the blame for his demotion at the doorstep of the high school principal, even though the superintendent had final say over transfers. Ensuring that Burkett became even more unpopular with the teachers, Salvator later surmised, may have been exactly the outcome Moskowitz intended; he had observed that competitive-spirited administrators sometimes played hardball with one another. (To those who had detected the superintendent's practice of elevating adjustable chairs to a height that allowed him to look down on everyone else at meetings, Moskowitz seemed a fairly competitive guy.) Although chief steward Esch circulated a petition asking that Burkett revoke the transfer, which was signed, as Salvator remembered it, by two-thirds of the faculty, the union's demands went unheeded. "You got too far ahead of your troops," former Army grunt Esch sympathized with former Navy swab Salvator afterward, "and you got picked off."

Local 795 was to prevail, however, in a contemporaneous protest that arose when Burkett encouraged the faculty to take advantage of a free summertime training program. The source of the controversy was a letter the principal sent teachers in early July 1988 informing them of an upcoming week-long workshop to be held at a local university on the pedagogy of Madeline Hunter. Burkett was an admirer of Hunter, an educator and psychologist who recognized that teaching methods were too often derived from such dubious sources as folklore, tradition, or individual idiosyncrasy. As an antidote, she had translated principles of instruction based on scientific research into a classroom decision-making model that Burkett believed might be of interest and benefit to the Heights High faculty.

Burkett's letter stated that there were openings for fifteen Heights teachers to attend the workshop at no cost, and invited the staff's participation. Glenn Altschuld immediately called the principal to complain that the letter violated the "voluntary and compensated" provision of the union's contract, as no mention had been made of paying the teachers for participating in what was obviously in-service training. Burkett was forced to withdraw his invitation. (This was precisely what Altschuld liked about the man: "He learned—if you just gave him a little help.")

Later that summer the union president described both the incident and the rationale for the "voluntary and compensated" provision in a letter sent to every teacher in the district, in the process revealing his disdain for professional development activities. "For sixteen years, our contract . . . has protected us," he noted, "from administrators who believe they are 'Educators', capital 'E', and should have the power to force 'teachers', small 't', to become trained in every new theory, or zany educational idea they have seen at some meeting."

The traditional midsummer planning meeting between the high school principal and the stewards took place shortly after the Hunter workshop incident. Still in high dudgeon, Burkett decided to exert the only control that he had over classroom performance. "Hugh grew fangs," said one of the stewards present, describing the principal's announcement of his intention to step up the pace with which faculty members were regularly evaluated. Some teachers, he forewarned the stewards, would be observed once a week, some every two weeks, some every two or three days. Theoretically, first- and second-year faculty members, candidates for tenure, and teachers in new assignments were to be evaluated once a year, and tenured faculty members once every three years.

Administrative scrutiny of a teacher's work was never a welcome prospect, even though it occurred only infrequently and consisted merely of an administrator's sitting in on a single class period and writing an evaluation that was later discussed privately with the teacher. The only real power an administrator had to ensure that the teacher heeded the evaluation's suggestions was that of persuasion, since tenure—which was awarded after three years of service in the district—and the unionization of the teaching profession had made it extremely difficult to fire the incompetent. Even so, teachers looked forward to being evaluated with the same relish that most people greet a visit to the dentist.

Despite Burkett's vehemence on the subject, the stewards perceived his promise that "the administrators are going to be *living* with the teachers" to be an empty threat. For one thing, there were too few principals to cover even the normal number of observations, with the result that the performance of veteran faculty members occasionally went unevaluated for years. But that did not deter one of the stewards, a physics teacher named Robert Quail, from voicing his opinion about the ridiculousness of Burkett's new policy proposal.

Seemingly the shyest of individuals, Bob Quail fairly seethed with resentment, an attitude generally shared by his fellow teachers. The fire in Quail's belly came from the sure knowledge that those in charge of the public education system to which he had devoted his life regarded teachers as their inferiors. Money issues provided the clearest indication of how little administrators valued teachers, in Quail's estimation. He still remembered the paltry sum of $5,900 that he earned in 1966–67, his first year at Heights High—a salary he had regarded as especially insulting because he held a master's degree.

At the time the Cleveland Heights–University Heights Teachers Association, an affiliate of the National Education Association, represented the vast majority of teachers in the district, while Local 795 boasted fewer than twenty-five recruits at the high school and no more than thirty-five members altogether. Despite its small numbers, the AFT unit was by far the more aggressive group, favoring strikes as an effective negotiating tool. Quail decided to cast his lot with the AFT because he perceived the Teachers Association as a "company union" that settled for whatever puny raises the district cared to offer.

Quail and his fellow AFT members also smelled something fishy in the teachers association's go-along-to-get-along negotiations, which from time to time seemed to precede the chief NEA contract negotiator's immediate promotion to an administrative position. When, in 1970–71, after the historic failure of a school levy two times in a row, the NEA proved unable to negotiate even a few dollars more in pay, the impasse paved the way for AFT's election as the teachers' collective bargaining agent.[6] The takeover was engineered by the AFT's newly elected president Glenn Altschuld, the first Local 795 officer to attempt to organize the traditionally less militant and overwhelmingly female elementary school staffs.[7]

Even after Local 795's ascendancy, the district persisted—much to Bob Quail's frustration—in its apparent belief that teachers should subsidize the financial operation of the schools. When levies failed and money grew tight, Quail had observed, it was the teachers who were expected to forgo raises, the teachers who were the first personnel to be cut, the teachers who were expected to do without needed resources. Colleagues still remembered the time when Quail sought unbudgeted funds to buy fifty rulers for his physics classes, only to be refused. He had been reduced to xeroxing his own ruler, fifty times.

In response to this and countless other examples of his employers' indifference to the teacher's lot, Quail had become as militant a unionist as his old friend and periodic dinner companion Glenn Altschuld. In Quail's view, it had been "fun" to picket the high school during the 1983 strike. He had enjoyed rolling tires and logs in the path of vans delivering substitute teachers to the building, while other teachers rocked the vehicles back and forth when they stopped at the front door.[8]

The year following the strike Quail made himself known to the new principal of the high school when he filed a class grievance on behalf of all Heights High teachers, protesting the administration's failure to inform faculty members of their teaching assignments for the subsequent year by the June 1st deadline stipulated in the teachers' contract. The following year

Quail filed a similar grievance, an action that was on its way to becoming a tradition until Hugh Burkett conceived of the stratagem of delivering tentative schedules (all the information he had) by the required date.

Quail could also be counted on to oppose any change that threatened to disrupt the status quo in his classroom, such as Burkett's plan to move to a seven-period day. Having calculated that the elimination of science labs would reduce the instructional time allotted to each of his physics classes by a month over the course of a year, Quail found the changeover traumatic.[9] The following year the administration disrupted Quail's routine once again when, as a result of Burkett's determination to erase the stigma associated with teaching standard-level courses by spreading them around, Quail was assigned to teach a smaller number of advancement placement physics courses than was normally his due—a schedule change he interpreted as Burkett's retribution for daring to disagree with him on the issue of the seven-period day.

After the Model School Project was announced in the spring of 1988, Quail let it be known that he opposed the project on the grounds that the impetus for school restructuring had come not from the faculty, but solely from Burkett. When asked several years later why teachers felt compelled to challenge the ideas of administrators, he answered: "Just because." Pressed to give a fuller response, he said, only half-jokingly: "Because it's good for morale." Pressed again, Quail finally acknowledged: "Because they think they're better than us. They think they know everything and we know nothing."

Quail was indeed an accomplished teacher, whose students consistently earned impressive scores on advanced placement physics tests. He was also one of the few members of the faculty who conducted his classes on the Sizerean principle of "the student as worker." Quail seldom lectured but rather made himself available to answer questions whenever his students found themselves stumped by some element of the experiments or problem-solving exercises he asked them to conduct almost daily, either on their own or as part of teams, using as their primary guide an exhaustive physics text that he had written because of his dissatisfaction with published manuals.

No matter that Quail ran a model classroom, which even during his lunch and planning periods was crowded with students eager to continue their work. His militancy was a source of continual aggravation to Hugh Burkett. Quail's protest of the principal's proposed new policy regarding teacher evaluations was the final straw. Burkett could no longer bear the union's thwarting him at every turn. He informed the stewards that he saw no reason to continue meeting with them in the future, as nothing but dis-cord had ever come out of their monthly discussions. Then he stalked out of the room, with Frank Walter following on his heels.

A contingent of stewards, whose number included Allan Wolf, was de-ployed the same afternoon to ask Burkett to reconsider. He agreed to resume meeting, if and only if the stewards committed to the concept of shared deci-sion making—a condition to which they felt comfortable acquiescing only after polling the faculty to solicit approval for such an unprecedented expan-sion of Local 795's union's role. Out of the ensuing conversations that fall came the suggestion that the stewards and the high school's entire adminis-trative team should start meeting regularly under the watchful eye of a trained group facilitator.

This plan was inspired by the example of the District Steering Commit-tee, a contingent of administrators and union leaders drawn from school buildings throughout the system who were ostensibly learning how to com-municate with one another with the assistance of the director of a university-based center for labor-management cooperation, who happened to be Allan Wolf's stepbrother. Neither Moskowitz nor Altschuld had sought to create such a forum; the School Consensus Project, a civic committee searching for solutions to the problems of the schools, had been the first to suggest the idea as a means of averting teachers' strikes. By most accounts, the two men par-ticipated reluctantly, their presence commanded by civic pressure and the union's executive board, respectively. (Moskowitz and Altschuld were also supposed to be meeting on their own once a month, again as a result of the School Consensus Project. However, those private conferences accom-plished little, according to the union president, because of "'The Man's' duplicity and constant con job.")

Because the formation of the District Steering Committee's high school offshoot was voluntary, its prospects for success seemed somewhat greater. Anticipating that an outside expert would be able to help them iron out their differences and coalesce as a management team, Burkett and the stewards optimistically decided to call their new grouping the High School Steering Committee (HSSC). Only Bob Quail declined to sit on the new committee, interpreting the HSSC as a clever ploy by Burkett to distract the stewards while he and his Model School cronies plotted their takeover.

Quail's boycott to the contrary, the creation of the High School Steering Committee during the 1988–89 school year, coming swiftly on the heels of the Model School Project's launch the previous spring, renewed Burkett's hopes that the administration might yet govern Heights High in partnership with the faculty. After five years of butting heads with the union every time he wanted to make a major move, Burkett had finally accepted that being a tough guy did not work with Local 795; it only stiffened union opposition to whatever innovations he proposed. But even should the experiment with the High School Steering Committee come to naught, the principal sensed that he had found in the Model School Project another way around his impasse with the high school's eight union stewards. If the teachers themselves were committed to making changes, how could the union thwart their wishes?

Yet the April 1989 summit between the building stewards and the project coordinators revealed that the two groups were working at cross-purposes. When the discussion turned to the Model School's consideration of a site-based management council of teachers and administrators, the stewards made clear their expectation that union stewards be the sole faculty representatives on any body created to govern the model school—an understanding to which Burkett had already given his assent in a moment of exuberance at a particularly productive High School Steering Committee session.

If the stewards were indeed serious about pursuing Burkett's unilateral agreement, it put the project coordinators in a fix. They and most members of the site-based management study team envisioned a more broadly based management council. Privately, the coordinators were of the opinion that teachers who had been elected steward largely for their willingness and ability to be pit bulls were not necessarily the best-qualified people to govern the school. (Indeed, it was rare when more than nine or ten teachers ran for the eight stewards' slots; most faculty members curled their lips at the thought of seeking such a combative job.)

The Model School coordinators refrained from articulating their point of view at the meeting with the stewards, however. They reasoned that it was premature to argue about the management council's composition before the site-based management study team issued its recommendations on the subject. It seemed wiser to defer the showdown with the union until later—a strategy of postponing inevitable confrontations on which the coordinators came to rely again and again, much to the project's detriment.

Part 2
Psychological Warfare

The freedom to be creative and innovative, the capacity to influence students, opportunities for feedback, recognition and support, and the chance to share with peers. . . . Such is the stuff of which empowerment is made.

—GENE I. MAEROFF
The Empowerment of Teachers, 1988

8

A Strategic Retreat

There cannot be significant change, certainly not a rebirth or a new beginning, through immaculate, painless conception.

—JOHN I. GOODLAD
The Dynamics of Educational Change, 1975

At the moment, the coordinators faced more immediate problems than the arrested development of the teachers' union. As spring beckoned, they were rushing to complete an interim status report, which they hoped would begin the process of shaping the study teams' work into a meaningful whole. After the five-page summary had been written and presented to the faculty, Steve Young received a letter from Bob Quail criticizing the coordinators' use of the word *proactive* to describe the mind-set of teachers in a model school. Noting that his dictionary defined the term as meaning "involving modification by a factor which precedes that which is modified," the physics teacher deprecated the coordinators' competency.

"Are you sure that the Model School Committee knows what its [*sic*] doing?" Quail asked, unaware that the missing apostrophe in his sentence opened him up to similar ridicule.

Young immediately took it upon himself to draft a sarcastic response, pointing out the various grammatical errors in Quail's letter and conveying *his* dictionary's definition of proactive as enterprising and involved. Yet the coordinators regarded it as an auspicious sign that Quail, whose opinions carried considerable weight with the rest of the staff, could find only a nit to pick with their report.

The coordinators next turned to the challenge of coaxing the study teams into making final recommendations, a task that they thought to speed by providing the teams with an easy-to-complete questionnaire. The responses, which dribbled in throughout the late spring of 1989, confirmed their suspicions. Most of the study teams did not know how to turn their guiding principles into action.

The student life study team, for example, desired to "develop a positive high school experience for all students." However, in the space provided for a list of recommendations, the team leader, having drawn a blank, instead enumerated "comments from group when asked about general feeling on project."

The comments revealed a dispiritedness that suffused the work of some of the other study teams as well. They were:

1. Feels lack of organization . . . "Spinning Wheels"
2. What will happen to info? Probably won't make a difference
3. Very interested in continuing to see total outcome of entire project
4. When is everything supposed to come together?
5. Frustration
6. Interest is waning
7. As long as there is an enstrangement [sic] by staff & teachers things won't change

Four other study teams also left the recommendations section of the questionnaire blank, although each team indicated that there were questions the members still wanted to research. The direction of the future inquiries did not look especially promising, however. The family relations team intended to find out "how responsible can we make the parents, in regards to the students [sic] behavior & academics?" while the high expectations team was, after six months of meetings, still puzzling over the issue of "how to make expectations (both academic and discipline) clear to all involved." Even the reports of some of the better-organized teams, such as curriculum, professional development, and site-based management, were essentially restatements of their previously announced guiding principles. While the curriculum team had recently begun to consider the merits of heterogenous ability grouping, and the professional development team had turned its attention to peer mentoring and review—innovations that were anathema to many members of Local 795, who feared that measures to self-police the profession would end up pitting union brother against sister—their members had reached no conclusions about these controversial topics.

Having satisfied their need to unmask one another's prejudices, the members of the race relations study team had settled down and produced the most coherent package of recommendations. The team called for an ongoing human relations program for teachers and students; the hiring of a human relations ombudsman and a multicultural-curriculum specialist; regularly scheduled social events for teachers; active recruitment of minority teachers and administrators (especially black males); human relations orientation for new staff members and a mentoring program for all students; instruction for teachers on the learning styles and behavioral patterns of black students; required courses in African-American history and African-American literature; all high school administrators to teach at least one course (to put them in better touch with the students and classroom realities); improved staff attendance at student activities and performances; and a clearer statement of discipline policies and the equitable enforcement of school rules.

But even the relative quality and thoroughness of the race relations study team's work could not hide the fact that the Heights High faculty had been unable to marshal the skills, knowledge, vision, and commitment necessary to reinvent Heights High School. As it turned out, the expectation that teachers could, without training or supervision, master the rudiments of strategic planning had been yet another flaw in Moskowitz and Burkett's thinking. This particular miscalculation looked as though it might prove costly.

By the time all the study team reports were in hand, Moskowitz and Burkett's original deadline for presenting a model school design to the board of education had passed, and the end of the 1988–89 school year was approaching. If decisive action were not quickly taken, the Model School Project would die. In this pressured atmosphere a new plan aimed at pushing the project to completion was hatched. It smacked of desperation. Elaborating on a solution proffered by Young (who shared Burkett's impatience with the tedium of group process), the coordinators decided that they, Burkett, and Frank Walter should pack up the study team reports and the piles of unread research articles and closet themselves in a hotel. Then over the course of a weekend this select group would attempt to formulate a design for a model school to be presented to the faculty for comment, criticism, and refinement. The group risked being lambasted by their colleagues for such presumption, but allowing the project to die for want of leadership seemed worse. Young put the decision in perspective (his penchant for sarcasm was redeemed by an unerring ability to cut through confusion and palaver to the crux of an issue). "We've got to do something, or we'll look like assholes," he argued at one of the coordinators' daily planning sessions.

Late one Friday afternoon in early May 1989, the six educators checked into a hotel conference center on the outskirts of greater Cleveland. For three nights and three days they discussed their individual conceptions of the components of a model school, sometimes presenting ideas from the study team reports or research articles they had read, sometimes speaking from personal experience or conviction. Over the course of the retreat they took time out only for room service, an occasional beer, and midnight poker games. By late Monday afternoon the small conference room where they had gathered each day for fourteen hours at a stretch was wallpapered with flip-chart sheets on which proposals, counterproposals, statements of educational philosophy, and inside jokes were scrawled in colored marker. Even with the end of the long weekend in sight, the energy in the room had not diminished; if somehow harnessed, it could have driven a turbine engine.

"I feel like I've just participated in the planning of D Day," enthused the high school's choral director, Bill Thomas. A round-cheeked, jovial man who favored short-sleeved shirts no matter the season, Thomas was, at age forty-seven, one of the high school's most senior teachers and perhaps the employee best known to parents. Secure in his status as a pillar of the school, he was occasionally given to making grand pronouncements.

"Except we hope nobody gets killed," responded librarian Fran Walter, a slender, earnest woman with short-cropped dark hair.

"Or gets shot by their own side," added Steve Young, who may have been feeling guilty that he had violated the number one rule in his personal survival manual—"Never, never, never, *never* trust an administrator"—by collaborating behind closed doors with two of them. A 1969 graduate of the then iconoclastic University of Wisconsin, Young liked to signal his disrespect for the bureaucratic administration of Heights High School by refusing to attend department meetings and dressing down in jeans or chinos, which he teamed, incongruously, with one of a seemingly endless number of expensive sweaters. Today, however, he wore a T-shirt emblazoned with the cautionary slogan: "It's a Jungle Out There."

"And dare I say that we may produce the same momentous, worldwide results?" Thomas remarked, enjoying the modest word play that his D Day metaphor had engendered.

"If you would like to present the project at some national education convention, I can arrange for that," Hugh Burkett offered, sharing in the feeling of accomplishment in the room.

"It's a measure of how sick I am that that sounds like fun." Cathleen McBride responded. A woman in her early forties with a wry sense of humor and a waterfall of waist-length black hair that she kept under wraps in a bun, Cas McBride was the kind of English teacher who compelled her students' love of literature by the force of her personality and convictions. As English department liaison, she held sway over her colleagues by much the same means, abetted by an ability to puncture the resolve of those who opposed her with icy silence or a withering retort. But her intimates in the department could not have hoped for a more nurturing and protective friend, as confidant Young could attest. She guarded his interests at scheduling time, promoted his opinions, and even tolerated his nonparticipation in departmental affairs. The two were so cozy they set up one another's jokes—a routine that had revealed itself Friday night during the opening session of the retreat, which the coordinators had decided that Young should conduct.

When the group had assembled in a small conference room at the hotel at approximately 7:00 P.M., they found Young rummaging through a black sports bag, from which he retrieved masking tape and thumbtacks. Then he began affixing to the walls large sheets of paper, each of which bore a different plan for scheduling the school day.

Young had started out with the Model School Project as chairperson of the school structure study team. He had volunteered for the position, he insisted, in order to ensure that the model school included in its schedule a winter intersession that would allow him the opportunity to go skiing—a cover story he apparently needed to avoid the razzing of his poker-playing buddies at school, most of whom had chosen not to participate in the project. Young's team had ended up issuing no recommendations, however, because its chairperson had come to realize that the structure of a model school ought not be dictated in advance, but should arise naturally out of its objectives.

Nonetheless, having sat in on the deliberations of the curriculum study team and done some reading on his own, Young had reached a conclusion about the structure that he thought would best serve to improve student achievement. Heights High should reorganize its ninth and tenth grades, he believed, into a series of interracial schools within a school. This was a concept advanced by some leaders of the national reform movement as an antidote to the cruel anonymity of secondary school education.[1]

As Young envisioned this new structure, each school within a school would consist of four teachers certified to teach one of the four major academic subjects. The teachers would be given a common planning period that they would presumably spend in one another's company. Such enforced togetherness would help combat their own feelings of isolation, make it possible for them to collaborate on an interdisciplinary curriculum, and encourage their use of such desirable practices as team teaching, peer mentoring, and collaborative problem-solving.

Each group of four educators would be assigned to a heterogenous cluster of one hundred students, whom they would teach for both their freshman and sophomore years. Such continuity would theoretically allow the teachers to develop an intimate relationship with each of their students, who, in turn, would have the opportunity to get to know all their peers in the "school." Who knew? In time the members of this close-knit learning community might come to regard one another with something approaching respect and affection.

At this point in Young's scenario, traditional thinking took over. For scheduling purposes, the "school" would be divided into four separate classes of twenty-five. Each class would spend either the morning or the afternoon together, studying math/science and English/social studies on an alternating-day basis, during two, back-to-back periods of eighty minutes in length. The remainder of the students' day would be devoted to electives taught by other teachers. Young had committed his plan to paper and posted it on the wall of the hotel conference room, along with nine other alternative schedules to be considered during the retreat.

"Okay, the school year would be one hundred days long," Young said, kicking off the discussion. Since the State of Ohio mandated that public schools must provide 180 days of instruction annually, it was obvious that the English teacher had planted his tongue firmly in his cheek.

"*Ninety-five* days would be devoted to the teachers' professional development," Young continued.

"But the other five days would be *quality* time," Cas McBride said without skipping a beat.

"I'm trying to catch up," Hugh Burkett said, missing the joke. "What is the basis for doing structure first?"

"We wanted to irritate you," said McBride, who enjoyed a love-hate relationship with Burkett. In spite of the principal's advocacy of shared decision making, he and McBride had yet to resolve the issue of who was ultimately in charge of the English department, and they frequently butted heads over the issue of authority.

"Don't jerk him around," Fran Walter said, rushing to intervene. Burkett had hired Frank Walter's wife (amid some grumblings about nepotism) to transform Heights High's traditionally run library into a user-friendly resource center for students and teachers alike. Walter took her responsibilities seriously. An English teacher by training, she had accepted Burkett's proposal that she leave the classroom and become a librarian because she found the task of grading students—making *judgments* about their worth and fate—an excruciating process.[2] Yet she continued to anguish over fine points of educational philosophy and rhetoric, driven by what she often joked was a heavy dose of Catholic guilt to make distinctions that to many of her colleagues were indiscernible. This conscientiousness, a trait shared by her husband, had earned the couple a teasing but affectionate nickname; a colleague called them, privately, the "Saint Francises."

In response to Walter's admonition, McBride decided to explain the agenda to Burkett. "We're looking at structure first," she said, "so we'll know whether the other things we want to do will or won't fit in."

The first schedule that the group examined had been drawn up by the science department liaison, a chemistry teacher by the name of Virginia Hellstern. In a never-say-die attempt to restore a science-lab period to the school day, Hellstern had suggested a return to shorter classes in order to accommodate an extended period at the end of the day, which would be parceled out to each of the student's five major courses once a week. As this schedule offered no other discernible benefits, it was quickly dismissed.

A trimester schedule that Burkett had unsuccessfully attempted to implement in Jackson Hole, Wyoming, prompted a lengthier debate. The Jackson Hole schedule proposed that students take only two 150-minute courses, plus one sixty-minute tutorial, every day for eleven weeks. At the conclusion of each seminar-length course they would have earned one credit. Such a schedule would reduce a teacher's class load to around sixty students a trimester.

"Are there some courses that don't lend themselves to such intensity, like math?" Frank Walter asked.

"This addresses so much of the literature out there that says that how we schedule kids is not how you do things in real life," Burkett responded.

"I've read that literature, too," Young interjected, "but any time period is artificial. Do all tasks take one hundred and fifty minutes?"

"How many books did you bring to read this weekend?" Burkett asked Young. His question seemed to be a non sequitur.

"One," Young responded, nonetheless.

"Why didn't you bring five books and read ten minutes of each?" Burkett challenged. "The question is: What time period is closest to the reality of how people think and work?"

"Doesn't this structure answer a lot of philosophical things we've been talking about, like getting to know the kids one on one?" Bill Thomas said.

"You still see one hundred and fifty kids a year; that's no different than now," Young observed.

"But you really get to concentrate on them when you have them," argued Burkett.

"And maybe never see them ever again," Young said. "I'm not crazy about this plan, but our agenda is not to argue but to look at our options."

"Some of this is starting to sink in," Thomas said. "With trimesters a kid has to concentrate on only three classes."

"Doesn't the literature say that learning is not episodic?" Young countered. "The biggest disadvantage of this schedule is that it's possible for a kid to take English the first trimester of his freshman year and not again until the third trimester of his second year."

"If we looked at trimesters for seniors only," Burkett said, "then the problem of sequential courses is taken care of."

Burkett's compromise was accepted, and the concept of seminar-length classes for older, more mature students became a working premise of the model school. Then the group moved on to look at a schedule that had appeared in a recent issue of a newsletter published by Ted Sizer's Coalition of Essential Schools. Basically an eight-period day, it featured several forty-five minute lectures interspersed with ninety-minute interdisciplinary seminars.

"Notice that the period that you take the same class varies from day to day," Young pointed out. "I like variety, but I wonder if you wouldn't have a lot of lost souls wandering around."

Burkett was suddenly seized by an inspiration. "To get the greatest amount of flexibility," he asserted, "you give X number of teachers Y number of kids and then you let them do whatever they want."

Although no one seemed to pick up on Burkett's observation at the time, his concept of a flexible block of instructional time constituted an epiphany. Later it would be incorporated into the school-within-a-school plan, an addition that empowered each team of teachers to reschedule the two eighty-minute periods that Young proposed be devoted daily to a core academic curriculum however they saw fit (provided that the team took care to ensure that each core subject received, over the course of a year, the exact number of instructional hours that the state required to award one credit). Rescheduling this block of time would be a matter of give and take. Say the science teacher wished all one hundred students in the school within a school to go on a half-day field trip (a current impossibility, given Heights High's rigid schedule). She simply agreed to give up science's share of an equivalent amount of instructional time on succeeding days, extra minutes that her teammates could then put to their own purposes. The same arrangement could be made when the social studies teacher wished to show a three-hour documentary on the Civil War in its entirety.

Or suppose the English teacher needed to tutor a few faltering students. She could arrange for the remainder of her class to spend the period with one of her teammates, in exchange for taking all these students under her supervision at the point in the day when they would normally be working with the other teacher. When the math teacher wished to introduce his students to a new algebraic formula, he could do so once (instead of four times), in an all-"school" lecture, then break up the students into small groups to work on problems collaboratively applying the new information. If the English and social studies teachers wished to team teach an interdisciplinary unit on the concept of war, they could be given use of the entire block for a number of days or weeks, freeing up their teammates to write their own interdisciplinary unit when they were not serving as their colleagues' classroom aides. The possibilities for utilizing such a large block of time seemed endless.

The group's discussion of scheduling continued well into the night. When the six educators reassembled early the next morning, five of the ten schedules had been eliminated as unacceptable, and the group set about examining the remaining five contenders (including the Young and Jackson Hole plans) in terms of their ability to abet Model School objectives. Earlier the coordinators had assigned a code letter and number to each of the study teams' guiding principles, and they planned to list on each of the schedules the codes of the objectives that the group agreed it would further, the thought being that such a tally would make instantly clear which of the five schedules best suited the model school's purposes. But their system soon broke down, a victim of the group's inevitable desire to reexamine each of the guiding principles, some of which they had had no hand in shaping. By early afternoon the coordinators had stopped charting code numbers and given themselves over completely to the heady pleasure of deliberating with their bosses as equals.

From time to time tempers flared between the administrators and the teachers; and while these emotional confrontations demonstrated the difficulties the project faced in producing consensus for even modest changes, they also represented a rare opportunity for mutual understanding. The group's discussion late Sunday afternoon of the ways in which the quality of students' nonacademic life could be improved, for example, turned tense when Burkett offered a seemingly innocent suggestion.

"What if we released a teacher to work on full-time special assignment as a student activities adviser?" Burkett said, pleased that this proposition would also speak to the Model School objective of providing the faculty with a menu of opportunities for professional development.

Despite the well-meaning nature of his intentions, Burkett's willingness to pay a teacher's salary for what seemed to be a cushy job unleashed the English teachers' anger. It confirmed what they had long suspected: administrators did not truly understand and value the work of teachers.

"Is there an advantage to full-time versus a supplemental contract?" Steve Young asked. A supplemental contract paid a teacher a modest amount of money for taking on additional responsibilities, such as coaching.

"Then we wouldn't get anything more out of the adviser than organizing school dances and Homecoming," Burkett responded.

"What else would this person do?" Young asked Burkett.

"They'd deal with the whole issue of student climate, like getting students to take 'ownership' of the cleanliness of the cafeteria," the principal explained. "They could promote memberships in clubs and organizations, deal with student grievances, supervise student government."

"Is there a time this weekend when we're going to talk about teachers in nonteaching positions?" Fran Walter asked. (Frank Walter had left the room earlier to attend a son's track meet.)

"What's your question?" Burkett asked.

"The coordinators had a conversation last week about the staff's resentment of teachers serving in nonteaching positions," Walter responded. At Heights High, two former teachers filled quasi-administrative positions in Cedar and Lee Houses, for example. Known as house coordinators, they processed disciplinary referrals and dealt directly with the less serious offenders.

"We talked about instituting a system of trade-offs," Young volunteered. "I can kind of see a deal where if you advise student council, you lose a class. But having someone released to do student activities full-time galls me. Maybe it's all those English papers I have to grade."

"It shouldn't," Burkett said.

Cas McBride literally growled: "Don't *ever* tell people that they shouldn't feel some way!"

"We've been able to keep our spending on administrative salaries flat over the past five years because we've used teachers to fill what were formerly administrative positions," Burkett said, attempting to explain his way out of this predicament. "It creates some leftover funds for other activities that we're committed to."

"Maybe I don't know everything the house coordinators do," Young said, "but I don't think that you need a master's degree to do this shit. It could be done by an efficient secretary."

"A secretary can handle it when a kid who's been referred to Lee House doesn't show up?" Burkett asked doubtfully.

"What does a first-year cop make?" Young asked Burkett.

"Twenty thousand dollars."

"He has to handle a gun," Young said. "So pay the House coordinators $16,000."

"Why isn't there resentment out there if an administrator gets paid an administrator's salary to do these jobs?" Burkett wanted to know. "The trouble is, the administrators didn't want to do them. When I first came on, referrals were backed up six to eight weeks; now we run only about two days behind. The difference is that we now have people who view dealing with referrals as their main job. But I'm willing to cash in all teachers in non-teaching jobs and replace them with administrators, because that would give me more people to supervise teachers." Now he was trying to bully his way out of the argument.

"If we envision these positions as a deserving perk," Young countered, "it would be less objectionable to the staff. When it's perceived by the staff that they go to a bunch of assholes who don't know shit from Shinola and who don't appear to have anything to do, at least in terms of class preparation, then the staff is perturbed."

"I'm not comfortable," Fran Walter said, "calling any of these things perks, because that sounds like a vacation or a car with a phone."

"The entire Model School Project has been a perk, from getting a class period off to getting your opinions listened to," Young reminded her, adding sarcastically: "even the acknowledgment that teachers might *have* an opinion once every sixteen months. So give the perks to people who deserve them."

"Look what we're doing to each other," Thomas interjected, "lusting after each other's jobs. When really we're all working hard but differently. We just don't trust each other. My God, no wonder we're the lowest profession!"

"I didn't realize this was such an issue," Burkett said. "But I'll just put in for an administrator who can do student activities. That would really help me."

"That's a stupid idea, if you don't mind my saying so," Walter said.

"We've expressed some concerns, so now you're going to punish the teaching staff," McBride chided Burkett, continuing, "There's an important philosophical issue here. You could hire an administrator or you could hire a teacher, *or* you could design a system that would rotate teachers in and out of jobs so that some years you wouldn't have to teach five periods."

"But rotating who holds these nonteaching positions will just rotate the people who you're jealous of every year," Thomas pointed out.

"And I'll have twenty-one people doing the job of three," Burkett added.

"Do not go to the opposite extreme to make my argument absurd," McBride said coldly.

"If you're looking toward a future that includes site-based management," Fran Walter said, "then to put all the responsibility up at the top instead of spreading it around doesn't make sense."

"That's why we wanted to get a teacher to do student activities," Burkett noted.

"Why not post that job with a salary that you think it's worth?" Walter suggested.

"Then any teacher who wanted that position would have to take a salary cut," Burkett said.

"We've talked all around this," Young said, "but the bottom line is that there's no mechanism in place to make teaching a doable job and to give you the feeling that what you're doing is valued, not only by students but by those who have authority over you."

"Right now it's an undoable job that administrators want you to do better," McBride said.

The conversation seemed to have reached an impasse. Then Burkett had an inspiration.

"It's a discussion like this that is the foundation of a model school," he declared. "This stuff," he said, waving his hand toward the numerous flip-chart sheets posted around the room, "is not going to make the final difference." Although no one recognized the import of his remarks at the time, Burkett had pointed the Model School Project in a promising new direction.

"Can I clarify what issues we're leaving for later?" Walter asked, unwilling to let the discussion end without some sort of resolution. "Did we write down the student activities job? I like that idea."

"I don't, but I don't know why," McBride said. "I guess because I see it as another person coming along who will ask me to fill out surveys and tell me how much *fun* being student activities adviser is."

"But it wouldn't matter how bouncy that person was if we have the students do a needs assessment, and we have a written job description, and we don't call that person a teacher and pay them a teacher's salary," Fran Walter said. "I think rotating teachers into other jobs at a teacher's salary is not the answer. It creates resentment. I'd rather fix your job so it's more doable."

"What ever happened to that idea of making the English teachers' fifth period a grading period?" Thomas asked.

"Everybody else complained," Burkett noted.

"Maybe that's still an answer, even though it got kiboshed," Walter said.

"What am I going to say to the teachers in the social studies department, who teach five classes, when English goes to four?" Burkett asked.

"The same thing," McBride said, "you've been telling me for years. 'Sit down and shut up.'"

"Not in those words," Burkett protested weakly.

"But sometimes you ride roughshod over people," McBride insisted, bringing up a particular sore point by way of example. "English teachers come to me and complain that their schedules have been changed. I say: 'No, that can't be. Hugh hasn't told me.' Then I find out you *have* changed their schedules, and I have egg on my face."

"Why do you do that?" Young asked. "To irritate Cas? Because you're stubborn?"

"Because I forgot," Burkett said sheepishly. "I really, really believe I never change an English teacher's schedule without telling Cas."

Burkett's admission of his own human fallibility eased the tension in the room and accomplished something that had generally eluded his grasp for five years. In an instant he had been transported from the ranks of the omnipotent and unfathomable other (as the Heights High faculty insisted on mythologizing its principals) to those of the merely mortal. Once the coordinators recognized its importance to the success of the Model School Project, the "de-fanging" of Hugh Burkett was to become a critical component of their second-year plans.

Finally the group moved on to debate other matters, and in the free flow of conversation around the conference room table, a structure for a model school that would accommodate a variety of academic and personnel needs began to take shape. When time ran out, the group had yet to agree on such important issues as the composition and responsibilities of a management council, the content of a core academic curriculum, and the details of a race relations program. Nonetheless, when Burkett, Walter, and the four coordinators emerged from the hotel late Monday afternoon, they were, for the moment, united in purpose and feeling like close friends. If they had failed to complete the design of a model school, they *had* settled upon a new strategy for involving Heights High's faculty in the Model School Project.

As the project's sluggish start had demonstrated, the teachers' lack of interest in taking charge of their own futures was an entrenched dynamic whose roots lay deep in the paternalistic way public schools were administered. But the project leaders were now confident that they had figured out a way to engage the hearts and minds of their colleagues. Their weekend together had proved so compelling an event, leaving them on an intellectual and emotional high note, that they were determined to duplicate the experience for their colleagues. They had decided to sponsor a series of weekend retreats at which small groups of teachers could build a spirit of camaraderie and establish a more trusting relationship with Burkett, while they examined, point by point, the components of a model school that the project leaders had just spent seventy-two hours hammering out.

By this means Burkett, Walter, and the coordinators hoped to reach agreement by the end of the summer on a structure for a model school with some thirty to fifty teachers, creating the broader base of support that the project needed to survive. They planned to continue hosting retreats throughout the following school year until no more teachers could be persuaded to attend. (The promise of an all-expenses-paid stay at a nice hotel—an unprecedented largesse for teachers accustomed to receiving few perks—would serve as bait.) At that time a "super-retreat" attended by one or two representatives from each previous retreat would be held to reach final agreement on which components of the model school should be developed more fully and implemented.

The process amounted to psychological warfare. It would be long, convoluted, and expensive. But the project leaders saw no other hope of transforming a passive, demoralized faculty into committed agents of change.

9

Intramural Rivalry

As in industry, the productivity of any school depends mostly on the skill of those who directly manage the workers (the teachers). But . . . their success depends almost completely on how well they, in turn, are managed by the administrators above them.

—WILLIAM GLASSER
The Quality School, 1990

Before the new plan could be put into action, the Model School Project lost one of its key supporters. In June 1988 Irv Moskowitz announced that he was resigning to accept the superintendency of a quickly growing, predominately Hispanic public school system in Pomona, California. Exemplifying a worrisome national trend that had seen the average tenure of superintendents of big-city school systems drop to an ineffectual two and a half years, Moskowitz decided to leave Cleveland Heights because he had found the community to be more interested in contention than cooperation. Even the schools' most enthusiastic supporters subjected the district to scrutiny so intense it approached "self-flagellation." With admirers like the members of the School Consensus Project, who needed critics?

Moskowitz had felt so stymied during his brief, three-year tenure that he was able to make only two contributions that he believed to be notable. After discovering that 150 Heights High students had flunked ninth grade in 1986—a statistic that gave a sense of the depth, if not the breadth, of the school's problems with achievement—Moskowitz initiated an internal discussion that resulted in the creation of Taylor Academy, an alternative, off-site high school created explicitly for failing ninth and tenth graders.

As for his second major achievement, Moskowitz pointed to the fact that he had reined in AFT Local 795, crying halt to its demands every three years for a hefty raise. The union's supposition that automatic salary increases were its "god-given" right had, in Moskowitz's estimation, wreaked havoc with the district's finances.[1] In the superintendent's view, the wage and benefit package he inherited was a sweetheart deal consisting of 6, 6, and 5 percent raises over three years and fringes whose final value totaled approximately 25 percent of the average teacher's salary. It was negotiated in 1985 by Moskowitz's predecessor, an interim superintendent who may have hoped that, by averting a repeat of the 1983 teachers' strike—a public relations disaster—he would further his chances of keeping the job permanently.

The 1985 contract was hailed as "the best the teachers of Cleveland Heights have ever had" by Glenn Altschuld. Yet the package so elevated the district's expenses that the board of education was forced to return to the voters three years in a row to ask for increases in property tax millage—an awkward development that turned some board members against the union.[2] The first two tax requests were immediately approved, but the third requested increase was defeated twice before it finally passed. This unsettling turn of events had shaken community confidence in the management and stability of the schools.

In order to avoid "giving away the store" once again during the 1988–89 contract negotiations, Moskowitz had dismissed the district's usual legal advisors and hired a local law firm specializing in labor negotiations that had a reputation for union busting. He also felt it necessary to enter into an unseemly dispute with Glenn Altschuld, highlighted by their exchange of increasingly intemperate open letters to the staff in which each man questioned the honesty, motives, and tactics of the other. For example, in the second issue of the *Bargaining Table,* his triannual newsletter to the rank and file detailing the progress of contract negotiations, Altschuld accused Moskowitz of intransigence, noting:

In June . . . the Local 795 bargaining team took the Board of Education and Superintendent to a private dinner and pleaded our case. We requested a return to non-confrontational, problem-solving bargaining. Such a return does not take great effort or understanding. You either instruct your bargaining team to get the best deal you can (confrontational) or you instruct your bargaining team to solve problems and settle fairly (non-confrontational).

. . . We have met a stone wall.

Moskowitz responded in kind:

To: Teaching Staff.

Circulating around are rumors, bits and pieces of information, misinformation and assorted facts concerning contract negotiations. . . . Let's see if I can provide you with some facts that are . . . certain:

. . . In various attempts to engage in problem-solving, the Union President has declined to participate. Here's an example: The offer was made by the Board's team to jointly review the budget and work together to find areas where reductions might be made. This was declined with the words, "That's your problem."

Watching the escalation of tempers, one union insider likened the effect that Moskowitz and Altschuld had on one another to that produced by gas fumes and a match.

In private, the superintendent was occasionally even less guarded in expressing his opinions about Altschuld. When the conversation turned to the subject of the union president at a luncheon meeting with a former top-ranking district administrator, Moskowitz asserted, "That man is evil."

"You found out," Moskowitz's luncheon partner thought to himself, "if by 'evil' you mean someone who believes in the end justifying any means, someone who believes you simply do what you have to do, with no remorse felt."

On another occasion, during the course of the lengthy contract negotiations, when it looked as if a strike were inevitable, the superintendent pulled teacher and friend Allan Wolf into his office and flatly informed him of his intention to destroy the union. Wolf vividly remembered Moskowitz's violent imagery, his talk of smashing Glenn Altschuld's head with a baseball bat and his vision of noses getting bloodied when the district took its gloves off. Performing what he apparently thought was a favor to a friend, Moskowitz advised the high school steward that it would be best for him not to cross the picket line.

The superintendent's statement, combined with an announcement he sent to parents that the district had lined up a sufficient number of substitute teachers to keep the schools open in the event of a strike, convinced Wolf that Moskowitz was willing to see the teachers stay out indefinitely in 1989, should that extreme measure be necessary to break the union's stranglehold on the school system's coffers. By contrast, the eight-day walkout in 1983 looked like a disagreement among friends. (Legend had it that the 1983 strike lasted only as long as it took for the teachers' lost wages to amount to the total needed to pay for the raise that Local 795 was demanding—a calculation that each side accused the other of cynically factoring into its strike strategy.)

The community had come to expect aggressive tactics from Altschuld, who once held up the district's receipt of a Cleveland Foundation grant that would have returned art instruction to the elementary schools (a "frill" that had been slashed from the budget) by paying professional artists to assist classroom teachers half a day a week. (In an attempt to protect union jobs, Altschuld objected to the fact that the artists had no liability insurance, which they could obtain only by joining the union.) A school superintendent, on the other hand, was supposed to be a diplomat, and, as a consequence of Moskowitz's public brawling with Altschuld, his reputation was tarnished.

The teachers' union president did not escape altogether unharmed, however. In the end, Moskowitz's intransigence forced Local 795 to back off from its strike threat and to accept a 1989 contract offering 0, 4, and 0 percent raises, with the right to reopen salary discussions in the third year. (A strike would not have produced more favorable terms, in the opinion of one of the union's negotiators, who perceived the superintendent's personality to be such that he would rather have seen the district in flames than give ground.) Shortly after suffering the humiliation of so public and thorough a trouncing, Altschuld was notified that he was being transferred immediately from his teaching assignment at the high school to one at Monticello Middle School. The decision was transmitted, Altschuld noted in a subsequent union communication, "without explanation, without even a day['s notice] to clean my desk or say goodbye."

Moskowitz had sought to minimize the union's influence and dethrone its powerful leader, bystander Burkett concluded, because the superintendent was after complete control of the district. Burkett also understood that it was largely because of his battles with Local 795 that Moskowitz had found it difficult to make things happen on the educational front. This was a lesson that the high school principal seemed to be incapable of applying to his own professional relationships, however. With Moskowitz no longer in a position to protect and defend him, Burkett appeared to be in danger of losing his job because of his own entanglement in several feuds.

Undeterred by the brevity and controversial nature of Moskowitz's tenure, several administrators in the district harbored ambitions of replacing him. Unfortunately for Burkett, the front-runner seemed to be Dr. Lauree P. Gearity, a former elementary school principal, whom the board of education had appointed to the position of interim superintendent in late June of 1989. If the board went on to award Gearity a permanent three-year contract, there was a good chance that she would not renew Burkett's contract when it came up for evaluation. During the 1988–89 school year, Gearity had served as Moskowitz's assistant superintendent, with responsibility for directing the work of the high school principal, and it was during this period that she and Burkett had learned to dislike and distrust one another.

As is true of many rivals, Gearity and Burkett had a lot in common, starting with their hard-driving personalities and addiction to cigarettes. Both came from poor families, although Lauree Pearlman grew up in an Orthodox Jewish home in Cleveland Heights, while Hugh Burkett was reared a Baptist fundamentalist near Kinston, North Carolina. Like Burkett, Gearity had not been a particularly good student; she, too, had "found" herself only after reluctantly going off to college. Each had begun a professional career in the classroom—she choosing to work at the elementary level because she liked kids, he wanting to be a football coach and seeing no other path than teaching to reach his goal. Both aspired early on to become principals.

Unlike the maverick Burkett, however, Gearity never strayed far from home professionally. Except for a five-year stint with the Cleveland public schools, she had spent her entire career in Cleveland Heights, from whose high school she herself graduated as a member of the class of 1960. Gearity went on to earn her bachelor's degree from Ohio University and a master's degree and doctorate from nearby Kent State, another Ohio university. Her experience with the educational policies and regulations of only one state may well have been one of the reasons why she liked to do things by the book.

Burkett, on the other hand, believed first and foremost in Burkett's Law, a self-reliance born of a career spent knocking about and of voracious reading in his field. By the time he arrived in Cleveland Heights, he had come to be convinced of the sureness of his instincts and the correctness of his educational views.

Irv Moskowitz, for one, admired Burkett as a man of unshakable integrity and supreme self-confidence, while acknowledging that other district administrators and certain members of the board of education found him arrogant and rigid. No matter how one characterized Burkett, the bottom line remained the same: Heights High's principal chafed at taking orders.[3] He and Moskowitz had been able to develop a relatively smooth working relationship only because Burkett respected the superintendent's intelligence and creativity. (It also helped that Moskowitz tended to give Burkett his head in running the high school.) The Model School Project was a good example of their ability to work together. But, perhaps because of his southern upbringing, Burkett had particular trouble accepting suggestions or direction from females, colleague Frank Walter noticed. This rule held especially true in the case of Burkett's relationship with Lauree Gearity.

Prior to her appointment by Moskowitz to the position of assistant superintendent, Gearity ran for ten years what was widely agreed to be the best elementary school in the district. The focused atmosphere at Belvoir did not escape Moskowitz's notice. One could not walk into another elementary school in the district that was more "on task," he often marveled to associates. Although Gearity lacked a similarly thoroughgoing understanding of secondary education—a qualification that one might expect in a candidate for an assistant superintendent's job with direct-line responsibility for a high school's operation—Moskowitz did not regard her inexperience in this area as a serious handicap. Moskowitz himself had come up through the ranks of secondary education and felt that he had that specialty covered. The superintendent was more concerned, frankly, about finding someone who could get along well with the other administrators in the central office, and he believed that Gearity's popular standing in the community and years of loyal service in the system augured well in this regard.

In naming Gearity to be his second in command (Moskowitz briefly considered Burkett for the job but decided that the principal's shortcomings as a team player made it politically impossible to offer him the position), Moskowitz was also motivated by a desire to change the district's record of promoting only men to such a position of responsibility. In Cleveland Heights, whose politics had become so progressive that the liberal Democrats who now controlled city council believed it reasonable to pass a resolution declaring the suburb a nuclear-free zone, it did not pay to be thought insensitive to feminist causes. Indeed, within a few years Cleveland Heights would become home to the first black female mayor of an Ohio city with a predominately white population.

Predictably, Gearity's promotion to assistant superintendent placed her on a collision course with Burkett. Having previously reported (without major incident) to a man who served as principal of Heights High during the late 1970s, Burkett judged that his new superior lacked her predecessor's qualifications to supervise and direct him. Consequently, he did not go out of his way to keep her apprised of his actions or seek her approval of his decisions. As Gearity was long accustomed to giving orders, Burkett's lack of respect for her authority must have offended her sense of professional order. Certainly, his failure to keep her informed placed her in an awkward position with Moskowitz, and periodically, the high school principal remembered, she would call him to complain about the lack of communication, charging that he was trying to make her look bad. By the end of the school year, they were barely speaking, as it had become obvious to Gearity that she and Burkett were miles apart philosophically and would never reach agreement on how to manage the high school.[4]

Another superintendent might have sat down with the two administrators and encouraged them to work out their differences; but Moskowitz preferred, in the main, to keep to his unwritten policy of nonintervention in the disputes of his subordinates, figuring that time would render these squabbles inconsequential.

In the case of Gearity and Burkett, this proved to be a major miscalculation. Gearity would make a move that deepened the rift after she became interim superintendent. When it came time to name an interim assistant superintendent, she bypassed Burkett—as the district's highest-ranking and highest-paid principal, Burkett theoretically stood first in line for the promotion—and instead offered the position to Burkett's right-hand man, Frank Walter. Walter declined the appointment out of loyalty to Burkett, which removed some of the sting from Gearity's slight.

Gearity had forewarned Burkett that he would be passed over, explaining that the board of education's president had made it clear to her that the high school principal was not a desirable candidate for the central-office position. Only a month before Gearity's appointment to the interim superintendency, Burkett had burned his bridges with the school board in a philosophical dispute. The issue that prompted the wrangle was Burkett's decision to deny permission to the Brothers and Sisters, Inc., a state-chartered organization of African-American graduates of Heights High, to present two $100 scholarships at the school's annual Senior Recognition Night. Burkett had concluded that to allow the organization to participate in the ceremony was to give official recognition to a group whose high school affiliate, he was later to claim, had "played an active role in fights, cases of intimidation, and hazing."

Unbeknownst to Burkett, the Brothers alumni decided to appeal his decision. They approached the president of the school board, an African-American attorney named Bernard W. Greene, who arranged for them to speak to his colleagues at what was supposed to have been an executive session of the board. The Brothers, Inc., representatives made a strong case for their organization, which Burkett was not present to counter. They argued that the only interest of the group, whose numbers included professional football players, attorneys, and politicians, was to serve as role models for their youthful affiliates, encouraging them to study hard, participate in sports, and perform community service.

Maureen O. Weigand, the vice president of the board and a prominent local Democrat whose husband was the mayor of Cleveland Heights, later explained that she found it inappropriate to discourage the attempts of upstanding citizens to help the school district. She suggested that the Brothers, Inc., be allowed to participate in the awards ceremony on the condition that the group make a statement that night explaining the difference between the adult and high school chapters and expressing its abhorrence of violence—a compromise to which four of the five members of the board agreed.

Irv Moskowitz felt that he understood why the board members voted as they had. They had asked themselves "who was best equipped to make decisions affecting the welfare of the district: 'We who live in the community and are of the community, or some guy who leaves for his farm in Ashtabula every night?'" But Moskowitz's acquiescence to the board's decision surprised Frank Walter, who wondered why the superintendent had not backed the high school's ban on gang activity more vigorously. Walter suspected that Moskowitz "had already left town; he just hadn't packed yet." On the other hand, Walter could see how the Burkett administration might have contributed to the decision by failing to keep the board fully apprised of adverse conditions at the high school. (There was a tendency on the part of building administrators, he admitted, to put one's best foot forward in presentations to the board.)

Unlike Walter, Burkett was in no mood to temporize. The role of a school board was to set policy, goddammit, not to run the schools. Although he usually preferred to stay well above the political fray, he decided that he must lodge an official protest against this particularly harmful instance of board interference.

"The high school administrative staff have worked for five years to neutralize the negative effect of gangs/groups in our schools and community," Burkett declared in the letter he sent to the board, which he also released to the high school faculty. "The distinction between the Brothers, Inc. and the Heights High Brothers is lost on our faculty, our students, our community, and our police force. Was the former Heights student who robbed the woman at the Mad Greek [restaurant] a Brother or a [member of] Brothers, Inc. or a former Brother? Was the former Heights student who trespassed in the cafeteria this year to confront another group a Brother or a [member of] Brothers, Inc. or a former Brother? . . . I cannot emphasize enough the negative impact your decision will have on the climate at the high school and on the dignity of the Senior Recognition Program."

Moskowitz warned Burkett that confronting the board would be a disastrous career move. Burkett ignored the advice. How could he not express his indignation with a board that had so blithely undermined his administration's five-year struggle to make Heights High School a safe and orderly environment for learning—even if it cost him his job? His outrage having overcome his better judgment, he concluded his letter to the board by saying that he planned to boycott the awards ceremony and dispense with the enforcement of school rules prohibiting the wearing of gang colors at the high school, an effort that he now saw as wasted energy. These statements, when somehow leaked to the Cleveland *Plain Dealer,* drew a rebuke from school board president, Bernard Greene, who suggested to the daily newspaper that the principal was "out of line" to announce that he would not comply with school policy.

The board president had no public comment when the *Plain Dealer* subsequently published an editorial chastising the board of education for weakening Burkett's message to students of the school's intolerance of aggressive social groups. Behind the scenes, however, the board was in an uproar. Although the principal insisted that the leak did not originate with him, some board members believed otherwise, informing Moskowitz of their dismay that Burkett had deliberately sought out this opportunity to embarrass them publicly.

For Maureen Weigand, the Brothers episode was "the last straw." Although Weigand had privately applauded some of Burkett's initiatives, such as his decision to close the high school campus and his encouragement of reduced ability grouping in math, she had long been troubled by his unforthcoming communication style. This latest example of his inability to convey his philosophy to his superiors before acting on it had convinced her of the validity of Burkett's reputation as a "loose cannon." Word began circulating around Cleveland Heights that Weigand was making no secret of her intention to "get Burkett." When these rumors reached Burkett's ears, he realized that it was highly unlikely that his contract would be renewed.

By the time he left the city in midsummer, Irv Moskowitz had modified his opinion of Burkett's effectiveness. Although still counting himself among the principal's admirers, Moskowitz now believed the apolitical Burkett to be a mismatch in a district in which everybody, but everybody, wanted to have his or her say. Burkett, too, seemed resigned to being forced out of Heights High, having already considered and discarded the idea of giving Gearity a run for the top job in the district. When he told Fran Walter that he had decided not to seek the superintendency, Walter wondered out loud about the reason why.

"Too much paperwork?" the librarian guessed.

"No," Burkett replied, "too much ass-kissing."

Instead, Burkett decided to focus his energies on the successful completion of the Model School teachers' retreats, a task that had taken on even greater significance and urgency in his eyes. Now that the board had demonstrated its willingness to interfere in the high school's daily operation and now that an administrator he perceived as uncomfortable with shared decision making had assumed the reins of the superintendency, the high school must make known its determination to move toward site-based management as quickly as possible. If Burkett's contract were indeed not renewed, it would expire during the summer of 1991. It was imperative that the model school be in place well before then.

10

Hearts and Minds

Bossing and kowtowing are so deeply engrained at the top of the system that my only hope for educational reform is to find enough principals willing to give up bossing and start leading.

—WILLIAM GLASSER
The Quality School, 1990

The first Model School Project teachers' retreat did not begin auspiciously. The opening session of the retreat was scheduled to start at 7:00 P.M. on Friday, August 11th, but as of 7:30, several of the twelve teachers and two administrators signed up to participate had not yet straggled into the meeting room at the Holiday Inn conference center, where the project leaders had booked a block of rooms through the following Monday. Pre- and after-school meetings at the high school invariably began ten or fifteen minutes late, as the staff seemed constitutionally unable to be punctual without the aid of ringing bells; but this degree of tardiness was unusual.

While those attendees who had arrived earlier chatted quietly among themselves at their places around a massive pink-clothed conference table, the coordinators fidgeted. They had returned that morning from the American Federation of Teachers School Restructuring Academy at Michigan State University and were eager to share some interesting news. The Model School Project, they had discovered, far surpassed in scope and ambition the piecemeal agendas for change of the thirty other secondary schools from around the country that had sent representatives to the five-day workshop. Surely their colleagues would be proud to learn that Cleveland Heights High School stood at the leading edge of education reform.

As the coordinators considered whether to begin the proceedings without the latecomers, Frank Walter busied himself setting out an impressive array of snacks, fruit, cold soda, and beer on several side tables. Walter had agreed to serve as the retreat's majordomo, and it was his responsibility to replenish the refreshments throughout the weekend. Only Hugh Burkett, clad in shorts and a polo shirt, sat patiently, leafing through a thick packet of journal articles that the coordinators had mailed in advance to the retreat participants in the hopes that they would familiarize themselves with such concepts as site-based management, schools within a school, and curriculum reform.

Although Burkett believed that, left to his own devices, he could probably design a model school in a few hours, he had come to accept the painful reality that a consensus for Heights High's reform would have to be built slowly, one teacher at a time. He was now committed to participating in as many retreats as were necessary to accommodate all the teachers who could be cajoled into attendance. If the retreats must be devoted to raising the consciousness of the participants, bringing them up to speed on the latest theories and developments in secondary education, and occasionally even to jollying them along—time-consuming and tedious processes that ran counter to his take-charge style and authoritarian personality—so be it.

The packet with which Burkett was contentedly whiling away the hour contained a twenty-page document that Fran Walter and Steve Young had coauthored shortly before the end of the school year. The task of collaborating on a summary of the May retreat had put a strain on their newly cordial relationship, and the tension between them would only increase during the Model School Project's second year. Although the coauthors had little in common stylistically, both enjoyed a high opinion of their own work, and it had proved difficult for each to make suggestions about how to meld their two voices without giving offense to the other.

Walter and Young found themselves in agreement, however, that the report should be disguised as a narrative describing what life would be like in a model school, a format that they thought might help to boost readership. Getting busy, distracted teachers to slow down long enough to read a document of more than a paragraph in length represented a communications challenge of the first order. The coauthors attempted to surmount the problem by means of a conversational tone and the plentiful use of bulleted highlights. Thus the section devoted to academic reform masqueraded as a description of the activities of students in a model school, who would:

> have demonstrated mastery of the materials they need to successfully begin high school work. . . .

> —know that they can learn, if given enough time to master the material. . . .
> —not jump from one course to another, but spend time and energy on exploring many possibilities within one subject; they are more involved with depth of investigation than with the quantity of material covered; they take part in longer class periods, but study fewer subjects per year
> —work with a few teachers every day, for sustained periods of time; they have the opportunity to know their teachers well, and their teachers know them well. . . .
> —focus on learning a common body of knowledge in the first two years of high school; this core curriculum prepares them to choose alternatives during junior and senior years
> —take courses driven by concepts, not solely by content. . . .
> —not [be] "tracked"; as often as possible they work in a heterogenous grouping that allows all students to . . . share ideas, and to learn from each other
> —learn to think critically as well as to read, write, and compute
> —become culturally literate; they know and appreciate the contributions of all world cultures. . . .
> —[be] offered many opportunities to demonstrate learning; they demonstrate mastery through projects, speaking, research, a variety of ways in addition to traditional tests. As many as possible of their mastery demonstrations are public; these demonstrations provide the school and the community a chance to acknowledge student progress
> —[be] recognized for academic achievement in many ways, from all-school assemblies to having their pictures in the "student recognition" showcase. . . .
> —see, hear, and work with many people who model adult success; they learn to break through stereotypes about achievement. . . .
> —perform community service as part of the work they complete toward graduation

—acknowledge their partnership in the success of the school. . . .

—participate in school-wide decision making.

Unfortunately, the effort devoted to making the narrative easy to digest delayed its presentation to the faculty until a week before the end of school, and there were few indications that the teachers found time to read it. Race relations study team chairperson Phyllis Fowlkes seemed to be one of the only exceptions to this rule. Encountering fellow team member Fran Walter in the building, she opined that the narrative watered down the team's race relations recommendations to the point of invisibility—a complaint that she also registered with Young. The coordinators had indeed chosen not to address the issue of race relations in a separate section, in part because of Fowlkes's decision to disband the race relations study team midyear so that its members could "infiltrate" the other study teams and encourage them to address equity issues specifically affecting their own areas of concern. They had also concluded that the topic was too hot to tackle head-on.[1]

Just as Fowlkes accepted no responsibility for the reduced visibility of race relations in the Model School agenda, so the coordinators shrugged off her criticism, attributing it to Phyllis being Phyllis. If revisions were needed, they decided, that fact would emerge at the retreats. It was the coordinators' intention to guide each retreat through a section-by-section examination of the model school narrative in the hopes of prompting a lively debate whose highlights would be recorded on a flip chart. These notes would serve as the basis for a revised draft of the narrative, which each retreat group was to prepare. In the process of thinking through their own conceptions of a model school, the retreat-goers would come to be convinced of the need for reform and committed to a written plan of action—or so the coordinators strategized.

At nearly twenty minutes to eight, the latecomers finally arrived, explaining that they had not had time to fix dinner before leaving for the hotel and so had wandered across the street to a McDonald's to grab a bite to eat. Stifling her anger at this display of thoughtlessness—over the course of the summer the coordinators had been trained in the art and science of facilitating group discussions by an organizational development consultant—Cas McBride issued a warm welcome to everyone and, as only a handful of her audience had previously been involved with the Model School Project, briefly explained its history. Then she asked the retreat-goers to introduce themselves and explain why they had decided to attend the retreat. Judging from their responses, many of the latecomers' colleagues suffered from a similar unreadiness for work. Most of the educators admitted that they had come in search of personal and professional renewal, perhaps calculating that three days of pampering at a nice hotel promised to be restorative, even if the retreat proved to be a bore.

"I don't know why I'm here," confessed Betty Levy, one of three English teachers in attendance, when her turn came to speak. "I'm an old teacher, the oldest person here, and maybe I'm a little stale."

Other expressions of burnout echoed around the table. They contrasted sharply with the enthusiasm of the coordinators' personal statements.

"I've never been involved in anything in education that's excited me as much," Fran Walter said. Bill Thomas agreed. "I came away from our retreat in May," he said, "with feelings for comrades and education that I never felt in twenty-five years as a teacher." Even Steve Young confessed to having caught the Model School bug. "I'm here because all those things we've bitched about for fifteen years can maybe change, and that's too good an opportunity to pass up," he said.

Jean King, a special education teacher who earlier in the summer had been tapped by the Burkett administration to become student activities adviser for the 1989–90 school year, seemed to be the only participant who came with a broad goal in mind. The sole African-American staff member who had signed up for the first retreat, she appealed to her white colleagues to make good on the Model School Project's promise of ensuring a quality education for all students. "I'd like to leave here," she said, "believing that there is unity because we all believe in what we're doing."

Given King's aspirations, it was ironic that her promotion to student activities adviser had itself contributed to the staff's disharmony. The job had not been posted, nor was the hiree's salary adjusted—suggestions that the coordinators had advised Burkett at the May retreat to follow in order to render the assignment of a well-paid teacher to what appeared to be less onerous work more acceptable to the faculty. The principal had not, however, heeded these recommendations.

Burkett's continuing inability to manage Heights High School in strict accordance with his professed belief in shared decision making suggested that his was more an intellectual appreciation of the concept. But an experience at the AFT's School Restructuring Academy, which Burkett attended in the company of the coordinators, had served to deepen his emotional commitment to teacher empowerment. At the AFT conference Burkett and the coordinators had heard Albert Shanker deliver a persuasive keynote address on the need for teachers to take back the leadership of the education reform movement, and they also had the opportunity to chat privately with the national union leader about school restructuring. The contact with the charismatic Shanker renewed Burkett's sense of the intertwining of national purpose and personal mission that had been leached from his conception of the Model School Project by its fitful beginning.

Inspired by Shanker's comments to take a more active role in the leadership of the Model School Project, Burkett planned to use the retreats to challenge faculty members one on one to examine the inconsistencies between their stated educational philosophies and their classroom practice, taking advantage of all the powers of persuasion at his disposal: reasoned argument, humor, biting sarcasm, and, if necessary, guile. When McBride asked him if he would care to make some opening remarks, he responded by asking the retreat attendees to treat him during the activities that followed as a fellow participant, not as their principal, a shrewd move that freed him to speak and act forcefully at the same time that it won him points for being "one of the guys."

The remainder of the opening session was devoted to the participants' statement of their expectations for the retreat, an activity that was happily abandoned when Frank Walter came into the room around 9:00 P.M. with a half-dozen boxes of takeout pizza. Work resumed the following morning at 8:30 A.M., with a roundtable discussion of concerns centering on the school's physical plant. The object of the session was to identify as many problems as rapidly as possible and get them down on paper, without any concern for order or continuity. As the high school had no skilled plasterers, painters, or carpenters at its disposal on site—the scheduling of major repairs and remodeling was handled at central-office headquarters on Miramar Road, several blocks away—the recitation of woes about "Miramar's" poor maintenance of the building and of the inadequacies of the facility itself was enthusiastic.

The group then considered possible remedies. At the outset of the Model School Project, superintendent Moskowitz had placed only one restriction on its outcome: he outlawed a recommendation that a new high school be built. Before inviting a consideration of possible measures to improve the appearance, cleanliness, and repair of Heights High School at each of the nine retreats the Model School Project eventually sponsored, the coordinators liked to explain Moskowitz's prohibition by saying, "The only thing we can't do is 'nuke' the high school." Invariably, their warning provoked a semifacetious response: "What about Miramar?"

When the discussion turned after lunch to the topic of students, the mood of the August retreat participants sombered. "Somehow we have to address the caste system at Heights High," said social studies teacher Cal Rose at one point during the group's listing of a staggering array of student problems.

"What do you mean by caste system?" asked Fran Walter, who was serving as discussion facilitator for the session, while Bill Thomas, magic marker at the ready, manned the flip chart.

"A standard track that's all black and an advanced track that's all white," Rose responded. "We have to encourage kids to leave the standard track." Although Rose, a Mick Jagger look-alike right down to the gap between his two front teeth, was a newcomer to the Model School Project, he was not shy about expressing his support of liberal causes ranging from integration to organized labor.

Bill Thomas used Rose's remarks as a wedge. "I'd like to put down as a potential solution the elimination of the grouping system," he said, prematurely attempting to press Rose's colleagues to come to consensus. Instead he opened up a floodgate of resistance.

"But are you going to be meeting the needs of the students? Are you going to deprive kids capable of doing more advanced work by teaching to middle?" Virginia Hellstern asked doubtfully. A petite woman with perfectly coiffed red hair, Ginny Hellstern was the science teachers' liaison to the high school administration. She predominated over her colleagues, among the school's most stubbornly opinionated faculty members, by virtue of an even more entrenched viewpoint. If academic departments at Heights High could be likened to states of the union, Hellstern was the faculty's most committed state's righter.

"How about putting down: 'Reevaluate grouping,'" Betty Levy suggested as a compromise.

"I haven't seen any proof it's benefiting either end," Thomas countered.

"I really agree with Ginny," English teacher Kathleen Blaine interjected. "I realize grouping has its problems, but I can't imagine putting students' names in a computer and coming up with a random class list and somehow meeting the needs of everyone in the room. You'd end up having to teach five different textbooks. I can't imagine that."

"It *is* hard to image," McBride agreed, "if we keep on imagining the classroom as it is. But it might be easier if we think of it in terms of cooperative learning, independent study, the teacher as facilitator and the student as worker."

"I don't see why we can't say I want to hear you play the trumpet before we allow you in the orchestra," Blaine responded in heated defense of ability grouping.

"Kathy, can I ask you a question?" Burkett said in a respectful tone. "Would you be willing to teach to five different levels in one classroom if you assume that you could do it well, efficiently, and you would love it?"

"Why would you assume that?" Hellstern snapped. "It's not true."

"Yes," Blaine said, "I suppose so, but it's not possible."

"Just leave it at 'yes,'" Fran Walter urged.

"Except for age, emotional maturity, and motivation," math teacher Mark Wessels chimed in, "there's very little difference in most students' ability to understand."

"I don't think you should discount motivational differences," Blaine insisted.

"Someone asked why we group," Cal Rose said. "I have the answer. Because it's the American way. We're very competitive here. The Japanese don't group. They reward hard work and cooperation."

"Yeah, but we're the only country that tries to educate everyone," Hellstern observed.

"How are we going to explain ungrouping to our community?" Levy worried. "We're going to end up losing all our top students, black and white."

"How do we honestly explain to the community that the kids in standard classes are not expected to get As?" Frank Walter countered, referring to an infamous memorandum issued to the faculty by the previous assistant principal for curriculum that discussed her philosophy of preestablished grading ceilings for each level. "I find that attitude quite distressing."

"I still think kids should have the choice between expanded and advanced placement chemistry; they're not the same," Hellstern insisted.

"I could make an argument for eight levels," Fred Mills said, taking up the banner for heterogenous classes. The social studies department's liaison spoke from personal conviction; he had not previously been involved with the Model School Project. "But then we're saying that students should come to school *physically* but not *mentally*. Standard kids might feel more challenged by being with kids who *are* motivated."

"Let's look at our history," Hellstern urged. "Let's look at when high schools were a melting pot. The graduation rates were a lot lower then."

"If we look at ungrouping without looking at how we teach," Burkett agreed, "then we might as well stay grouped."

"It's going on four o'clock," Fran Walter noted. "We could stay here until Monday and not solve the issue of grouping."

"Maybe we ought to come back after break to talk about what Hugh said," Levy suggested, "the way we teach."

"I hope our final report won't say that we should eliminate grouping," Hellstern said, as the session ended. "We haven't reached a consensus on that. I wouldn't be able to hold my head up with my colleagues."

While the retreat participants stretched their legs during break, the four coordinators huddled together at one end of the hallway leading to the conference room, assessing the success of the session. Having observed Hellstern and Blaine's negative reaction to being pressured, Cas McBride proposed that the coordinators limit themselves to asking questions rather than making comments. Such a procedure, she suggested, would help to head off the suspicion that they were trying to steer the retreat participants toward a preconceived plan. It was a rule that McBride herself would have difficulty observing, so eager were the coordinators to impress upon the retreat-goers how well various Model School Project concepts answered the concerns that they were articulating.

Steve Young was to prove over the course of the nine retreats best able of the four facilitators to hold his tongue during the discussion sessions, and Fran Walter's and Bill Thomas's continuing inability to refrain from commenting would begin to grate on him, a development that would eat away at the unity of the project's leadership. Even so, he shared the others' optimism that once all of the Model School concepts were fully understood, they would be accepted as reasonable. It was merely unfamiliarity with alternatives to homogenous classes that had motivated Hellstern and Blaine's resistance to ungrouping, Young assured his colleagues. "They don't know yet what replaces grouping, so they just see chaos in the classroom. But when they find out about four teachers assigned to one hundred kids," he predicted, "they'll say: 'Well, that's not so bad.'"

When break ended and everyone had reassembled in the conference room, Fran Walter advised the group that its final report and the statements recorded on the flip chart were not one and the same. "It's really important not to go away with the impression that the Model School is a done deal," she explained. "This discussion is just a way to get people to generate ideas, but nothing is going to be done just because it got written on the chart."

But the divisive issue of grouping could not be put to rest so easily. It arose again the next day during the Sunday-morning session on family and community, which Bill Thomas led. After a brief consideration of the strengths of the community, among which the suburb's strong commitment to integration figured prominently in the discussion, the group turned its attention to problems that the participants had encountered in their dealings with parents or citizens. Math teacher Carol Shiles shattered the self-congratulatory mood. Shiles pointed out that many Cleveland Heights residents paid lip service only to a belief in integration. "A lot of people," she noted, "don't send their kids to public school, or they move when their children get to be of school age."

"There are a lot of closet bigots out there who are uncomfortable with integration when they're in the minority," Cal Rose agreed.

"It concerns me," Fred Mills interjected, "when our concept of the vitality of the school is dependent on the number of white students."

"But white flight is a problem," Rose insisted.

"Why is that?" asked Mills, a soft-spoken, sensitive man with black hair and pleasant features.

"It's all the problems associated with low-income families, like the condoning of pregnancies," Hellstern volunteered. "It's more than racial."

"What I'm talking about is gearing our actions to keeping white students," Mills explained. "It's as if white students legitimize us. If our priority as a system is to hang on as tightly as possible to white families, what does that say to our black families?"

"Because so few communities are trying to maintain integration, there's not much of an understanding of what we're trying to do in Cleveland Heights," Fran Walter complained.

"I'm just saying I don't feel we convey to the community that everyone is equally important to us," Mills said. "I'm going to play devil's advocate here: Are we really integrated, or are we just interested in statistics and appearances?"

"You can't control what goes on in people's brains," Hellstern responded, "but if you put people together, maybe that brain activity will occur."

"Are you saying we have integration because we have blacks and whites in the same building?" Wessels challenged. "I see a lack of shared experiences. Look in the courtyard. The punkers hang together, the skateboarders hang together."

"Why is that so bad?" Levy wondered.

"If we value integration, then we should do things to promote it," said Wessels, a sandy-haired, hazel-eyed man, whose thin frame exuded restless energy. It troubled him that to date the Model School Project had prompted nothing but talk.

"May I suggest that, rather than argue, we look at solutions for furthering integration," Steve Young interjected.

"Being the *in-house* black expert," Jean King said, ironically referring to her status as the only African American at the retreat, "it seems to me that one of the biggest problems is attitude. Someone said to me: 'I know you got your new job because you're black.' I like to think I got it because I'm qualified and if my blackness enters in at all, it's a plus. We have a lot of antiquated ideas about blackness. Even some black kids use their blackness as an excuse to fail."

"When our school began to change," Hellstern said, picking up only on King's final statement, "it became readily apparent that the people we were getting needed more structure—I hope I won't be accused of racism."

"I'm *trying* to understand," King said.

Hellstern continued: "They need more—"

"Who is '*they*'?" King interrupted, calling Hellstern on her tendency to generalize about African-American youth.

"Lower socioeconomic—"

King cut Hellstern off impatiently, saying: "With every new freshman class, we get something new. It amazes me how many educators defend the way things have always been done. Why do we have to do it the same way if it needs to be changed?"

"Since we're dropping bombs here, I'd like to say let's eliminate grouping for those teachers who want to do it," Wessels suggested.

"How would that work in the math department?" Hellstern asked.

"You'd put all ninth, tenth, eleventh, and twelfth graders in the same ungrouped Algebra I class," Wessels explained.

As a matter of fact, the math department had decided to undertake this modest experiment with ungrouping when school started in the fall. Burkett had been pressing the department to make this change for some time, going so far as to suggest that the Algebra I teachers give the same test to their standard- and expanded-track students in order to see if their respective scores would be significantly different. They were not, and the statistical evidence had helped persuade the math teachers to give heterogenous Algebra I classes a try.

"But you're still tracking in middle school," Hellstern noted, referring to a sequence of preparatory courses that middle schoolers in the district were required to take if they were planning to follow an accelerated course of study in high school and enroll in geometry and biology rather than Algebra I and general science in ninth grade.

"Yeah," Frank Walter agreed, "if there's a sequence in junior high, the damage from grouping has already been done." Indeed, enrollment records showed that African Americans accounted for fewer than 5 percent of the students taking advanced math courses at Heights High School, despite growing evidence that mastery of advanced mathematics was the gateway to economic success.[2]

"Let's forget the details of how to ungroup," Burkett commanded. "Would the elimination of grouping enhance integration?"

"Not that alone," Wessels responded. "You'd have to force some kind of cooperative learning experiences on the students."

"Then the minority kids—lower-class, I mean—would underperform," Hellstern observed.

King rolled her eyes at Hellstern's statement, but said nothing.

"I disagree," Wessels said, "but on to another thought. If you have ungrouped classes, where whites sit on one side and blacks sit on the other, that's not integration. So you assign seats black/white/black, just like boy/ girl/boy."

"And teach teachers how to deal with the complaints, like 'How come I can't sit with my friends?', so they don't feel like they're being thrown into a snakepit," Fran Walter added.

"But as long as there's a choice—" The words were barely out of Hellstern's mouth before Burkett was mocking them.

"As long as all black kids *choose* to take general science instead of biology," he said sarcastically.

"Oh, *Hugh*," Levy blurted out.

"What do you mean: 'Oh, Hugh?'" Burkett asked Levy angrily.

"Maybe I'm naive," Levy said, "but I don't see black kids being told they can only take general science."

Burkett responded, "Oh, we don't *tell* them . . ."

"Grouping benignly allows racism to go on," Bill Thomas said, picking up on the principal's train of thought.

"But then we're taking away students' choices," Levy objected. "I don't know why a black male can't eat lunch with another black male."

"Oh, he can," Burkett said. "But if we *promote* segregation, we shouldn't insist: 'It's the *kids'* choice.'"

"Virtually all the exceptions to the standardized test placements that kids and parents ask us to make in their grouping assignments are toward increased segregation," Frank Walter pointed out. "Virtually all the white kids choose up and the blacks down."

"Same thing happens with vocal music," Thomas confirmed. "Gospel Choir is 99 percent black."

"The choice to move up or down is based on the perception of the degree of difficulty of the standard classes," Burkett asserted. "Another perception in the community is that the people who teach standard classes are the people we are attempting to punish."

"The students perceive that, too," King reminded him.

"It's rather ironic that minority kids 'choose' the poorest teachers," said Levy, who may have been unique among the Heights High faculty in volunteering to teach nothing but standard courses. Her voice rising, she continued: "I can't believe that they assume that. Their parents *kill* to get them into Heights, and then they purposely *choose* the poorest teachers? I didn't know that I was thought to be a pile of shit! I love my standard classes!"

A painful silence descended. Thomas, looking for a way to ease the tension, called for a ten-minute break. Levy, who was wearing an orange T-shirt bearing the words, "No Problem," immediately rushed off to the sanctuary of her room, while Burkett took up his usual position in the hallway, where he leaned against the wall and smoked a cigarette. He had grown accustomed to such outbursts from teachers, students, and parents. If one wanted to see a display of real agitation, wait until the first day of school, he thought, when certain members of the faculty were sure to claim, "Did you hear Burkett is going to eliminate grouping?" and "Did you know that Burkett said all standard teachers are incompetent?" The high school principal was willing to bet that by the time of the second Model School retreat, which was scheduled for late September, the rumor mongers would have succeeded in mobilizing the attendance of a progrouping contingent.

The coordinators did not share the principal's blasé attitude toward the real-life psychodrama that had played out unexpectedly before them. Fearing that the incident would have a chilling effect on the participants' willingness to speak candidly, they decided to attempt to restore the group's emotional equilibrium by refocusing the discussion on practical solutions when the session resumed. Bill Thomas accomplished the task with a small dose of humor.

"I want to compliment everyone on how well it's going," he said, chuckling. "I had no idea that on Sunday morning at 8:00 A.M. we'd be dealing with such *weighty* issues. I'd like us to continue, but I'm concerned that issues like eliminating grouping have the power to blow away other ideas. Would you be willing to jot down some thoughts for dealing with integration? They could be much more personal, something you could do in the class-room or with a buddy teacher."

After a few minutes of silence, Thomas called for the group's ideas. Fred Mills started off this round of talks, saying, "We need to find ways to increase integration as a part of the curriculum, not just through extracurricular activities."

"Seat assignments by alphabet," Levy suggested.

"But Jones and Adams are common black names," Carol Shiles said, pointing out the flaw in that strategy.

"How about assigning lab partners on a racial basis?" Hellstern suggested.

"And teach them how to work together," Diana Tuggey said, breaking a long silence. Tuggey no doubt felt a bit of an outsider, as she taught at Second Site, an off-campus school set up in 1987 by the Burkett administration as a place to send expelled students (after they had served out their expulsion) until they were judged ready academically and emotionally to return to the high school. "I used to do group work and get awful results. One kid would do all the work and the others would slide by."

"I need help with teaching kids to work together, too," Kathy Blaine said. For teachers to admit publicly to having gaps in their expertise meant that a certain level of trust had finally been achieved in the room.

"There are some ramifications for professional development in ungroup-ing," Thomas said, trying to make clear how the various components of a model school were interconnected.

"Assuming grouping stays," Mills said, "we have to limit the occasions that we allow kids to drop down a level."

"Maybe we could reduce the number of levels as a transitional step," Blaine suggested, softening her earlier stance.

"Be careful what you say," Burkett teased. His implication was that her colleagues in the English department might frown upon a public change of heart, since to date the department had been successful in resisting the Burkett administration's blandishments to make such a change.

"We're playing games here," Hellstern objected. "I find that really repel-lent. Is the purpose of education to mix bodies? If so, we could just put ev-erybody out in the courtyard."

"What if," Frank Walter countered, "we divide the school into smaller segments in which the students and staff all know each other personally? Then all kinds of activities, forums, and small group discussions could be handled in a manageable way."

Despite Young's hope that the Model School concept of schools within a school would prove instantly compelling, Walter's advocacy of this structural innovation sparked no debate. In fact, his comment seemed to take the edge off the discussion, perhaps because its ambition was so much greater than that of the previously noted suggestions. Thereafter the group meandered from considering one half-measure for promoting integration to another. Jean King finally called a halt to the apparently pointless discourse.

"A lot of good things have been said," she affirmed, "but until teachers walk into a classroom and see twenty people with individual histories—not just colors—then you still don't have integration. Right now there's fear between the races at Heights High because of misconceptions, but no one wants to talk about it because they don't want to hurt people's feelings."

As if to prove King's point, the group readily agreed with Cal Rose's observation that the time had come to break for lunch. But the welcomed respite from confrontation and controversy was to be short-lived.

That afternoon's session centered on the topic of staff. When asked by facilitator Cas McBride to say what troubled them about either the teaching or the administrative staff, the participants once again found themselves wrestling with issues and emotions that some of them would have preferred not to address directly. This time the debate was sparked by Frank Walter's complaint about "staff members who let union attitudes drag their feet."

"What do you mean," his wife asked.

"Glenn Altschuld saying teachers shouldn't call homes outside of the contract day," Walter said by way of example.

"Then you should say 'Glenn,'" Rose insisted, "rather than 'union.'"

"Let's stay away from names," Levy pleaded.

"I'm uncomfortable with this 'union' thing," Rose continued. "There are many dedicated unionists who are dedicated teachers."

"If this report is going out to the whole staff, shouldn't we be careful what we say?" Hellstern advised.

"We'll have full editing power," someone reminded her.

"If these charts are typed up," Burkett disagreed, "what we say *will* get out there."

Frank Walter was not so easily silenced. "Take last summer's Madeline Hunter fiasco," he said, continuing to cite the sins of the Local 795. "Sending a letter to teachers inviting them to attend was viewed by the union as a hostile act. Or that you would need a union directive before you could be part of the Model School Project."

"You're saying that the union is confrontational," Levy summarized.

"I would object to that going up there, unless you also say that the attitude of the board of education gets in the way of education, too," Rose said.

"I'll agree with that," Walter responded.

"Can't we compromise?" Mills suggested. "The chemistry of the two groups causes confrontation."

"I'm willing to substitute 'outside sources' that prevent people from being all they could be for the word 'union,'" Walter conceded.

"I guess I'm uncomfortable with *not* putting the union up there as a problem," Burkett said.

"I'm concerned that we'll be sending the perception that Model School is antiunion," Rose said.

"When we say union, aren't we really saying union leadership?" Wessels suggested. "The union leadership in my opinion *is* too confrontational."

"If we start undermining our own, then we're turkey meat," Hellstern asserted. "It's one thing to talk like this among union people."

"But we *are* the union," Thomas responded. "And I think the union needs to accept responsibility for educational issues."

"I'm not sure the Model School Project can mandate anything to the union," McBride said.

"We won't have a model high school," Burkett insisted, "if we and the union don't get together to work on educational issues."

"What kind of union would close this project down for one remark?" Frank Walter asked rhetorically.

"Fran," Hellstern said, looking for an ally, "am I being alarmist?"

"I'm at the point," Fran Walter responded, "that if this is what people feel, it needs to be said. We need to get this stuff on the table."

"I just think we ought to show a little political savvy," Hellstern explained. "The union has done a good job with benefits. That was their role. Reform is new to them. If we don't like the leadership, we should work to change it."

"I'd hate to think that a 'Dump Glenn' movement emerges from this weekend," Rose interjected.

"I don't hear that," Levy assured him.

"It's true that we sometimes neglect our jobs because of an attitude or something someone tells us to do," King said. "This is a legitimate concern. I don't feel that because I don't agree with the union position, I'm less than a unionist. Sometimes we have to take risks, if we want something good to result."

"We need to spend time on other issues," McBride said, effectively putting an end to the argument. "Shall we move on to solutions?"

By lunchtime Monday the retreat participants had been put through nine such grueling work sessions. Although none of the others had inspired as much anguish as the debates about grouping and the leadership of the teachers' union, each session had produced moments of enlightenment. Having arrived seventy-two hours before blaming the system for their feelings of demoralization, the retreat participants had glimpsed the extent to which their own attitudes and beliefs stood in the way of their success as educators and the resolution of Heights High's problems. Now they were primed to accept responsibility for making some changes.

Upon announcing after everyone returned from lunch that the final session of the retreat would be devoted to a discussion of next steps, the facilitators walked out of the conference room, leaving the participants free to decide for themselves what, if any, actions they wanted to undertake toward the realization of a model school. The decision to absent themselves was a strategic move on the coordinators' part; they wanted to see if the fledgling reformers would be able to fly on their own.

Without prompting, the participants decided to split up into teams to initiate a number of school improvement projects. Most of the ventures were on the scale of the after-school mixer that Burkett, not wishing to be outdone, volunteered to host for the professional staff the first Friday after classes started. Nice gestures, but nothing yet amounting to a revolution. Mark Wessels alone seemed unwilling to await the Model School millennium. Displaying a degree of initiative rare among teachers, he would go on to conceive, find the funding for, and supervise a major new program aimed at increasing the number of African-American students enrolled in advanced math courses at Heights.[3]

Surprisingly, when it came time to deal with writing a retreat report, no one tried to dodge this difficult chore. So proprietary had the group become about the direction of the Model School Project that they decided the report's composition must continue to be a joint effort, to be accomplished in as many future meetings as were needed to produce final agreement on the broad outlines of a model school. In the interim, it was agreed that the flip-chart sheets, with their telltale evidence of the Model School's conspiracy against the powers-that-be, should be locked in the high school's vault, where they could not prove incriminating.

The transforming powers of shared decision making could be seen again when the group's written report was finally issued in December 1989. The product of several intensive after-school work sessions, it contained seventy-one restatements of basic Model School principles on which the group had been able to achieve consensus, including an unexpected concession from the more conservative thinkers. While not yet ready to recommend a move to heterogenous classes, these educators had agreed with their colleagues that "a Model School will not support a grouping policy that isolates people racially, culturally or sexually." And the staunch unionists had revealed their willingness to envision a new era in labor relations, agreeing that "in a Model School, union and management cooperate in an atmosphere of mutual trust."

But these were not the most important changes of mind that the retreat experience had effected. The educators' sense of what constituted professionalism had also been reconstituted. In a section devoted to school culture, which the report defined as "who we are, what we do and what we believe," the retreat participants declared their liberation from Heights High School's deadening culture of inertia, stating:

In a Model School
—there is a willingness to change;
—there is a supportive collaborative environment;
—there is constant self examination and improvement;
—there is the willingness to deal with the diversity of our students and staff. . . .
—there is an environment which supports healthy debate and ways to resolve conflict;
—there is a spirit of optimism;
—there is a united approach.

The August retreat report was signed by teachers Kathleen Blaine, Edith Delman, Virginia Hellstern, Jean King, Betty Levy, Fred Mills, Charlene Morse, Cal Rose, Carol Shiles, Mark Sutter, Diana Tuggey, and Mark Wessels, and Lee House principal Ursula Busch and assistant principal for school operations Lawrence Mlynek. With this flourish of the pen, fourteen additional members of the Heights High faculty and administration officially signaled their desire to break with failed tradition and move toward a radically different future.

That left 140 converts to go.

11

Hidden Agendas

Schools are not factories using any means at their disposal to turn out young people who can read, write, and spell. They are social work places . . . where people of various ages live together five or six hours a day. . . . If they are failing . . . , they are failing because they are . . . more preoccupied with maintaining their daily routines and regularities than with creating a setting where human beings will live and learn together more productively and harmoniously.

—JOHN I. GOODLAD
The Dynamics of Educational Change, 1975

With the exception of the events surrounding the first Model School retreat, the 1989–90 school year began normally for the teachers of Heights High. To make sure that its employees arrived on the first day of classes ready to teach, the district required all teachers to show up at their schools the day before to prepare. Traditionally, this "Professional Day" started with a districtwide faculty meeting at which administrators redundantly explained procedural information that they also presented in memorandum form. The teachers were then dismissed to attend another faculty meeting, this one conducted at their home schools, after which they were required to spend the remainder of the day working in their classrooms.

Many teachers deemed Professional Day to be an insult to their professionalism, but most, having resigned themselves to their lack of autonomy in matters of school governance, complied with its requirements without complaint. This rule did not hold true, however, for a certain group of male

131

teachers at Heights High, a cadre of malcontents who styled themselves as the "Mutherfuzzards." The members of this semisecret society displayed their cynicism as if it were a badge of honor. For them the highlight of each school year was not prom night or graduation day, but rather their annual stag evening of softball, beer, and dirty movies, which was capped off by the presentation of rudely named awards to colleagues who had made the year more difficult to endure—or worse yet—had been observed trying to win points with an administrator.[1] Even cheerful participation in school events at which the presence of teachers was not a matter of choice could put one on the road to nomination, so it was not surprising that, as members of this rebellious band showed up for the Professional Day meeting in the high school's "social room" on Tuesday, September 5, 1989, they pointedly made their way to seats at the back. From this disdainful distance the men proceeded to issue a running commentary on the meeting, secure in the knowledge that their remarks could not be heard by the presiding administrators.

The casual atmosphere in the social room suggested that most of the other teachers at Heights High were less preoccupied with the need to affirm their professional independence. As was their wont, few of the teachers, male or female, wore suits. Most preferred to work in informal attire, and as the weather was warm some of the men wore shorts. One of the teachers was even accompanied by her children.

The gathering's relaxed air was in keeping with the status of Professional Day as a nonevent. Only a handful of insiders knew that for two of the leading participants there was serious business to be conducted. The search for a new superintendent was soon to begin. Although the teachers would have no say in naming Irv Moskowitz's replacement—the board of education traditionally made that hiring decision—the aspirants for his job understood the public relations value of having the professional staff in one's corner. Jockeying to win the tacit support of the high school teachers, front-runner Lauree Gearity had decided to put in an appearance at their Professional Day meeting.

Only a few of his close friends knew that Hugh Burkett would also be trying to ingratiate himself with the teachers. Shaking off his fatalistic acceptance of the inevitability of not being renewed, Burkett had decided that he would give Gearity a run for the superintendency, after all. His entry into the race, which he never made public, had been prompted by the emergence in early August of a slate of reform candidates who were vying against two incumbents for three seats on the board of education that came up for election in November. Should the slate be elected (a prospect enhanced by the recent decision of board president Bernard Greene not to seek reelection), Burkett's chances for the superintendency increased from slim or none to even or better. Although the slate had promised to conduct a national search for a new superintendent, Burkett planned to meet privately with the three candidates in order to make them aware that he was interested in the district's top job. For those teachers who knew of these developments, Burkett's newly intensified rivalry with Gearity imbued the tedious Professional Day meetings with a welcome element of drama.

At approximately 8:30 A.M., Frank Walter stepped up to the microphone at the front of the social room. Like the preponderance of the high school's teachers and administrators, Walter was at midcareer, and his future as the next principal of Heights High School seemed fairly assured, especially should Burkett gain the superintendency.

As he stood at the front of the room looking out over the crowd, Walter could not help but be reminded of his first years on the job. He had come to the district eighteen years before as an idealistic young English teacher, straight from a rigorous Jesuit education. It was the exhilarating era of the national student-protest movement, and student and parental interest in finding an alternative to the traditional curriculum had prompted the creation of an experimental program within the high school.

New School, as it was called, offered its two hundred or so students such unconventional courses as "Ascent of Man," "Zoology," and "Juggling." They were also given the option of taking classes on a pass-fail basis and even the opportunity to teach. Fred Mills and Mark Wessels were New School teachers, a position to which Walter also aspired, despite the fact that New Schoolers were viewed by mainstream students and teachers as lazy hippies or worse. (There was no telling what his colleagues thought of Walter himself, who wore his hair cascading down to his shoulders and rode a bicycle to and from work.) Walter remembered with pleasure how it blew everyone's mind when he and the New Schoolers managed to pull off polished productions of *One Flew over the Cuckoo's Nest* and two Woody Allen one-acts, *God* and *Death,* on the social room stage in front of which he now stood.

New School, which was housed in its own wing of the high school, had provided students and staff with a real sense of community, especially since the students enjoyed a say in the school's governance. Walter missed this feeling of closeness and connection, which he hoped would be permanently restored when the Model School Project put into effect its plan to create a series of schools within a school. The New School spirit of togetherness had proved to be all too fleeting. The desire to be part of a community of scholars that had prompted the New School's creation had gone the way of peace symbols and love beads sometime in the early 1980s. For Walter, the death knell had sounded when New School students began stealing not only the doughnuts he brought in fresh every morning to be sold on the honor system, but also the money in the kitty.

When he became Lee House principal, Walter tried to create a new feeling of family by making a point of affirming his commitment to integrated education during the opening-day assemblies for ninth and tenth graders over which he presided for two years. The privilege of working with so many fine African-American students and teachers had enriched his life, he wanted them to know. Walter was surprised and disappointed by the lack of reaction to his comments each year. Only one teacher ever came up to him to express that he, too, shared Walter's commitment to making the integration of Heights High work.

Yet the teaching staff at the high school was not unique in its disunity, as became obvious after most of the stragglers finally took their seats at tables in the social room and Walter convened the Professional Day meeting. "Good morning," he said. "Welcome back. This meeting will take the place of the usual one at Wiley auditorium, but I promise that we'll only take twelve minutes instead of an hour and a half."

Even as he acknowledged the welcome decision to dispense with the districtwide faculty meeting (held, inconveniently, at the central-office complex on Miramar Road) that normally started off Professional Day, Walter could not resist taking a swipe at "Miramar." Burkett was not alone in chafing under the rule of a distant bureaucracy. The relationship between district-level administrators and most building administrators was complicated. Building administrators shouldered the responsibility of running their schools on a daily basis, but they were accountable to Miramar for their decisions. This chain of command often proved cumbersome and untenable, with the predictable result that the high school administrators tended to view their central-office counterparts as a bunch of know-nothings, foot-draggers, and second-guessers, while district-level administrators tended to see the high school principals as secretive, uncooperative, and irresponsible.

Tension between Miramar and Heights, which was to be expected in such a hierarchical relationship, had only grown worse when the board of education appointed Lauree Gearity as interim superintendent. The strained nature of Burkett's relationship with her undoubtedly explained why the honor of introducing Gearity to the high school faculty on Professional Day fell to Burkett's diplomatic envoy, Francis Xavier Walter.

When Gearity, a silver-haired woman of forty-seven clad in a print dress and carrying a handbag over her arm, stepped up to the microphone in the social room, she was greeted with tepid applause. The interim superintendent's matronly appearance belied a tough-as-nails manner. As a member of the Moskowitz administration's contract negotiating team, she had played a role in persuading the union to accept an agreement that denied any raise for the 1989–90 school year. It was widely believed that Moskowitz had pushed such an insulting offer not for lack of financial wherewithal, as the superintendent claimed, but because he was determined to break the power of the union. For this reason Gearity was not particularly popular at the moment with the high school faculty.

Now that she was in the running for superintendent, however, it behooved her to try to repair management's shattered relationship with union leadership and to mend fences with the rank and file. Because the Model School Project seemed to be generating some interest and excitement among teachers who only six months before had been demoralized by the protracted and acrimonious nature of the contract negotiations, she made it the focus of her remarks.

"I'm anxious to see what happens to the Model School Project this year," she informed the teachers. "I see it as a chance for you to become masters of your own destiny. This project could be revolutionary, and it has my full support, although that doesn't mean I won't disagree with the fine points of your plan. Teachers can make Heights what it can be; the rest of us are just a necessary evil."

Gearity's statement was deft. It positioned her administration to share in the credit should the teachers produce an acceptable plan, while giving her the ability to backpedal if they did not. Most public school superintendents appreciated the value of circumlocution; in Cleveland Heights it was an essential survival skill. The board of education had a long record of commissioning faculty and lay committees to study problems and make recommendations, only to find it necessary to dismiss the proffered solutions as unworkable when they proved (as was invariably the case when changes were proposed) too controversial. Over the years, Heights High's veteran faculty had observed the board of education back and fill with some regularity, and the change in command at Miramar had only served to exacerbate the widespread suspicion that the model school design would end up gathering dust on somebody's shelf. It was axiomatic that a new administration would care more about programs of its own invention than those it had inherited.

The Model School Project coordinators themselves had been uncertain of the new interim superintendent's attitude toward teacher empowerment.

Gearity had often accompanied Moskowitz to project briefings at the high school the previous year, but, unlike the former superintendent, she seldom offered comments or criticism.[2] Yet, in order to be able to move ahead credibly with their second-year plans, the Model School coordinators had greatly needed a public statement of support from the new interim superintendent. While Gearity's Professional Day remarks seemed to have made little impression on her audience, who awarded them polite applause, they were a source of relief to the project coordinators—despite their suspicions that the talk of a Model School–inspired "revolution" had been meant only for show.

There was some basis for this hunch. Privately, Gearity found many of the concepts advanced by the Model School Project untenable, if not ludicrous. (Even her admirers felt compelled to note that Gearity was not an "idea" person.) While she favored teachers having a say in the design of educational programs and the selection of their principals, she could not envision the day when buildings should be given absolute control over their budgets. In her opinion, most building principals lacked business acumen and should not be encouraged to turn their attention away from educational matters, in any event.

She was also opposed to the idea of instituting a common academic curriculum. After all, Heights High was not "Harvard on the Hocking," she maintained, referring to an Ohio river. It needed to serve a wide range of students who were not (in her opinion) all created equal in ability or interests. And the recommendation that class sizes at the high school be reduced to twenty or fewer students was to her truly laughable. How could one justify such a luxury in a district where some elementary teachers were struggling along with classes of thirty or more? However, there was no reason for Gearity to create a ruckus by voicing her concerns before the Model School Project issued its final report.

After the interim superintendent departed, Frank Walter asked the teachers to reconvene in the high school library. The move was symbolic. The library, which boasted relatively new furniture and carpeting, an inviting color scheme, and twin banks of windows that flooded the interior with light sufficient to maintain a variety of green plants, was the coziest space in the school, and its use was meant to suggest to the teachers that now that the outsiders had left, the remainder of the Professional Day meeting would be carried out among friends. A buffet of coffee and pastries enhanced the feeling of camaraderie.

In the library Burkett stood before the assemblage in shirt sleeves and tie.

The principal's appearance at the microphone was a sign that something unusual was up, because he normally delegated to Frank Walter the task of presiding at faculty meetings.

Walter was also frequently called upon to represent the high school at civic gatherings, partly because his roots in the community were deeper than Burkett's, and partly because he was an articulate and inspiring public speaker.[3] Burkett, on the other hand, had discovered that the job of front man was not one he liked or believed that he performed extremely well. He preferred to work behind the scenes, refusing even to make the school's daily P.A. announcements. He had decided to preside at today's faculty meeting, however, because he wanted to reconfirm the importance of the Model School Project to the future of the high school and to reposition himself as a visionary (and more visible) leader.

As his first order of business, however, Burkett was contractually obliged to introduce Daniel MacDonald, Heights High's newly elected chief steward. In an earlier era the frequency and agenda of faculty meetings had become the subject of collective-bargaining sessions when teachers complained that administrators were calling needless meetings and wasting their time. Subsequently, a provision giving the Cleveland Heights–University Heights Board of Education the right to require teachers to attend up to, but no more than, fourteen faculty meetings a year was written into the contract.[4]

The contract also provided that one-sixth of the time allotted for each faculty meeting was to be turned over to a representative of Local 795 for a discussion of union business and concerns. This provision explained Burkett's introduction of Dan MacDonald, a slim, shaggy-haired man in his early forties wearing modish glasses and a gag tie, one of a collection of outrageous neckwear for which he was notorious.

Perhaps because he was a guidance counselor, MacDonald paid attention to the "affective," or emotional, side of things. Today, for example, to demonstrate his school spirit, the tie he wore was adorned with a tiger's head. Like Burkett, MacDonald was angling for higher office—that of the union's vice presidency (a position that might lead to the presidency)—so he planned to give the teachers a rousing pep talk. Yet the new chief steward was not typical presidential material. MacDonald's sensitivity to others' feelings and his unauthoritarian leadership style made him a standout among union activists, who as a type tended to be more obdurate personalities.

Hugh Burkett had been elated to see MacDonald given the position of chief steward. Now that a progressive—at least, someone who passed for a progressive in Local 795 circles[5]—was serving as the union's main liaison to the high school administration, Burkett felt that he finally had the union "in his pocket." His confidence had also been buoyed by a significant change in the teachers who would serve under MacDonald's leadership for the year. While Bob Quail had been reelected steward, two other hard-liners and the mercurial Allan Wolf had decided not to run again, and they had been replaced by three moderates, including, much to her delight, Fran Walter.

Walter had received the least number of votes of any person elected. (No doubt many members of the faculty shared the discomfort of one teacher, who complained to union leaders about the dangerous loophole that allowed an administrator's wife to run for steward.) But no matter how thin her victory, Walter had succeeded in achieving her private objective. A proponent of the Model School Project had now infiltrated Local 795's power structure, from which vantage point she could better feel out and perhaps even influence the union's stance toward the restructuring project.

As Dan MacDonald approached the microphone, Burkett felt prompted to celebrate the harmonious new era in labor relations that he believed lay ahead. "We're going to have a wonderful working relationship this year, aren't we, Dan?" he called out.

Burkett's remark was greeted with scattered laughter, because the Wagnerian clashes between the high school stewards and the principal were legendary (at least in union circles). MacDonald himself was so taken aback by the principal's unexpected warmth that the normally loquacious steward seemed momentarily at a loss for words. In the silence that followed, Burkett walked over to MacDonald's side, hugged the chief steward and said helpfully, "Well, moving right along."

Recovering his equilibrium, MacDonald introduced his fellow stewards and then launched into his pep talk.

"As we move into the 1990s," MacDonald said, "let me quote Mark Twain: 'Thunder is good, thunder is impressive, but it is lightning that does the work.' By that I mean this is the year that we have to quit talking, bitching, and move on to action. Every member of the union needs to get more involved." The plan MacDonald set forth, however, revealed the poverty of the union's vision. "I encourage each of you," he continued, "to pick out a kid who seems likely to fail and help him through the semester. Politically, we are going to ask you to get behind our candidates for the board of education elections that are coming up in November. Socially, many things will be going on, and I'm hoping that everyone will go to some or all of these events."

MacDonald then segued into the introduction of twenty-two new faculty members, a contingent sufficient to staff a medium-sized elementary school. He presented each one with a long-stemmed yellow carnation purchased with money from the union's "Sunshine Fund"—the system's first and only recognition that novice teachers and those new to the district might need moral and other kinds of support. (If the newcomers somehow survived twenty-five or thirty years until retirement, they would receive, upon their departure, another carnation at the traditional year-end faculty breakfast.)

When MacDonald concluded his remarks, a vocational education teacher and former union steward by the name of Richard Wirth stood up on the far side of the room. A twenty-three-year veteran who taught courses in secretarial skills, Wirth was the ranking member of the Mutherfuzzards by virtue of his invention of the club, and he had a bone to pick. The school year was barely one hour old.

"The real source of our problems," Dick Wirth said, "is Miramar, not Fairmount Road." (The headquarters of Local 795 were located on Fairmount.) "You should be urging everyone to work *on* the board of education, not *for* them."

Wirth's remarks were met with an uneasy silence. More a school personality than a faculty leader, he was not exactly the type of person everyone rushed to follow; on the other hand, his comments hit home, as they tapped into the ever present undercurrent of faculty frustration and discontent with central administration. In terms of advancing Burkett's agenda, Wirth's comments came as an unexpected but welcome gift; he could not have provided Burkett with a better counterpoint for his own talk. Despite his uneasiness with public speaking, Burkett hoped to deliver a message that would inspire the teachers to greater heights of endeavor, rather than continuing to sit back and blame others for the high school's failures.

"I want to tell you how I spent my summer vacation," Burkett began, somewhat unpromisingly, when he returned to the podium. "I spent most of it thinking about today and what I wanted to say," he continued, going on to paraphrase his new guru, AFT leader Al Shanker, "about how the work of teachers, students, and administrators needs to change. I'm convinced that the answer to the national problem in education lies in what we decide to do right here in this building. We need to restructure for the kids' sake. If we don't restructure, it will be done to us. My goal is to make sure that *we* decide how *we* want to look.

"I want to throw out a couple of terms," Burkett added. "They aren't new; I just want us to talk about them more. They're *vision* and *mission*. Let me give you something that speaks to this."

The principal handed a sheaf of yellow paper to a teacher sitting near the microphone to pass around the room. The previous year he had attended a seminar on corporate culture, where he had picked up the concept that businesses known for the excellence of their products are able to articulate their mission in a phrase or two. On the yellow handout were typeset three lines that Frank and Fran Walter had helped Burkett compose. A mission statement that he hoped would become the teachers' watchword, the lines read:

Staff • Students • Families • Communities
In Schools That Work, Everyone Works—
Together.

As copies of the mission statement were passed around the room, Burkett resumed speaking.

"I want my role to change," he said. "I want to get out in front—in the community, with parents—with a vision. My vision for the high school is that we need to share management. It's not easy for me to give up control—what little I had—but I want to be your leader.

"As your leader I would tell you that it's no longer enough for teachers to say, 'I'm really good at what I do in the classroom.' You need to be concerned about what's going on in the next room, down the hall. I want you to look at the big picture. The Model School retreats are an opportunity for all of us to think about how we can improve the operation of the *entire* school.

"Six years ago I couldn't have talked to you about these issues; my thinking hadn't really crystallized. I just had some beliefs that led me to today. Now I know that we need autonomy over our budget and things like hiring. We can't have autonomy unless we all come together as a staff and demand it. *I know we can do it.*

"Have a good year. We're out of here!"

After being dismissed, some of the teachers lingered in the library to chat with one another. Four or five people came over to shake Burkett's hand, saying "Nice job," and "That was a positive note." Most of the faculty members headed straight for the peace and quiet of their classrooms. Once ensconced at their desks, some of the teachers may have glanced again at Burkett's mission statement before sticking it in a folder with all the other administrative notices, reminders, and dictums handed out to the faculty on Professional Day. Most, however, simply tossed it in the trash.

Part 3
The Backlash

Proponents for change proceeded in ways that . . . guaranteed conflict and failure precisely because the needs and self-interests of significant people were ignored. It was less that they were ignored, because that implies a conscious decision, than it was a failure to recognize what should be obvious: an effort at institutional change, however circumscribed it may be, is observable by, has different meanings for, and will be differently judged by a variety of people in the setting in which change is being sought.

—SEYMOUR B. SARASON,
The Culture of the School and the Problem of Change, 1982

12

A Minor Uprising

You come to school to learn, we tell him, as if the child hadn't been learning before, as if living were out there and learning were in here, and there was no connection between the two. . . . Your experience, your concerns, your curiosities, your needs, what you know, what you want, what you wonder about, what you hope for, what you fear, what you like and dislike, what you are good at or not so good at—all this is not of the slightest importance, it counts for nothing. What counts here . . . is what we know, what we think is important, what we want you to do, think and be.

—JOHN HOLT
How Children Fail, 1964

By the end of September, twelve teachers had signed up to attend the second Model School retreat. This hopeful sign of renewed interest in the project overshadowed what was to be a more telling development, although no one recognized it as a portent at the time. Caught up in their preparations for the retreat scheduled for the weekend of September 29th, the project coordinators paid little attention when, the Monday before, a small group of students began boycotting Heights High's cafeteria.

Their numbers swelling as the week progressed, the boycotters refused to purchase items from the cafeteria steam table, opting instead to pack their lunches, in order to protest an increase in food prices that had gone into effect at the beginning of the school year. By the end of the week, revenues from the sale of hot meals and à la carte hamburgers, french fries, and pizza were off by 50 percent, and the school district's business manager had agreed to sit down with the leaders of the boycott to discuss their grievances. The boycott ended the following week when the business manager announced a modest reduction in prices. "For once everyone got together to do some good rather than work against the school," one of the boycott leaders rejoiced.

Although organized protest was a new experience for most members of the student body, veteran teachers could recall the days when demonstrations were as common a feature at Heights High as pop quizzes. Thus, a sense of déjà vu may have prompted the coordinators' indifferent response to the boycott, even though it was not their first indication that Heights High students were fed up with the quality of their school life.

The previous spring the administrators and stewards on the High School Steering Committee had arranged for the student body to be surveyed professionally. They took this action on behalf of the Model School coordinators, who had despaired that the study teams' search for reliable information about student attitudes would ever bear fruit. The preliminary results of the nationally normed survey, which were in hand before the end of the 1988–89 school year, revealed that students found the climate at Heights High to be singularly oppressive.

Only in its effort to ensure personal safety had the high school ranked above average nationally. When it came to the students' perceptions of whether they wielded influence and were respected and treated fairly, the school received below average scores. The survey had not caught the student body in a temporary funk. The following year the graduating class of 1990 raised money by selling a T-shirt that expressed the students' trapped feelings even more vividly. It featured a drawing of a tiger languishing behind prison bars.

In retrospect, the survey findings and the boycott could have been interpreted as wake-up calls indicating that the student body was on the verge of mutiny. But neither development seemed to ruffle the composure of the Heights High's principal. As the boycott was directed at central-office policy, Burkett decided to play no direct role in its resolution. Behind the scenes, however, he lent the boycotters a hand, advising them about the proper procedures they needed to follow and giving them access to the copier in the high school's main office to make protest flyers. (Burkett's benign treatment of the boycotters stood in sharp contrast to his normal policy regarding student demonstrations. Having come up through the administrative ranks during the turbulent 1960s and 1970s, he had learned that it was counterproductive to attempt to quash nonviolent protest by force. The superior tactic was to "let the students do whatever they needed to do, but never give an inch.")

There were those who suspected that the high school principal had an ulterior motive for assisting the boycott: he wanted to see the fledgling Gearity administration embarrassed. If that were indeed Burkett's aim, he realized it; the suburban newspaper gave front-page coverage to the proceedings. Yet, in the end, the boycott had far more serious implications for the political viability of *his* administration. It served notice that the current generation of students intended to make themselves heard about the kind of school they wanted Heights High to be. It also provided them with a powerful advocate in the person of recently appointed student activities advisor Jean King, whose handling of the boycott had placed her at odds with the very administrators with whom she had sided during the debate about the teachers' union at the August Model School retreat.

Hugh Burkett had promoted the special education teacher to the quasi-administrative student advisory position because he and Frank Walter were impressed by her presence at so many of the school's extracurricular activities, a record of attendance that signaled an unusual degree of concern for the self-esteem of students.[1] King, in turn, counted herself among the high school principal's biggest fans. Yet the two educators envisioned the job of student activities advisor quite differently.

Burkett expected King to serve as his liaison to student council and to work on strengthening and expanding the existing extracurricular program. He also wanted her to handle special projects. An idea for one such endeavor—outfitting the cafeteria tables with white cloths and fresh flowers in the hopes that the students would then take pride in the space and stop trashing it on a daily basis—emerged from a Model School retreat. But it was never implemented because King saw student advocacy as perhaps her most important responsibility. She wanted to "be there" for kids, especially the disaffected African Americans who preferred affiliations with gangs to membership in the French or drama club.

The discrepancy in their outlooks first became apparent during the cafeteria boycott. As the idea for the boycott had come from members of several unchartered fraternities and sororities, whose presence on campus the high school administration had officially banned, Burkett asked King to help him effect a transfer of organizational responsibility for the protest to student council. King showed no interest in cooperating with the plan to strip the unchartered groups of their newfound credibility as spokespeople for the student body.

No matter how firm a stance the high school administration took with underground social clubs and groups, she had observed, the district had never been successful in controlling their existence. In King's opinion, it was better to try to control the *behavior* of group and gang members by involving them in community service activities, such as food drives and charitable fund-raisers. She failed to understand why Burkett and Walter, her immediate supervisor, did not want her to work with problem students. If she dealt only with recognized student organizations, she would have to turn away half the kids who came to her for help. Perhaps, she speculated, the high school administrators felt threatened by those who were able to forge relationships with kids they themselves could not reach.

For their part, Burkett and Walter dismissed King's definition of her duties as self-serving. Having watched her hog the microphone at after-school pep rallies, they had come to believe that King enjoyed being the center of student attention. Unwilling to continue subsidizing King's freedom to act as a "self-styled gang mama"—Walter's description of her approach to her job—and unable to resolve their differences, Burkett decided to send King back to classroom teaching part-time at semester's break in January 1990. The demotion embittered her toward Burkett, whose private insistence that she follow his orders seemed to King disturbingly at odds with his public profession of belief in teacher empowerment. She was left with the conclusion that the man she had once admired was a fraud.

Like the smoldering frustrations of the student body, King's disillusionment with the Heights High School administration was tinder awaiting a match.

Actually, Burkett's unwillingness to allow King to function as a sort of student ombudsman was consistent with another set of even more deeply rooted convictions: his conservative philosophy of student rights. A progressive on most educational issues, the high school principal still held to the old-fashioned view that adolescents lacked the maturity and experience to make appropriate decisions on their own behalf and thus should not be afforded the same rights to free expression and independent action as adults. Having consigned students to the ranks of second-class citizens, it was easy for Burkett to discount their desires as frivolous and their complaints as exaggerated.

Burkett's ability to shrug off the unflattering findings of the Model School Project–inspired student survey was an example of his immunity to student opinion. After sharing the preliminary survey results with the project coordinators at the May 1989 retreat, he and the coordinators never again discussed them. Perhaps because all of them were working hard to make Heights a better school "for kids" (as they liked to describe their motivation), they felt no pressure to respond immediately to the students' concerns. When the model school was finally in place, *it* would answer most of the complaints uncovered by the survey.

Neither Burkett nor the coordinators questioned whether the student body would embrace changes that it had had no part in recommending, nor did anyone suggest that students should be seriously involved in Model School deliberations. And when, during the late fall of 1989, the coordinators began to talk anew about the need for student input into the Model School Project (the national survey having been filed and forgotten), a concern for public relations, more than a desire for enlightenment, motivated their discussion.

To preempt a lengthy consideration of the best way to solicit student opinion, Steve Young volunteered to prepare a worksheet inviting students to list up to five problems at the school of greatest concern to them. Then he made arrangements with a handful of teachers to have the worksheet filled out by their classes during the first semester of 1989–90. Young attempted to tabulate the responses, but he soon lost interest in this impossible chore and began filing the worksheets in a folder. Crammed with recurring complaints about the school's overcrowding, the absence of study halls, class periods that were too long (i.e., boring), poor teachers, the unfairness of ability grouping, the administration's hostile treatment of unchartered organizations, and the prevalence of fighting, social segregation, and racial tensions, the file grew to be five inches thick before Young consigned it to oblivion in a desk drawer. To the leaders of the Model School Project, students seemed to exist merely as abstractions—"our greatest asset," as Burkett was to describe them at the second Model School retreat in late September—not as individuals whose ideas and feelings must truly be taken into account.

Yet the project leaders were not unique in paying only lip service to student opinion. With a few notable exceptions, such as the staff members who had recently volunteered to serve as faculty advisors to Unity, a student-organized effort to improve race relations at the school, Heights High's teachers and administrators talked about and treated young people as if they were incapable of making a significant contribution to the solution of problems. There was a sad inevitability to the educators' dismissive behavior. It echoed the way in which their own superiors treated them.

While typical of the low regard for the adolescent mind expressed in both the repressive atmosphere of many public schools and the heavy emphasis that public education placed on rote learning, their exclusion from meaningful participation in the Model School Project did not go unnoticed by Heights students. In fact, it generated a fair amount of ill will. Some students grumbled to their parents that the Model School Project was disrupting their education by pulling teachers out of the classroom. Others imputed sinister meaning to the fact that Model School retreats were held outside the building. Bethany Aram, a member of the class of 1990 who was editor of the *Black and Gold* during her senior year, knew a number of students who regarded all the time Burkett spent off-site at retreats as proof that he hated Heights High, a perception that had its origins in the principal's tendency to cloister himself in his office and his preference for operating through surrogates.

For her part, student body president Traci McLin thought it injudicious that students had not been consulted about their concept of a model school simply because they were "kids." It was just like Heights High, McLin observed, to make things more difficult than they needed to be. "How can you fix things," she wondered, "if you don't ask what's wrong?" A junior with ambitions of becoming a spokesperson for a major corporation, McLin could easily have summed up the students' perspective. "We can't do this, we can't do that, we can't *breathe*," she complained. But no one representing the Model School Project sounded out the thinking of the student body's elected leader.

The ritualistic nature of the project managers' interest in student opinion became unmistakably clear in their ongoing discussions about the proper composition of a site-based management council. Bill Thomas, whose chaperoning of the Heights Singers' annual tour gave him the opportunity to get to know the members of the chorus informally, consistently argued in favor of allowing student representatives to participate in the school's governance. None of his colleagues expressed lasting enthusiasm for the idea, however, and Burkett was vehemently opposed to it.

Students did not possess the qualifications to make decisions on educational matters, Burkett insisted. (Thomas's recommendation that parents, community members, and representatives of the high school's support staff should also be given seats on the management council was vetoed by Burkett for the same reason.) The high school principal also pooh-poohed the suggestion that at the very least the management council should build in a method for obtaining student input.

"I can meet with the students once a year and know all their issues," he countered. "They never change."

If there was indeed a repetitiveness to student demands, it was because the conditions to which Heights High students objected went unaddressed semester after semester. Each year the incoming student council could be counted on to request that the campus be reopened at lunchtime. Remembering the security problems in the building and the chaos in lot 5, Burkett steadfastly refused to reconsider his decision. For reasons of safety, he also resisted student council's perennial suggestion that the school sponsor more dances. (Experience showed that these events invariably attracted troublemakers from other communities.) When Traci McLin took over the reins of student government in the fall of 1989, she, too, presented the principal with a list of "fun" activities that student council wanted to organize, including an intramural talent show. Since, early in his tenure, an assembly showcasing student acts had ended in an outburst of vandalism, Burkett nixed the idea, all the while wearing a big smile that struck McLin as phony.

The new student council president decided to fight back. At McLin's urging, Burkett began attending student council meetings, where he was pressed again on the issue of dances and the talent show and reminded of the students' interest in cleaner bathrooms, new lockers, and a rec room in which they could socialize. Cordell Pace, a junior class representative at the time, remembered that Burkett made a show of taking notes at the four or five meetings that the principal attended but never took action on any of the student council's suggestions or complaints.[2]

When Burkett finally stopped coming to meetings altogether, Cordell Pace decided that the principal had intended only to pacify the students with his presence. He had not really come to listen. Pace was unaware, of course, that Burkett had tried to be more flexible with an earlier generation of Heights students only to discover that they refused to live up to their promises to behave appropriately in exchange for certain privileges. The disappointing results of the attempt to regulate group and gang behavior via the Non-Chartered Organization Council in particular had soured the principal on the benefits of compromise.

If Burkett had his reasons for behaving dictatorially with the students of Heights High, he was nonetheless flying in the face of established community values—to say nothing of national trends. Thanks to new theories of child rearing popularized by Dr. Spock (a one-time resident of Cleveland Heights), progressive parents no longer ascribed to the notion that children should be seen but not heard. The federal courts had helped to dispel the view of children as chattel during the postwar years by granting them the same rights to freedom of speech, association, and assembly as adults. Because earlier generations of students had waged and won the battle to ensure that the Cleveland Heights schools followed suit, the community no longer accepted the district's once unquestioned authority. There was another reason why the schools' ability to act in loco parentis had been weakened. In an integrated district such as Cleveland Heights, the issue of student rights was imbued with racial as well as legal and political significance, a reality guaranteeing that some African-American parents would regard with suspicion any attempt by the predominately white-run school system to correct their children's conduct, no matter how well-intentioned.

As a relative newcomer to Cleveland Heights, Burkett might have been excused for lacking an appreciation of its record of political activism against the ironfisted rule of administrators, if only his ignorance of community norms and expectations had seemed less willful. (No one laughed at the September Model School retreat when Burkett, responding to a teacher's profession of her belief that students have rights and responsibilities, asked sharply, "Who says?" They knew he was probably not kidding.) It seemed only a matter of time before the zeal with which Burkett fulfilled his obligation to maintain order on campus would offend a sizable enough group of students and parents who prized individual expression over self-discipline to undermine his standing in the community and that of his most visible adherents, the leaders of the Model School Project.

To appreciate the extent to which Burkett was out of step with prevailing community values on the issue of student rights and the degree to which this placed his otherwise progressive administration at risk, it is necessary to have an understanding of the intensity of the struggle to win for Heights High students protection of their basic civic liberties.

There was, of course, a time in Cleveland Heights (as elsewhere) when children were routinely treated as if they had no civil rights. When seven Heights High students were caught lobbing eggs, bricks, and firecrackers at the home of an unpopular teacher on Halloween eve in the early 1950s, for example, the response to the prank was hardly in keeping with the severity of the crime. Declining to handle the incident internally, the high school administration allowed the vandals to be turned over to juvenile court, where they were sentenced to terms in the state's Boys Industrial School. The parents' only recourse was to complain to the papers that their sons had been the victims of hysteria.

Yet before long the high school's seemingly boundless jurisdiction would begin to crumble. Challenged by such visionary leaders as John F. Kennedy and Martin Luther King Jr. to become politically active, a new generation of students would bring its interest in changing the world to bear on the public schools, compelling them to become less restrictive institutions.

Although Heights High was never a hotbed of radicalism, it was not at all unusual during the 1960s for some Heights students to spend their summers tutoring inner-city children in Cleveland or registering black voters in the South. Even though students with a liberal social conscience were still greatly outnumbered by those of a more conservative bent, this vocal minority exerted disproportionate influence over the tenor of the high school. In 1966 they raised such a stink about the elitism of the school's National Honor Society chapter, which each year invited a select number of juniors and seniors with good grades and demonstrated leadership abilities to become members, that the faculty disbanded the prestigious recognition program. Twenty years passed before the chapter was invited back on campus, its recall yet another academic initiative of the Burkett administration.

Even the school's custom of raising the American flag in the courtyard every morning during homeroom to the accompaniment of drums and bugles was not safe from challenge. Al Abramovitz, then the district's director of secondary education, remembered the morning in 1968 or 1969 when several students, wishing to register their unhappiness with the government's involvement in Vietnam, grabbed the flag before it could be hoisted and set it on fire. After the principal intervened to break up the demonstration, the protesters organized a mass walkout, charging that school authorities had infringed upon their First Amendment right of free speech. As a result district administrators deemed it wise to suspend the flag-raising ceremony, at least for a few weeks. After a suitable cooling-off period, the flag could again be seen flying over the campus—only now it was raised without pomp and circumstance by a lone custodian at six in the morning.

In order to contain student unrest, the high school was forced to loosen up in other ways. (The process may have been speeded by a mid-1960s threat to blow up the building, a scare that Abramovitz attributed to students who thought its rules were too rigid.) The second half of the decade saw Heights High eliminate mandatory study halls, open the Tiger's Den as a student hangout, dispense with such policing tactics as hall passes, create an independent study program, and give students a voice on the faculty's Curriculum Advisory Committee. Even so, the principal who initiated most of these changes (a longtime employee of the system who "saw himself as the last anchor stopping the community from going off the edge," according to Abramovitz) was forced into reluctant retirement because of continuing criticism of his administration as too strict.

The first victim of the community's growing ambivalence about the authority of public school educators—a new dynamic that would help turn the job of running Heights High into a no-win proposition and give the school a tainted reputation as a "principal's graveyard"—the retiring administrator was to exact a measure of revenge. (Or so the legend went.) During his final year as principal in 1968–69, he liberalized the school's dress code, in effect saying to students "anything goes" while giving teachers the option to object to distracting clothing. Pandemonium promptly broke out, and the house offices were flooded with young women whose teachers objected to their wearing of slacks. One young man sent to the office for sporting cutoff jeans was instructed by a harried administrator not to wear them again for a few weeks "until the teachers cooled off."

The next principal of Heights High, a recruit from the East Coast, recognized that the better part of wisdom lay in embracing change rather than continuing to fight it. "I don't intend to be a policeman," he told a reporter during his first months on the job. "I want to be an educator . . . someone who works with kids on an intellectual, physical and emotional level." The board of education gave its imprimatur to this approach by approving a policy statement in October 1969 that acknowledged the basic civil rights of students.

Not everyone in the district welcomed these developments. In the spring of 1970, the Heights Women's Republican Club, whose members had for decades provided formal and informal leadership of school affairs, made a last-gasp attempt to restore the old order. They went before the board of education, then presided over by a prominent Jewish attorney, to complain about the presence at Heights High and Roxboro Junior High of active chapters of the Student Mobilization Committee (SMC). SMC was a national antiwar organization that some of the club members claimed was an extremist group with connections to drug traffickers. Declaring that her children had no civil liberties "except what I give them," the leader of the Republican women's protest asked the board to prohibit antiwar meetings from taking place on any of the district's campuses. Under pressure the board agreed to ban the Student Mobilization Committee.

The following month SMC's local attorney appeared before the board to demand that its members rescind their decision. "If you muzzle people in these times, young people will turn to much more violent means," the attorney argued. "Do you want them to be vegetables—apathetic to the issues of our times?" At the conclusion of the attorney's impassioned thirty-minute speech, the president of the board said only that he and his colleagues would take the matter under advisement. At its next meeting, however, the Cleveland Heights–University Heights Board of Education reaffirmed the students' rights of freedom of speech and peaceful assembly in a statement notable for its straightforward language and conviction.[3]

The surprise decision would have lasting significance for the district in that it established an institutional tolerance of student activism and legitimized organized protest as a valid means for students to express dissent. As a result, political engagement was to become an honored tradition at Heights High School. Long after the majority of America's youth abandoned the idealism of the 1960s and became preoccupied once again with personal economic advancement, many Heights High students remained socially conscious. During the Reagan and Bush eras, Heights students recycled aluminum pop cans, marched on downtown Cleveland to protest apartheid, and organized an in-house blood drive in response to the news that fear of contracting AIDS had drastically reduced donations of blood to the local Red Cross. The drive netted more than 125 pints.

To be sure, the ambiguity of the line between student rights and administrative authority resulted in occasional abuses. When a portrait of Mickey Mouse was emblazoned on the high school's clock tower sometime during the 1970s, this symbol of student rebellion was allowed to loom over the campus for many years. Even when Mickey sprouted genitalia in the early 1980s, school authorities did not deem it time for his removal. Only when the clock tower was undergoing restoration in the fall of 1986 did the Burkett administration seize this opportunity to have Mickey painted over. After he magically reappeared the following summer, Burkett, for whom matters of image and public relations were of tertiary importance, decided to let Mickey stay. One of the few known instances in which the principal allowed someone to get the better of him, the incident no doubt lingered in Burkett's mind as yet another example of the student body's immaturity.

Heights High's predominately black student council was not the only group to encounter the principal's jaundiced views on student rights. *Black and Gold* editor Bethany Aram, a member of the school's advanced placement elite, also ran into the brick wall of Burkett's closed mind when she attempted to establish a written editorial policy for the student newspaper during her junior year in 1988–89. Disturbed by the implications of *Hazelwood School District v. Kuhlmeier*, a 1988 Supreme Court decision that upheld a Missouri principal's right to censor his high school's newspaper, Aram was looking to ensure the continuation of the editorial freedom that the *Black and Gold* had enjoyed since the 1970s, when the paper was transformed from a sophomoric mouthpiece for the school administration into an opinionated journal that almost lived up to its editors' description as "a thought-provoking masterpiece of penmanship issued by the energetic and highly creative journalists of Heights High."

Aram's proposed editorial policy was a thoughtful document that prohibited the *Black and Gold* from publishing material that was libelous or obscene or that encouraged student strikes, violence, or defiance of lawful school regulations. However, it placed final control over the newspaper's content in the hands of its student editors. The policy statement went through several drafts under the watchful eye of the newspaper's faculty advisor, also assistant principal for curriculum, Walter, before it was sent to Burkett for approval. Much to Aram's dismay, the high school principal refused to sign the agreement, which stripped him of the power granted his office by the board of education to shield the district and the community from irresponsible student commentary.

Having invested a year in drafting the editorial policy, Aram was not willing to accept Burkett's turndown as final. She attempted to reason with him, assaying a counterargument that she later reprised in a guest column published in the suburb's newspaper. "Limiting student freedoms and responsibilities seems to be a trend in public education, perhaps as a reaction to the presence of drugs and to an increase in gang involvement across the country," she wrote in the *Sun Press*. "While administrative control of student activity may seem warranted in the short term, it will inevitably be detrimental to the long-term future of the nation. How can we function as productive, thinking individuals when we are restricted physically and intellectually during our young adulthood?"

Although Aram's concerns echoed those that had prompted the creation of the Model School Project, Burkett remained unmoved by her arguments. Rather than seek a mutually acceptable resolution, he chose to stonewall, stating flatly that "I have my rights and responsibilities, and I'm not going to sell out to the students, who are going to create anarchy" (according to Aram's reconstruction of their conversations). A National Merit Scholarship semifinalist and accomplished bassoonist who would go on to study at Yale University, Aram decided that Burkett was just being stubborn. He hailed from the South, after all, and his mentality simply was not that of Cleveland Heights.[4]

Aram also had difficulty countenancing the behavior of Frank Walter, who she felt had not been sufficiently vigorous in defending the editorial policy he and she had negotiated. Walter's apparent willingness to do the principal's bidding even when it contradicted his own beliefs puzzled the young woman. How could a person of such obvious integrity play Burkett's games?

Aram would later conclude that Walter's wife shared her husband's misguided sense of loyalty. In the fall of 1989, Fran Walter approached her with a suggestion that the student newspaper publish a story about Burkett's recent move into Cleveland Heights. Walter explained that the principal's decision to sell his farm in Ashtabula and rent quarters in town was newsworthy because it demonstrated his ongoing commitment to Heights High. This kind of publicity would have been helpful in positioning Burkett as a viable candidate for the superintendency, if only the editor of the *Black and Gold* had accepted Walter's argument. However, the way Aram saw it, Burkett had moved into a cheap place in town because he was planning on getting the heck out of a district he hated.

Buoyed by the successful completion of the first Model School retreat and believing that he still had a shot at the superintendency, Burkett had made no formal departure plans as of early autumn 1989. But Aram's instincts were sure in one regard. The unpopularity of the principal's approach to discipline and student rights was about to catch up with him and help to seal the fate of his administration.

13

The Question of Exclusion

Children are taught a host of lessons about values, ethics, morality, character, and conduct every day of the week, less by the content of the curriculum than by the way schools are organized, the ways teachers and parents behave, the way they talk to children and to each other, the kinds of behavior they approve or reward and the kinds they disapprove or punish. These lessons are far more powerful than the verbalizations that accompany them and that they frequently controvert.

—CHARLES E. SILBERMAN
Crisis in the Classroom, 1970

Burkett's prediction that a progrouping contingent would crash the second Model School retreat did not come to pass. The mood of the September retreat was surprisingly muted.

Like dutiful students, the participants waited their turn before speaking and seemed disinclined to argue with or even follow up on the comments of others. The coordinators found it impossible to ignite a debate about grouping—or any other subject, for that matter. As the weekend wore on, a few of the male teachers began reading newspapers or wandering around the conference room during sessions. Burkett, too, seemed disengaged from the discussions. He rarely commented and, in sharp contrast to his assertive behavior at the August retreat, displayed little interest in challenging the group's preconceptions.

When the coordinators met afterward to assess why the retreat had failed to spark a serious dialogue, they concluded that the fault lay in the personal dynamics of that particular group of teachers. This interpretation permitted the project leaders to cling to their optimistic view of the retreats as magical experiences, capable of infusing the participants with a lasting commitment to the objectives of the Model School Project. Unfortunately, their steadfast faith in this particular strategy preempted a consideration of additional steps that could have been taken to strengthen and expand interest in the plan to restructure the high school.

The coordinators were not inclined to shoulder more work, in any event. Although they had now been freed from class two periods a day to conduct Model School business, they would have been required to give up their own time to lead supplementary activities, which would have to be scheduled during after-school hours, when the other teachers were at liberty. To keep the faculty continuously engaged in Model School deliberations, they would also have to work with groups independently of one another, a concept with which they had never been comfortable. (None of the four felt that he or she had been given an individual mandate to lead.) It was easier to focus on tasks that they could accomplish together during their "release" time, such as reviewing the by now familiar preparations for the upcoming weekend retreat scheduled for late October. They also began laying plans for several two-day retreats to be held during the school day in November and December for those teachers unable or unwilling to give up a weekend.

At the moment the coordinators' single-minded determination to host retreat after retreat until no more teachers volunteered to attend was producing gratifying results. Twelve more staff members signed up to attend the October retreat, and places at subsequent sessions were filling up fast. But the participating faculty members would be afforded no other significant contact with the Model School Project during the first semester of the 1989–90 school year. And the rest of the teachers were left out of the loop altogether.

The previous year volunteers had published a monthly Model School newsletter featuring progress reports and excerpts from books by leading education reformers, but, like the concept of the study teams, this tool for perpetuating interest in restructuring had been lost. Rumors filled the vacuum created by the absence of Model School announcements and activities. Feeling ignored, several former study team chairpeople began grumbling that the coordinators had thrown away all the teams' research and hard work, and one of them made known his intention to boycott the retreats, a decision that he said he would reverse only if he received a personal invitation to attend from Burkett.

Although they seemed impervious to the small signs of discontent emanating from their colleagues, the coordinators were all too quick to respond to Burkett's midautumn complaint that the retreat process was consuming too much of his time. Without thinking through the consequences of the decision, they abandoned their strategy of asking the retreat participants to achieve consensus on the basic outlines of a model school. Now the groups would be allowed to use the coordinators' loose transcription of their discussion sessions as their final reports rather than be required to follow the example of the August retreat-goers, who continued meeting for weeks afterward until they produced a written agreement.

For all these reasons, the faculty's commitment to restructuring had dangerously shallow roots.

During their debriefing sessions following the lackluster September retreat, the coordinators also expressed concern about the causes of Burkett's atypically poor showing. Fran Walter proffered the information that the principal's back was hurting him. As Burkett had undergone back surgery two years before, the other coordinators accepted this explanation for his subdued performance. His back was not the only thing preoccupying Heights High's principal, however.

The new year was barely a month old, and already the school had been rocked by a couple of unusually disturbing assaults committed by female students. One incident involved a young African-American woman who had struck several white girls with a belt. The second incident was even more bizarre. It occurred in the main hallway on the first floor of the high school. While the security guard normally stationed in the hallway was called away from his post, two young black women had cornered a white student and proceeded to cut her hair.

Alarmed by the apparent racial overtones of the assaults, a small group of concerned students and parents immediately requested a meeting with the high school administration. "The girl with the belt does not represent black people in the school," Frank Walter assured the gathering. "I'm sure many black people are equally outraged." Beth Aram, who had accidentally stumbled onto the meeting and begun taking notes on the discussion, later asked several African-American students for their interpretation of the attacks for a story she had decided to prepare for the *Black and Gold*. They, too, condemned the assaults. "These girls did it to be ignorant," a young woman in the class of 1991 told Aram. "All they do is go around making trouble. They know that [if they picked on a] . . . black girl, they would have gotten into a fight. They see white girls as defenseless."

Aram did not personally believe the haircutting incident to be racially motivated. She knew the victim to be one of those expanded-track girls who cared only about her clothes, hair, and makeup and looked down on anyone who did not share her narcissistic interests. There were days when Aram herself felt like taking scissors to the snob's hair!—a confession she later made to bolster her argument that the incident had not been motivated by racial animosity. For a while after the assault occurred, Aram made a special point of going up to her black friends and saying, "What's up?"—just to let them know that she did not regard the haircutting incident as a cause for alarm.

Recognizing that other students might be upset and angry, however, she felt it important that the *Black and Gold* publish something that would put the assaults into perspective and help to defuse racial tensions. To that end she wrote a news story that concluded with a quote from a skills-for-living teacher that sounded a plea for students and staff to act rationally. "I was confused, angry and depressed to hear about these things," the teacher told Aram. "Any kind of incident is so sensitive. People start to generalize and people start to stereotype. It just precipitates what has been an upsurge in racial prejudice [nationally] in the last ten years."

The story might have served to initiate a much needed dialogue between students and staff about the causes of and cures for racial prejudice, an issue that lost a prominent place on the Model School agenda after the study teams were disbanded. But the story never saw print. Perhaps envisioning that hordes of outraged and frightened parents would descend on the high school should word of the black-on-white assaults spread, Burkett censored it. He had enough trouble on his hands.

Unbeknownst to all the coordinators save Fran Walter, Burkett's relationship with Lauree Gearity had collapsed, a state of affairs that did not augur well for the principal's ability to push the model school design through channels at the board of education once it was completed. The issue of discipline was the latest cause of contention. The climate in the district had changed since Burkett was hired with a board mandate to restore order. In recent times the words and deeds of white teachers and principals had come under intense scrutiny from a small group of African Americans who called themselves Cleveland Heights–University Heights Concerned Parents.

Cleveland Heights–University Heights Concerned Parents had established itself as a force with which to be reckoned after its members broke ranks with a more moderate organization of concerned black parents who declined to join them in opposing the creation of Taylor Academy, an alternative school for students flunking ninth or tenth grade at Heights High.

The militants charged that Taylor segregated failing black students from the mainstream of high school life. Although their picket lines and demand for a civil rights investigation of the alternative school by the state department of education had not prevented Taylor's opening, the leaders of the new parents' group continued to make it their business to monitor the school system for instances of racist behavior and policy. When they learned of black students who believed that they had been "disrespected," discriminated against, or unfairly suspended or expelled, they immediately stepped forward with offers to assist the aggrieved parties in seeking redress. Because the student advocates were quick to use allegations of racism as a hammer for driving home their demands, their main accomplishment in the past had been to inspire fear and loathing in the hearts of those educators whose practices they challenged. Irv Moskowitz, for one, had dismissed their protests as "street theater."

Now the group appeared to be influencing policy at Miramar. During the first two months of the school year, the new interim superintendent would overrule four expulsion recommendations sent to the central office by the Burkett administration for approval. In the assault cases, Lauree Gearity signed the expulsion papers but agreed to allow the female offenders to be enrolled at Second Site, provided that they obtain counseling.

Reporting on these developments at the October faculty meeting, the high school stewards complained that board policy did not permit conditional readmittance of students who had been expelled. Burkett's adverse reaction was much more emotional. Gearity's actions made him sick at heart. How would his administration ever maintain control of the high school, he despaired, when his superior was sending a message to the community that violence and aggression would be winked at?

Not every administrator at the high school shared Burkett's sense of grievous injury. (There was dissension among the building administrators over the issue of discipline, too.) At least one house principal found Gearity's decisions to be fair. It was not as if the female offenders had been allowed to escape unpunished; they had all served ten-day suspensions, reasoned Jeffrey Forman, the white assistant principal of Lee House. Having served as an assistant principal at all-black Shaw High School in impoverished East Cleveland for fifteen years before Burkett hired him, Forman had a more nuanced approach to discipline than his recruiter. He believed that disciplinary action should be therapeutic as well as punitive, tough but not fatal—a philosophy born of his long association with extremely needy students, he speculated.

Forman had not been able to exercise his own judgment in disciplinary matters at Heights High, however. For one thing, Burkett was a firm believer in what Forman thought of as "cookbook" discipline: that is, "If you fight, you're *gone*." No exceptions made. Forman also felt the presence of Local 795 at his shoulder. Here was a union so strong that it had been able to win for teachers the right to specify on the referral form how they wished a troublemaker to be punished. After accommodating the views of his superior and the referring teacher, Forman did not have much room to see to matters he believed to be paramount: involving the troublemaker's parents in the disposition of the case (they were, after all, paying the bills) and making sure that the punishment did not leave the student permanently scarred.

Forman's colleague, Clarence Mixon, the African-American principal of Cedar House, shared Forman's belief in leavening discipline with affection. Mixon tried never to let a student who had been severely disciplined leave the office angry. If necessary, he would delay processing the student's referral until he had a chance to talk with the young man or woman. At the end of such conferences, Mixon always told the student the same thing: "Remember, I still love you; I just don't like what you did." Then he would put his arm around the offender, even if he were a big strapping guy. Mixon had a hunch that many of these kids had never been hugged, at least not by a male.

Both Forman and Mixon saw themselves as dispensers of justice rather than as purveyors of punishment. They were willing to consider mitigating factors in making their decisions and sought, whenever possible, to involve the offender's parents in the disciplinary process, thus turning them into allies. Burkett frowned on both practices, Forman had learned. Heights High's principal believed that any response to serious misbehavior other than the consistent, swift imposition of the school's stated disciplinary consequences was dangerous waffling. A willingness to negotiate reduced punishment with some students and their parents encouraged others, Burkett was convinced, to test the school's determination to enforce its rules.

Given Burkett's inability to conceive of workable alternatives to suspension and expulsion, it followed that he could find only one explanation for Gearity's overrulings. Unlike her predecessors, the interim superintendent must have caved in to pressure from Cleveland Heights–University Heights Concerned Parents to lessen the district's use of disciplinary exclusion from schooling. Neither she nor the black parents seemed willing, he lamented, to acknowledge the fact that acts of aggression were unacceptable under any circumstances or to accept the reality that only when student conduct improved would there be a concurrent reduction in the number of suspensions and expulsions. Burkett felt that they just wanted to see lower numbers, period.

Actually, pressure to do something about the overrepresentation of blacks in the disciplinary system had been building in Cleveland Heights schools for years. As early as the mid-1970s, a handful of African-American parents who had banded together as the Committee to Improve Community Relations (CICR) decided to investigate their children's complaints that they were being punished more harshly than their white peers. Among other actions it took, CICR asked to study the district's disciplinary records. "If you saw those figures, it would have scared you," remembered committee member Lacy Lott. "You would have thought all the black students were hoods or part of the Mafia, the way they were treated."

Eventually, CICR wrested a written agreement from the Cleveland Heights–University Heights Board of Education requiring the superintendent to meet annually with committee members to review the year's suspension and expulsion figures. According to Lott, the owner of a small construction business who had moved to Cleveland Heights in the mid-1960s because he wanted his two sons to attend quality schools, CICR's scrutiny made little difference. Semester after semester black students continued to be kicked out of school at rates disproportionate to their numbers.

In 1984, the year that Hugh Burkett arrived in Cleveland Heights, the district's disciplinary practices were once again called into question. This time the school system suffered the embarrassment of receiving unfavorable notice in a statewide citizens' report on the issue of disciplinary exclusion. The report's author, an educational researcher and Cleveland Heights resident named Susan C. Kaeser, found the disparity between the suspension rates for black and white students to be greater than the statewide average in fifteen of forty-seven districts in Ohio with substantial minority enrollments. Cleveland Heights ranked near the top of the list. "Efforts to remove any doubts about fair treatment of all children should focus on these districts," Kaeser asserted in the report, which went on to explain how racial discrimination could indeed occur during the referral process because administrators had to rely on the subjective judgments of individual teachers about what constituted student misbehavior.[1]

Because of her authorship of the report, Kaeser believed that she had become persona non grata at Miramar. She suspected that central-office officials had subsequently blocked her nomination to the School Consensus Project, a biracial task force formed in 1985 when several civic organizations approached the district with an offer to assist in the preparation of a school-improvement plan. Kaeser finagled her way into the deliberations, nevertheless, by volunteering to serve as a resource person for the SCP disciplinary subcommittee. The experience modified her thinking about the practice of disciplinary exclusion. Previously she had believed that education was so basic a civil right, and the social and economic consequences of being excluded from school so dire, that no student should ever be dismissed for any reason. However, after talking with Burkett and other Cleveland Heights administrators about the realities of running large, quasi-urban public schools, she "came down from her ivory tower."

Now she found herself agreeing with Burkett's contention that public schools must be allowed to establish and enforce clear expectations about student behavior. A line had to be drawn somewhere. Much to her surprise she also discovered that Burkett, whom she had previously known only by his reputation as a hardnose, agreed with *her* on certain matters. For example, Burkett shared her conviction that the only sure way public schools could lessen the need for disciplinary exclusion was to improve dramatically the quality of education they were providing to minority students. Burkett's Model School Project was, in her opinion, a means to that end. Certainly, it was the best hope the district now had of achieving that objective, given the ignominious end of the School Consensus Project.

"Motivated students: a key to order" had been a major theme of the School Consensus Project's final "Report to the Community." Published in October 1987, this executive summary of SCP's work asserted, "When we can help more students to be successful academically, then we will also have more orderly schools."

No matter how ringing its pronouncements, the report was a poor substitute for the community forums SCP leaders had asked the school board to sponsor. But the board declined to act on SCP's request that the recommendations for reform on which the task force had been working for two years be presented to the public. A much needed property tax levy—it would pay for the hefty salary increases Local 795 had negotiated in 1986—was coming up for a vote, and the board may have feared that the forums would disintegrate into school-bashing sessions and jeopardize the levy's passage (or so SCP leaders speculated). Consequently, the question of the best strategy for reducing the number of suspensions and expulsions in the district—to say nothing of the other important equity and excellence issues on which the School Consensus Project took a stand—never received a public airing.[2]

That shriller voices had, however, succeeded in making themselves heard on the issue of discipline became clear later, when Irv Moskowitz called a special meeting of all the district principals to present data showing that suspension and expulsion rates in Cleveland Heights were higher even than those for the Cleveland public schools. At the meeting Moskowitz made plain his belief that the district's figures were out of line. Hugh Burkett took Moskowitz's lecture to mean that the reduction of suspensions and expulsions was now an unwritten goal of the central administration. Even so, Moskowitz had never undercut Burkett's authority in an attempt to mollify such pressure groups as Cleveland Heights–University Heights Concerned Parents. (Although the former superintendent suspected that Burkett overreacted to disciplinary problems, Moskowitz had been loathe to overrule the principal's recommendations for expulsion, recognizing that to do so would damage Burkett's credibility.)

Moskowitz's successor felt no such hesitancy. Lauree Gearity tended to sympathize with parents, who (she felt it safe to say) did not take well to having their children suspended or expelled. If Burkett were indeed treating students fairly, why was it that the African-American community did not buy into his disciplinary policies? Gearity wondered. (It had been her experience that minority parents usually *favored* a "structured" school environment for their kids.) While Gearity was willing to grant that Burkett had been largely successful in ridding Heights High of what she called "deviant" behavior, she questioned the high cost of his success. In short, the new interim superintendent considered herself quite willing to reexamine the issue of discipline, and she found it a major failing on Burkett's part that he had not demonstrated a similar open-mindedness.

A few weeks after the haircutting incident, Gearity overturned yet another recommendation from the Burkett administration that a student be expelled for assault. This time it was a teacher who had been attacked. The incident occurred when the teacher attempted to break up a fight between two African-American students. One of the combatants had turned on him and attempted to push him down a flight of stairs. District informed the high school that it could not uphold the recommendation for expulsion because there were conflicting reports about which student attacked the teacher—a justification that Burkett and Frank Walter found patently ridiculous.

Walter had attended a sufficient number of expulsions hearings to know that contradictory testimony was invariably presented; it was the responsibility of the hearing officer to decide whom to believe—in this case, the high school's football coach, or a student who had been previously expelled. It was to be expected that the district's hearing officer had decided that the evidence against the student was shaky; having formerly worked as a guidance counselor, she was naturally reluctant to expel students. But Walter concluded that there was no reason other than Gearity's lamentable inexperience with expulsions—a draconian punishment that elementary principals rarely meted out—for the interim superintendent's decision to accept the hearing officer's judgment casting doubt on the word of the football coach.

In desperation Burkett decided to play the union card. At his next meeting with the high school's chief union steward (Dan MacDonald had followed his predecessor's practice of conferring privately with the principal every Monday morning—over the objections of some of his fellow stewards, who worried that deals might be cut at these get-togethers without their consent), Burkett brought up the problem he was experiencing with expulsions. Burkett asked MacDonald what the union intended to do about the situation, a question the principal knew would have the same effect as throwing chum to a shark. The maintenance of discipline being one of Local 795's preeminent concerns, the high school stewards decided to call for a job action. At the October 1989 faculty meeting, they encouraged their colleagues to write letters to the interim superintendent expressing dismay at the disposition of the assault cases.[3]

"Lightning struck," MacDonald crowed in a memo to the faculty distributed five days later. MacDonald reported that because of the job action a central-office administrator had agreed to meet with him to explain "the Board position regarding the four students and the overall Board goal of the reduction of suspensions and expulsions [through the] 'use of alternatives where possible.'" As it turned out, MacDonald had exaggerated the success of the job action, no doubt for reasons of troop morale. Later he let slip that only four teachers had penned letters of protest. It was Local 795's concurrent decision to file four grievances—one for each student that the district had declined to expel for assault—that had most likely prompted Miramar's interest in discussing the matter.

MacDonald emerged from his summit deflated. For one thing, he felt as if he had been sandbagged by Burkett, who had neglected to inform him that district administrators had what they considered to be legitimate reasons for overturning the expulsions. They protested that the high school's written documentation of the assault cases was inadequate. This contention had caught the chief steward off guard. Reflecting upon the matter later, MacDonald realized that the complaint about incomplete documentation was a red herring; disciplinary paperwork was always "dirty" to some degree. The real problem was the bad blood between Miramar and Heights High.

The situation reminded MacDonald of that between the United States and the Soviet Union at the height of the Berlin Wall crisis. Each side was entrenched in its perception of the other as subversive. With Cleveland Heights–University Heights Concerned Parents making loud noises about the high number of suspensions and expulsions in the district, Miramar felt that Burkett was pushing matters that should not be pushed. But when the chief steward attempted to persuade Burkett to talk over his differences with the interim superintendent and the district hearing officer, the principal had pounded his desk and shouted, "I'm not going to have them in my building!" When it came to the issue of discipline, MacDonald decided, Burkett lacked peripheral vision.

If the district's top two administrators remained unwilling or unable to resolve their differences, the interim superintendent and the teachers' union were beginning to forge a working relationship. This welcome turn of events would have an unexpected impact on the cause of school reform. Soon Gearity would have to choose sides in a major disagreement between the leaders of the teachers' union and the Model School Project. But for the moment the thaw in labor-management relations seemed to have only an upside.

For starters, Gearity and Glenn Altschuld were able to settle the four disciplinary grievances that the union had filed in the fall of 1989 without resorting to government arbitration. In January 1990 the union announced that the grievances had resulted in Altschuld's appointment to the newly created position of technical compliance officer. Henceforth it would be Altschuld's responsibility to review all teacher-originated referrals and, if he determined that a teacher's paperwork was not in order, to assist the author with a rewrite. Although the resolution was somewhat empty—when later asked to describe his duties as technical compliance officer, Altschuld could remember only that the job had been "fun"—its amicability stood in sharp contrast to the endless labor-management bickering of the Moskowitz years.

As it turned out, Gearity had wasted no time in seeking a rapprochement with Altschuld after Moskowitz departed. "Dr. Gearity made it plain that she did not want [a] breakdown to occur a second time," the union president explained in a confidential letter to his executive board written shortly after Gearity's promotion to the interim superintendency in June 1989. As one of her first acts, the interim superintendent reinstituted a practice that had been recommended by the School Consensus Project: regular private meetings of the superintendent and union president.

Finding the school's new chief executive a "more predictable and constant personality" than her predecessor, Altschuld responded favorably to
Gearity's request that they reopen discussions of the changes to the contract
sought by both sides that had been left unresolved during the previous year's
negotiations. Within the space of three months, Gearity and Altschuld were
able to come to agreement on a dozen new provisions, with the union gaining the right to negotiate the terms of all supplemental contracts, for example, and the board of education gaining the go-ahead for such changes in
staffing as a reduction in the number of elementary school librarians.

Altschuld, whose transfer back to the high school had also been among
the concessions made by the new administration, called upon rank and file to
ratify the new contract proposals at a union meeting held shortly after the
start of school in the fall of 1989.[4] Quoting Gearity, he hailed the contract
agreement as "a new beginning" in labor-management relations.

Gearity later attributed her success in reestablishing a working relationship with Local 795 to the fact that she had more respect for teachers than
her predecessors. She was quick to point out that, in her ten years as principal
of Belvoir school, only two grievances had been filed against her administration—a record that testified, she believed, to her ability to deal fairly with
teachers. The reopened negotiations may also have been sped along by
Altschuld's impending retirement as union president. Not only did the labor
leader wish to depart on a good note, Gearity perceived that he also wanted
to prove that his inability to work with the previous superintendent had
been Moskowitz's fault.

Indeed, both Gearity and Altschuld had much to gain from putting an
end to labor-management conflict and public disputes. She would be seen
by the members of the board of education as a diplomat who possessed the
consummate negotiating skills needed in a superintendent, and he would be
perceived by the union membership as having rebounded from the disastrous 1988–89 contract negotiations. Even before Altschuld had been outmaneuvered during the contract negotiations by Irv Moskowitz, there had
been a movement afoot to put together an opposition slate to run for the
union's leadership positions. No challengers had appeared, however, and
Altschuld needed to create the impression that he was once again in control
of Local 795's destiny to ensure that no one would emerge in the coming
year to oppose his handpicked successor.

The lengths to which both labor and management were prepared to go to
restore good relations became clear when, shortly before the ratification
vote on the new contract provisions, the State Employment Relations Board

found probable cause that the Cleveland Heights–University Heights Board of Education had violated fair labor practice by instituting a seven-period day without Local 795's approval and by issuing letters of reprimand to those union members who had actively protested the decision. Although some Local 795 leaders thought it likely that the union would win compensation should the cases go on to a formal hearing, the union's executive board agreed to withdraw the complaints, and the board of education dropped its countercharge protesting the union's job action as illegal.

Anticipating that this unusual act of accommodation might inspire some second-guessing, Altschuld promptly issued a note of explanation. "We were browbeaten and pushed around by a Board of Education and Administration and when we were finally vindicated, our own union comes to us and requests that we let . . . all be forgiven. It is a bit much to take," he acknowledged. "[But] I believe it is better to build a bridge than fall into the same canyon twice. And I do not see the special value in pushing the other guy into the canyon when we can both use the new bridge."

The wisdom of Altschuld's homily was lost on Hugh Burkett. The constant wrangling with Miramar had taken its toll on the high school principal. His back was killing him, he was having trouble sleeping, and he was up to two packs of cigarettes a day. What would happen to his health if the unthinkable occurred and Lauree Gearity became superintendent on a permanent basis?

By the time of the third Model School teachers' retreat in late October 1989, Burkett's résumé was in the mail to school systems across the country that were advertising for top administrators. The job search was a matter of sensible precaution on his part. He did not really believe he would be forced to abandon all the hard work that he and his Model School compatriots had poured into their campaign to save Heights High School. Burkett was simply hedging his bet that the upcoming board of education races would result in an outcome favorable to him.

14

The Silent Majority

Even if . . . community involvement should interfere with profession-
als or otherwise reduce the "efficiency" of the school, such participa-
tion is the paramount way of preserving the democratic process in the
schools as in other public institutions.

—MARIO FANTINI ET AL.
Community Control and the Urban School, 1970

Much to the relief of the coordinators, the October retreat did not turn out
to be a disappointment like its predecessor in September. In fact, the opening
session on Saturday was so animated, with teachers drowning out one
another's comments in their rush to list their pet problems with students,
that the coordinators were forced to abandon their casual approach and give
every person in the room a formal opportunity to speak.

"At least we don't have to worry we won't get into the issues," Cas
McBride sighed during the morning break.

After lunch the retreat participants showed no signs of tiring. They dove
into the afternoon's task: identifying problems that centered on the family
or the community. This particular group of educators had a lot on their
chests. Their biggest complaints concerned the negative perception of
Heights High School that was prevalent among some white residents and
the seeming lack of interest many black parents exhibited in their children's
educations.

169

Science teacher Anne Austin began the discussion with a criticism of "parents who do not provide time or space for quiet home study."

"And/or: 'enough supervision,'" added Bill Thomas, who was serving as the facilitator for the discussion. This was the first of Thomas's allotment of two remarks per session. Steve Young had imposed this strict limit on his fellow coordinators when he was unable to win their agreement to stop monopolizing the retreat discussions. Thomas invariably exceeded his limit.

"Parents who have thrown in the towel" was history teacher JoAnne Broadbooks's complaint. "They say, 'I can't do a thing with him.'"

"What would you suggest?" English teacher Joseph Geiger asked.

"Buy them a bus ticket," responded Broadbooks, whose sense of humor asserted itself consistently throughout the weekend.

"There's a perception among many community members that they have no stake in the success of our kids," Geiger noted, changing the topic of conversation to racial prejudice.

"What about the negative image of school in the community?" offered Hyla Winston, the high school's new part-time public relations person. "Willing to believe the worst, nitpicking—that's our community. They're eager to perpetuate a negative image, rather than build something better."

"People see the school as belonging to another subgroup of the community," music teacher Roger Clary explained. "Black members see it as belonging to whites and vice versa."

"Blacks *know* it's being controlled by whites," Dan MacDonald insisted. No one challenged the chief steward's statement.

"Excessive absences are enabled by families," guidance counselor Judy Grenda said, returning to the subject of parental apathy. "They operate on a four-day week."

"Parents don't follow through when you let them know that their kid isn't doing his homework," complained Sharon Drake, a special education teacher who was only the fourth African-American faculty member to attend a retreat to date.

"You don't get any response at all to Fs on report cards," JoAnne Broadbooks reported. "But you do get hostility from parents to disciplinary action."

"Families don't know what their kids are doing, where they are, or when they're supposed to be home," said physical education teacher Larry Hoon.

"Not knowing is a big problem," Hugh Burkett agreed. "I've never once convinced a parent whose son was a member of the Home Boys that they are *not* a dance group."

"Some parents follow through," Joe Geiger said, picking up on an earlier comment. "'I'll purple his behind,' some parent said to me when I called about a problem. Well, that's not what I wanted at all. Also," Geiger continued, "write down: 'fear of the high school.'"

"Just the sheer size of it," math teacher Dave Muthersbaugh affirmed.

Muthersbaugh and MacDonald were the first of the high school stewards to take the time to attend a retreat. MacDonald had also gone out of his way to encourage the faculty's participation in the Model School Project in his October newsletter to the high school rank and file. "Talking to one another can only help us grow closer," he wrote, echoing the positive responses circulating about the retreats.

"We keep saying fear, but did we say 'fear for one's safety'?" asked Kaye Price, the high school's coordinator of pupil services. "Some members of the community are afraid they might get mugged in the school."

"They're afraid of school-age looking kids in general," JoAnne Broadbooks responded. This time she was not joking about the reaction that the sight of hundreds of black teenagers pouring out of the high school at the end of each day elicited in some white residents.

At this point Bill Thomas asked the members of the group to present solutions to the problems they had raised. Why not provide free tickets and bus transportation to the high school's music programs? someone suggested. Or encourage businesses to "adopt" high school clubs? When one of the teachers praised the middle schools' practice of inviting senior citizens to tea, JoAnne Broadbooks cracked, "Do they wait until after the students leave?"

Resisting the temptation to slacken the pace because of the late hour, the group produced a long list of recommendations, such as scheduling regular parent-teacher conferences, recruiting security monitors or students to act as official greeters, organizing a Heights High speaker's bureau, and offering courses in parenting skills as part of the adult education program in Cleveland Heights. On a smaller scale, someone suggested that the standardized form teachers used to send "supplemental" reports to parents be redesigned so that it would include space for positive as well as negative comments. The retreat group decided to carry out this suggestion as one of its school-improvement projects.

It was no accident that most of the ideas generated by the October retreat dealt with ways to increase the minimal attention the high school staff paid to community outreach. The teachers shied away from embracing a more experimental antidote to fear—community participation in school governance—because they did not welcome the prospect. Like most other professionals, they regarded the involvement of lay persons in their affairs as meddling.

Even the coordinators were not immune to this particular allergy. When in their private planning sessions they had begun to consider whether parents and community groups should be involved in designing the model school, Cas McBride spoke for much of the faculty in exclaiming, "I don't want people coming in and telling me how to teach!" To buttress her objection, she offered an example of the unhappy consequences of soliciting noneducators' opinions. "At a PTA meeting at my kids' school, a man suggested that teachers should hit students who sleep in class," she warned. "If we allow parents to have input into the design, we won't be able to cope with their solutions."

At the October retreat the usually tough-minded Hugh Burkett did not challenge the erroneous assumption underlying the teachers' preoccupation with community outreach: that those controlling the purse strings would accept having no real role in a model school district. Burkett was well aware that the literature on shared decision making called for public schools to be managed in partnership with parents and community members, but, since he shared the faculty's aversion to "outside interference," he did not press his colleagues on that point. On the contrary, his habit of giving the Model School Project credit for the high school's employment of PR person Hyla Winston reinforced the faculty's inclination to view bigger and better outreach programs as the solution to Heights High's image problems.

Actually, the idea to hire Winston had been Burkett's exclusively. Only superintendent Moskowitz had been asked to okay the move. And Burkett alone had determined what Winston should do. He immediately put her to work organizing the publication of a new school paper to be mailed every month to Cleveland Heights and University Heights residents. A twelve-page exemplar of one-way communication—and crammed with upbeat stories, photos of student activities, and information of use to parents—the inaugural issue of *Heights High News* appeared in October 1989. Featured prominently on its front page was an essay on the characteristics of effective schools penned by Burkett himself.

The first issue of *Heights High News* caught the eye of Moskowitz's successor, who informed Burkett that it was not appropriate for the high school administration to publish its own newspaper. Reminding the high school principal that all communication with the community must emanate from the board of education, Lauree Gearity said that he would henceforth be given several pages for the high school's use in the district's monthly

newsletter. Burkett suspected that something other than attention to protocol had prompted Gearity's actions. He surmised that she did not want a rival
stealing her limelight at a time when the superintendency was up for grabs.

If people in the central office were feeling some anxiety about the subject
of Moskowitz's successor, it was understandable. The upcoming school
board races promised to be perhaps the most fiercely contested and unpre-
dictable of any such election in the history of Cleveland Heights. By the filing deadline, ten candidates had declared their intentions of running for the
three available seats on the five-person school board, whose members were
elected at large. The candidates represented a spectrum of educational philosophies and all of the district's major racial and religious groups. Clearly,
the future of the school district rested in the hands of three of these individuals. They would help to determine who became superintendent and
whether the Model School Project's most powerful proponent and protec-
tor would continue to be employed as Heights High's principal. But who
would win seemed almost impossible to forecast.

One thing was clear. The overabundance of contenders indicated that every segment of the community felt disenfranchised from the operation of the
Cleveland Heights schools. Even the system's staunchest supporters—white
liberals and moderate blacks—had put together a reform slate that pointedly
promised in its campaign literature to "engage in positive problem-solving
and provide the leadership that this district needs to reach its potential as a
national model of quality integrated education."

Chief among the groups that the present members of the board of education had alienated was AFT Local 795. The teachers' union usually sought to
influence the results of board elections through endorsements and contributions, but the unproductive contract negotiations of the previous spring had
given the union an especially large stake in the outcome of the 1989 race.
Two of the ten candidates were incumbents, and one of them had prominently allied himself with Moskowitz's attempt to hold the line on salary
increases.

The other incumbent was University Heights resident Judith Glickson, a
communications consultant who had first run for election in 1986 on a one-
plank platform: "no more strikes." Some of her fellow school board members suspected that Glickson had attempted to make good on her campaign
promise by leaking information to the union about board strategy for the
1988–89 contract negotiations. While these charges had never been proven,
Glickson made no secret of her prolabor sympathies. She alone objected to
the terms of the board's tightfisted contract offer, calling it an invitation

to strike. And she alone of all the 1989 candidates won Local 795's endorsement and financial backing.

The union's campaign was only a sideshow to the main event, however. Greater interest centered on the prospects of the reform slate. Only if all three members of the slate were victorious would it be possible to break the hold that vice president Maureen Weigand exerted on the board now that president Bernard Greene had decided not to seek reelection. Weigand, whose own seat was safe for two more years, already controlled two votes— her own and that of her former campaign manager, who had recently been appointed to fill a two-year vacancy.[1] Burkett's rumored adversary would soon control a third vote on the five-person board, should one of the winners be the candidate backed by many of the leaders of the local Democratic Party (of which Weigand's husband, the mayor of Cleveland Heights, was the titular head). Short of a sweep by the reform slate members, there was a strong possibility that Weigand, a capable politician in her own right, would find a way to put together a majority coalition with herself at the helm, no matter who won.

While it was fairly clear what the ascendancy of a Weigand-controlled board of education would mean for Heights High's principal, its possible significance for the Model School Project was harder to forecast. To date, the board's involvement in the project had been limited to rubber-stamping the acceptance of planning grants from the Cleveland Foundation. However, foundation officials had made clear that funds to implement Model School programs would have to come from the school district. This meant that at some future date the board of education would have to agree to allocate scarce resources to pay for the high school's actual restructuring.

In spite of the project's ultimate dependence on board approval, the coordinators paid little attention to the upcoming school board races. The Model School Project endorsed no candidates (although Fran Walter worked for the reform slate after hours). Nor did the coordinators consider how to go about winning the victors' support. Should Weigand become board president, would she encourage her colleagues to act on the high school faculty's ideas for change? That was a question the Model School coordinators felt could be addressed at a later date.

Had the coordinators taken a closer look at Weigand's track record, they might not have been so indifferent to the outcome of the election. When Weigand sought reelection to a second term in 1987, her first-term performance had sufficiently impressed Local 795 to win its endorsement. But doubts about the sincerity of her interest in the teachers' well-being had arisen in union circles during the 1988–89 contract negotiations, when she had voted to approve the board's hard-line offer. Her unenthusiastic reaction to the School Consensus Project's proposals had also called into question her openness to reform. After six years of service on the board, Weigand seemed to be suffering from what one SCP leader described as "hardening of the intellectual arteries." Other SCP members found her much too quick to greet new ideas with the negative retort "It won't work." They wondered whether Weigand had despaired of the likelihood of improving the quality of education in the district.

Indeed, Weigand had reached the conclusion that the job of school board leader was a no-win, thankless position. Only administrators possessed the power and information necessary to run the schools; yet it was the members of the board of education who took the heat for administrative decisions, fielding late-night calls from angry parents and shouldering public criticism. Having originally run for office because she was tired of complaining about the quality of education Cleveland Heights provided her four children, she had soon discovered it impossible, even as an insider, to effect major changes. As a result, she had adjusted her sights accordingly and now operated by a few simple rules: "You figure out what's important to you and chip away at it. You don't try to please everyone, because you can't. And you don't make your decisions based on the last person you talked to."

Not yet similarly disillusioned, the leaders of the School Consensus Project decided to ignore their rebuff by Weigand and the other members of the school board. They had continued meeting one Saturday a month to discuss how their reform plan could be salvaged. Eventually they reached the conclusion that the current board of education must be replaced with far-sighted leaders willing to address, rather than run from, the district's many problems. Taking the name Heights Committee for Educational Leadership (HCEL), they had begun laying plans to encourage qualified citizens to seek election to the school board in 1989. The three who made the best impression on HCEL's screening committee would be invited to form a slate that the group would resoundingly endorse. More important, HCEL would provide its candidates with a ready-made campaign organization and financial support.

In exchange, the slate would be required to commit to certain principles and courses of action. In terms of its bearing on the district's future, the most important of these pledges was the slate's agreement to conduct a national search for a new superintendent. Although this was not necessarily HCEL's intent, a serious headhunt lessened the likelihood that Lauree Gearity would win the position by default, thus averting a scenario that spelled the end of Hugh Burkett's tenure and, perhaps as a result, weaken the impetus behind the Model School Project.

At the time of its formation, HCEL was unaware of the existence of another grassroots citizens' group with similar objectives. Residents and Educators for Action (REA) shared Local 795's interest in defeating or isolating antiunionists on the school board. When the leaders of REA and HCEL became aware of one another's plans, they decided to join forces. In early August 1989, after reviewing seventy-five résumés and interviewing seventeen potential candidates, the two groups jointly announced their endorsement of a multicultural, all-male slate. One member of the slate was Jewish, another Italian-American, and the third African-American—Steve D. Bullock, the executive director of the greater Cleveland chapter of the American Red Cross and a former leader of the School Consensus Project. If elected, Bullock would become only the third African American ever to serve on the Cleveland Heights Board of Education.

The at-large election of school board members did not fully explain why the board remained so firmly under white control at a time when Cleveland Heights's black population was approaching the 40 percent mark. Doris Allen, one of the community's pioneering black activists, offered another possible explanation.

In 1970 Allen had helped to organize some of the suburb's first black residents into a loose confederation that seemed to have the makings of a political caucus. The impetus behind the formation of the Committee to Improve Community Relations was the local police's seeming indifference to the harassment black children encountered on the streets and in other public places in the suburb.[2] The members of the parents' organization had initially hoped to ensure that blacks took part in the decision-making process of every governmental and civic board in Cleveland Heights. But they ended up concentrating most of their energy on fighting inequity in the public schools.

"We felt like we didn't have the time to play electoral politics," Allen explained. "Our children's lives were too important."

Other longtime black residents of Cleveland Heights acknowledged that part of the blame for their lack of political clout lay with themselves. To pay for a home in the suburb, both heads of African-American households usually had to work (incomes for blacks being lower on average than those of their white counterparts). Consequently, many black mothers and fathers were either too busy or too worn out to become active in civic or school affairs—or so Luke Isler had observed. One of the founders of Heights Concerned Parents (HCP), Isler had encountered this phenomenon in trying to build the membership of the new advocacy group, which replaced the aging Committee to Improve Community Relations as the suburb's most prominent black parents' organization in the mid-1980s.

Unlike other African-American parents of his acquaintance, Isler, a labor agency employee, had rearranged his own priorities in order to monitor more closely the education of his three offspring. He shouldered this responsibility after discovering how his six-year-old daughter had been treated by her first-grade teacher. Having enrolled in elementary school in the middle of the 1972 school year, his daughter had been shunted to the side of the classroom, away from her white classmates, by the teacher, who apparently had not wanted to take the time to redraft her seating chart. The Islers became aware of this peculiar arrangement during a parent-teacher conference scheduled after the teacher sent a note home informing them that their daughter was having trouble adjusting to her new surroundings.

Isler's wife, who herself worked in the field of education, took the situation in hand, suggesting, politely but firmly, that a change in the seating chart could easily be accomplished. But Isler realized that other black parents felt uncomfortable challenging the practices of teachers, who often were better educated than themselves. This uneasiness often translated into the avoidance of any involvement with schools.

For these and other reasons, no black counterpart of the Heights Committee for Educational Leadership had emerged in Cleveland Heights, which meant that African-American candidates had to take on the daunting (and expensive) challenge of running for the school board without the benefit of an established campaign organization or ready sources of financial support. These built-in disadvantages had discouraged the political aspirations of all but the most ambitious or angry black residents.

Both adjectives described Barbara Madison, the militant president of Cleveland Heights–University Heights Concerned Parents, who was among the ten candidates running for the school board in 1989. Dismissed by whites and moderate blacks alike as power-hungry and divisive, Madison nonetheless understood and was able to articulate the disaffections of a silent majority: the working and lower-middle-class blacks whose children were the predominate clientele of the school district. To trace her rise to local notoriety was to better understand the long-simmering frustrations of the average African-American parent, whose alienation so perplexed the majority of Heights High's faculty.[3]

Barbara Madison, a registered nurse and the mother of two teenage sons, had first become active in school affairs when she joined Luke Isler and others as a member of Heights Concerned Parents. But she soon broke ranks with the parents' organization because she perceived it to be a sellout. Heights Concerned Parents had been formed to address the academic problems of black students. In its early years the organization decided that it could do the most good by sponsoring a series of coffees at which African-American parents new to the district could be introduced to the ins and outs of dealing with an unwieldy and frequently unresponsive school bureaucracy. But even though superintendent Moskowitz had helpfully provided HCP with the names of newcomers to the community, the group's outreach program never attracted large numbers of participants.

HCP's game plan seemed strange to Madison, who wondered why the group's middle-class leaders were reluctant to place the blame for the problems black students were experiencing where she felt it rightfully belonged—with the school system. She could not believe her ears when HCP members pointed to students who had come into the system straight from the Cleveland public schools or lower-class black parents who failed to give their children the proper encouragement as the causes of the school's performance problems.

Her sons having attended Cleveland Heights schools since their elementary days, Madison was convinced of the folly of depending on the goodwill of whites when it came to the education of one's children. The realization that white educators viewed her children quite differently than she had begun to dawn on Madison when her younger son's elementary teacher called to complain that the boy was fighting with another child in his class. When Madison confronted her son, he admitted that he had punched the other child on several occasions.

Why? Madison wanted to know.

"I hit him every time he called me a nigger," her son replied.

The incident convinced Madison of the school system's inherent racism, although at that point she hesitated to raise such a charge publicly. Then one day she received a frantic call from her older son's school informing her that he had been caught carrying a weapon. Madison rushed over to the principal's office, expecting to be confronted with a confiscated knife or gun, only to discover that the weapon in question was a slingshot. Her son was subsequently suspended for three days, a punishment Madison regarded as grossly unfair given the fact that nothing was ever done to a white student she believed had been caught selling firecrackers in the boys' bathroom around the same time.

Madison acknowledged that she could not document her charge that white youths received preferential treatment. "If they're not punished," she had learned, "there is no paper trail." She grew determined to find some way to challenge what she saw as a racist bureaucracy adept at covering its tracks.

In the spring of 1987, when no one else volunteered to run for the presidency of Heights Concerned Parents, Madison stepped forward to claim the position. That summer the board of education announced its intention of sending failing high school students to the newly created Taylor Academy in the fall. At a subsequent board meeting Madison voiced her fear that, because Taylor's enrollment was likely to be all black, the alternative school represented a return to the days of segregation. Feeling that her concerns were brushed aside by board president Bernard Greene, she "decided to go to war." Using the HCP presidency as a soapbox to promote her own views, she blasted Taylor Academy on a local radio program.

As Madison had staked out this controversial position for HCP without consulting its members, some of them asked her to cease and desist. When she refused, she was voted out of office. In defiance Madison formed the rival Cleveland Heights–University Heights Concerned Parents organization and continued her unsuccessful campaign to prevent Taylor Academy's opening. (She managed only to force the board to make enrollment at the alternative school "voluntary" rather than mandatory.)

Neither parents' organization was seriously damaged by the split. After passing a resolution in support of Taylor Academy, the HCP stalwarts soon found that they had a new status in the district. District administrators began as a matter of course to seek HCP's counsel on major decisions. ("The school system was under pressure," Luke Isler explained, "and basically needed friends anywhere it could find them.") Madison, for her part, continued making the rounds of local public affairs talk shows. An attractive and well-spoken woman who was a popular guest because of her controversial views on public education, she always seized the opportunity to broadcast a phone number so that parents who believed that their children had been unfairly treated by the Cleveland Heights public schools could call her organization for assistance.

As a student advocate, Madison specialized in arranging private meetings between aggrieved parents and school principals, to which offending teachers were summoned to defend their actions. At the start of these sessions,

Madison usually announced that she had come only in the interest of protecting the student's rights. She was not there to make trouble, she would inform the principal, adding, "That's up to you."

As Madison's tactics became general knowledge, some faculty members began to request that a union steward accompany them to these sessions, and on one occasion a teacher flatly refused to meet with her. Madison called superintendent Moskowitz in protest, only to be informed that the union contract did not require teachers to attend parent-teacher meetings they considered threatening. So be it. If the teachers would not come to her, Madison decided, she would go to them; and she began to request permission for parents to attend their children's classes. If the parents did not like the practices they witnessed, they were to write a letter of complaint to be put in the offending teacher's file.

Madison spent so much time in the district's various front offices that she was sure most of the principals in the system thought that she was on welfare. (Madison worked as a freelance nurse from three in the afternoon to eleven at night.) At one point she decided to check out for herself several standard-track classes in which her youngest son was enrolled at Heights High School. She was horrified by what she saw. The standard-track classrooms she observed were invariably overcrowded, nearly all the standard students were African Americans, and the teachers sat oblivious to the "yelling and screaming" going on around them.

Even the most outrageous behavior seemed to be tolerated, Madison concluded. In one classroom, a girl had begun painting the fingernails of a boy sitting next to her without attracting the attention of the teacher. In another class Madison noticed that most of the students had fallen asleep during the screening of a film. She asked the teacher why she had not reprimanded the students for dozing off.

"Well," she remembered the teacher had responded, "at least they were quiet."

No *wonder* black students are failing, Madison thought after completing her stint at the high school. Nonetheless, she decided not to take on the policy of ability grouping. The issue of disciplinary exclusion made a better target, she figured, as the discrimination involved in the latter practice was much more blatant.

Madison came to codify her experiences as a classroom monitor into a motto: "An informed parent is a dangerous parent." It was hard-won insights such as this that she liked to pass along to other black parents, whom she likened to rape victims because they had been so demoralized and intimidated by their encounters with the local school system. Madison, by contrast, felt that she had only to show up at certain Cleveland Heights schools and the principals would grant her whatever concessions she demanded. Ego-satisfying though her advocacy work might be, Madison was aware that it produced only case-by-case results, if that. It was in the hopes of gaining a real say over the governance of the Cleveland Heights public schools that she decided to run for the school board.

The smart money dismissed Madison's candidacy as a long shot, given her reputation as a rabble-rouser. But if Madison could be written off as an outside agitator, she was nonetheless plugged into a basic political reality. The overrepresentation of whites on the Cleveland Heights–University Heights board cast African-American parents into the untenable role of petitioners. In order to be treated as partners, they would have to wrest for themselves a greater measure of political power. Only then might the black community be able to temper the subtle white, suburban bias of the school board.

Because the Cleveland Heights system had learned the hard way about the pitfalls of openly resisting its black constituents' wishes, most African-American parents in the district had come to believe that they could afford the luxury of moderation. The present generation of Heights Concerned Parents's leaders (whose numbers included reform slate candidate Steve Bullock) preferred to work with the school system, rather than attack it.

"To blame everyone else for the ills of our kids isn't quite right," said one past president in attempting to explain HCP's temperate approach. "Besides, finger-pointing and backing people into a corner is not my style. I don't want to live my life as a bitter, angry person," she added, obviously referring to the confrontational style of Barbara Madison.

Madison, for her part, saw HCP's desire to be cooperative as a major tactical error. Collaboration simply played into the hands of the white-run board of education. In order to get away with mistreating black kids, she had concluded, the public schools needed the camouflage provided by a group of African Americans willing to support the system publicly and without question. Barbara Madison would not be counted among them.

With black parents differing greatly on the best means to resolve their problems with the schools, it was difficult for those who aspired to represent their interests to meld the African-American community into a united front. Despite his commitment to improving the academic achievement of black students, Hugh Burkett made no attempt to rally the support of black parents for the Model School campaign. Nor did he attempt to explain the connection between his crackdown on tardiness, truancy, and troublemaking

and his desire to increase the uninterrupted time students spent in meaningful contact with their teachers. Instead he succeeded in alienating such vocal
proponents of change as Barbara Madison.

Madison should have been a natural ally of the principal in his plans to
reshape Heights High into a school where all students—not just a white elite
—received a rigorous academic education; but the black activist considered
Burkett an "idiot." She reached this conclusion after a particularly frustrating encounter with him. Madison had made an appointment to talk to
Burkett about the union-mandated practice of sending tardy students to an
isolation room. It did not make sense to her that the punishment for missing
the start of class was being compelled to miss the *entire* class. The day of the
meeting she called the high school to tell Burkett that she was going to be a
few minutes late. "I hope we can still keep the appointment," she said.
When Burkett assured her he would wait, she informed him that she was
pulling his leg. He merely laughed, missing what Madison felt to be the
whole point of the exercise.

Instead of seeking to make allies of disaffected black parents, the constituency most likely to support his school restructuring plans, Burkett kept the
Model School Project largely under wraps. Only when he began eyeing the
superintendency did he belatedly attempt to build a support base for himself
and the project among the affluent white liberals and moderate, middle-class
blacks whose willingness to participate in such school-improvement efforts
as the School Consensus Project and Heights Committee for Educational
Leadership indicated a certain interest in reform.[4] During the fall of 1989,
Burkett began to schedule talks with the predominately white PTAs in each
of the district's elementary and middle schools. Running well into the
winter—a stretch of time that coincided with the district's search for a new
superintendent—these presentations served as an opportunity to introduce
the district's traditional supporters to the Model School Project and the
promise it held for improved student achievement at Heights High.

Burkett also made himself available to the HCEL reform slate, volunteering to brief the three school board candidates about conditions at the high
school so that they could speak authoritatively about Heights High's problems during the campaign.

The effort made by those interested in seeing three progressive and like-
minded leaders elected to the Cleveland Heights–University Heights Board
of Education came to naught, however. The evening of November 7, 1989,
Hugh Burkett stayed up late to listen to the election returns, only to learn
that the voters had denied HCEL its hoped-for sweep. While slate members

Steve Bullock and Stuart M. Klein, a professor of labor-management relations at Cleveland State University, proved to be successful vote getters, it
was maverick Judith Glickson who won the third seat on the board of education. Maureen Weigand's potential ally ran fourth, while Barbara Madison
finished third from last in a field of ten.[5]

The election boiled down to a draw: neither the proponents of change
nor the protectors of the status quo had gained clear control of the board. It
now appeared that the most important decision facing the new board—a
decision that had great bearing on the future of the Model School Project—
would end up being negotiated behind closed doors in a smoke-filled room.
Whichever faction of the board succeeded in putting together three votes
would name the next superintendent of schools.

15

A Failure to Communicate

*Fundamental changes cannot occur unless those who have control
over the resources of the organization (the moral and symbolic . . . as
well as the financial and physical . . .) can be persuaded to use their
control in ways that support the change.*

—PHILLIP C. SCHLECTY
Schools for the Twenty-first Century, 1990

Three weekends after the conclusion of the eighth and final faculty retreat,
Hugh Burkett, Cas McBride, and Steve Young left the motel where they
had gathered to resume designing a model school and drove into Cleveland
Heights to the board of education building. They arrived at Miramar a little
after 10:00 A.M. and were soon joined in the lobby by Bill Thomas and Fran
Walter. Aware that the members of the new school board were meeting in
executive session only a wall's breadth away to consider whether to conduct
a national search for superintendent, the group stood around nervously. At
10:36 McBride asked, "If you have to wait fifteen minutes before walking
out on a professor who's late, how long do you have to wait for a board of
education?"

At Burkett's urging, the coordinators had scheduled a meeting for 10:30
that morning—Saturday, February 3, 1990—to introduce the new school
board to the details of the Model School Project. The imminence of the
performance was not the only reason for the self-conscious small talk. The

184

coordinators were angry with one another, and Burkett was sitting on an uncomfortable secret. Only Fran and Frank Walter knew that in two days Burkett would be flying to Virginia to interview for a job as area superintendent of the Prince William County public schools.

The previous evening at the motel, Burkett, McBride, and Young had begun to refine the model school design in response to the retreat groups' suggestions. They intended to devote the weekend to readying the model school's conceptual framework for review by the entire Heights High faculty. Thomas and Walter had been conspicuous by their absence, having been banned from the proceedings by Steve Young. Fed up with Walter's and Thomas's volubility—a tendency that had only grown more wearisome in his eyes when, the retreats now ended, the project leaders began to debate a plan of action—Young had informed the two coordinators point-blank that he thought it would be more efficient if the conceptualizing of the framework were done by a group smaller than five. Walter and Thomas were so stunned by the baldness of Young's put-down that they had accepted without protest his suggestion that they come out to the motel on Sunday to approve the finished design. But weeks later they still harbored grudges against him.

Thomas assuaged his hurt feelings in displays of obstreperousness. One outburst came as the coordinators were preparing for their presentation to the school board. When the discussion turned to the kinds of supportive actions the coordinators wanted to ask the board members to take on behalf of the Model School Project, Thomas suggested that they demand to be allowed to interview and evaluate candidates for the superintendency to ensure that an educator sympathetic to the concepts of site-based management and shared decision making was hired. The others thought such a confrontation unnecessary and ill advised. Fran Walter reminded Thomas that, in accordance with their campaign pledge to foster an open decision-making process, new board members Steve Bullock and Stuart Klein had "promised that everyone including my mother is going to be involved" in the search. Thomas threatened to issue his demand anyway when it was his turn to address the board.

Instead of licking her wounds openly, as Thomas had, Walter distanced herself from the others. Walter had traditionally acted as the group's spark plug. It was she, for example, who had pressed the coordinators to begin serious future planning as soon as the final retreat was scheduled. (Walter's conscience was bothering her. She felt bad that the group had been "frittering" away costly release time on details.)

Attempting to compensate in one blow for not having built external support for the restructuring project, the coordinators, at Walter's urging, went on to conceive a whirlwind outreach campaign. They decided that Thomas would organize one or two mini-retreats for the high school's secretaries, custodians, and security monitors; Young would attend selected classes to ask students to fill out a one-page questionnaire listing their most pressing concerns; and McBride would brief central-office administrators and building principals on the project's progress at a district-level administrators' meeting. Always a glutton for hard work, Walter volunteered to call a dozen or so community organizations and schedule a time for the group to make a formal presentation about the Model School Project to each.

Although she soon discovered that it was impossible to get an immediate hearing with any local organization, Walter kept her troubles to herself. She would be darned if she let the other coordinators know that she needed help. As a result, the five members of the board of education were practically the only community leaders to be made aware of the project's existence and objectives.

Ten minutes after the Model School presentation to the board of education was scheduled to begin, the door of the boardroom finally swung open, and the contingent from the high school was invited to enter. Inside, the group found the members of the board and the interim superintendent seated imposingly on a dais. As the project leaders took their seats, board member Judith Glickson acknowledged their presence not with words of welcome but with a brusque inquiry as to which member of the high school contingent was emceeing the presentation.

In January Glickson had been elected president of the Cleveland Heights–University Heights Board of Education, beating out longtime opponent Maureen Weigand for the leadership position. Reform slate members Bullock and Klein had given the sixty-one-year-old Glickson the votes she needed to win. This was an ironic turn of events. Although the labor-oriented Residents and Educators for Action had wanted Glickson to become a member of the reform slate they jointly endorsed with Heights Committee for Educational Leadership, HCEL's members had vetoed her inclusion because they perceived her to act erratically. Bullock and Klein, who themselves lacked the votes to gain the board presidency, had been forced to choose between what their supporters saw as Glickson's unpredictability and Weigand's consistent nay-saying.

Their gamble on Glickson backfired almost immediately. While the Model School Project leaders waited outside in the hall, the new board president put a stop to Bullock and Klein's attempts to persuade the district to conduct a national search for superintendent. Faced with impending contract negotiations with the teachers' union and a decision as to whether to place a new tax proposal on the ballot, the district could not afford to conduct a lengthy search, Glickson argued. The schools needed a superintendent who could hit the ground running. "Besides," Klein remembered that Glickson had warned, "the last time we conducted a national search, we got Irv." Weigand and her board ally agreed with Glickson's recommendation that only internal candidates be considered.

Some HCEL insiders would later speculate that Weigand had sided with Glickson for the first time in recent memory against political rivals Bullock and Klein in order to make the latter look like "chumps." But Klein thought he detected a feminist agenda behind the move to restrict the pool of prospective candidates. "It was a woman thing," he concluded. The three female members of the board clearly wanted Lauree Gearity for superintendent. "They saw a competent woman, and they wanted to give her a chance. Steve and I were left sucking our thumbs."

Unaware of this fateful development, the coordinators threw themselves into the task of selling the board on the merits of restructuring Heights High School. McBride spoke first. She related the chronology of the project, noting with pride that 80 percent of the faculty—124 teachers, to be exact—had participated in the recently concluded retreats. Young then described the consensus-building activities planned for the remainder of the school year.

In March, Young explained, the coordinators planned to present a schematic of the model school framework and a written explanation of its components to two elected representatives of each retreat group, who would be asked to critique the framework at an all-day conference. This "super-retreat" would serve as a reality check. If it turned out that a representative sampling of teachers could not live with certain aspects of the model school design, the coordinators would have time to modify the conceptual framework before its official unveiling to the rest of the faculty at a workshop in early April.

Young explained that the workshop would run for two weeks in a multipurpose meeting room at the high school. This would give Heights High teachers the chance to examine the schematic and accompanying explanation at their leisure during their planning and lunch periods. If they had questions or comments, they would be encouraged to post them in writing on a large-scale version of the schematic or to make them known to the coordinators, at least one of whom would be on duty every period of the day. After the workshop, the project leaders would use the criticism received to once again refine the model school framework, which would then be taken back to the faculty for final review.

At this point in the plan the coordinators had allowed their imaginations to soar. They fantasized that the revised framework would be approved by acclamation at a "convention"—complete with balloons, placards, and a keynote address by an educational reformer of the stature of Ted Sizer or Al Shanker—to be held in late spring. The convention would be capped by a formal dance that would take place under twinkling lights in Heights High's courtyard. (Young had been given the assignment of finding just the right rock band. As he made no secret of his admiration for the hedonistic lyrics of singer Jimmy Buffett, he was thought to be knowledgeable about such things.)

After the convention, the faculty would be divided into task forces responsible for transforming the conceptual framework into detailed program designs. Assuming that some task forces would be willing to work over the summer, certain aspects of the model school could begin to be implemented in the fall of 1990. It was a beautiful dream that the coordinators liked to visit again and again, but in his presentation to the board, Young downplayed the plan's more fanciful elements. Instead he stressed that one of the project's major objectives was to alter the way decisions were traditionally made in the school district.

How were the coordinators chosen? Stu Klein interrupted, taking McBride up on her invitation to board members to ask questions at any point during the presentation. Although Klein's query about the representativeness of the project's leadership seemed to have come from out of the blue, Fran Walter was not surprised to see Klein home in on a decision that had *not* been made in consultation with the high school faculty. She had heard through the grapevine of his concern that the Model School Project represented the viewpoint of only a limited number of teachers, and she suspected that Allan Wolf's soured experience as project manager had something to do with his brother-in-law's impression, which she attempted to alter with a detailed explanation of how the coordinators had been drawn from the ranks of the study teams.[1]

When the presentation resumed, it was Bill Thomas's turn to speak. He described the ways in which the Model School Project hoped to improve the high school's tenuous relationships with parents and community members—and said nothing about his desire to see teachers involved in the selection of the next superintendent. Walter followed Thomas with an explanation of the kinds of innovations that would best serve to nurture students' self-esteem and develop their critical-thinking skills.

During Thomas's portion of the presentation, Judith Glickson spoke up. "A thought came to me," she said. "The high school has produced a lot of great alumni. Maybe you could build a sense of pride with an active alumni association."

"There have been a number of suggestions about starting an alumni association," Thomas said. "It's a good idea, but a lot of kids have trouble relating to the graduates of the 1950s and 1960s."

Glickson did not catch Thomas's allusion to the changed racial makeup of the high school's student body. "I graduated with the class of '46," she protested. "It was a *wonderful* class."

The new board president also seemed to misinterpret the aims of school restructuring, judging by her response to the plea with which emcee McBride concluded the presentation.

"Change is scary," McBride summarized. "It means having to acknowledge that what we are doing is not necessarily successful and that we need to do things differently. You can best support what we're trying to do with your own openness to change, whether that be in the formulation of new policies, the negotiation of the new teachers' contract, or"—here she made a concession to Thomas—"your choice of superintendents. As you are the official representatives of the community, we need . . . we *beg* you . . . for your support."

"You know you have that," Glickson responded. She immediately qualified her statement by adding, "Unless you mean financially." Then she mentally dismissed the group. "Please get back to us," she said, "when you decide what you're going to do about the building."

The coordinators had made no mention of capital improvement plans. An astonished Hugh Burkett could only conclude that Glickson had little conception of the nature of the endeavor to which she had pledged her support.

Board member Maureen Weigand, on the other hand, understood enough about the project's objectives to spot a potential problem. "The project implies a great deal of change in working conditions," she noted when it was her turn to speak. "Is the bargaining unit involved enough in the project to support these changes?"

"Good question," Fran Walter said, revealing her skepticism about her fellow stewards' interest in reform.

"Does the leadership of the bargaining unit understand what you're proposing?" Weigand persisted. Despite her upbringing as the child of a labor organizer and her former career as a first-grade teacher, Weigand had learned during her tenure on the school board to view teachers' unions with a jaundiced eye. The actions of Local 795's officers invariably impressed her as having little to do with the education of children and everything to do with enhancing the union's power.

"May I read a paragraph to you from Dan MacDonald, future vice president of the union?" said Steve Young in response to Weigand's need for assurance.

"You know that?" asked Weigand, impressed with the English teacher's possession of this piece of common knowledge. Lack of independent information on which to base decisions was one of Weigand's most serious complaints about the largely volunteer school board job. Too pressed for time by career and family obligations to do much homework, school board members were of necessity forced to rely on data and analysis supplied by the central administration, however one-sided or incomplete that information might be.

"We predict the future," Young joked, as he searched his notes for a quote from the latest issue of the chief steward's newsletter. He then proceeded to read it aloud.

"I continue to urge your support of Model High School," MacDonald had written, garbling the name of the project. "We need a process by which each of us can share our ideas to help Heights students. Model High School will hopefully implement a more responsive process than we currently have."

Young's dramatic reading was disingenuous. The union's power to quash changes in working conditions of which it did not approve posed a serious challenge to the teachers' ability to implement desired innovations. The portion of MacDonald's rumination that Young did not quote made the threat of obstructionism quite clear. "As to the Model High School super committee," MacDonald harrumphed, "I worry and have all along that Hugh Burkett is an active member of all Model High Schools. Be aware that no matter how subtle his imprint is on the Model High School. . . . The super committee . . . [is] about to give birth to an idea. . . . Make it liveable and not something that will be assaulted by grievances for the next decade."

Outmaneuvered, Weigand backed down from her line of questioning. "You talk to us about making a careful choice for superintendent," she said. "Let me ask something from you—remember the same thing when you elect your union stewards."

"If you've got the masses to the point of commitment, I don't worry about the union president," Steve Bullock weighed in. His reaction to the presentation as a whole had reflected a similar can-do spirit. "This is so exciting for me," he had said earlier, "for selfish reasons. These are my goals. I have lots of questions about how we could better support this, including with dollars."

"Any afternoon," Young informed Bullock, "you can find us meeting at the high school."

"I'll be over," Bullock said, making a promise that he did not keep.

When the board completed its questioning, Lauree Gearity spoke for the first time. "You know you'll be invited back," she said, indicating to the group that its allotted forty-five minutes had come to an end.

Outside in the lobby, Burkett gave his colleagues a rare compliment. "You made me proud," he said. But it was not clear what the coordinators had accomplished. Of the five board members, Bullock was the only one to embrace without apparent reservation the project's objectives. Taking her cue from her superiors, Lauree Gearity had said nothing to indicate whether or not she supported the goals of the Model School Project. But Stu Klein suspected that Gearity was uncomfortable with both the untraditional design of the model school and the prospect of allowing the high school to move away from central-office control. Klein, too, harbored doubts about the feasibility of site-based management councils. Having consulted for various public schools on labor-management issues, he had gained an appreciation of the difficulty of, first, engaging the interest of parents in governance and, then, reining in their emotionalism.

While she considered herself sympathetic to the concept of site-based management, Maureen Weigand was having a hard time disentangling the Model School Project agenda from that of Hugh Burkett, in whom she had lost confidence. Weigand later admitted that members of the school board and central administration had probably lost sight of the value of the Model School proposals because of this confusion. As a result, the board's stance toward the restructuring project remained consistently ambivalent. Its members neither enthusiastically promoted nor vigorously opposed it.

This display of fence-sitting was precisely the outcome predicted by the only coordinator who made a point of following district-level politics.

"The board's attitude is always wait and see," Fran Walter had warned her colleagues. "It saves energy. They're masters at letting things die a slow death."

16

Masters of a Slow Death

By conducting "local experiments," making advanced policy statements, doing studies [and] giving technical and administrative explanations as to why more change was not practicable . . . the board . . .
has . . . been able to absorb virtually every major protest that has
been made.

—DAVID ROGERS
*110 Livingston Street: Politics and Bureaucracy
in the New York City Schools,* 1968

The board of education's history of resistance to previous proposals for
sweeping educational reform shed light on the obstacles awaiting the Model
School Project leaders. On past occasions when the need to take action was
similarly urgent, the board's impulse to preserve the status quo—a finely
tuned responsiveness to community pressure deriving from the need for
votes at reelection time—had usually prevailed. Such was certainly the case
during the turbulent transitional period in which the Cleveland Heights
schools were integrated.

On average only thirty or so African-American families had moved into
Cleveland Heights each year between 1960 and 1970. Yet the opposition
mounted against this modest influx resembled the civil rights strife making
headlines in the South. It was not uncommon for the newcomers to be
snubbed by their next-door neighbors for years, or to wake up and find their
windows broken and paint splashed on their cars. Cases of racist-inspired

arson and bombings mounted in numbers sufficiently great to give Cleveland Heights the unofficial nickname of the "Bombing Capital of the North."

The violence shamed other residents into taking action. Concerned citizens organized block clubs to welcome newly arriving blacks, and they asked the Cleveland Heights–University Heights Board of Education to form a human relations task force that would advise the school system on ways to smooth the onrush of integration.

The members of the resulting lay committee decided that the school board should take a firm stand against discrimination. In 1966 the task force recommended to the board that it adopt a progressive human relations policy. The proposed policy called for the recruitment of new teachers only from institutions of higher education whose admissions policies conformed with civil rights legislation; the letting of service contracts only with firms conforming to fair employment practices; and the purchase of textbooks restricted to those publishers whose lists were free of prejudice.

The hard-hitting policy was the product of two years of deliberation. But it took only a few months to dismantle it. Over the course of three noisy public hearings, during which time twelve hundred residents signed petitions opposing these measures, the board of education completely rewrote the policy statement, excising the offending clauses. The document that was finally approved espoused such toothless goals as a recommendation that the district's staff should be "generally representative of the diverse world our students will encounter as adults."

The pressures on the board to moderate its stand on human relations could be seen in the adverse public reaction to a section in the original policy draft advocating an aggressive minority recruitment program. The questionable passage stated that new teachers would be assisted in obtaining housing and that only those landlords who operated in accordance with fair housing principles would be permitted to list property with the schools. When the school superintendent was accused by audience members at one public hearing of "going into the real estate business," he pointed out that the school district had always maintained a list of available housing. The district now needed to police the list, he explained, because several home owners on it had denied teachers the right to rent or buy because of their race or religion. The superintendent's explanation did not quiet the audience's objections. One citizen charged that the policy statement smacked of "Communist-style" social engineering. "Let's keep our neighborhoods nice," he commanded.

Yet the dismantling of the human relations policy could not be attributed entirely to community pressure. The school board was a willing partner in the process, as the businessman who was then board president would make clear twenty-five years later when he felt free to voice his suspicion that the human relations policy had been a "bill of goods" foisted on the school system by those with an interest in "steering home sales to Negroes." Judging by contemporaneous newspaper accounts of the proceedings, some of the board president's colleagues had also shared the sentiments of the outraged whites who attended the public hearings. The eagerness with which "the board took its policy, already completely revised once since its first presentation, and revised it again in front of an audience of 500, incorporating many of the changes which had been suggested by members of the audience," spoke volumes about the segments of the community to which the school board paid its greatest allegiance.

Even the liberal members of this particular board of education displayed a tendency to frame minority issues from a white perspective. When the board member who cochaired the human relations task force gave a progress report to a sister organization in early 1966, she lamented the difficulties that the Cleveland Heights schools had encountered in attempting to recruit minority teachers. But her elaboration of the problem betrayed the bias of the Cleveland Heights system. "'Up until three years ago they couldn't find a Negro who would fit in,'" the minutes of the meeting quoted the board member as explaining. She offered two reasons for this situation—according to the minutes: "1. She wanted the first Negro to be equal to or superior to the white teachers on the staff. 2. It's a little silly to hire teachers if in spite of an 'all out effort' you could not get them a place to live."

Laxity on the issue of minority hiring was to pit the all-white board of education against the interests of its African-American constituents again in the mid-1970s. At the time the number of black students enrolled in the district had reached nearly 30 percent. Persons of color accounted for only about 5 percent of the teaching staff. In the eyes of the Committee to Improve Community Relations, the shortage of black role models was one of several trends and practices adversely affecting the equitable operation of Cleveland Heights public schools.

The trailblazing parents' organization (whose members included Lee Road homeowner Doris Allen and her neighbors Bernice and Lacy Lott) had first become involved with the schools because of an outbreak of racially related fights at Heights High. After black parents, with the permission of the high school administration, began patrolling the hallways, the fights stopped. But CICR's attempt to resolve the problem did not end there.

When its members investigated the reasons why black students were acting up, they determined that the troublemakers had cause. Black students suffered from what one member of the Committee to Improve Community Relations characterized at the time as "benign administrative neglect."

The building and central-office administrators with whom CICR members subsequently met were sympathetic but largely unresponsive to the group's requests for new programs and policies that would nurture black students' self-esteem. Lacking other alternatives, the leaders of CICR decided to make their dissatisfaction public. In June 1974 they presented the board of education with a comprehensive list of demands representing what CICR claimed to be the wishes of three hundred black families with children in the school system.

In addition to petitioning the board to hire more black teachers, the Committee to Improve Community Relations called for mandatory black studies, training in black history and culture for all teachers and administrators, and the recognition of Martin Luther King Jr.'s birthday as an official Black Achievement Day. CICR also demanded the elimination of dual standards of punishment for black and white students, an end to racist remarks and actions on the part of staff, and the reevaluation of Heights High's guidance department (which had gained a bad reputation among black parents for its alleged practice of advising black students that they were not college material).

The board's written response to CICR's demands was presented at a public meeting in midsummer. The board members agreed to form a lay committee or devise "some other in-depth process" to evaluate the guidance department and to offer teacher training in black history and culture beginning in the fall. They pointed out that the system's human relations policy condemned racial or ethnic slurs and that a reevaluation of disciplinary procedures was already under way. The concept of mandatory black studies was rejected out of hand.

As an alternative to making King's birthday an official school holiday, the board suggested the establishment of a Recognition Week that would acknowledge the contributions of all races and cultures.[1] It also downplayed the importance of minority recruitment. "Last year and this year 40 percent of the new teachers hired have been black," the board's statement noted. "This represents an increase of fourteen black teachers in 1973–74 and twelve black teachers in 1974–75. [However], we do not have a racial quota. We have a quality quota of 100 percent to which we rigidly adhere."

The leaders of the Committee to Improve Community Relations felt as if they had been stonewalled. That fall the parents' organization took its case to the U.S. Department of Justice, asking for an investigation into racial discrimination by the Cleveland Heights public schools. "We have not charged the board of education with willful discrimination against blacks, but the results of institutional racism have the same effect," CICR's press statement read. "Whether by design or accident, black students are being denied equal opportunity of education and services."

By January 1975 the board of education had agreed to meet with the Committee to Improve Community Relations in the presence of a mediator from the community relations service of the Justice Department. These high-level talks—and the media's continuing scrutiny of them—produced the results that CICR desired. In April the Cleveland Heights–University Heights Board of Education announced that it had executed a written agreement with the parents' organization. The keystone of the agreement was the board's promise to increase minority staff employment to 15 percent by 1980. The board also agreed that CICR representatives would assist the social studies department at Heights High in preparing a new course outline for U.S. history that would incorporate materials describing the history and contributions of black Americans. Furthermore, January 15th—King's birthday—was to be recognized henceforth as an official school holiday, and charges of racist behavior of staff members were now to be investigated promptly by the administration, with written warnings issued to those employees found guilty. On paper at least, CICR had gained the changes it sought.

Getting the school system to honor its promises was a different matter. The agreement stipulated that representatives of the board of education would meet annually with the Committee to Improve Community Relations to discuss the district's progress in recruiting black teachers. Every year CICR members would troop into the superintendent's office and hear the same story about the difficulties of finding qualified black educators. By the 1980 deadline, blacks constituted only 13 percent of the district's total professional staff, and it had become clear to CICR member Lacy Lott that the group's dream, which was to see minority employment in the district reach a level commensurate with minority enrollment, would remain elusive.

Even so, Lott perceived that CICR's written agreement with the board of education, which had had no official termination date, was an albatross around the necks of the district's succession of superintendents. It was Lott's opinion that Al Abramovitz had attempted to disentangle the district from the agreement by endorsing the formation in 1984 of a potential organizational rival, Heights Concerned Parents. In Lott's version of events, Abramovitz did not necessarily share HCP's interest in doing something to reverse the failure rates of black students. Rather, he had an ulterior motive—that of wanting to see a new advocacy organization (with which the district had signed no agreement) replace CICR as the leading voice for black parents' concerns. This scenario had in fact taken place. By the end of the 1980s CICR's influence had dwindled, not only because of the rise to prominence of Heights Concerned Parents, but also because its members no longer had an immediate stake in the public schools. Their children had graduated.

In addition to enforcing the school district's commitment to minority hiring, CICR's most lasting contribution was to knock down the color barrier that stood in the way of African-American representation on the Cleveland Heights–University Heights Board of Education. In the fall of 1974, CICR spokesperson Bernice Lott was appointed to fill a board vacancy, making her the first black ever to sit on the school board.[2] When she eventually won the seat outright, she became the first black woman ever to serve in an elected capacity in Cleveland Heights. According to her fellow school board members, it was Lott who quietly encouraged the district to develop a plan during the mid-1970s to reverse the increasing segregation of its schools.

Once again, however, the white-dominated board proved itself unable to swallow the recommended remedies. To a great extent, the board's interest in combating racial isolation had been motivated by fear. The National Association for the Advancement of Colored People was filing—and winning—federal discrimination suits throughout the North against school districts that the NAACP believed guilty of de facto segregation (segregation arising not from legislative mandate but from housing patterns, economic disparity, and social prejudice). At the time, the percentage of minority students enrolled in the local elementary schools ranged from 9 percent at Belvoir school in University Heights to 69 percent at Boulevard school in Cleveland Heights.

Fearful that, should the district become the target of a lawsuit, the courts might view this imbalance as justification for imposing an unpopular and costly desegregation plan, the board of education deemed it wise to try to head off the nightmare of federal control. In December 1976 it formed a lay committee to recommend the best means for the system to desegregate. One evening shortly thereafter, a shotgun blast shattered the front window of the home of the board member who had made the motion to authorize the desegregation study. Fortunately, no one was injured, but the board member could not help seeing the incident as a warning.

The following April the lay committee returned with two different plans for reassigning children throughout the system's eleven elementary schools, neither of which could be accomplished without busing. The estimated cost of either plan hovered around $1 million. The recommendations elicited little reaction from the black community, one committee member recollected. The adoptive white father of minority children, he sensed that black parents felt they were powerless to affect the final decision, given their still small numbers in the suburb as a whole. Believing that in the final analysis the white-dominated board would act to protect its own self-interest, they had resigned themselves, he believed, to living with an outcome that was probably not going to be advantageous for their children.

White parents, on the other hand, greeted the proposals with an outpouring of anger, arguing that desegregation spelled the end of the sacrosanct "neighborhood" school to which their children could walk. "I don't want the school board to decide what social atmosphere is best for my children," said a Belvoir parent at one of three public hearings held to discuss the desegregation recommendations. "I chose the community and school I wanted my children to attend when I bought my house." Highly aware that the most vociferous objections were coming from the residents of predominately white University Heights, whose votes played a critical role in the passage of school levies, board members tabled action on the report. They explained that they needed more time to assess such costly remedies.

When assistant superintendent Albert Abramovitz became superintendent in early 1978 (after his predecessor was fired), he began looking for a resolution to the impasse. Revealing himself to be a master politician who understood how to achieve consensus by preselling his ideas to leaders throughout the community, Abramovitz put together a compromise plan within six weeks. It called for the closing of a primary school in a predominately black neighborhood, the redistricting of several other K–6 buildings (which required a limited amount of busing, primarily of students from black neighborhoods), and the creation of two magnet elementary schools offering specialized curriculum and instruction to which children from throughout the district would theoretically be attracted on a voluntary basis. Belvoir, which was located in a largely Jewish neighborhood in University Heights and had the highest percentage of white students of any elementary school in the district, was chosen as the site for the first magnet program.

Boulevard school in Cleveland Heights, which was predominately black, became the second magnet school.

As it happened, Lauree Gearity, who was then principal of Northwood elementary school in University Heights, had already begun investigating the concept of magnet schools on the district's behalf with the aid of a federal grant. She seemed the logical choice to design the Belvoir magnet, and her capable handling of this tricky assignment gave a boost to her administrative career. Gearity, it turned out, had a gift for group process. She shrewdly quieted opposition to what amounted to Belvoir's overnight integration by involving parents in each step of the redesign.[3] Although some Belvoir families made good on their threat to move out of the district should black children be encouraged to attend their neighborhood school, the new magnet program proved attractive to other parents. When Belvoir opened as a magnet in the fall of 1978, it boasted 575 pupils, an enrollment far surpassing that of any other elementary school in the district. Twenty-five percent of the magnet's enrollees were black.[4]

But the district's achievement in restoring the racial balance of its schools was short-lived. By the time Lauree Gearity moved over to Miramar, having cemented her reputation as a talented administrator by making sure that Belvoir never lacked for resources or excellent teachers, the continuing effects of white flight had undermined the attempt to maintain integration. By the late 1980s only one of the district's eleven elementary schools had less than a 50 percent minority enrollment; at the Belvoir and Boulevard magnets, black children accounted for 51.3 and 68.9 percent of the student body, respectively.

If Gearity's magnet program had failed in its mission to stem white flight, her experiences in soft-selling voluntary desegregation reconfirmed a lesson that she had already taken to heart during her many years of dealing with angry or upset mothers and fathers: in the end, parents, not educators, must be allowed to have the final say in determining what is best for their children. A truism especially applicable to the primary years, it was yet another philosophical point on which she and Hugh Burkett differed, as the latter was a firm believer in the primacy of the professional educator. But this belief was to put her in good stead with the members of the 1990–91 board of education, who, despite the divergence of their politics, were able to agree on at least one point: that a demonstrated commitment to working with parents and residents was one of the major attributes they sought in a new superintendent.

Four days after the Model School coordinators asked the board to take care in choosing the next superintendent, Frank Walter went to what he expected would be a routine board of education meeting. A discussion of the district's budget was the only announced item on the agenda. The meeting started at 7:30 P.M., and when Walter arrived at 7:55, he was startled to discover at the front of the boardroom a blackboard on which was written a list of the qualifications of the ideal candidate for superintendent. The items listed included budgeting expertise, experience in curriculum and program development, knowledge of contract negotiations, a history of commitment to the Cleveland Heights schools, an appreciation of cultural diversity, and a willingness to work with residents and staff.

In the view of the three female members of the board, Dr. Lauree P. Gearity was the educator who best exemplified these qualities, and by the time Walter arrived at the meeting, her appointment as superintendent had already been announced by Judith Glickson (whom Gearity largely credited for her promotion). Gearity was offered a three-year contract starting at $82,000 a year, a decision that Klein and Bullock had decided to make unanimous when they realized that they had been outvoted.

Walter was astonished by the appointment. He could think of no reason a school district of the stature of Cleveland Heights could not have had its pick of outstanding superintendents. It looked as if the Cleveland Heights–University Heights Board of Education had once again opted for expedience over excellence.

Later, after he recovered from his surprise, Walter tried to figure out the board's rationale. He decided that the members must have been operating according to what he called the "pendulum theory" of hiring superintendents. In order to avoid repeating the mistake that had been Irv Moskowitz's unproductive tenure, the board had looked for someone who was his diametrical opposite. It was easy for Walter to tick off a half-dozen obvious differences between Moskowitz and his successor. Irv was, of course, a male, and Lauree was a female (a consideration, Walter believed, of no small importance to the three women on the board). Irv was a "loosey-goosey" manager, in Walter's opinion, while Lauree was no-nonsense and fiscally tightfisted. Irv had no prior experience in dealing with unions; Lauree knew how "to cut a deal, if that was in her best interests." Irv had abandoned the school system after only three years of service; Lauree had clearly made a lifelong commitment to the district.

Fran Walter's interpretation of events, on the other hand, tended more toward the conspiratorial. She sensed the fine hand of Glenn Altschuld in Judith Glickson's championship of Lauree Gearity, who even as interim superintendent had informed the union that she was carefully laying aside what Altschuld described in a November 1989 memorandum to Local 795's executive board as "a saved money amount to fund a raise in January, 1991." Indeed, Glickson had made a special point of praising Gearity's ability to work harmoniously with the teachers' union in explaining to the media the reasons why the board had not seriously considered any other candidates. "It boiled down to the fact Dr. Gearity fit all our criteria," Glickson said. "We were comfortable with her and satisfied with her performance thus far. Morale among teachers has gone up and relationships with employees have done an about-face. Dr. Gearity has set a positive tone for the district, and we wanted to continue along that line."

Maureen Weigand agreed that change was unnecessary. "When I looked at what I thought were important qualifications," she told reporters, "maintaining stability and continuity were tops."

17

The Walkout

The "parents association" . . . is essentially a middle-class device and is not consonant with the style of low-income, poorly educated minority parents.

—MARIO FANTINI ET AL.
Community Control and the Urban School, 1970

The Model School coordinators greeted the news of Gearity's appointment to the superintendency with varying degrees of equanimity. When a crestfallen Fran Walter walked into the Model School offices the morning after the February 7th board meeting, Steve Young, remembering that the librarian had once called Gearity's frumpiness an affront to the professional image of the school system, used the remark to poke a little fun at both of the women. "When are you taking Lauree shopping?" Young teased.

McBride shared Young's sense of gallows humor about the news. As Thomas handed out copies of a feature story on the Model School Project published in the suburban newspaper that morning, she deadpanned: "Staple it to my résumé."

"Which we are all now quickly preparing," Walter responded, speaking in earnest. Only she knew that Hugh Burkett might soon receive a job offer from the Prince William County schools, whose superintendent was planning to fly to Cleveland the following week to interview Burkett's colleagues. Now that Gearity had been named chief executive in Cleveland

Heights, it seemed almost certain that Burkett would accept the offer, should it be forthcoming. Walter intimated as much to her colleagues. "I think Hugh's degree of discomfort with Lauree's being superintendent will be pretty high," she warned.

Although Walter feared that Burkett's departure would prompt a rapid decline in the district, neither Young nor McBride found the prospect of a change in the high school's administration particularly alarming.

"I know it's difficult to foretell the future or even to plan for contingencies, but we have to think about what happens to the project if he leaves," Young said, without a hint of gloom. "At the very least we should be involved in interviewing his replacement."

"Would you be willing to try to talk Hugh into the viewpoint that leaving is unacceptable?" asked Walter. "I don't know how integral you feel he is to the success of the Model School Project."

"I think he's integral," Young responded. "But, while I'm willing to say to him that the project will move along a lot faster if he's here, who are we to say he can't leave if Lauree riles him up?"

Walter saw things differently. "It is so self-indulgent to say that I don't get along with so-and-so, so I'll let everything get flushed down the toilet," she protested. "A lot of people's aspirations and dreams are hanging on a personality conflict."

"How one would characterize his decision to leave," McBride interjected, "depends on whether you believe in the American system, where everyone is out for himself, or the Japanese system, where you need to honor your promises.

"Anyway," she continued, "Hugh is facing a staff who are real good at talking at retreats, but are willing to make changes only as long as it doesn't upset what they've been doing for the past fifteen years. Can we ask him to make a commitment to one hundred and fifty people like that?"

"I don't believe most of the teachers are going to throw themselves in front of the train of restructuring and say stop," Walter said incredulously. "Are we the *only* people who want things to change?"

"No," McBride responded, "*we're* the people who want everyone *else* to change."

"What does it say about someone," Walter persisted, "when they realize, 'Uh, oh, here comes the hard part,' so they leave and go somewhere else and pump other people up?"

"Throw that up to Hugh, then," Young suggested.

McBride disagreed. "The only thing we can say to him is that he's integral, and that the project will go in a different direction if he leaves, and that people have built on their trust of him personally," she argued. "Those are facts, although I don't know that I would present to him the conclusion I would draw from those facts."

"I would," Walter said. "I guess I'm in a more ranting and raving mode."

Bill Thomas had remained uncharacteristically silent throughout the co-ordinators' discussion, but he had taken Walter's desperate proposal to heart. Without telling anyone, he subsequently made an appointment to see Burkett. A year before, when the high school principal had asked Thomas to become a Model School coordinator, the music teacher had agreed to risk such an extraordinary commitment only after extracting from Burkett a guarantee that he would not resign halfway through the restructuring pro-cess. After twenty-five years as a teacher, Thomas believed that such a sce-nario would surely lead to the project's collapse. The following week, when the music teacher met with Burkett, he tried to encourage the administrator to make good on his promise. "Can't we here in the building circle the wag-ons and work out what we want for ourselves," Thomas pleaded, "in spite of Lauree, or maybe even bring her along?"

Thomas did not actually expect that Heights High's faculty would rally to Burkett's cause should the new superintendent or the school board decide to terminate his contract. He knew that his colleagues generally perceived Burkett to be a "company man" like most of his ilk—an image that had been reinforced the previous winter when the power went off in the building and Burkett had kept the teachers on duty in their dark, cold classrooms, even though the students had been sent home. No one, Thomas realized, had stopped to think Burkett was merely carrying out one of Miramar's "stupid" orders. No, his colleagues believed that the high school principal enjoyed exerting his power over them in an arbitrary manner.

Nevertheless, the music teacher felt safe in encouraging Burkett to stay on, because Thomas had hatched a salvage plan. It was Thomas's intention to intercede on Burkett's behalf with Gearity, whose performance as the principal of Belvoir elementary school had earned his respect. He intended to ask her whether she and Burkett could not, as professionals, put aside their differences and negotiate a truce "for the sake of the kids."

Burkett did not disabuse Thomas of the notion that something could be worked out. A part of him wanted to stay in Cleveland Heights. Never be-fore had he invested so much in a school district, and it pained him to have to leave before his work was done. Never before had he become so emotion-ally involved with his colleagues, and the thought of leaving behind some very good friends brought tears to his eyes. However, the superintendent of the Prince William County schools had already given Burkett an unofficial job offer. Should the Virginia school board approve the hiring decision, Burkett had decided to take the position.

The necessity of his leaving had been reconfirmed when he informed Gearity of the developments in Prince William County. A few days before their conversation, a tabulation of first-semester grades revealed that Heights High students had earned the greatest number of As since a comparable grading period in 1981. The school's grade point average had now inched up to 2.02, a solid C. Upon hearing that Burkett had entered into serious job negotiations in Virginia, however, Gearity agreed that the principal's departure would be for the best. The town, she observed, was not big enough for the both of them.

As if to confirm this analysis, Gearity and Burkett were to butt philosophical heads once again. One week after Gearity was named superintendent, their in-house dispute over discipline escalated into a pitched public battle whose shock waves inflamed the entire community, shifted the balance of power in the district, and blew the Model School Project off its shaky underpinnings.

The stage for these developments was set when four hundred students walked out of Heights High School at midmorning on February 15, 1990, to join a small group of parents protesting the suspension and/or expulsion of more than twenty African-American youths ordered by the Burkett administration as a result of a rash of off-campus fights. Ignoring a cold, steady drizzle, the demonstrators marched two miles to Cleveland Heights City Hall, where the protest organizers demanded to speak with the chief of police, whose officers they accused of conspiring with the high school administration against African-American teenagers.

The protest had been conceived by Barbara Madison's advocacy group, Cleveland Heights–University Heights Concerned Parents, after five African-American youths were suspended and recommended for expulsion because of their participation in an after-school fight that had taken place several blocks from the high school. The incident occurred on February 6th at four in the afternoon when members of the rival Brothers and Home Boys gangs encountered one another near Taylor Academy in a quiet retail district fronting on Taylor Road. Fighting ensued. When one of the youths pushed his opponent into a large storefront window, breaking it, the confrontation ended. The alleged combatants were subsequently apprehended by the Cleveland Heights police and charged with disorderly conduct and vandalism.

School board policy mandated that district administrators cooperate with the police. "Information pertaining to the identity and whereabouts of alleged offenders, victims and witnesses, shall be supplied to police upon request," board policy stated. Because the Burkett administration had gone out of its way to provide information of this nature to the police whenever it was requested, it had become routine for officers to return the favor by informally alerting the high school whenever its students ran afoul of the law. Burkett learned of the Taylor Road arrests in this manner.

Fearful that the February 6th dispute might "carry over" to the high school, Burkett ordered his house principals to suspend the potential troublemakers when they arrived at school the following day and begin proceedings to expel them. Burkett acted with dispatch to remove the gang members because he feared they might turn on one another again in the hallways and seriously injure themselves or others.

There was some basis for the principal's apprehension. Less than two weeks before, on January 24th, six or seven students had begun fighting in the courtyard during their lunch hour. Burkett, who, because of the fight, had missed the Model School luncheon at which super-retreat representatives were elected, traced its cause to another brawl at a public dance attended by hundreds of African-American teenagers in Cleveland Heights the previous Saturday night. According to Burkett's police sources, at the conclusion of the event, a group of students from Shaw High School in East Cleveland waded into the departing crowd and beat up several Heights High students. Having stood by helplessly as their "brothers" were pummeled, the victims' fellow gang members apparently felt compelled to restore their reputations as tough guys.

Or so Burkett speculated, based on the numerous displays of machismo—the bouts of bumping in the hallways, the staring matches in the cafeteria, the fight in the courtyard—that he and other administrators witnessed the following week. One of the students involved in the latter fray told the principal that he had jumped in only to protect a friend, but Burkett, who had rushed out of a meeting to assist the security monitors in breaking up the clash, felt that he detected in the would-be hero a greater degree of enthusiasm for the rescue work than was necessary. The student was suspended and recommended for expulsion.

No one had been seriously hurt in the courtyard fight, but later that afternoon, a fifteen-year-old member of the Kappa Phi Nasty gang was attacked by a group of Home Boys as he played basketball in a park near the high school. Knocked to the ground, slapped, punched, and kicked, the teenager was finally rescued by his friends, who rushed him to one of their homes, with the rival gang members in hot pursuit. The Home Boys were in the process of breaking down the front door when the police arrived. Five of the alleged attackers were ultimately arrested on charges ranging from vandalism to aggravated rioting, felonious assault, and aggravated burglary.

Earlier in the afternoon the Cleveland Heights police had been called to another residential neighborhood, where they found a large brawl in progress. Some forty African-American youths were fighting in the street. The young men fled at the approach of the police, but ten of them were apprehended and charged with aggravated rioting. All those arrested were Heights High students, who had been dismissed early because the school was operating on a half-day schedule owing to final exams. When Burkett learned of the incident from the police, he ordered the students' suspension for ten days, believing that the continuing presence of warring gang members at the high school posed a real threat to the safety of the student body and faculty. (Also caught up in the principal's dragnet was a young woman who had been questioned by police about her presence at the scene.)

Burkett justified his precautionary actions to the house principals by citing the board-approved policy that governed "misconduct away from school." The policy stated: "Students who engage in an assault upon a school employee or other person off school property or at a school-sponsored or related activity, function or event, or on school property before or after school hours may . . . be subject to suspension or expulsion from school." Lee House carried out the suspension orders, but the African-American principal of Cedar House mutinied. He refused to process the appropriate paperwork, believing that it set a bad precedent for the high school to attempt to police all of Cleveland Heights all of the time.

Observing this whirlwind of disciplinary activity, a leader of the African-American staff concluded that Burkett had a hidden motive for his actions. It seemed to guidance counselor David Smith as if the high school principal were turning up the pressure in order to pave the way for certain changes he desired, such as the reforms soon to be proposed by the Model School Project. Burkett was smart enough to realize (Smith figured) that change was not going to occur simply because one administrator and a few teachers wanted it. Change would arise only from "pain within the body." By expanding his use of disciplinary exclusion even after district officials had indicated their displeasure with this approach, Heights High's principal seemed to Smith to be trying to force the board of education and the community to actively respond to the gang problem and other kinds of student misbehavior and to deal constructively with its causes.

Smith applauded Burkett's determination to put a halt to fighting, provided that the high school administration made sure its disciplinary policies were equitably enforced. But the parents of the disciplined students saw the crackdown in a different light. Instead of reaffirming Burkett's message that acts of aggression were totally unacceptable, they loudly protested their children's innocence. The high school's information exchange with police, its assertion of off-campus jurisdiction over students, the severity of the consequences it had recommended in certain questionable cases, and its mechanical handling of the disciplinary process—all these seeming injustices contributed to the parents' mood of denial.

"When James brought home the suspension papers with the recommendation for expulsion, I could have fainted, it was that devastating," said the mother of one of the young men involved in the Taylor Road fight. The grievances Nita Heard expressed were typical. "I could have seen it," she said, "if he had been a chronic discipline problem and couldn't be controlled, but he had never been in trouble before."

Heard knew her son to be a member of the Brothers, but insisted that the group had "high standards" and provided a "positive motivating experience" for its members, which was why she had not prevented her son from joining. ("These kids need *something* to encourage them," she said of James, a former Taylor Academy student who was a sophomore at the time of his suspension.) The Home Boys, on the other hand, attracted "a different set of boys, who were more aggressive." Indeed, Heard was of the opinion that the Home Boys had initiated the Taylor Road confrontation when they approached James and two of his fellow Brothers, whose car was stopped at a streetlight. The Home Boys were carrying sticks, and, in James's retelling of the incident, the Brothers were thinking only of avoiding possible damage to the car, which belonged to the mother of the driver, when they decided to park the vehicle and jump out to face their foes on the street.

But the Burkett administration would have none of that. Believing that "Dr. Burkett was not a person you could really reach," Nita Heard instead scheduled a meeting with the principal of Lee House to plead her son's case. The administrator declined to reconsider the terms of James's punishment. "In the high school's eyes," Heard discovered, "James was no longer an individual; he was a Brother and that was a gang." Contrary to her belief that each disciplinary case should be judged individually, the high school administration preferred to "lump everything together as gang-related." Heard found her encounter with the disciplinary system extremely chilling. "It was like they felt that we as black parents didn't care. There was no phone call [to inform the family in advance that James was being suspended]; 'no, we didn't need to come in and talk seriously about this.' But we did take it seriously."

As it happened, one of the other Taylor Road mothers served as treasurer of Cleveland Heights–University Heights Concerned Parents. After the Burkett administration had denied their individual requests to revoke the expulsion recommendations on the grounds that they were excessive and unjust, she suggested that the aggrieved parents make a joint appointment to see the superintendent. "My son is not an A student, but I didn't want the opportunity for him to get an education snatched from him," Heard said by way of explaining why she decided to join in the new offensive. "Some kids don't recover from expulsions. When you just throw a child out and he doesn't have an education—especially for a black kid, he can't get a job and you open him to a life of crime. I was fighting for my child's existence."

Superintendent Gearity met with the group briefly on February 8th. "Oh, these kids won't be expelled," Gearity assured Nita Heard and the other parents, making a prediction that was to prove true.[1] But the treasurer of Cleveland Heights–University Heights Concerned Parents was not satisfied by the superintendent's promise to meet again. "She was on Barbara Madison's committee that helped parents whose kids were being suspended," Heard explained, "and she knew there was no stopping the system."

As a last-ditch measure, Madison's lieutenant conceived of the idea of organizing a demonstration to call for the ouster of Burkett and his house principals. "We needed something spectacular to show there was a problem," said Barbara Madison, who stepped in at this point to help organize the parents' protest, which they decided should take place at the high school on February 15th at ten in the morning. "We had had so many arguments with the school system about racism. Now we had to prove it."

On Wednesday the 14th, a flyer encouraging participation in the demonstration began to circulate at Heights High School. "Your child may be innocently walking home from school . . . or buying you a gift for your birthday at the neighborhood shopping center [when he] can be picked up by the police," it stated. "Bring a stop to false arrest, slanderism [sic], police brutality and harassment." When word of the planned demonstration reached Hugh Burkett, he decided to follow his usual policy toward organized protest and do nothing to stop the demonstration.

Burkett's boss was of a different mind, however. Early in the morning on the 15th, Lauree Gearity called the high school to say that she was coming over and to inquire whether additional backup was needed. As Burkett had not yet arrived, her call was transferred to Frank Walter, who felt that he lacked the authority to tell the superintendent to sit tight. Walter's timidity infuriated Burkett, when he arrived, because he believed it the responsibility of the high school administration alone to deal with such protests.

Gearity soon appeared with several other central-office administrators and the district's maintenance crew, determined to deploy the burly crew members at entrances around the building to prevent students from joining the protest. Burkett spent the next few hours arguing the superintendent out of that potentially explosive strategy. Gearity refused, however, to accept his suggestion to return to Miramar and thus leave responsibility for events in the hands of a person she no doubt figured for a lame duck. Nor did she follow Burkett's advice on the best way to contain the protest, which was, he asserted, a posture of nonengagement: "Do not allow the demonstrators on campus, do not negotiate with the students, do not talk to the media (at least not while the demonstration is taking place)."

When Barbara Madison and a contingent of fewer than fifteen parents showed up, Gearity instructed Burkett to permit them to enter the school's grounds. Madison picked the courtyard for use as a soapbox. "We want a more positive atmosphere at the high school. We are tired of our kids being labeled criminals and looked upon as members of gangs," she told the reporters who had descended on the school—"like piranhas," in Burkett's eyes. Gearity did not share the principal's disgust with the media's taste for controversy at Heights High. Even before students began exiting the building to join the parents' protest, Burkett saw the superintendent, surrounded by television crews, standing in the courtyard giving "eighteen thousand interviews."

At no time during the weeks-long media circus that surrounded the demonstration did Gearity publicly deny the charges of racism leveled at the Burkett administration or express confidence in the principal himself. Neither did she defend the high school's disciplinary policies as appropriate nor maintain that those policies were fairly enforced. Instead she repeatedly proclaimed her empathy for the aggrieved parents and her willingness to investigate their complaints. "There are new powers-that-be," she told reporters. "And if I have anything to do with it, things will change." As far as Gearity was concerned, the district could survive bad publicity. But it would not survive for long if racial tensions were not forthrightly addressed.

Burkett, on the other hand, steadfastly refused to talk with the press. If the person who knew the least about Heights High's gang problem insisted on being at the center of the debate, there was no use, he reasoned, in his attempting to explain the rationale for the high school's strict disciplinary policies. In fact, Burkett believed that were he to speak up, it would be to the community's detriment. The more he said, the less competent he suspected the new superintendent would appear—an impression he feared would only sharpen the widespread perception that the Cleveland Heights schools were on the decline.

Burkett decided to swallow his pride, hold his tongue, and allow himself to be labeled a racist. He consoled himself on the loss of his reputation with the thought that at least he was in the right. If dealing firmly and swiftly with aggression and violence made him a racist, so be it.

Burkett's public humiliation contrasted sharply with the case of Joe Clark, the baseball-bat-toting black principal of a predominately black high school in Paterson, New Jersey, who two years earlier had become a national folk hero for a similar stance. Clark had refused to back down when the Paterson Board of Education threatened to fire him for expelling without due process or board approval sixty-six students he considered "hoodlums and thugs and pathological deviants." Clark's life story had been turned into a movie, but there would be no similar star treatment for the white Burkett.

As the parents' protest got under way outside, several hundred students congregated inside the main building in the first-floor lobby and front hallway. Rumors that Black History Month had been canceled and that black students had been sent home for wearing African paraphernalia had added to the size of the milling crowd. Most of the class cutters were black. In advanced placement classes throughout the building, white students groused to their teachers about the disruption of their educations, while the members of the Summas, an affluent white fraternity, took advantage of the confusion to escape outside for a smoke.

It was clear to Frank Walter that the would-be demonstrators did not know how to get organized. Seizing the opportunity to control the action, the administrators on patrol in the front hall suggested that the students reassemble in the social room. Some students brought along placards that read "Prejudice and Injustice Are Not Part of a School's Curriclum [sic]" and "Stop Suspension and Expulsion Of[f] School Property" and "Mandella [sic] is Free Why Can't We Be[?]" However, the bedlam in the social room convinced Walter that most of those gathered there had no idea of the issues that had prompted the parents' protest.

Student activities advisor Jean King also recognized that the individuals in the social room were "really confused—so many little things were upsetting them."[2] She took it upon herself to bring order out of chaos, informing the students of the media's presence and encouraging them to make sure that they had straightened out the issues at stake before they decided to join the protest. "You need to take a stand for something," she instructed the assemblage, "and it should be one for all and all for one." King knew that she would be faulted by the Burkett administration for her failure to encourage the students to return to class, but she felt that their having to make a decision as to whether or not to join the parents' protest afforded students a rare opportunity to practice critical-thinking skills.[3]

Having received King's permission to do so, most of the students in the social room decided to walk out. Student body president, Traci McLin, did not join them, a decision for which she was later verbally abused by her peers. But McLin had concluded that racism was not her cause. (She "could not care less whether white people at the high school liked her." She was concerned only with getting an education.) In any case, the student demonstrators seemed to her hotheaded and ill informed. If people were going to disrupt school, they better have a strong reason, she felt. Yet it was clear to her that some kids had joined the walkout simply to get out of class.

The sight of hundreds of students pouring out of the high school elicited a different reaction in Barbara Madison. It reminded her of the civil rights movement of the 1960s, an exciting era in which she had unfortunately been too young to participate. An exhilarated Madison took charge of the new recruits, instructing them to stay on the sidewalk as they marched to city hall so that they could not be arrested for jaywalking. Later she crowed about the fact that "all of these supposed troublemakers" had shown up at their destination without having engaged in a single fight. Madison arrived at city hall before the students, having driven over in her car to avoid getting wet in the rain. There she discovered that city officials had locked the entrance to the building.

"Pompous idiots," Madison thought. "Is this how they deal with taxpayers?" She banged on the door and demanded a meeting with the chief of police. A city spokesperson opened the door and said that the police chief was willing to meet with Madison and one other parent. When Madison indicated that the protesters would return the following day should the chief refuse to meet with all of the parents immediately, the adults were admitted into the building.

The police chief and the city manager met with the group for forty-five minutes. When Madison emerged from behind closed doors, she summarized the parents' demands for reporters. "We want the police to leave our kids alone and to stop the police state at Heights High," she explained. The police chief declined to talk to the press about the group's demands, but Madison told the media that he had pointed out to her that his department had no jurisdiction over the public schools. Although she later admitted that "nothing much came out of the meeting," Madison counted the confrontation with Cleveland Heights officials a success. "We shook up city hall," she would say later, "and that's what they needed."

In contrast with the police chief's strategy of distancing himself from the controversy, the superintendent of schools acted as if she were determined to resolve it single-handedly. Gearity followed the students to city hall, where she promised to meet with them to discuss their grievances in exchange for their agreement to return to class. Rather than end the student protest, the superintendent's openness to discussion escalated it. The following day some six hundred students cut their first-period classes to stage a sit-in in the social room. They insisted that they would not leave until they were granted a personal audience with Hugh Burkett. Burkett acceded to the demand. If the students' "script" called for him to be taken hostage, then he would playact that role for them.

For the next four hours, a parade of angry African-American students stepped forward to express their concerns and frustrations directly to the principal. "It was a chance for them say to 'Mr. Invisible': 'You're never around and yet you have all this power over me,'" recalled Jean King, who was again on hand to help the students organize their thoughts. The litany of grievances ran the gamut. Students complained about the lack of African-American teachers and black studies courses and the quality of food in the cafeteria. They called for the return of daytime pep rallies and an open campus and questioned the fairness of ability grouping.

Steve Young peeked into the social room during his planning period, coming away with the impression that what the demonstrators really wanted was to hear themselves talk. When Burkett attempted to categorize their complaints by type in order to facilitate discussion, Young observed, the students brushed him off. It was not, agreed *Black and Gold* editor Beth Aram (who was there taking notes for a special issue of the newspaper to be devoted to the protest), an atmosphere conducive to problem solving, but Aram took pride nonetheless in the fact that her peers numbered censorship of the student paper among their concerns.

Chief steward Dan MacDonald also stole in for a few minutes and came away disturbed by the students' humiliation of Burkett. The sit-in reminded him of nothing so much as Pontius Pilate's grilling of Christ. But a significant number of the African-American faculty found the student uprising inspirational. They decided to begin meeting privately to formulate positions on the issues the demonstrators had raised, adding to the discussion concerns of their own, such as the all-white leadership of the Model School Project. "The kids put it out there for us," Jean King later explained. "We realized we needed to do more and be more clear in our stand. We needed to show the kids they didn't need to distrust the whole staff."

Although some white teachers greeted word of the closed-door sessions with alarm, fearing that they would lead to the faculty's enduring racial polarization, the black staff justified its decision to meet separately as a means to an end. The only way justice would ever be achieved at the high school, guidance counselor Dave Smith now believed, was for Heights High's black educators to throw off their accustomed passivity and mobilize.

If the sit-in called up a host of emotions in those who observed it, it seemed to have no visible effect on the person who endured it. Having dealt with student demonstrations before, Hugh Burkett knew the game plan by heart, and, painful though it was, he was determined to follow it. He would listen to the students and take their abuse and be careful not to agree to do anything or give anything away, and somehow he would get through the day.

In contrast to Burkett's stoic approach, the superintendent of schools (who arrived at midmorning after the demonstrators called Miramar to request her presence) once again attempted to take charge. At one point Gearity struggled with a student for control of the microphone, but ultimately she found it impossible to cope with the cacophony. Proclaiming her inability to work under such adverse conditions, she proposed that the demonstrators put together a written list of concerns, which she promised to try to resolve by meeting with them in the future in small groups. Gearity's suggestion set off a noisy new round of complaints about the Burkett administration, which showed no signs of ending until Jean King announced around one o'clock that she had to return to class and asked the students to do the same. Much to the onlookers' astonishment, they complied.

The following Monday the high school was quiet. Madison and her followers were hard at work behind the scenes, attempting to persuade the Twenty-first District Congressional Caucus, an alliance of local African-American politicians headed by U.S. Representative Louis Stokes, to take up their cause. Eventually, the Office of Civil Rights of the U.S.

Department of Education would decide to investigate a class-action complaint filed by Cleveland Heights–University Heights Concerned Parents against the district, but Cleveland's black political establishment declined to intervene, instead encouraging Madison's group to work out its differences with the school system. In the meantime, Madison and her followers decided to stage a second protest at Heights High School on the morning of Wednesday, February 21st.

By this time, Lauree Gearity had marshaled her own political allies. Hearing rumors of the second demonstration, the new superintendent enlisted the services of a prominent African-American member of the state board of education, who spoke over the high school P.A. on the morning of the 21st, encouraging students to remain in class. The speaker, a former employee of the district, congratulated the student protesters for having brought Heights High's problems to the forefront, where the "best minds in the district" could now begin to work on resolving them. Then she reminded those who were contemplating cutting class to think of black South African leader Nelson Mandela's prescription that the best way to combat racism was to get a good education.

Gearity had also rallied the support of Heights Concerned Parents, some of whose members attended the Wednesday-morning protest in the high school auditorium in order to demonstrate to the media that not all African Americans in Cleveland Heights believed the public school system to be guilty of racial discrimination. But they were drowned out by the members of Madison's contingent, who had finally bearded Burkett in his den and were not going to be denied the opportunity to excoriate him in person. As the television cameras rolled, one of the Taylor Road mothers provided the evening news with a colorful, if not particularly illuminating, sound bite. "We haven't seen you for three years," she accused Burkett. "All you do is sit back in your office and eat doughnuts." Adhering to confirmed practice, Burkett declined to dignify the ranting with a reply.

Unlike that of the adult demonstrators, the anger of the African-American students had apparently played itself out. There was no exodus from class on the 21st, and when the district subsequently attempted to involve the student body in constructive problem-solving activities, the effort met with mixed success.

As a member of an internal crisis-management team that Gearity had assembled the weekend after the walkout, Frank Walter suggested that several student committees be created to advise the high school administration on desired improvements. Although two hundred students subsequently indicated an interest in serving on Heights High's new "Quality of Life" team, attendance was poor at many of the committee sessions, which began late in the summer of 1990. Walter served as the administrative liaison to the Rewards and Recognition Committee, and frequently only he and the student chairperson attended its regularly scheduled meetings the following year. Given the circumstances under which the students had come to participate in the walkout and the ephemeral nature of their interest in school improvement, Walter wondered in retrospect how anyone could have responded to the demonstrations as if they were "the voice of the people."

Part 4
Business as Usual

Will American political and educational leaders seriously rethink what their schools are and what they do? I remember that they have not . . . and I worry that they will not, this being a day dominated by the politics of slogan and sound bite, of short-range gain. . . . I fear that the preferred alternative to careful rethinking will be continued pushing, prodding, testing and protesting our largely mindless, egregiously expensive, and notably unproductive current system. It is not a pretty prospect.

—THEODORE R. SIZER,
Horace's School: Redesigning the American High School, 1992

18

Management by Crisis

It is relatively rare to find schools with a sense of destiny. They do change when prodded from the outside, the impetus for change falling off with the departure of the change agent or pressure. And they change under the leadership of an energetic, inspired person, change again falling off when he or she goes on to bigger and better things. But some continuing, productive movement to stay relevant or meet newly defined expectations . . . is rare, indeed.

—John I. Goodlad
The Dynamics of Educational Change, 1975

Although he had trouble admitting it to himself, his public lambasting had caused Hugh Burkett to begin to reexamine his philosophy of discipline. In his zeal to promote academic achievement, maybe he *had* "overstructured" the administration of Heights High School. At the beginning of the school year, he had instructed the house principals to place same-day calls to parents whose children were marked absent in order to verify that the students were not truant. Now he found himself thinking: Maybe we should not be checking up on kids. Maybe our attitude should be "If you come to school, fine; if you don't, fine."

Burkett's reflective mood was not typical of the response other white staff members displayed toward the February demonstrations. Some teachers were consumed with feelings of white guilt. Others shared Frank Walter's concern that the significance of the demonstrations had been blown out of

219

proportion. They felt betrayed by the district's unquestioning acceptance of the demonstrators' point of view, as the need to maintain public safety at the high school seemed to them self-evident.

The first bursts of resentment surfaced at a regularly scheduled faculty meeting held the same afternoon as the second parents' protest. The opening statement from the floor came from standard-track English teacher Betty Levy, who had taken personally the frank discussion at the first Model School retreat of the poor image that standard classes had. Levy voiced dismay over the board of education's handling of the previous week's events. Not only had the superintendent undercut the Burkett administration's authority by making public her view that its routinely prescribed punishment for fighting was too severe, she had subsequently overturned Burkett's chosen disposition of the students who participated in the walkout and sit-in. His mandate that all demonstrators be given unexcused absences from class and prohibited from making up the work was overruled. Levy feared that students were being sent the wrong message.

"I'm very upset about the fact that no one has yet said that with privileges come responsibility for one's actions," she complained. "We have to spread that message because right now the students are laughing at the rules."

A weary Burkett fielded her comment. "Friday was not a time to tell students what to do," he responded. "It was a time for them to vent." Then, for the first time since the controversy over discipline erupted, he seemed to have second thoughts about his punitive approach. "My administration has felt personally responsible for student behavior," he continued. "I in particular have 'owned' all the inappropriate behavior. We've put into place a number of restrictive measures and had sort of a siege mentality, which maybe now we need to move away from. We need to get students to take responsibility for their own behavior."

Although he numbered among the faculty's reenergized black activists, guidance counselor Dave Smith shared Burkett's new perspective on the ingredients of a model discipline policy. Smith, too, believed that the time had come for the administration to stop spending all its energy on the 10 percent of students who caused the biggest headaches. Better to start teaching the other 90 percent a sense of personal responsibility by awarding them certain privileges and showing them how to handle such freedom. After all, Smith liked to point out, the word *discipline* derived from the Latin word meaning "to teach."

There was no real possibility that the demonstrations might lead to a rational consideration of the discipline issue, however. The community at large was in no mood for a philosophical debate. A public forum hosted by the board of education on February 24th attracted more than 125 residents to Wiley Junior High School, an exceptional turnout for a wintery Saturday afternoon. Intended to produce a meeting of the minds with Cleveland Heights–University Heights Concerned Parents, the forum immediately disintegrated into a shouting match between Barbara Madison and Lauree Gearity over the question of which side should chair the proceedings. Madison refused to concede that the board had called the meeting and controlled the podium, prompting Gearity to stalk out of the Wiley auditorium. She took with her about one hundred members of the predominately black audience (among them, Nita Heard and her husband, who were embarrassed by Madison's blatant power play).

The defectors were not necessarily supporters of the school system, as the superintendent discovered when she reconvened the meeting in Wiley's library. Most had come to complain about specific instances of mistreatment endured by their children. Occasionally, someone would disagree with the common refrain that the school system was prejudiced against African Americans. "Making choices, understanding consequences, and accepting them—that's what life is all about," one of the few whites in the audience said. "If my son gets in trouble, I *want* him to hit the trail. Put him in the courtyard in shackles—I don't care. He knows the rules."

Discovering such stalwart defenders of the school system to be rare, Gearity attempted to temper the audience's anger by talking about the district's strengths. She mentioned that a recently completed evaluation of the district by the Ohio Department of Education had pronounced it one of the most outstanding school systems in the state. She also assured the audience that "99.5 percent of the teachers in the district do well by your children."

Mary Watson, a remedial reading teacher at Heights High School, had come to the forum intending merely to listen. However, when Gearity praised the caring nature of the district's staff, Watson felt she could not let the remark pass unchallenged. If nothing were said to counter the false impression that the superintendent had created, Watson feared that the African-American community would be made to look like "jerks" for raising such a needless stink. Believing that one had to "go all out for the black cause—the battle was so large that one could not be only part way involved"—she decided to speak up.

"Dr. Gearity," Watson called out. A willowy former New Yorker, Watson could be an intimidating presence because of her height, accent, and loud speaking voice. "I've been a teacher in this district for eleven years. I'm proud that Cleveland Heights is considered one of the top high schools in the state. But there *is* racism in the district. I feel racism in our school. I feel racism in our staff meetings. Tension in the building is overwhelming."

Watson's remarks, which were quoted in the daily newspaper, were greeted with contempt by some of her colleagues, whose reaction might have been more tolerant had they been aware of the innocent origins of Watson's stentorian voice. (A member of a family of eleven, Watson had learned to speak loudly in order to make herself heard at the dinner table.) The following week anonymous hate mail, a job application, and an article on black racism showed up in Watson's faculty mailbox, delivered by teachers whom she believed had mistakenly attributed her "problack" sympathies to antipathy toward whites.

Watson's observations also had a profound effect on the superintendent, knocking her off balance. At Wiley, Gearity had been operating on the principle that the best defense is a strong offense. Now she retreated. "Based on what you say," Gearity responded to Watson, "it sounds a lot worse than I thought it was." The superintendent's concession was widely reported, adding fuel to the continuing story of alleged racial discrimination at Heights High.

Responding to the media's unrelenting coverage, the Cleveland Heights mayor and his fellow city councillors sent a strongly worded letter to the editor to the area's major newspapers. It defended the Cleveland Heights police, pointing to the department's "long-standing tradition of fair and equal enforcement of the law," and decried the media's distortion of the "reputation of our city and our schools with sensationalized coverage."

Officials at Miramar shared the fear that the controversy posed a threat to the suburb's social and economic stability. "These kinds of visible conflicts will be the death of Cleveland Heights," the district's community relations director lamented in private. "They lock up the undecided vote against the schools." Yet the district's top two administrators were unable to emulate the united front presented by the city against the media onslaught, and the new superintendent's noticeable lack of support for the Burkett administration helped to keep the controversy alive.

Whatever its public relations flaws, the superintendent's strategy of conciliation won backing from the board of education. "We are all united behind a very intelligent superintendent, who is not afraid to say, 'Maybe we are doing something wrong,'" board president Judith Glickson told reporters. According to the district's community relations director, Miramar believed that the white-run school system could not have credibly defended its disciplinary practices, even if it had wanted to. "That has to come from black parents who say, 'Yes, they're taking the right approach,'" he explained sotto voce at a board of education press conference held the week after the walkout to assure reporters that the district would not sweep the problem of racial discrimination under the rug.

As a matter of fact, the board had little interest in mounting a vigorous defense of Burkett's strict enforcement of the "no fighting" policy that had been approved by a previous board. Ironically, veteran Maureen Weigand was perhaps the last remaining supporter of this approach. Newcomer Steve Bullock tended to believe that Madison's charges about race-based inequalities in the district's disciplinary system had some foundation in truth, even though he did not condone her confrontational approach. And while Stu Klein was confident that Burkett did not have a "racist bone in his body," he had begun to suspect that the high school principal was an ideologue who ignored evidence that conflicted with his educational philosophy.

For example, there was the procession of misfits who appeared before the board in the winter of 1990 to appeal their expulsions from Heights High. Might not these youngsters have benefited from a more creative approach to dealing with their gang membership? Klein wondered. "To a person they were punks, not very bright, failing students; they were little kids or big fat kids," he recalled. "It was heartbreaking and eye-opening. You saw why they were attracted to gangs. The affiliation made them feared and respected in other people's eyes." Klein concluded that the Burkett administration had failed to diagnose and treat the real cause of the high school's disciplinary problems: lack of self-esteem among young black males.

In quest of alternatives to expulsion and true to her public promises of change, Gearity had by the end of February set in motion a formal review of the district's disciplinary policy by an internal committee consisting of union and management representatives. Her crisis-management team began looking into ways to increase the racial sensitivity of teachers and administrators throughout the district, and Gearity herself began to pay closer attention to the opinions and desires of the African-American staff. When members of Heights Alliance of Black School Educators (HABSE), a coalition of the district's African-American professional staff, requested a private summit with central-office administrators, Gearity promptly set up the meeting for early March.

The title of a confidential document compiling the prepared statements HABSE members read at the meeting summarized the caucus's agenda: HABSE demanded that the district stop treating black staff as a "Forgotten

Resource." The first speaker, high school reading teacher Mary Watson, who believed black educators possessed a special understanding of the "culturally diverse student," suggested one place in which their knowledge could immediately be put to use. She requested that the superintendent install African-American teachers at the highest levels of the Model School Project leadership. Gearity duly attempted to relay this message to the Model School coordinators through various intermediaries, obviously hoping that they would expand the project's inner circle without her having to confront them directly.

At the HABSE summit Watson stopped short of arguing the case for an all-black professional staff, a reform that would not be necessary, she privately believed, if white teachers were willing to acknowledge their racism and work on becoming "recovering racists." To do so, she felt that they must first address their ignorance of what she saw as the unique learning styles of blacks. To that end Watson recommended at the HABSE summit that the district seek out qualified African Americans to conduct cultural awareness workshops for the staff. Her suggestion and others in a similar vein captured the imagination of Larry Peacock, the district's African-American director of staff development, who immediately began work to obtain foundation funding for an intensive multicultural training program.

Miramar also embraced black board member Steve Bullock's suggestion that a fact-finding committee be created to investigate the truth of accusations that the school system was racially biased. In late February 1990 the board of education announced the creation of the Heights Commission on Excellence and Equity in Education. The responsibility of chairing the lay commission was given to a Heights Concerned Parents founder, an African-American woman named Phyllis Evans, who had earlier answered the call to speak in support of the district at the board's February 21st press conference.[1] The proposed investigation did not pacify Barbara Madison, however, who regarded it as a "bunch of crap." It was impossible, she thought, for an organization to police itself.

Viewing these developments from the vantage point of a student of political action, it looked to Heights social studies teacher Cal Rose as though the community had veered completely off track. It seemed to Rose that controlling the spread of gangs should have been the main focus of the debate. If the gang problem were not addressed, Rose was convinced, Cleveland Heights would follow Los Angeles and New York City "right down the tubes." Perhaps more than most residents, Rose (who had been among the first Model School retreat-goers) was aware of how prevalent gang activity had become in the suburb. Rose's son owned a police-radio scanner, and within a few hours of the student sit-in denouncing the repressive atmosphere at Heights High School, the scanner crackled with word that yet another gang fight had broken out in Cleveland Heights.

The next day the social studies teacher attended a Saturday-afternoon basketball game at the high school, where he gained a firsthand appreciation of the reasons why Burkett had been forced to spend "half his time as sheriff." After the game ended and most of the fans had departed, Rose spied Burkett riding around in a police car, monitoring the activities of a group of about one hundred youths who were roaming "like a wave" over municipal parking lot 5, a pack of teenage girls in tow. Whenever it appeared that something might be "going down," the young women screamed their delight. Rose looked around for reinforcements, but, with the exception of Burkett, Frank Walter, and a couple of police officers, there were no other adults in sight.

Where were all those parents *now*, Rose had wondered, who dismissed Burkett's disciplinary practices as excessive?

The community's refusal to acknowledge its gang problem was soon to claim another victim. On Sunday, March 4, 1990, at 5:30 P.M., Wilbert Stallworth-Bey II, a fourteen-year-old Cleveland Heights middle school student, was walking down South Taylor Road with a group of friends. Members of the Kappa Phi Nasty gang, they were coming from a meeting convened to consider the gang's response to a recent provocation. The night before, ten members of a gang named MOB (an acronym for Men Over Boys) had attempted to crash a Kappa party in Cleveland Heights, and a street brawl had taken place. Later that evening, several Kappas threw bricks through the windows of the home of a reputed MOB member, who, at age eighteen, had recently left Taylor Academy to join the tenth grade at Heights High.

The next day the tenth grader and his cousin were driving around with a loaded .38-caliber revolver when they came upon the group of Kappas walking down the street. According to police reports, the Heights student, who was a passenger in the car, shouted death threats at the Kappas, prompting them to throw rocks at the vehicle. To ward off the attack, the tenth grader fired the revolver in the Kappas' direction. Wilbert Stallworth-Bey fell to the ground. A bullet had pierced the fourteen year old's right side and lodged in his heart. He died in the arms of his older brother.[2]

City officials immediately proclaimed that the murder vindicated the public schools. The mayor went so far as to speculate that the controversy over the schools' role in enforcing public safety might have indirectly caused the shooting. "I feel that it was being suggested possibly to some of these kids that they had carte blanche," he observed to reporters. "Maybe they felt less restrained in their activities." Breaking his silence, the chief of police hastened to add that the interviews with some of the youths involved in events preceding the shooting confirmed the mayor's "keen insight." "Some of these kids did have that feeling," the lawman said.

Upon reading these remarks in the newspaper, Barbara Madison felt a shiver of fear. The timing of the shooting seemed to her too pat, neatly putting an end to her protest before it had been resolved. Kids were so easily manipulated, it would not have surprised her if the youths involved in the shooting had somehow been set up. The officials' remarks showed her just how little they respected young black men.

Madison's cynicism was not shared by the community at large. Perceived as a regrettable incident of gang violence, the shooting accomplished a goal that had eluded the Burkett administration for six years. It drove home the reality of the gang problem in Cleveland Heights.

Even before the murder victim was buried by his sorrowful mother (who pleaded at the gravesite with the youth of Cleveland Heights to "reevaluate your goals . . . don't let Will's death just go to waste"), the tone of the community debate over discipline underwent a sea change. An emotion-charged meeting organized by Heights Concerned Parents the week after the shooting attracted more than two hundred African-American residents, who were now prepared to acknowledge the seriousness of the gang problem. "This is not a racial issue," one concerned mother insisted. "These are our black children and they are running amok, killing each other in the street and tearing down our schools. We as parents must say we will not put up with it anymore."

Members of the audience volunteered to start patrolling the high school campus after school and to pass along to other parents the suggestion that they not allow their children to host weekend parties without adult supervision. Some even espoused the idea of fining adults whose children committed disruptive or criminal acts. "These problems will have to be dealt with at the roots—at home," argued an audience member. "Our property values can even go down if we don't nip these things in the bud." Her remarks drew loud applause.

Black parents were not alone in reassessing the severity of the gang problem. The board of education also experienced Stallworth-Bey's senseless death as an epiphany. "I'm sorry it took a tragedy for some members of the community to wake up," Judith Glickson told reporters a few days after the shooting. The board president's dramatic about-face on the need for stringent disciplinary policies ushered in a new flurry of activity at Miramar. The role of the superintendent's crisis-management team was expanded, and it now began organizing an in-service workshop aimed at educating staff systemwide to recognize signs of gang membership in students. Another lay committee was formed, this one charged with coordinating offers of assistance pouring into the school system from local civic and religious organizations.[3] The district also decided to avail itself of the services of the National School Safety Center (NSSC), a California-based consulting firm specializing in gang violence.

In mid-March the school system flew in two NSSC representatives for three days of meetings with parents and community leaders. The consultants warned that the presence in Cleveland Heights of at least five gangs (defined as such by their involvement in initiation rites and turf disputes) and three times as many underground social groups represented a ripe recruitment opportunity for larger criminal organizations. They stressed again and again that only a coordinated community effort would be effective in combating the spread of gang activity. The message was one that Burkett had tried to convey several years before, when he invited NSSC consultants to town in the vain hope of raising awareness that the gang problem was not the schools' alone.

Other developments, such as those spawned by the parents' protest, helped to place the charges leveled against the Burkett administration in clearer perspective as well. For example, the internal committee created to review and revise the district's disciplinary policies recommended their tightening and strengthening.[4] That the school system emerged intact from this challenge to its disciplinary authority was not particularly surprising. Three of the six policy review team members were top officials of the discipline-conscious teachers' union and the fourth was the union-endorsed school board president.

After collecting data and testimony for ten months, the Heights Commission on Excellence and Equity in Education issued a report in February 1991 absolving the school district of institutional racism. The report pronounced the high school's disciplinary policies and practices fair, while recommending that the staff be better educated about the self-image of African-American youth in order to eliminate complaints about the rates at which and reasons why black students were referred for disciplinary action.[5]

Several months later, the U.S. Department of Education's Office for Civil Rights (OCR) offered a different interpretation of the evidence, releasing a report that found the district's disciplinary procedures to be racially biased. However, OCR's findings paralleled those of the district's lay commission in one respect. OCR investigators also pointed to the subjectivity of the referring teachers as the cause of the perceived inequitable treatment of black students, rather than placing the blame on building administrators or policies.[6]

As a result of its investigation, OCR determined that the Cleveland Heights system had violated title 6 of the Civil Rights Act of 1964, which prohibits federal funding of programs that discriminate on the basis of race or national origin. To avoid losing its federal assistance, the district agreed to start monitoring disciplinary referrals systemwide for evidence of racial bias and to train staff members to be "race neutral" in their disciplinary practices.

Shortly after the Office of Civil Rights report was released in May 1991, Lauree Gearity called an emergency faculty meeting at the high school to explain why her administration had decided not to dispute OCR's findings. Her remarks shed light on her handling of the parents' protest as well.

The superintendent began by noting her agreement with Local 795's written criticism of the OCR report, which union officials described as a flawed piece of analysis based on incomplete statistical evidence and subjective testimony presented as fact. However, Gearity argued that it was counterproductive to ignore the report's findings. "If there is any possibility at all that teachers are handling referrals in a manner that is not race-neutral, then the problem must be rectified," she insisted. "The data collection will allow us to identify teachers who are having trouble managing their classrooms and intervene."

The new president of Local 795, who had accompanied the superintendent to the faculty meeting, also took pains to balance his comments so as to offend neither blacks nor whites. Despite reservations about the accuracy of the OCR report, union officials had concluded that it would be too expensive to fight the federal finding, he informed rank and file. Instead Local 795 would concentrate its energies on determining "appropriate" ways to support Miramar's attempt to ensure the race neutrality of the district's disciplinary processes, while standing ready to defend any teacher the district sought to remove because of persistent prejudiced behavior.

Local 795's uneasy endorsement of the mandatory disciplinary monitoring system did not deter former union steward Lou Salvator from rising to his feet to protest the OCR report's methodology. Salvator pointed out to

Gearity that its charges that teachers were guilty of making racially biased referrals were based primarily on allegations of unnamed *administrators*.

Salvator's argumentative attitude drew a sharp retort from the superintendent, highlighting her sense of the larger issues at stake. "You can play that
us-versus-them game if you want," Gearity admonished, "but if we don't all
work together on resolving these complaints, this district is going to be
down the creek."

Needless to say, these new understandings came too late for Hugh
Burkett. Twelve days before Stallworth-Bey was shot to death, Heights
High's principal sent a terse memo to the faculty announcing his resignation,
effective at the end of the 1989–90 school year. The memo noted that
Burkett had decided to accept an appointment as area associate superintendent of the Prince William County schools. As several cynics on the high
school staff had predicted, Burkett's leadership of the Model School Project
had indeed served to advance his career. One of his duties in Virginia would
be to help the twenty schools under his supervision make a transition to site-
based management.

Even though the Virginia job had been in the offing before the walkout,
the timing of Burkett's resignation led some observers to believe that he had
been driven out of the district. Barbara Madison received several calls con-
gratulating her on ridding the district of a pernicious racist, exactly as she had
promised. Madison herself took little pleasure in the news of Burkett's resignation. It was of no import to her who occupied the main office at Heights
High School. As far as she was concerned, public school principals were
"monkeys" who had to do what they were told. It was the system that had to
change!

Madison did not occupy herself with the question of how change would
be instigated now that the irritant causing such "pain in the body" had finally
been expelled.

19

Deadly Decisions

Failure to discipline shared decisions by results means that the decisions will be disciplined by reference to the interests of factions, groups and parties, rather than the interests of children.

—PHILLIP C. SCHLECTY
Schools for the Twenty-first Century, 1990

When Bill Thomas found Burkett's resignation notice in his mailbox on February 22, 1990, his first impulse was to hand in his own resignation from the Model School Project. The longer Thomas contemplated taking that action, however, the more uneasy he felt. To resign would be to admit that teachers were incapable of self-governance, that nothing could be accomplished at Heights High unless an administrator willed it. By the time Thomas bumped into Steve Young later in the day, he had abandoned the notion of quitting and was already thinking about how to remedy the vulnerable state in which the newly leaderless Model School Project found itself.

Thomas and Young agreed that the high school faculty must have a say in the selection of Heights High's next principal. They decided to prevail upon Lauree Gearity to make her choice in partnership with the high school staff. If Gearity agreed that the coordinators should draw up a selection plan involving the teachers, it would represent an important vote of confidence in the concept of site-based management. It would also constitute a tacit acknowledgment that the Model School Project was still viable, even without its erstwhile administrative leader. There was another benefit to be had. If Model School representatives were involved in selecting the new principal, it increased the chances that Burkett's successor would be sympathetic to the project's proposals. Maybe Burkett's departure was for the best, Young found himself thinking. It might actually speed the onset of shared decision making at Heights High School.

At the coordinators' next planning session, Thomas reported that an appointment with Gearity had been arranged for February 27th. He also passed along the superintendent's comment that the coordinators should not be panicked by Burkett's resignation, as she was of the belief that the project should proceed.

Fran Walter took no solace in Gearity's reassurances. Hurt and angered by Burkett's decision to leave Cleveland Heights, she and her husband had both begun to distance themselves emotionally from their departing mentor and friend. Hoping to become the next principal of Heights High School, Frank Walter threw himself into the work of the superintendent's crisis-management team, while Fran Walter brooded. February's demonstrations had prompted her to question whether the model school design adequately addressed issues of discipline, race relations, and multiculturalism. Perhaps their plans to present the model school framework to the faculty should be put on hold, she suggested to her fellow coordinators, to give the group time to rethink certain proposals. "Otherwise I'm afraid the staff's reaction will be 'This is the least of our worries,' or 'Forget that—it's the product of the white staff,'" Walter said.

Young suggested a more conservative reading of recent events. "We need to be careful that we don't equate those who scream the loudest," he responded, "with—"

"Sanity?!" Cas McBride interjected sarcastically. Then she let down her guard, confiding, "I feel like all these years I've been walking on solid ground and the whole earth just fell away. Mary Watson's accusations have devastated me. I go home crying every night."

"We can't let Hugh's resignation and racial unrest generated primarily by three people dictate the future of the high school," Thomas insisted. "May I suggest a wild idea? I think the Model School Project represents stability, that amidst this insanity we teachers are continuing to take control of our destiny."

"So you're saying there are a lot of needy people out there who need something positive," Walter said, trying to shore up her confidence in the project's validity.

"And we can give it to them!" asserted Young, who was privately of the opinion that the still-reeling board of education would have no choice but to acquiesce to the Model School Project's proposals should the coordinators and faculty emerge united behind a plan to restructure.

As a precautionary measure, however, Young decided to look again at how the proposed design dealt with equity issues. He double-checked the completed draft of a framework for the model school against the first-year recommendations of the race relations study team, which had been reissued to the Heights High faculty by the team members shortly after the walkout in the hopes that the long-forgotten report would suggest some immediate solutions to the controversy. Young determined that twenty-two of the study team's thirty-three recommendations had been incorporated into the model school's design, a finding he later reported to the other coordinators. "Two-thirds isn't too bad," he commented, "so let people go ahead and scream." Young's cool confidence in the soundness of the model school design ended all talk of delaying the super-retreat and workshop.

Like most of their white colleagues, the coordinators were not yet aware of a subtle shift in power that had occurred in the district. In the aftermath of the walkout, the newly organized African-American staff had won the ear of the superintendent, who took seriously the black educators' complaints about practices they considered to be reflective of institutional racism (such as the all-white leadership of the Model School Project). That seeds of doubt about the coordinators' credibility had been successfully planted in the superintendent's mind became apparent at her February 27th meeting with them. Although Gearity indicated that she intended to consult with the high school faculty before making the final decision as to Burkett's successor, she declined to give the coordinators an official go-ahead to develop a consensus-based principal selection plan.

"You four know how impressed I am by you and how you have moved the Model School Project forward," Gearity said. "But I don't know where the staff is or how representative you are, so you won't be the only group I talk to."

"Would you at least put out that you're working with the Model School Project to develop a selection process?" Thomas asked.

"My saying that could be a fiasco," Gearity responded. "I don't know your credibility with the staff."

"Eighty percent involvement in the retreats hints at the project's acceptance," Thomas said in rebuttal.

Outmaneuvered, Gearity came up with a no-risk compromise. She suggested that the coordinators prepare a proposal for involving the faculty in the selection of the next principal and present it to the high school staff for *its* approval.

"That doesn't require my coming to you," she noted.

A Model School Project update handed out to the faculty in early March 1990 announced that the coordinators were working out the details of a principal selection plan. When news of this development reached Glenn Altschuld's ears, the teachers' union president expressed sincere admiration for the superintendent's slyness. "You have to love that lady," he thought. Of *course,* Gearity would allow the four "pussyfooters" of the old principal to have a say in choosing the new one. The superintendent was *dying* to have teachers sanction the fact that they had a boss. Altschuld, who claimed to recognize no one as his superior, realized that he would have to put a stop to this dangerous example of "sucking up."

Unaware of Altschuld's misgivings, the coordinators met again with Gearity on March 16th to review their principal selection plan. It called for a twelve-member search committee consisting of two administrators, two parents, two students, and six elected staff members. The coordinators recommended that, at a minimum, the committee should screen and interview prospects in order to produce a shortlist of mutually acceptable candidates. By the end of the meeting, however, the coordinators had worn down Gearity's resistance and wrested from her an important concession. Rather than having final say, the superintendent reluctantly agreed to be a member of the selection committee and make the hiring decision by consensus, provided that her teammates understood *her* definition of the term, which was that she refused to hire a candidate favored by everyone else against her will or better judgment. Hoping that the process would not lead to such an impasse, the coordinators began preparing a memo to the high school faculty announcing this major step toward the realization of site-based management.

The Model School Project seemed to be drawing toward a happy dénouement as well. Two days before their meeting with Gearity, the coordinators had presented the completed model school framework to the super-retreat representatives at an all-day conference. Assuming that most members of the group had probably not read "War and Peace," as Steve Young half apologetically referred to the lengthy written exposition of their proposals, the coordinators presented the material orally, allowing plenty of time for questions and discussion. The interactive format permitted the project leaders to engage in some gentle arm-twisting, which they supplemented with earnest assurances that any lingering concerns the super-retreat representatives might have about the framework would be ironed out by the faculty task forces responsible for designing various program components long before the model school was created. By the end of the day, these tactics had elicited a generally favorable response to the Model School proposals from the sixteen teachers in attendance (four of whom were African American). Having passed its test run, the restructuring plan now seemed to the coordinators virtually unstoppable.

Then they met with the high school stewards. After a year-long lapse in official contact with the project, the stewards had asked to be the first group to examine the model school framework. Not wanting to undermine the authority of the super-retreat representatives as the staff's elected spokespeople, at least in Model School matters, the coordinators offered instead to give the stewards a special preview of the design after the super-retreat took place.

The preview took place after school on March 20th, two days before the Model School proposals were scheduled to be unveiled to the faculty at large at the workshop. After the coordinators had explained the components of the framework pictured in a line drawing, or schematic, that Young had prepared, they turned to a discussion of the future. When mention was made of the faculty task forces that would be created to design and implement those programs the teachers approved at the workshop, steward Bob Quail interrupted. "My understanding from Glenn Altschuld is none of this can be implemented without this going through the District Steering Committee," Quail said, referring to the informal labor-management committee that the teachers' union now desired to transform into the chief internal decision-making body for the school district. "The superintendent told him that."

Quail's latter assertion took the project leaders by surprise. This was the first they were aware that union officials had complained to the superintendent about the fact that the coordinators had briefed the board of education on the project's progress without first making a presentation to the District Steering Committee (DSC). The necessity of winning the DSC's approval of the model school framework did not come as welcome news to the coordinators. Unlike the administrators on the committee, who defined its function as a funnel through which proposals flowed to the board of education, committee member Glenn Altschuld saw the DSC as a "bottleneck," an assured point at which Local 795 could put the stopper on bad ideas bubbling up from district schools.

Such as the Model School Project. In private conversation, Altschuld dismissed teacher empowerment as a waste of time. Desired reforms could simply be mandated by the union, he liked to insist. The coordinators doubted, however, that the veteran labor leader would support the kinds of changes they were about to propose, such as creating a school within a school for every one hundred ninth and tenth graders and supplying a counselor, or "dean," for every two "schools." As these innovations would considerably increase the ratio of staff to students, Altschuld would no doubt view them as a luxury that could be afforded only at the expense of salary hikes—the cause to which he had devoted a quarter century of his life.[1]

Of course, Altschuld did not need to rely on the DSC to block the Model School Project (although the committee did serve a useful purpose by masking obstructionism as a labor-management impasse). In the final analysis, only the union had the contractual authority to negotiate changes in working conditions with the board of education. The Model School proponents were powerless in this regard, as Bob Quail was quick to note at the stewards' preview of the model school design. "Everything you're proposing changes working conditions," he informed the coordinators, "and if your proposals are not put through Steering Committee, I'll file a grievance."

Hoping to forestall a public showdown with the stewards that they knew they would only lose, McBride, Walter, and Young listened to Quail's threat in silence, their eyes glued to their laps. Thomas alone rose to the bait. "Why are we willing to turn decisions about the future of the high school over to other people?" he asked combatively.

"Because teacher empowerment has to be negotiated through the union," Quail responded.

"If the high school staff agrees that this is what they want to do," Thomas countered, waving the schematic, "then we go to the District Steering Committee and tell *them* what *we* want them to negotiate."

"This is not the time to address that question," Steve Young said, hoping that Thomas would take the hint.

"We need to," chief steward Dan MacDonald responded, "or the model high school will remain a bunch of lines."

Now that the restructuring project had moved beyond the talking stage and was poised to become a reality, MacDonald had cast aside his cheerleader's uniform for sterner garb. The coordinators' only hope of overcoming the stiffening opposition of Altschuld, MacDonald, and other top union officials was an overwhelmingly successful workshop.

That hope evaporated when the two-week-long workshop opened on March 22nd. Instead of the expected acclamation, the unveiling of the model school framework was greeted with yawns. Those faculty who did not ignore the proceedings dropped by the workshop site only to partake of the free lunch served there on opening and closing days.[2] And the small number of teachers who took the time to study the Model School proposals reacted with an outpouring of criticism. When the workshop ended on April 6th, a blizzard of Post-it note protests covered the large-scale schematic that the coordinators had taped up for examination.

To make matters worse, the superintendent had notified Heights High's faculty midway through the workshop that she would not be proceeding with the announced principal selection plan. "I have been informed by the President of Local 795, AFT, that he was instructed by the Union Executive Board that there was to be no teacher involvement in the selection of the Administrative Principal," Gearity stated in a March 27th memo. "Although Mr. Altschuld and I discussed our philosophical differences on the issue and agreed not to agree, I will abide by the Union's position."

Local 795's decision to kill the Model School initiative had been made without consulting the high school faculty or taking a formal vote of the union's executive board. The executive board had accepted unquestioningly Altschuld's characterization of the plan as a clever management trap. His hangup: Unless the high school faculty was also given the right to fire the new principal, Altschuld feared the teachers could be stuck with the blame when he or she made a major mistake. The union president repeated this warning at a heated question-and-answer session he was forced to hold one afternoon in order to put down a groundswell of protest.[3] Twenty or so teachers showed up to dispute the union's unilateral decision, but the coordinators were not among those who spoke out. They had deemed it hopeless to fight what appeared to be a fait accompli. With Gearity unwilling to risk her newfound harmony with Local 795, they recognized that the principal selection plan had lost its only powerful ally. And, in light of the beating they perceived the model school design had taken during the workshop, they felt as if they lacked a clear mandate from the faculty to continue their pursuit of site-based management.

However, a closer reading of the criticisms heaped upon the Model School proposals showed that they boiled down to a highly predictable concern for preserving the status quo. "How would special education classes and staff fit into this scheme?" wrote one teacher. "Where's grouping/tracking especially in English?" worried another. "The needs of highly intelligent, skilled, and motivated students are not addressed," asserted a third.

The most vociferous objections came from teachers of elective subjects, who could not see the value of requiring ninth and tenth graders to master the major academic subjects before they were allowed to pursue elective interests. "One period is left for an elective which (as compared to three available now) is not enough" was a typical complaint. "Students need to be successful, and electives help them find success." Other criticisms of the concept of a core curriculum betrayed a departmental bias. "Do you really expect to honestly address cultural and racial diversity and differences by ignoring the arts?" or "Why no foreign language until 11th or 12th [grade] . . . terrible to wait that long!"

Also drawing fire was a Model School proposal calling for an entrance examination to determine whether graduating eighth graders had mastered the skills needed to succeed in high school. The underlying idea was that summer-school or off-site remediation would be provided free to those students found to lack the necessary competencies, but the African-American faculty saw the exam as a plot to deprive black students of a mainstream education. "High School entrance exam makes this a private school and is racist," wrote one black teacher. However, this was the only feature of the proposed design to which members of the African-American faculty publicly objected. Most of the black teachers had simply ignored the workshop. Instead they had chosen to present a list of fourteen demands that represented, in effect, their vision of a model school to the faculty the day before the workshop opened.

Reaffirming their solidarity with the student protesters, the black teachers had called for the reexamination of the school's disciplinary and ability grouping systems. They recommended the infusion of Afrocentric materials into all high school courses and the regular provision of mandatory staff training aimed at eliminating racist behavior. To humanize the school environment, the black educators requested that more guidance counselors be hired, that the students' right to wear African dress and jewelry be reaffirmed, and that homeroom, study halls, and spirit assemblies be restored to the school day. And they asked that black staff members and students be included in the highest levels of leadership of the Model School Project.

In terms of their thrust, if not necessarily their particulars, the changes sought by the African-American faculty echoed many of the proposed Model School reforms. However, as emotions on both sides were running high, neither the black educators nor the coordinators seemed to appreciate that they wanted the same things: to create a nurturing school environment that would foster students' self-esteem and achievement, and to elevate the status and authority of teachers.

The unfavorable reception that the model school framework received in some quarters threw the coordinators into a foul mood. Although they had made a great show of welcoming feedback, explaining that they would be present at the workshop not to defend the framework but to give serious consideration to questions and comments, the coordinators felt personally insulted when some of their colleagues actually criticized their year-long labor.

"Did you see the six-page typewritten response Dan MacDonald submitted?" Fran Walter asked at a debriefing session following the workshop. "He didn't like anything about the design."

"Fuck him," Young said.

"If only we had asked Dan in the beginning," McBride added sarcastically, "this would have all gone differently."

The demands of the black staff seemed to the coordinators to be more of the same kind of carping.

"On the last day of workshop," Walter reported, "Phyllis Fowlkes came in, made her sandwich, and said, 'You know *my* feelings on the project— there need to be *six* African-American coordinators,' and left. This in spite of the fact that not a single black teacher had written down a comment. Guess theirs," Walter added with unusual venom, "is an oral tradition."

Walter continued, "I thought, 'I'm not going to allow Phyllis to bait me,' but then she babbled on about how the black staff was not going to settle simply for being given a few task force positions. So I said, 'But that's where the action is. The coordinators are *never* going to be allowed to make decisions.'

"Do we personally need to be brought low or replaced," Walter asked, "to have the mob satisfied?"

"I don't think so," Young said. "We just have to add other coordinators. They don't believe whites can create a satisfactory program for blacks."

"Do you believe that?" Walter asked.

"To a certain extent," Young replied.

"It's frustrating that there is no willingness to examine the project on its own merits," Walter concluded.

The coordinators could be accused of a certain amount of blindness, as well. They had allowed the wounding of their egos to affect their judgment. Instead of using the criticism of the model school framework to strengthen and refine it (as promised), they mistook the negative opinions of a vocal minority more interested in protecting their turf than promoting reform for a blanket rejection of restructuring.

With Burkett's mind on other matters, there was no one to check up on the project's progress and nudge the coordinators into action with a few pointed questions. As a result, the question of what to do next was debated for weeks. Unable to reach any satisfactory solutions and overwhelmed by feelings of isolation, despair, and weariness, the project leaders allowed most of the remainder of the school year to slip away.

Finally, after nearly two months of indecision, they decided to put together a poll asking the faculty to indicate approval or disapproval of key components of the model school framework. The survey results revealed that there was more support for the restructuring plan than the coordinators had believed true after their frustrating experience with the workshop.[4] But the survey was conducted in late May 1990, when there was no time to resume work on consensus building until the fall. The project's forward motion had once again fallen victim to its organizers' lack of management experience and training.

The coordinators' handling of their African-American colleagues' demands betrayed a similar inexpertise. But in this case their inexperience would prove to be much more costly. During the month of April, the coordinators had managed to take one or two positive steps. They began a search for an organizational development consultant who could suggest ways they might regroup, and they scheduled a summit meeting with Heights High's black staff members. But the meeting turned tense almost from the start. Fearing that they might be pressured into making injurious concessions, the coordinators decided that only Young and McBride should attend the summit, thus giving the pair an excuse to avoid making decisions on the spot— they had to consult with their missing colleagues. Unfortunately, the absence of Walter and Thomas was interpreted by the black staff as a slighting commentary on the meeting's importance.

In addition, hoping to negotiate an acceptable compromise that would not result in the coordinators' losing control of the project's overall direction, an unusually nervous Young came across as rude. When the black staff members asked the coordinators point-blank about their intentions of naming one or two African-American counterparts, spokesperson Young did not answer directly. Instead he asked whether he could be honest, a gambit that did not win him any points for diplomacy. Nor did his response to assurances that it was all right to be candid. "I never know for sure," he replied.

When it finally came, Young's answer seemed lame. "An African-American should have been appointed a coordinator a year ago," he conceded. "On the other hand, while the four of us don't always agree, we've learned to work together very intensely, and to bring in another person—regardless of race—would upset the balance. I wonder if there's not another alternative. We envision the task forces as very powerful."

"Is the balance of the group more important than the statement we would be making about working together, more important than perpetuating what students perceive the problems to be?" Jean King asked. "The bottom line is: Where are our priorities? A new balance can be established."

"How can you have a model school without having a model staff?" Mary Watson wanted to know.

"When Hugh chose the coordinators, I felt powerless to change his decision, so I said, 'Forget it,'" admitted Dave Smith, a mountain of a man with a soft voice that he seldom exercised, giving his infrequent remarks unusual gravity. "But the time has come to talk about how we're going to achieve *real* integration."

Privately, the coordinators considered statements such as these to be prejudiced and insulting. They interpreted them as code words for the black faculty's belief that the white faculty did not have the best interests of black students at heart. Nonetheless, King, Watson, and Smith had succeeded in couching the argument in terms impossible to refute without sounding insensitive. By the end of the meeting, Young and McBride had agreed that the coordinators would give serious consideration to naming an unspecified number of African-American teachers as project leaders. However, as even this modest concession was clearly grudging, it did not buy the project leaders any goodwill with their black colleagues.

More than a month elapsed before the coordinators acted on their promise. Recharged by the results of their poll and a strategy session with an organizational development consultant from a local university, they were finally able to put aside their personal objections and agree among themselves that an African American should be appointed to their ranks at once. The appointment was one part of a new plan of action conceived as the turbulent 1989–90 school year drew to a close. The other part of the plan called for the super-retreat representatives to be reconvened in the fall as the Model School Planning Team to help the coordinators make needed changes to the model school framework.[5]

Three days before school let out for the year, the coordinators presented their reorganization plan to the superintendent. They had scarcely finished their explanation when Gearity began chastising them for the project's lack of progress, again warning that they and it were losing credibility.

The source of the superintendent's impatience soon became clear. After indicating her dismay that the coordinators still had no firm idea of the costs of restructuring, she explained that she hoped to point to the creation of a model high school as one of the reasons why the voters should support a property tax levy planned for the fall ballot. (A proposed increase in the local income tax for use by the schools had been overwhelmingly defeated at the polls that spring, in part because the district had not made a convincing case for its necessity.) Brushing off the coordinators' plans to continue consensus building in the fall with the warning that "you can study something to death," Gearity asked them to cost out the components of the model school framework over the summer.

Talking afterward in the parking lot at Miramar, the coordinators voiced concern about Gearity's instructions to establish a budget. Such an exercise seemed to them premature, given the fact that the faculty had yet to approve the proposed model. They also worried that if they were to put a price tag on a model high school, it might place them at further odds with the officers of Local 795, who were scheduled to begin salary negotiations with the school district that August. The coordinators feared that management might use as a bargaining tool the argument that the community could not afford to raise salaries *and* implement the Model School Project, too.

Wanting to move ahead with at least some aspects of the reorganization plan, the coordinators decided to set up a meeting with the black staff to discuss the selection of a fifth coordinator. Fran Walter volunteered to make the arrangements, but she was unable to do so before the last day of school, an occasion traditionally marked by a faculty breakfast.

Friday, June 15, 1990, was also Hugh Burkett's last official day, and there were some furtive looks cast in his direction when Lauree Gearity appeared that morning in the high school cafeteria. The superintendent had come to the breakfast at the request of Dan MacDonald. The chief steward wanted her to inform the faculty of an important development, so that the teachers would not be surprised when they read the news later in the papers. After being called up to the podium, Gearity announced that she had offered Heights High's principalship to C. Michael Shaddow, a veteran Cleveland public schools administrator. "He's someone the students and community will enjoy," Gearity said by way of explaining why she had chosen the forty-three-year-old white educator. "He's married, has children, and," in what appeared to be a Freudian slip, she blurted out, "he's little."

Frank Walter had been one of three finalists for the job, and some

Miramar watchers regarded Gearity's decision not to hire the only candidate clearly committed to carrying out the Model School Project as a sign of the project's lack of standing with her. Others attributed Gearity's rejection of Walter, whom she had once found sufficiently qualified to be assistant superintendent, to her need to demonstrate that business at the high school was not proceeding as usual.

After Gearity made her surprise announcement, MacDonald began the morning's program by acknowledging the staff members who were retiring or leaving for other jobs. He called them to the podium to receive a certificate and a long-stemmed flower. At the end of the ceremony, MacDonald noted that there was "another person who won't be here in the fall."

"Hugh, come up here," the chief steward said. "We have something for you."

Burkett walked up to the podium from his seat in the back of the cafeteria, received his flower, and turned to face his colleagues. He stood for a long time, seeming to gather his thoughts, before he finally spoke. "Goodbye," he said simply and returned to his seat. Tears sparkled in his eyes.

Then Frank Walter rose from his seat. Hiding his great disappointment that he had been passed over for promotion because (he suspected) he was too closely identified with the tarnished Burkett administration, Walter commandeered the microphone and launched smoothly into a prepared speech summarizing the many tangible accomplishments of his departing mentor and friend.

"But your impact goes far deeper than all of these external items," Walter observed. "You challenged this staff to think. You read the educational research and you encouraged us to do the same. You asked hard questions. You forced us to examine some of our educational traditions here at Heights High and to make changes where necessary.

"I hope," Walter concluded, "that the teachers here realize that they have been a part of something very special. We are never again going to meet a principal who asks so much of us."

Obviously moved, Burkett returned to podium to embrace Walter. Now he felt like speaking. He said that his six years at Heights had helped him to "grow, change, listen, and learn."

"I always thought I would leave here angry and tell you to stick it," Burkett confided.

Indeed, a part of him *had* decided that Gearity, the board, Madison, Altschuld—the whole contentious lot of them—were welcome to Heights High. After six years of struggling to help the district make good on its published mission statement—to recognize and challenge the unique potential of each student—he felt that he had paid his dues. "I had done more for black kids in that school than anybody ever had in terms of program design, expectations, changes that you could see in test scores and grades and attendance, reduced failure rates, black kids being less isolated," he would later observe. Yet no one in Cleveland Heights had ever acknowledged or appreciated his championship of black students. As a result, he had vowed he would never again take on the thankless job of trying to save a minority school.

But the sight of so many familiar faces—some of them belonging to persons he had come to regard as comrades in arms—touched another, deeper chord in him. "However, I do not leave by choice," Burkett concluded. "I've come to love you."

Perhaps a third of Burkett's colleagues gave him a standing ovation when he finished speaking. But most of them left the cafeteria without personally wishing him goodbye. The coordinators were also in a rush to get on with their summers. Their post-breakfast conference lasted only a few minutes. Fran Walter reported that the meeting with the black staff would now have to take place later that month. As no one else seemed enthusiastic about the prospect of giving up a lazy afternoon, Young (who taught tennis mornings for the Cleveland Heights parks system during the summer) volunteered to stick around town and represent the coordinators at the meeting. Walter promised to call him with the date and time.

Walter and Young's relationship still bore the scars of previous run-ins over the wording of Model School documents and the amount of speaking the coordinators should do at retreats. When the meeting date with the black staff was finally set for the afternoon of June 25th, Walter put off calling Young with the information until the last possible minute. She finally picked up the phone at eleven the morning of the 25th, only to learn that Young was not at home. Walter left a message, but Young did not return to his home until after the meeting had begun. As a result, no one from the Model School Project showed up for the session.

Deeply insulted by this seeming display of indifference, the black educators in attendance rebelled against the previously announced game plan. Walter had informed the African-American teachers that they could nominate up to four persons to fill the new coordinator's slot, from which shortlist the existing coordinators would make the final selection. Instead the black educators decided to appoint four coordinators. When Young heard this news from one of the appointees, a math teacher named Carol King who had served two years before on the original Model School Steering Committee, he responded that he would have to confer with McBride, Thomas, and Walter before accepting the counterproposal. The project probably could not afford to pay the release time of eight teacher-leaders, he explained to King.

Having, himself, succumbed to the summer doldrums, Young saw no reason to hurry along this unpleasant negotiation. It was not until mid-July that he spoke again with Carol King. Noting that the other appointees (one of whom was Mary Watson) were less suitable choices, he suggested that King alone join the project's leadership team. The math teacher demurred, saying she would have to consult with the other black teachers.

Had the coordinators been on better terms with their African-American colleagues, the latter might have accepted Young's compromise—to say nothing of his explanation of the snafu that had resulted in his missing the June 25th meeting. Ironically, the black teachers had come to that meeting prepared to accept the offer of a single coordinator's position. Now their backs were up. For starters, Young's assertion that Walter had failed to notify him of the meeting in time did not seem credible. Fran was too organized to slip up in such a fashion. They also questioned Young's authority. "Why do we have to get his permission? How does Steve get to choose?" was the general reaction of the math teacher's colleagues to Young's final proposition. Via phone the black educators decided that they had no other recourse than "to tell his mother," as King put it.

Calls were placed to the superintendent, who agreed to meet with representatives of the African-American faculty on July 23rd. At the meeting Gearity sympathized with the concerns expressed about the coordinators' insensitivity to equity issues, confiding that she had her own set of problems with them. Although the superintendent made no specific guarantees regarding the future composition of the Model School Project leadership team, she agreed that changes would have to be made. The new program officer in charge of education at the Cleveland Foundation had also voiced concern with the all-white leadership of the project the foundation had underwritten, Gearity noted.

Several weeks later, toward the end of August, Fran Walter received a call at home from Gearity. The superintendent reported that she had recently met with the education program officer of the Cleveland Foundation, from whom the district was seeking nearly $150,000 to underwrite the multi-cultural training program that it had been urged to start in the fall by various members of Heights Alliance of Black School Educators. The foundation representative (an African American who had formerly directed a program to promote the retention of minority undergraduates at the University of Maryland at Baltimore) shared Gearity's impatience with the Model School Project's lack of progress. It reflected poorly on both the foundation and the school district, the program officer felt, that so much money had been spent without a reasonable product to show for it.

The foundation official, who held a master's degree in education from Teachers College of Columbia University, also held the leadership abilities of the coordinators in low regard, noting that they had not "moved off the dime" even though the Model School Project was clearly "going nowhere." She was even less impressed with their belated reorganization plan, which, to mollify the officers of Local 795, called for District Steering Committee approval of all Model School proposals. From her elevated perspective, the program officer theorized that the plan ceded too much control over restructuring to the teachers' union, while not making sufficient provision for the involvement of the high school's minority faculty, the district administration, and the community.

For all these reasons the foundation's representative decided to prescribe harsh medicine for the project's ailments, and Gearity swallowed it. She had little choice, the program officer perceived. The superintendent did not want to jeopardize the district's future relationship with its most reliable source of soft money.

The Cleveland Foundation has decided not to release any additional funds to the Model School Project until a way can be found to ensure that the project's future leadership is more "inclusionary," Gearity informed Walter in late August 1990. Walter could not hide her disgust. How could foundation officials have made such a momentous decision about the project's fate without talking to the "peons" involved? Walter demanded of Gearity. Whatever happened to the foundation's objective of teacher empowerment? She pleaded with the superintendent to meet with the coordinators to discuss what could be done to reverse the foundation's decision.

Later McBride persuaded Walter that such a meeting was a waste of time. Why listen to Gearity repeat something they already knew? The Model School Project was over.

Epilogue

The Model School Project's reorganization took almost a year. Responsibility for some of the delay could be laid at the door of the Cleveland Foundation, which had offered to pay for an organizational development expert to advise on the most suitable reconfiguration of the project's leadership. Because philanthropic institutions move slowly and deliberately, a consultant was not hired until the late fall of 1990.

Then, after interviewing the concerned parties, the consultant deemed it unwise to dictate a specific course of action. Instead she advised superintendent Gearity to create an ad hoc reorganization committee made up of the four coordinators and two representatives each of the African-American faculty, the union stewards, and the high school administration. This committee was given responsibility for restructuring the project's leadership. Even with the consultant staying on to mediate, four months of discussion ensued. Finally, in February 1991, the ad hoc committee resolved that a formal deliberative body called the Model School Planning Team should be created to take charge of devising the model school.

The proposed organizational structure of the Model School Planning Team closely resembled that suggested by the four coordinators seven months previously, with one unfortunate exception: its members were to be

246

nominated by Heights High's eleven academic departments to represent departmental (as opposed to buildingwide) interests. On the plus side, the ad hoc committee reserved the right to pick which of the three candidates nominated by each department would sit on the planning team. It also claimed authority to name several at-large representatives—a prerogative aimed at ensuring that the team's membership reflected the desired sensitivity to issues of racial balance, adequate union participation, and project continuity insisted upon by the various factions of the ad hoc committee.

An acrimonious debate took place when the committee began to make its at-large selections. One of the committee's administrative representatives, a new assistant principal, set the tone of contention. The first of a succession of black administrators hired away from inner-city schools during Gearity's tenure—in response to pressure from the black professional staff to increase minority recruitment—this committee member attempted to deny Local 795 a place on the planning team by withholding her approval of the at-large appointment of two union representatives. Because the committee operated by consensus, her open hostility toward labor had to be painstakingly overcome. Then one of the African-American faculty representatives, math teacher Carol King, objected to the at-large appointment of Cas McBride, who alone among the coordinators had not managed to win a seat on the planning team by other means.

Saying that she meant no personal offense, King insisted that there was no need to guarantee all four coordinators a seat on the planning team, especially since their management skills had been called into question by their failure to bring the Model School Project to fruition. The coordinators refused to accept the math teacher's argument at face value. They perceived the motivation for her power play to be revenge for sins they had committed against the black faculty, but they were unable to mount a sufficiently persuasive counterargument to prevent McBride's exclusion. (McBride bemoaned her fate for a few weeks, then figured out a way to circumvent it. She made a successful run for union steward and was appointed to fill a vacant union seat on the planning team the following year.)

The twenty members of the Model School Planning Team were presented to the Heights High faculty at a brief induction ceremony on April 24, 1991. Elsewhere that spring two school districts better known for their experimentation with teacher empowerment were also, in effect, starting over with restructuring. In Dade County, Florida, members of the school board unanimously reaffirmed their commitment to a site-based management pilot program launched in 1987, even though average standardized-test scores at the thirty-two schools chosen to participate had not improved during the course of the three-year pilot. And in Rochester, New York, where teachers had been granted record-setting salaries in 1987 in expectation that they would willingly accept more on-the-job responsibilities, the teachers' union was forced to ratify a new contract in which a now wiser school board had strictly linked salaries to job performance under a new evaluation system.

In Cleveland Heights, the Model School Planning Team came together too late in the year for any real work to begin. Behind the scenes the more militant members of the black faculty complained that none of the eight African Americans on the team spoke for them, but the anger and urgent need for redress that characterized their mood the previous spring had disappeared. In the fourteen months that had transpired since the student walkout, the black community had solidified its influence on the Cleveland Heights school system. Now, in addition to Steve Bullock, there was a second black member of the board of education, appointed as a result of the midterm resignation of Maureen Weigand. A third African American would be appointed to the seat left vacant by the death of Judith Glickson the following December, giving blacks a majority say on the board for most of 1993.[1]

In addition to securing a representative voice for its black constituents at the highest levels of power, the school district renewed its commitment to providing intensive race relations training for its professional staff. Gearity's decision to proceed in 1991–92 with a second year of mandatory sensitivity training required her to ignore the howls of outrage that surrounded the first year's "multicultural workshops." Many white teachers had taken offense at the agenda of the initial workshops, which sought to help Caucasian teachers and administrators arrive at a working definition of racism so that they could more easily identify incidences of racist behavior—their own and that of other individuals and institutions. (The two-day sessions also tried to impress upon the African-American staff the ways in which blacks made possible their own victimization.)

The presence of Mary Watson and other black teachers regarded as strident separatists among the ranks of the workshop leaders made it all that much harder for some of the white participants to accept the charge that they were prejudiced. Adding insult to injury, many white veterans were dismayed to discover that some of their black colleagues did not share their commitment to integrated education—at least, that is how some whites interpreted the pressure put on them at some of the workshops to acknowledge that Cleveland Heights was a predominately *black* school system, as opposed to an *integrated* one. For the black educators who propounded this view, refusal to confirm this simple demographic fact was a sign of racism, proof that white teachers were trying to distance themselves from an association the latter obviously believed to be inferior.

By placing the taboo issue of racism on the table for discussion, Miramar hoped to encourage its painfully divided staff to take the first steps toward mutual understanding, but, in the end, the first-year workshops served only to exacerbate the racial tensions still simmering at Heights High School in the aftermath of the 1990 walkout.

During the year following the walkout, Miramar also tried to satisfy (at least in part) another postwalkout demand issued by the black activists on its professional staff: the call for the district to adopt an Afrocentric curriculum. The superintendent's crisis-management team countered with a more moderate proposal to form a new districtwide committee to suggest ways that the elementary and secondary curriculum could be made to reflect more emphatically a multicultural point of view. The committee recommended that the district hire a "multicultural coordinator," whose job it would be to make teachers aware of the wealth of multicultural textbooks, films, and supplementary materials available for classroom use. Instead of earning praise, however, the superintendent's decision to appoint a white educator to this part-time central-office post enraged many black staff members, who made their unhappiness known. In short order Gearity appointed a second part-time coordinator, this time choosing an African American.

Gearity would also hire blacks to fill central-office positions as executive director of secondary education and community affairs coordinator, and in the spring of 1992 the school district began an aggressive minority recruitment effort, sending representatives to visit a number of predominately black colleges located on the East Coast. Perhaps the most visible sign of Miramar's recognition of a new political order came later, in the summer of 1993, when the district promoted the black principal of Taylor Academy to the bellwether central-office position of curriculum director.

(Barbara Madison, the instrument of the board of education's heightened sensitivity to the diversity issue, watched these developments from afar. After her son completed his studies at Heights High, Madison resigned as president of Cleveland Heights–University Heights Concerned Parents, moved to another Cleveland suburb, and dropped from view.)

Aware that a greater emphasis on the principle of inclusion was taking hold in the school district, the Model School Planning Team selected, as one of its first acts, a well-liked although politically moderate African-American woman to serve alongside Steve Young as the team's cochair. This appointment put an end to grumbling at the high school about the planning team's representativeness. Within a few months of its official reorganization, the Model School Project disappeared as a worrisome blip on the radar screen of the black faculty activists.

Local 795 had done nothing to obstruct the planning team's formation, either. Glenn Altschuld having reached retirement age, the local was now under the uncertain direction of a new president, who represented an advance over Altschuld's shop floor–style leadership only in that he pronounced himself open to the union's becoming more involved with education reform while simultaneously declaring his disinclination to "go against the grain" of his membership. As a result, Local 795 once again decided to take a wait-and-see attitude toward the newly revived restructuring project.

The Model School Project posed no immediate threat to the status quo, in any event. During its eight-month hiatus the plan to restructure Heights High had lost its momentum. Many faculty members now labored under the impression that the project had died. Its rebirth in the form of a formal standing committee served only to relieve the 140 noncommittee members of their personal responsibility to act as agents of reform. Thereafter general interest in restructuring remained at a low ebb.

Even Bill Thomas lost heart, resigning from the Model School Planning Team early in its first months of operation. When the social studies representative followed suit midway through the 1991–92 school year, no one from the department could be persuaded to replace him. (Not even former planning team aspirant Phyllis Fowlkes expressed an interest. She was too busy with her work on the district's multicultural curriculum committee.) By the time the second round of Model School Planning Team elections were held in the late spring of 1992, several other departments had developed such jaundiced attitudes toward the project that they failed to nominate new members.

For all the high school faculty knew, the planning team was simply another in a succession of do-little committees. In the waning days of the 1990–91 school year, the team had decided to go back to square one, breaking up into small study groups. Each group was charged with the task of reviewing one or two proposed components of the model school framework. If a group found a proposal to its liking, its next step was to prepare a detailed plan for implementing it. This disjointed review process, which ensured that any changes made to the high school's organizational structure and operation would be piecemeal at best, took up the first semester of the 1991–92 school year.

During that time the planning team presided over a few modest improvements. It hired a student to serve as a part-time public "greeter" in the front office and produced an appointment calendar in which daily homework assignments could be recorded. The calendar was given free to ninth graders in the hopes that they would become better organized. The team's most visible accomplishment was to underwrite the Professional Development Institute. Organized by a planning team subcommittee that was cochaired by former team exile McBride, the on-site "institute" offered the high school faculty a choice of five free courses on topics ranging from "Cooperative Learning" to "Use of Macintosh Computers." Taught after school by professors from the department of education of a local university and counting as one hour of advanced-training credit on the salary schedule, the courses were so popular that they were offered again later in the year.

Institute organizer McBride took little pleasure from the program's success, however. Instead she decried the loss of vision that had accompanied the Model School Project's reorganization. "It feels like we've sold our birthright for a mess of potage," she privately complained, noting that Model School programs now under way or in the works merely represented reworkings of the usual administrative solution to educational problems, namely, "teachers working harder and smarter."

Indeed, it was Heights High's new principal, Charles Michael (Mike) Shaddow, who had conceived and aggressively promoted the professional development program as a worthwhile expenditure of the remaining Cleveland Foundation monies. Shaddow was highly aware of the foundation's interest in seeing tangible results. Otherwise he demonstrated a perfunctory interest in the planning team's activities, especially after he discovered his relative lack of influence on its deliberations. A twenty-two-year veteran of the Cleveland public schools whom Gearity hired more because of the favorable impression he made on the parents and high school students on her search committee than for his familiarity with the concepts of teacher empowerment and school restructuring, Shaddow seldom attended in their entirety the team's biweekly meetings, finding them too much like a "debate society" for his taste. After a time, he began skipping the sessions altogether, relying on the assistant principal who had attempted to keep the union from participating on the team to represent his administration's views.

As a matter of fact, Shaddow questioned whether Heights High School needed to be restructured. Having come from an inner-city school that did not even boast such amenities as a flagpole at the time he took over as principal, he did not see anything wrong with the academic program at Heights High. "Heights is not a school that needs to be turned around," he said publicly early in his tenure. "The kids who come here get the finest education possible."

Instead of embracing the Model School Project agenda of reform as his own, Shaddow preferred to concentrate on changes aimed at restoring the goodwill of the community and the damaged school spirit and pride of the student body. (This was, after all, his mandate from the superintendent, who had upped the stakes by promising the public that her appointee could "walk on water.") During his first year as principal, Shaddow concentrated on cosmetic improvements. He brought back daytime pep rallies and presented all the teachers with lapel pins in the shape of a tiger's head, in the mistaken belief that they would proudly wear them. (Few did.) Finding the shabby condition of the main lobby disgraceful, he located $75,000 to have it remodeled, recarpeted, and outfitted with sparkling new display cases. He also ordered a signboard installed on the Cedar Road side of campus, on which the high school's activities and victories could be publicized, and had the clock tower restored to working order and stripped of its offensive Mickey Mouse iconography.

Shaddow's concern for appearances (a preoccupation that also manifested itself in his coiffed hair, fashionable suits, and heavy gold bracelet) arose from his personal philosophy of education. Having improved "one of the worst schools in Cleveland—the kids were rotten and the teachers were rotten"—with similar sprucing-up and sports-recognition programs, the forty-three-year-old principal had come to believe that fostering students' self-esteem was the most important thing he could do to promote academic achievement. "It doesn't take a lot to provide a successful experience for kids," he suggested shortly after he assumed administrative responsibility at Heights High. "It can come from a teacher, custodian, counselor. Kids must be made to feel good about themselves."

Noting how greatly the Shaddow administration differed in substance and tone from that of the academics- and discipline-first Burkett administration, the latter's loyalists took to calling the new principal "Dr. Shallow" in private conversation. They sneered at the superficiality of his initiatives and innovations, such as his idea of awarding quarterly certificates of perfect attendance to teachers with no absences. Intended to satisfy Model School Project talk of the need for outstanding teachers to be recognized, the gesture served only to insult the faculty's sense of professionalism.

Other proposals that Shaddow began to broach with the high school stewards during his second year as principal revealed his discomfort with his predecessor's organizational innovations. Shaddow indicated his desire to return to the traditional eight-period day (a schedule that the Burkett administration had abandoned as not conducive to learning and proper discipline) and to reinstitute study halls and homerooms (features that the Burkett administration had banished as a waste of students' and teachers' time). Shaddow also expressed a desire to hire more administrators to "run" the school. And he wanted to dismantle the school's outreach-oriented guidance department in favor of restoring the traditional system of "assigned" guidance counselors (which his predecessor had replaced after determining that such a system was capable of meeting the needs of only about 20 percent of the student body). Even one of Shaddow's biggest fans on the teaching staff joked about the new principal's single-minded determination to see Heights High become "organized—just like his hair."

Shaddow's relative lack of interest in the academic side of the high school's operation came as a grave disappointment to Frank Walter. The assistant principal of curriculum was still mourning the loss of his dream of becoming Heights High's principal. Adding to Walter's misery, he now recognized that he would probably have to leave Cleveland Heights in order to realize his ambition of becoming a high school principal. This was a wrenching realization, as Walter had happily planned to devote his entire career to Heights High School. "It's the kind of place," he had once said admiringly to his wife, "from which you could retire." So certain had the future once seemed that the Walters had even figured out where they wanted to be buried—in nearby Lake View Cemetery.

In a less unsettled state, Walter might have been able to put aside his need to be a team member and resign himself to the fact that he and his new boss might never achieve a meeting of the minds. Given Walter's agitation, however, his lack of rapport with his superior assumed tragic proportions. There was only one good thing to be said for Mike Shaddow, Walter despaired. He gave Walter carte blanche. The assistant principal used his freedom to advance the work of ungrouping the high school's curriculum begun by Hugh Burkett.

During Burkett's tenure, Heights High's elaborate four-tiered system of ability grouping had been quietly dismantled, piece by piece by piece. While leaving the sacrosanct fourth-tier advanced placement and international baccalaureate courses untouched, the Burkett administration had succeeded in persuading the faculty to ungroup all elective subjects and eliminate third-tier accelerated courses in all but the English and social studies departments. Required subjects in the English, social studies, and science departments were still taught at the standard level, as were second-, third-, and fourth-year Spanish and French, but all other standard-level courses had been discontinued.

In the late fall of 1990, Walter wrote a series of three quietly impassioned memoranda recommending to the faculty that the remaining standard and accelerated courses be abolished. "The highest number of failures, truancies, and disciplinary referrals occur in standard-level classes," Walter noted. "The important question to ask is whether this is entirely the students' fault, or whether ability-level grouping actually helps to create the climate for failure, truancy, inappropriate behavior, hopelessness, and racism." Already softened up by the Model School Project's insistent promotion of heterogenous courses, the holdout departments gave an inch. Foreign languages agreed to ungroup French and second-year Spanish, while English and social studies dropped accelerated courses from their repertoire.

When weighed against his monumental unhappiness at finding himself a team player without a team, this accomplishment appeared mean and insignificant to Walter. Fran Walter was no better pleased with the snail's-pace progress of the Model School Project. By the end of the 1990–91 school year, Fran and Frank Walter had decided that the time had come to move on. That summer they uprooted themselves and moved to Prince William County, Virginia, where, with the help of Hugh Burkett, they had secured jobs in the public school system. The departure of the Walters, who were perceived (by their white colleagues at least) to be among the staff members most committed to the ideal of quality, integrated education, was taken by some as a sign of the further decline of the Cleveland Heights system. Although Frank Walter blamed his misfortune on Lauree Gearity, who he felt had chosen political correctness over merit in denying him the principalship, the Walters' friends fingered Mike Shaddow as the villain in this unhappy domestic drama.

In spite of his image problems at the school, Shaddow was at first generally well regarded throughout Cleveland Heights. Parents took appreciative note of the speed with which the new principal responded to negative news coverage with lengthy letters to the editor defending the high school. Residents who had no occasion to witness the increased incidence of gang graffiti in the high school's stairwells the year Shaddow took over as principal were reassured by his first-semester statements to reporters that the school's problems with gangs were now nonexistent. In fact, gang fighting in Cleveland

Heights would escalate by the following summer to such a point that the police began stopping, questioning, and sometimes ticketing or arresting black youth they encountered in problem neighborhoods in an attempt to discourage trouble on the streets.[2]

The police crackdown had no lasting effect. Two years later school and city officials felt the need to sponsor yet another public forum on the gang problem, at which time yet another authority on gang violence stated that collective community action was the answer. This reiteration of the advice the school district had received from other consultants following the gang-related murder of Wilbert Stallworth-Bey elicited a despairing response from a former member of the Cleveland Heights school board. "Our own community seems uninterested in solving this problem," he said. "As taxpayers, we are afraid and . . . struggling with our own problems. The chief of police is following the needs of the people in getting these kids off the streets."

Eventually Shaddow, too, could no longer credibly deny the existence of gangs at Heights High School. Switching tactics, he began to promote his administration's efforts to deter gang membership. "Straight talk and tough actions . . . are not our only approach," he asserted in a letter to the editor published in Cleveland's daily newspaper during his second year as principal. "We also work diligently at creating an atmosphere so good and so positive within our school that young people will not want to be on the outside looking in."

The latter statement was not merely savvy public relations. Shaddow had favorably impressed Heights High's students with the pains he took to greet them by name, make himself visible in the hallways, and show up at their sporting events. Unlike his predecessor, Shaddow extended his presence in the building by frequent use of the public-address system. On Fridays the principal liked to congratulate students for "a good week," after which he would exhort them not to smoke in the courtyard, or leave the campus during lunch hour, or hang around on Cedar Road after school—his "good cop/bad cop" approach in keeping with his philosophy of discipline, which could be summed up as "nurture" and "negotiate."

Predictably, Heights High's stewards perceived Shaddow's empathetic treatment of students as a sign of weakness, and they began complaining that discipline at the high school had become too lax. Whether students were responding to Shaddow's "nurturing" by behaving themselves or the house principals were "negotiating" reduced consequences for misbehavior, it was true that during Shaddow's first semester as principal the number of suspensions decreased by 20 percent from the comparable period the previous year.

By the conclusion of the first semester of the following year, however, Shaddow's honeymoon with the students was clearly over. Not only had the number of suspensions increased dramatically over the comparable period in 1990–91, they now surpassed by nearly 12 percent the number of students ejected by the hard-nosed Burkett administration during the penultimate semester of Burkett's tenure.

Moreover, the problem of the overrepresentation of blacks in the numbers of those disciplined had not gone away. Although Heights High's black enrollment continued to hover around 63 percent, nearly 92 percent of those suspended during the first semester of 1991–92 were African Americans. Predictably, the bureaucratic system set up that semester to monitor teachers' referrals at the behest of the Justice Department's Office for Civil Rights had failed to produce a race-neutral disciplinary process. As always, "the greatest number of referrals were from originators teaching standard classes at the ninth and tenth grade levels," Miramar noted in its first-semester report to OCR.

The perennial question of how to maintain proper discipline was not the only subject on which the new administration and the building stewards disagreed. Shaddow experienced no greater success than his predecessor in trying to transform the high school's unproductive steering committee of stewards and administrators into a problem-solving body. Despite years of encouragement to join the administration as full partners in governing the school, some stewards still clung to their traditional role as the watchdogs of the contract. This faction's resistance to change could be seen in the printed campaign statement physics teacher Bob Quail composed to solicit the faculty's support of his bid to serve as steward during the 1992–93 year. What has the High School Steering Committee accomplished? Quail asked. "Absolutely nothing," he declared. "The first three years were pretty much wasted in deciding on an agenda. Nothing of significance has been accomplished this year. While the stewards are discussing how to improve student achievement with the administration, you are probably wondering why they are not dealing with your specific problems and reporting back to you."

Shaddow shared Quail's low opinion of the steering committee, calling it a "joke." But HSSC's continuing paralysis seemed more of a tragedy than a farce. The monthly tug-of-war between stewards and administrators was to remain the closest approximation of shared decision making at Heights High, because, as it turned out, the Model School Planning Team's year-long review of the concept of a high school management council failed to produce any consensus.

In the end the planning team managed to launch only two full-fledged pilot programs. The first was designed to help eighth graders make the transition to high school. In early 1992 guidance counselor Dave Smith and his subcommittee won funding from the board of education for a summer institute program consisting of two three-week-long orientation sessions to be offered incoming ninth graders for a nominal fee.

Conceived as a humane alternative to the controversial ninth-grade entrance exam originally proposed by the Model School Project, the summer institute program was supposed to give the district an unencumbered shot at teaching new arrivals study and survival skills, career awareness, and cultural appreciation before they disappeared into the crucible of high school life. Unfortunately, Smith's subcommittee did not complete its preparations for the orientation sessions until late in the school year, leaving little time to publicize the new program and solicit applications. As a result, fewer than seventy incoming ninth graders took advantage of the two hundred available spaces.

Neither was the pilot school within a school that opened in the fall of 1992 an unqualified success. Despite coaching by chairperson Steve Young, the subcommittee in charge of creating the school found it impossible to persuade the Model School Planning Team of the need for a heterogenous enrollment. Although the subcommittee report pointed out the benefits of an ungrouped school, in which students were exposed to peers of diverse backgrounds and skills but all were expected to achieve at a high level, and in which the enthusiastic performance of the most highly motivated might serve to stimulate the slumbering interests and talents of the rest, these arguments left most members of the planning team unmoved. (No one wanted to cross the music department representative, who complained that, if the school's students were chosen on a random basis, a certain number of aspiring musicians would no doubt be assigned to its classes, making it highly unlikely that they would be free to take freshman orchestra the sole period it was offered. If that happened, he hinted darkly, the orchestra might not be able to field enough players to perform.) The planning team ultimately decided to mandate that the enrollment of the school within a school include neither the top nor bottom students but be drawn solely from the middle.

A reduced student-teacher ratio was the next crucial element to go. After receiving the board of education's approval of the school within a school in late January 1992, the subcommittee rushed into action, sending out a memorandum to the Heights High faculty soliciting applications from teachers interested in filling the school's four staff positions. Among the proposed job benefits described in the memo was a reduced teaching load of eighty students. In other words, class sizes in the school within a school would be reduced to twenty, well beneath the district's average.

Officials of Local 795 immediately filed a grievance against the pilot program with superintendent Gearity on behalf of the high school faculty, some of whose members had made known their fear that they would be asked to shoulder heavier class loads as a result of the school's creation. Subcommittee chairperson Young had been operating under the assumption that responsibility for fleshing out the pilot program lay with the Model School Project, but he was soon set straight by Gearity, who called him to a meeting in Shaddow's office and informed him that she could not live with a student-teacher ratio of less than twenty-five to one.

This sharp reminder of the teachers' place in the district's decision-making hierarchy served to crush Young's optimism about the prospects of site-based management. Angry and deflated, he mentally rejoined the ranks of those colleagues who felt that their only means of asserting authority was to ignore the dictates of administrators. Gearity could attempt to mandate whatever student-teacher ratio she chose. Young consoled himself with the knowledge that class size in the school within a school would ultimately be decided by a factor in his favor—that is, the probability that only a small number of students would volunteer to participate in the prototype program.

The settlement of the grievance against the school within a school revealed that Local 795's officers had an ulterior motive for taking action against the Model School Project. They were displeased that the planning team had bypassed the districtwide steering committee of union officers and administrators in the process of securing board approval of the pilot program. By filing the grievance, union officials hoped to force the superintendent to enter into formal negotiations with them about the types of policy and program decisions that must be reviewed by the District Steering Committee before being presented to the board of education.

In the past Gearity had fought off Local 795's requests that the DSC be written into the contract as an official decision-making body, believing that it would be unwise to dictate to future superintendents the manner in which they must work with the union. This time she agreed to talk, even though an attempt to formalize the status and powers of the DSC would move the district one step closer to granting the union an official role in such matters.

Gearity obviously did not wish to risk damaging the solid working relationship that she had forged with the new union president and his vice president, Dan MacDonald. Its value had been clearly demonstrated to her in December 1991, when the Cleveland Heights teachers ratified a new three-year contract *before* their old contract expired—the first time in recent memory that the triennial negotiations had been so rapidly concluded. (The board's offer of a cumulative 11.2 percent raise helped to speed an agreement.)

When the teachers' contract was signed, the members of the board of education commended Gearity for her nonconfrontational style. But there was a downside to purchasing the goodwill of the union. It became apparent two years later when the school system's treasurer reported that the district would end the 1993–94 school year with a deficit of at least $5.2 million. In response, the board of education placed a 8.9-mill operating levy on the November 1993 ballot, explaining that the new tax was the only way to avoid "tremendous financial jeopardy."

The voters of Cleveland Heights and University Heights had turned down three previous funding attempts by the district, and circumstances did not bode well for the passage of the latest tax proposal. During the summer of 1993, Lauree Gearity died at the age of fifty-one, less than a year after she was diagnosed with brain cancer. Credited by many with having prevented the district from self-destructing, Gearity was sincerely mourned, and after her death one of the system's elementary schools was renamed in her honor. Unfortunately, the loss of such a popular superintendent added to the impression of instability created by the February 1990 demonstrations.

Subsequently, Steve Bullock and Stu Klein announced that they would not seek reelection to the board of education. Having persuaded Gearity to involve the community in the preparation of a districtwide strategic plan— due to lack of financial resources, most its recommendations ended up on the shelf next to those of the School Consensus Project—the putative reformers felt that they had largely accomplished their main mission of legitimizing the school system's decision-making process. However, their desire to pass along their time-consuming responsibilities to a new generation of leaders only heightened the sense in some quarters that the district was rudderless.

A protest campaign to challenge the high school's reduction of ability grouping launched by a small but vocal band of affluent white parents further complicated matters. The campaign had been inspired by the parents' belief that the learning environment at Heights High had collapsed into chaos. As these were the constituents upon whose goodwill the passage of school levies depended, their outcry initiated a year-long lay study of grouping. In early winter 1993 the lay study committee proposed that ability grouping be reinstituted at the high school the following autumn. As one of her last acts, superintendent Gearity recommended that the board of education accept the committee's basic proposal, which it did, while modifying the committee's suggestion that fully *six* ability groupings be established. (That number was whittled down to the accustomed pre-Burkett level of four.)

This concession to white concerns about integration in the classroom helped persuade the school system's traditional supporters to return to the fold. Despite the lobbying efforts of an organized antitax group, the 8.9-mill levy passed in November 1993 by a comfortable margin. Once again financial ruin of the Cleveland Heights schools had been staved off at the eleventh hour. However, the public debate over the schools' educational practices and structure continued unabated.

The following year the board of education reaffirmed its support of ability grouping by voting down a proposal to reduce grouping in the middle schools. Under study by the middle school faculty for two years and presented with the support of Miramar's top African-American administrators, the proposal (among other things) would have required all sixth- through eighth-grade students, black and white, to take advanced math courses in preparation for studying high school algebra and geometry. The board's action prompted another group of parents—this one led by a former African-American appointee to the board, who had been defeated in her bid to win an elected term—to file a complaint with the U.S. Department of Education's Office for Civil Rights, alleging that the district's grouping policies were racially discriminatory. OCR promised a formal investigation into the parents' charges, but, even if the federal agency ultimately ruled against the district, previous experience suggested that its findings would do little to change educational practices in Cleveland Heights.

While the school community indulged its seemingly unslakable thirst for controversy and contention, the school system's performance problems went unameliorated. However, with the onset of educational proficiency testing in Ohio in 1990, its dismal educational record could no longer be kept strictly an internal matter. When the results of the first round of tests, which measured achievement at the ninth-grade level in reading, writing, mathematics, and citizenship, were published in 1991, it became a matter of public record that Heights High students had scored beneath the state average on each part.

The proficiency tests had been mandated by the Ohio legislature in an attempt to promote school reform. It was the legislators' intent that Ohio students must pass all four proficiency tests at some point during their high school careers in order to receive a diploma. Otherwise, they would merely be awarded a "certificate of attendance," even if they had earned the necessary high school credits to graduate.

This economic disaster-in-the-making seemed to await the majority of students in Heights High's then ninth-grade class. Less than one-third of them had been able to demonstrate ninth-grade proficiency in all four subjects on the first go-round. A closer examination of the scores revealed that 58 percent of the Caucasian students who took the first tests passed—hardly a cause for celebration. "A cause for panic" was how the Model School Planning Team interpreted the revelation that only 12 percent of the African-American students who took the first tests were able to demonstrate proficiency.

The disillusionment about the strength of the Cleveland Heights schools was accompanied in some quarters by a growing recognition that perhaps property values in Cleveland Heights were not inextricably linked to the quality of public education, after all. At least one prominent local political observer, a one-time Democratic mayor of the suburb, thought that he had detected a subtle change in attitude among his former constituents. "If the Cleveland Heights schools become 100 percent black, does that make any difference anymore?" John J. Boyle mused in 1991, shortly after the U.S. Census Bureau released data showing that, fully a quarter of a century after the first blacks moved into Cleveland Heights, the suburb remained 63 percent white. "The more the country moves toward the concept of school choice," Boyle continued, "the more likely public schools are going to be seen as schools of last resort. People no longer believe that the community will go to hell if the public schools are not strong."

In this financially straitened and beleaguered atmosphere, it was difficult to make meaningful plans for the future. Thus it came as no surprise when Miramar decided that it did not have the monies to pay for continuing Model School release time. Upon the termination of its foundation grant in June 1993, the Model School Project became a voluntary after-school activity. The last remaining participants formed a task force interested in discussing for yet another nine months the reorganization of the ninth grade.

Five years had elapsed since the project's conception. During this time little progress had been made toward achieving its goals of empowering the faculty and restructuring the high school. District officials had learned how to work more closely with Local 795 and listen more carefully to their black constituents, but the increased influence that the teachers' union and some members of the African-American staff and community enjoyed over the direction of the public schools had yet to produce noticeable improvements in student achievement.

Nor was it clear that in time it would. If the district's newly enfranchised and expanding staff of black professionals, for example, possessed ready answers to the persistent underperformance of black students, the results of the third year of state-mandated proficiency testing did not support that assumption. The percentage of ninth graders at Heights High who were able to read, write, compute, and demonstrate a mastery of civics appropriate to their grade level remained fixed at less than 30 percent.[3]

In the five years that transpired between the Model School Project's birth and demise, there had been time enough for one accomplishment, however. An entire generation of young men and women had passed through Cleveland Heights High School and been sent forth, prepared or not to function as responsible citizens and productive adults.

Afterword

The myriad ways that public schools work (wittingly and unwittingly) to suffocate change were made clear to me as I followed the progress of the Model School Project over the course of four tortuous years. As a freelance journalist who became an independent observer of this ambitious restructuring attempt, I was able to study at close range the workings of an entire school system. I witnessed destructive practices of which most outsiders are unaware, and to which even teachers, administrators, and school board members have become oblivious.

Many of these practices originated independently in earlier times as protections of the public interest or expressions of enlightened self-interest. Yet their convergence has now produced what I have come to call "the culture of inertia"—a systemic paralysis that can overcome even the most committed attempt to introduce meaningful change.

The components of the culture of inertia include, as I see it:

—the passive-conservative sociology of the teaching profession;
—the "revolving-door" nature of administrative leadership;
—centralization of school management;
—militant unionism;

—the institutionalization of turf and power disputes;

—the pervasiveness of "us versus them" thinking;

—racism, sexism, and classism and the interpersonal conflicts to which they give rise;

—lack of communication, miscommunication, and intimidation;

—lack of institutional memory;

—the political underpinnings of school boards;

—the dependence of public school financing on the whim and means of local homeowners;

—the market-driven nature of school curriculum and programs;

—educational policy making based on the race, gender, and class biases of dominant constituencies;

—limited resources (money, time, hard data and research, vision, community goodwill, parental involvement).

Because the basic organization of most large, comprehensive secondary schools mirrors that of Heights High, it seems reasonable to conclude that the entrenched behavior and counterproductive attitudes that bedeviled the Cleveland Heights reformers are endemic to the structure of public education in almost every community of size. In other words, the chronicle of Heights High School's attempt to restructure its operation may be used as a magnifying lens through which one can take the measure of the intractable nature of America's large urban and suburban school systems. In fact, readers may find it solidifies their understanding of the culture of inertia at their public school to call to mind from the preceding narrative examples of each of its components and to recollect the ways in which each impeded the progress of school restructuring at Heights High.

The insights gained are of no little moment. While about three-quarters of the nation's twenty-two thousand public high schools are much smaller than Heights, schools similar to Heights in size and structure enroll more than half of all public secondary students. The hidden dynamics that derailed the restructuring of Cleveland Heights High School make her sister schools similarly resistant to change.

It is my hope that, by exposing the culture of inertia that exists at Heights High School to the light of public examination, parents, politicians, and other concerned citizens may better reckon with the inhospitable climate their efforts to reform public education will encounter. Perhaps the story of Heights High's failed attempt at restructuring will also sound a wake-up call to teachers, administrators, and school board members, pointing out to them, by way of a close-to-home, "real-life" example, that the behavior, policies, and practices they hold dear are limiting their success as educators. Without question, *Welcome to Heights High* seeks to challenge all Americans to search their consciences for the answer to a haunting question first put to the nation more than a quarter of a century ago.

"Are Negroes such—in terms of innate incapacity or environmental deprivation—that their children are less capable of learning than are whites, so that any school that is permitted to become integrated necessarily declines in quality?" Kenneth B. Clark, a professor of psychology and pioneering black activist, asked in *Dark Ghetto* in 1965. "Or has inferior education been systematically imposed on Negroes in the nation's ghettos in such a way as to compel poor performance from Negro children—a performance that could be reversed with quality education? . . . If the first is false and the second true—and the community can be convinced of the fact—one of the basic injustices in American life could be corrected."

Appendix

Note on the Research

Between the spring of 1988, when the Model School Project began, and the spring of 1992, when its first major initiatives were in their final planning stages, I spent countless hours at Cleveland Heights High School as an independent observer and freelance documenter of this ambitious restructuring attempt. During the first two years of the project's life, I observed only Model School–related activities. I attended Model School committee meetings, staff retreats (eight in all)[1] and central-office or board of education briefings, as well as most of the private planning sessions conducted by the project leaders. By winter 1989 these had become a daily event.

At all meetings I took nearly verbatim notes on what was said in order to be as accurate as possible in reconstructing the chronology of the project, its changing strategy and objectives, and the various challenges to its proposals. My observation also afforded me a gold mine of insights into school procedures (formal and tacit), staff dynamics, and the teachers' and administrators' perceptions: of their roles, of their students and superiors, and of the high school's problems.

During the 1990–91 school year, when the Model School Project was placed on hold so that its all-white leadership could be reconfigured, I spent nearly every day at Heights High. To gain a firsthand appreciation for the caliber of the teaching, I attended classes in all of the high school's eleven academic departments except art and physical education, taking care to observe a mixture of standard, expanded, and advanced placement courses where they were offered and the work of both black and white teachers in the same department whenever possible. In order to better understand the school's culture and mores, I immersed myself in other aspects of daily life, attending student assemblies and pep rallies (as well as faculty meetings and the annual banquet hosted by the teachers' union), eating frequently in the faculty cafeteria, touring the sprawling high school complex from top to bottom, and observing important board of education and school-community meetings.

During this third year of research I took as my base of operations a small, glass-walled study room adjoining the high school's third-floor library, which contained computers and an abundance of professional journals and books—all exclusively for the teachers' use. When not otherwise occupied with classroom observation or interviews with teachers, administrators, and students, I situated myself at a table in the professional room (as it was called). There I reviewed back issues of the student newspaper and yearbook, read books that had influenced the "excellence in education" movement, and waited for opportunities to chat with faculty members. As a goodly number of teachers had reason to come to the professional room to use the computers at some point during the day, I was able to enter naturally into conversations with them. (By this time most of the staff had come to accept my presence and questions.) In this way I easily kept up with news, gossip, and gripes—informal intelligence that sharpened my understanding of the teachers' perspective.

During my fourth year of involvement with Heights High School, the Model School Project was drawing to a close. Although I continued to attend Model School meetings and chat informally with high school personnel, my time was consumed largely by the writing of *Welcome to Heights High,* a task that took yet another eighteen months to complete.

In addition to the above-mentioned sources of information, I drew upon coverage of the Cleveland Heights–University Heights school system by the *Cleveland Press* and the Cleveland *Plain Dealer* dating back to the high school's inception in 1904. I also conducted more than one hundred formal interviews of teachers, administrators, union leaders, students, and former students. Most of the leading proponents and opponents of the Model School Project were interviewed at least twice, some exhaustively. I also talked with a spectrum of local officials and civic leaders, past and present, in order to understand the community's perspective on the school system's history and problems.

Notes

Mise-en-Scène

1. In school districts elsewhere racial isolation was similarly on the rise. By the early 1990s two-thirds of America's black youth attended predominately minority schools.

Chapter 1. A Simple Remodeling Job

1. At the start of the 1989–90 school year, black students constituted 60 percent of the high school's total enrollment of twenty-five hundred.

2. National educational standards moved a step closer to reality during the presidency of former summiteer Bill Clinton. In 1994 Clinton signed the Goals 2000: Educate America Act, whose provisions include the development of national curriculum standards that states may voluntarily use as guidelines in their individual attempts to improve public education.

Chapter 2. A New Principle

1. Because of its proximity to several universities, college students and professors alike found Cleveland Heights a convenient and affordable place to live; among their numbers was (the soon-to-be-famous antiwar activist) Dr. Benjamin Spock, who taught at the medical school at nearby Western Reserve University. In this fertile soil chapters of the Student Mobilization Committee, Students for a Democratic Society, and even the Weathermen took root during the 1960s, all of them with followers at Heights High School. Although certain neighborhoods of Cleveland Heights continued to be attractive to the wealthy, these residents, too, tended to be of a liberal bent, at least insofar as in their willingness to live in a diverse community.

2. Altschuld had a favorite story about his rise to power. He claimed that during his first three years as a member of the AFT, he had not said a word at Local 795 meetings. One day Altschuld finally decided to make a few comments, and when he had finished, an older teacher turned to the group and said, "We've either heard the voice of the future or the world's biggest bullshitter." (This teacher retired after Altschuld became union president, but Altschuld continued to send him a copy of each new contract. Pleased to read of an especially healthy raise, the teacher once sent the union president a congratulatory note that concluded: "Now I know which it was: a little of both.")

Eventually the other members of Local 795 recognized Altschuld's leadership abilities and attempted to draft him to run for president. Initially he declined the honor, relenting only on the condition that henceforth Local 795 would be run "his way." While Altschuld declined in an interview with me to elaborate on his meaning, a retired union official codified Altschuld's strategy as "Might made right; and rank and file had to be loyal to him, as dissension would weaken the union."

3. In the old days turf issues had centered on the Tiger's Den, a large room, named for the high school's black-and-gold-striped mascot, across from the cafeteria that had been set aside in the late 1960s as a place in which students could hang out, play music, and talk. But the Tiger's Den had not long survived as a communal meeting place after the school's integration. Depending on one's perspective, the lounge had either been taken over by the black students, who made the white students feel unwelcome, or the white students had stopped frequenting the Tiger's Den because they did not want to associate with blacks.

4. Research on the effects of ability grouping on elementary students, the most studied area of this controversial educational practice, has been ongoing for more than fifty years. For a comprehensive review and analysis of the findings of this research, see Robert E. Slavin's "Ability Grouping and Student Achievement in Elementary Schools: A Best-Evidence Synthesis" (*Review of Educational Research,* Fall 1987, pp. 293–336). An excellent overview of the various criticisms of ability grouping can be found in *Keeping Track: How Schools Structure Inequality* by Jeannie Oakes, a social scientist at the Rand Corporation.

5. The Civil Rights Act of 1964 called for a study concerning "the lack of availability of equal educational opportunity for individuals by reason of race, color, religion, or national origin in public educational institutions at all levels in the United States." Conducted by James S. Coleman of Johns Hopkins University, the study unsuccessfully attempted to correlate achievement test scores from some four thousand schools with such traditional measures of a school's quality as teacher-pupil ratios, teachers' salaries, and expenditures per pupil. Ironically, the results of the highly publicized "Coleman report" contributed to the gloomy climate of opinion regarding the educability of minority children that other such Great Society programs as Head Start sought to dispel.

6. Edmonds deemed a school "effective" if it succeeded in eliminating the relationship posited by the Coleman study between student achievement and family background.

Chapter 3. Discipline First

1. One of Kunjufu's main messages was that educators must appreciate the importance black males place on oral expression—a tradition he believes can be traced back to the African "griot," or storyteller—if educators are to experience success in teaching them. "Teachers must understand that Black boys value their peers, walk, hat, 'rap' and signifyin more than anything else," Kunjufu writes.

By engaging in "signifyin"—"verbal duals [sic]" in which the opponents make derogatory comments about one another and one another's family members in the presence of an audience that urges them on—black males demonstrate their ability, Kunjufu argues, to suppress their emotions and think quickly on their feet. This test of their verbal competency makes "signifyin" an important rite of passage into manhood. "Unfortunately, when Black male children volley verbally in an aggressive, threatening manner," Kunjufu notes, "some teachers don't understand it, and interpret their behavior as fighting, when actually they were 'signifyin' to relieve tension and avoid a fight."

Kunjufu advises teachers to see "signifyin" in a new light—as an interest in public speaking—and to capitalize upon this interest by engaging black male students as frequently as possible in debates, dramatic presentations, word and rhyming games, and spelling bees and other oral contests.

2. The security staff's new skills represented a marked improvement over its former level of professionalism. "Before Burkett came, the hall monitors were of the Mod Squad variety," Frank Walter remembered, citing the day one of them spotted a trespasser in the building. The monitor pulled out a weapon and began firing at the intruder. School authorities were not aware that the monitor had taken the untoward precaution of arming himself; fortunately, no one was injured.

3. The crushing anonymity of student life was not a phenomenon unique to Heights. While about three-quarters of America's twenty-two thousand high schools have enrollments of fewer than one thousand students, the adolescents who attend the remaining quarter account for more than half of all secondary students.

4. By the time Walter became Lee House principal, 57 percent of the student body at Heights was black, yet 87.1 percent of the high school students suspended that year were of African-American descent.

5. For example, a program called PRIDE (Prevention, Referral, Intervention, and Drug Education) sought to direct students suspected of abusing alcohol or drugs to outside agencies for help, while GRADS (Graduation, Reality, and Dual-role Skills), a vocational home economics program, enabled pregnant students to stay in school by funneling them into Cleveland's social-service network and providing them with classroom instruction on subjects ranging from prenatal care to parenting.

School authorities estimated that up to one hundred students in the district became pregnant each year. This perplexing trend of babies having babies was made somewhat more understandable to one English teacher at Heights after she received a paper entitled "How to Have a Baby" in fulfillment of an expository essay assignment. The paper provided an object lesson in the high cost to ambition and self-esteem of low expectations for women.

"First you make love to someone, worthy of conceiving your child," its author explained. "Secondly, you miss a menstrual cycle. At this point you realize that you're either pregnant or you have a problem with your cycle. But you know that sooner or later you'll know the problem.

". . . [After] . . . going through the months . . . you're off to the hospital. You're in the delivery room getting on the table, the doctors rushing and getting cleaned up. Eventually they give you some medicine to soothe the pain. Afterward you should breathe deeply and be calm, the doctor coaches and beyond this point you breathe and you push and before you know it, you hereby have a baby."

6. Burkett was not unique in his inordinate attention to discipline. As a rule, high school administrators spend the better part of their professional lives pursuing truants and responding to disciplinary referrals. Burkett's predecessor complained that he was so

frequently pulled out of meetings to quell disturbances that he found matters of curriculum and instruction had to be relegated to after-school hours, a situation he lamented as grossly unfair, but which is actually intrinsic to the nature of public schools, as Philip Cusick's seminal study, *The Egalitarian Ideal and the American High School,* makes clear.

Because their tax-supported status obliges schools to accept all school-aged children regardless of their ability or interests, administrators are forced to devote whatever time and energy is necessary to compel the unwilling to attend and keep them under control. It would be much easier to tolerate class cutting and kick out the troublemakers. But with state aid tied to a school's average daily attendance, even a handful of truants or dropouts can result in a loss of funding equivalent to a full-time teacher's salary. And if students were to stay away in droves, the school would lose its claim to credibility.

7. By the end of Burkett's fifth year as principal, the number of students suspended from the high school had decreased by 48 percent, while the number of students recommended for expulsion had declined by 55 percent. These statistics do not necessarily indicate that Burkett's strict disciplinary policies and his no-exceptions enforcement of the rules were serving as a deterrent. It should be noted that during this period Heights High experienced an 8 percent drop in enrollment, in large part due to the creation of Taylor Academy, an alternative, off-site high school for failing ninth and tenth graders. Suspensions and expulsions were rife at the new school, suggesting that some of the high school's disciplinary problems had simply been transferred to other shoulders. Of the two hundred or so students who attended Taylor during the 1988–89 school year, eighty-one of them were suspended at least once, and twelve Taylor students were expelled.

Nor had incidents of violent behavior been completely eradicated at the main school. Failure to comply with directives, fighting, and truancy were the top three causes of all secondary school suspensions in the district in 1988–89. Possession of a weapon or dangerous instrument, assault, and failure to comply with directives were the top three reasons why Heights secondary students were recommended for expulsion that year, followed closely by fighting.

8. The disturbance began when "a tough white kid got the best of a tough black kid in a fight. The black kid went and got his friends, who beat up on the tough white kid," Cleveland journalist Ken Myers, a junior at the high school at the time, would later write of the events of January 24, 1975. "By lunchtime, packs of black kids were roaming the halls, sucker punching white kids who were standing at their lockers. The hallway leading to the cafeteria . . . was ringed with angry blacks, who smacked white kids 'upside the head' as they walked by."

When the administrators proved unable to quell the fighting, they called the Cleveland Heights police, who arrived on campus around 2:30 P.M. with "billy clubs ablazing," Myers recalled. Within fifteen minutes the police had restored order, but not without cost. Five officers and two students suffered minor injuries, and three black teachers claimed that they had been manhandled by the police as they were attempting to escort a pupil who had been fighting to an office. Apparently mistaking the struggling teachers—two women and one man—for students, the police officers rushed to separate the group. The officers threw the women against the wall and grabbed the male teacher around the neck, in the process knocking his glasses to the ground, according to the teachers, who all but said to reporters that the officers' zeal had been racially motivated.

Chapter 4. Time for Reflection

1. As the chairman of Heights High's science department, Al Abramovitz had been instrumental in the district's adoption of the grouping. Having found the nationally recognized advanced placement program too "canned" for his liking, he pushed his science department colleagues to collaborate with nearby Case Institute of Technology on the creation of a custom-tailored honors curriculum, an innovation that eventually spread to the school's other academic departments. Abramovitz's concern that the best and the brightest students be challenged to perform at their fullest potential survived his rise to the superintendency.

To carry out the task of writing new, "improved" guidelines for grouping in 1980, Abramovitz formed a task force on which key members of the internal curriculum committee and a prominent official of the Urban League were invited to sit. (The superintendent understood the political utility of citizens' committees, having written his doctoral dissertation on the subject. After examining the work of every lay committee formed by the Cleveland Heights–University Heights Board of Education between 1955 and 1975, he concluded that their purpose fell somewhere between placation and partnership.)

Deliberating for nearly a year, the task force finally suggested that the number of groups should be reduced from four to three and renamed, and that criteria for placement should be expanded beyond achievement test scores, grades, and staff recommendations to include parental or self-nomination. It also advocated that learning centers in math, English, science, and social studies be established to tutor those who needed extra help in order to advance to higher groupings and that students' placement profiles should be reviewed annually. Designed to promote the upward mobility of lower-level students and ease racial isolation in the high school, these new measures had by and large been proposed by Abramovitz himself prior to the task force's formation, in response to the internal curriculum committee's call for reform. With an eye to public relations, the task force dubbed its plan Project Student Achievement.

The impact of Project Student Achievement was assessed three years later by the School Consensus Project (SCP), a committee of concerned citizens trying to develop a school-improvement plan that would help to dispel the perception that the quality of the Cleveland Heights–University Heights schools was declining (an impression, SCP leaders privately believed, that seemed to grow in direct proportion to the increasing number of black students enrolled). An SCP subcommittee on curriculum found grouping practices at the high school substantially unchanged.

The subcommittee attributed the lack of progress in part to scheduling difficulties. Although it had been contemplated that "average" students would be able to put together a mixed schedule of standard, expanded, and gifted and talented classes to correspond with their varying abilities in different subject areas, this kind of flexibility had proved next to impossible to achieve because of the way course offerings at each ability level were blocked out in flights.

Negative peer pressure had also played a role in limiting upward mobility, the subcommittee reported. Black students who qualified for entry to upper-level classes risked being shunned by their peers as "white," a powerful incentive to stay put in standard or expanded courses with the majority of their peers. (Incredibly, Project Student

Achievement policy allowed students to enroll in courses one level of difficulty below that indicated by their placement profiles as appropriate.)

The report also found fault with the degree of subjectivity surrounding the guidance department's placement decisions, noting that there was a "lack of clarity about . . . criteria, goals and procedures." Among the areas of confusion cited were the weight that should be given to the recommendations of parents or teachers in placing students in upper-level courses; the frequency with which placement profiles were to be reviewed; and the degree to which such profiles should be used to determine ability level. Lacking consistent criteria for placement, it was not surprising that Heights High's guidance department was an object of suspicion among some black parents involved in the School Consensus Project. However, no mention was made in the report of the criticism that some black parents voiced in private conversation about the department's general assumption that their children did not have what it took to succeed in upper-level classes.

Nor did the SCP report make mention of the fate of the achievement centers. This part of Project Student Achievement had not worked as planned, either, having attracted the most-highly motivated students rather than those who could have most benefited from individual tutoring. A year after the SCP subcommittee report was issued, three of the four achievement centers closed due to lack of funds. The math achievement center remained open only because its teacher-tutors volunteered to donate their services. The operation of the achievement centers had originally been underwritten by a Cleveland Foundation grant, and when these soft monies ran out, the district chose not to allocate its own resources to keep the centers open.

2. It should be noted that Burkett did not oppose special programming for the truly gifted or the genuinely slow, who constituted the top 5 percent and the bottom 5 percent of all students, in his estimation. In fact, it was his administration that moved to replace the high school's in-house gifted and talented program with participation in the widely accepted advanced placement program, allowing high achievers at Heights to study college-level courses in a variety of subjects in anticipation of receiving college credit or being able to waive required college courses should they do well on a standardized exam given upon completion of the course.

3. The community foundation's record of supporting civic- and school-improvement projects in Cleveland Heights stretched back to the mid-1960s, when it began to realize that the suburb's success or failure in coping with integration would influence public policy and private pursuits throughout greater Cleveland. Among the many activities made possible by foundation underwriting were Project Student Achievement and the School Consensus Project.

Chapter 5. The Dilemma of Leadership

1. Heights administrators had long ago abandoned as quixotic their insistence upon the use of this daily planning tool, which most of the faculty disdained as busywork.

2. At the same time that the Model School Project was getting started, Burkett was also attempting to encourage the restructuring of the high school guidance department. With the assistance of a local university, the department's eight overburdened staff members conducted an intensive self-examination that resulted in their agreement to

become teacher-counselors who anticipated how to solve student problems through classroom instruction, innovative programming, and group work, rather than continuing with their Sisyphean attempt to respond meaningfully to whatever crises walked through their office door. The department's new structure was known in educational circles as a "competency-based" model, whose chief virtue lies in making sure that those students who, for whatever reasons, decline to visit the guidance office are given access to needed information and services.

Chapter 6. Less Is More

1. Sizer went on to create the Coalition of Essential Schools, a network of fifty reform-minded schools interested in attempting to put his ideas into practice. By the mid-1990s the network had grown to five hundred member schools and attracted a $50-million grant from publishing magnate Walter Annenberg to support its members' efforts at restructuring.

In both his writings and his actions Sizer posed a significant challenge to the "comprehensive" high school, a populist trend in American public education that gained final ascendancy in the post-Sputnik era of school consolidation and strengthening. In the name of ensuring equality of opportunity, comprehensive high schools provide vocational and business training in addition to the traditional liberal arts education of the public academy. To Sizer and other leaders of the excellence in education movement, however, comprehensive high schools are profoundly undemocratic. They symbolize the failure of public education to teach critical-thinking skills necessary to succeed in a postindustrial society to the majority of students.

A follow-up to Sizer's *Horace's Compromise* went further in assessing the failings of the comprehensive high school, arguing that, in seeking to be all things to all students, it ends up underserving most. Sponsored by the National Association of Secondary School Principals and the Commission on Educational Issues of the National Association of Independent Schools (the partnership that commissioned Sizer's original study), the second book was entitled *The Shopping Mall High School*. The authors deemed the analogy an appropriate description for a "universal public service" that offers "learning and mastery [as] just one among many consumer choices."

2. Indeed! Public school bureaucracies are accustomed to measuring success according to quantitative, rather than qualitative, norms: the number of days and hours students spend in class, the number of Carnegie units (credits) they complete, the grade point average they achieve, and so on.

3. Burkett believed that it might be possible to reduce the average student load without hiring more teachers. His reasoning: If fewer students had to repeat courses due to failure because they were now benefiting from greater personal attention, then more teachers could be released from remediation duties and made available to take up the slack arising from the decrease in the average workload. Frank Walter agreed with Burkett's analysis. "It's failure that's uneconomical," he insisted.

4. At one time the English department alone offered upward of fifteen electives ranging from "Sports Hero in Literature" to "Values of Life and Death" with which students could fulfill the graduation requirement for senior English. Those hoping to

slide through their final year in high school favored "Take Your Pick" over traditional college-prep courses such as "World and British Literature," in that the former allowed the students to inform the teachers which three or four novels they intended to read that semester. Similarly, the department's decision to offer "Shakespeare" and "Hemingway and Fitzgerald" as electives meant that students would not read these important authors in their mainstream English courses. By encouraging departments to take responsibility for scheduling and the provision of equitable student loads, the Burkett administration had reduced the number of superfluous, marginal, or elitist electives that found their way into the curriculum largely because individual teachers had proved effective at lobbying previous administrations on behalf of their pet offerings. And Burkett's model school proposed to carry the telescoping trend even further.

5. African-American literature and African-American drama and poetry were also offered as electives, and an elective in African-American music would be added to the curriculum in 1990–91.

6. French teacher Reva Leizman was among the team members who favored taking this moderate approach. Leizman had herself attended Heights High School during the 1960s. Despite the fact that they were then in the majority, she and her fellow Jewish students had endured their share of discrimination, she remembered. Only one Jewish American had ever been considered worthy of mention by her American history teachers, for example. While these kinds of hurtful experiences made her empathize with other victims of prejudice, Leizman thought it unwise to dwell upon obstacles to success. "Eventually, you have to get beyond worrying about what's holding you back and just do the best you can," she reasoned.

To illustrate how hypersensitivity to racial prejudice can become a trap that she hoped the race relations study team would avoid, Leizman liked to tell a joke. A Jewish girl asks a Gentile friend if she may borrow the friend's comb.

"Fine," the friend responds.

"May I borrow your brush?"

"Fine," the friend responds.

"How about your toothbrush?"

The friend demurs.

"Anti-Semite!"

Chapter 7. Solidarity Forever

1. In 1987 the Rochester Teachers Association negotiated a landmark contract in which the teachers agreed to take on additional after-school duties in return for salary increases that would make them among the best-paid public school educators in the nation. Most notably, the teachers' union promised that its members would accept the responsibility of monitoring the academic progress and attending to the personal needs of twenty students. The new contract also exposed teachers to greater professional scrutiny in the form of peer mentoring and review. The same year the United Teachers of Dade agreed to help the Dade board of education launch a pilot program of site-based management and shared decision making in thirty-two of the district's schools.

2. In its nearly two decades as the Cleveland Heights teachers' bargaining agent,

Local 795 only once threatened a walkout for reasons other than money. In 1975 Glenn Altschuld warned the community of the teachers' intention of striking should the board of education not meet a contract-mandated deadline for adopting the district's first detailed discipline policy, a possibility the board had raised as a trial balloon. The policy was approved a week later.

3. Glenn Altschuld watched the "negotiations" with interest. He regarded Burkett's plan as proof positive that the high school principal knew nothing about education. To the labor leader's surprise, Burkett had turned out to be a nice guy—Altschuld would not have hesitated to invite him to his poker table had he been a fellow teacher—but the principal obviously had no understanding of the fact that the attention span of the average high school student was "only about twenty seconds."

Altschuld would never dream of subjecting his students to a fifty-minute lecture. Midway through he would have to give them a break, "let them chew gum or something." To do otherwise, he thought, would be counterproductive, to say nothing of unconscionable. However, Altschuld knew that about half of the high school faculty supported the concept of a seven-period day (the union having polled its membership), so it looked as if all the stewards could accomplish in their negotiations with Burkett was to delay the inevitable.

4. Burkett also decided to act upon his belief that high schools should get out of the business of providing vocational education, if not because of concern for the issue of educational equity, then for the pragmatic reason that it was impossible for them to keep abreast of technological innovations in the workplace that they were purportedly preparing students to enter. Along with dropping study halls and homeroom, he virtually eliminated two of the school's vocational divisions that were no longer attracting sizable enrollments: home economics, which offered a number of cooking and sewing classes, and industrial arts, which taught courses in elementary electronics, machine tools, and woodworking. (In the latter, students learned to make such high-tech products as carved-wood address signs, examples of which proudly dotted the front porches of homes throughout Cleveland Heights.) Despite the dead-end nature of these classes, their termination did not sit well with the departments affected, adding to the unpopularity of the decision to switch to a seven-period day.

5. Failure to take Local 795's side in a dispute with administration could lead to unpleasantness, as Model School coordinator Cathleen McBride could attest. McBride crossed the picket line during a one-day strike in 1980 because at the time she considered such pressure tactics to be unprofessional. After the strikers returned to their classrooms, McBride walked into the teachers' lounge one day, only to discover her picture mounted on the wall accompanied by the caption: "Scab." McBride's punishment did not end with the public put-down. For years after the strike, she continued to be snubbed by some of her fellow teachers, who pointedly refused to say hello upon encountering her in the building.

6. The Teachers Association's defeat was tied to the perception that the NEA affiliate lacked the clout to negotiate even a modest pay raise. This was not at all the case, according to Michael G. Ferrato, Burkett's immediate predecessor as Heights High principal, who was a young association activist at the time. Association leaders had felt ethically bound not to discuss the progress of the talks at the time, Ferrato claimed.

The salary increases AFT Local 795 later won in 1971 were very close, he asserted, to those discussed with the association. Rather, it was the board of education's refusal to accommodate the association's desire for partnership in governing the schools that had prevented the finalizing of a new contract. In Ferrato's view, the central administration had preferred to take its chances "duking out each concession or teacher right" by means of collective bargaining rather than voluntarily ceding some of its power to a collegium. Apparently the board had not expected to so weaken the association that it would be swept aside by the more militant AFT.

7. Frances Herskovitz was one of the first elementary school teachers in the district to join Local 795. If Herskovitz's experiences on the job were typical, the women teaching elementary school in Cleveland Heights in the early 1970s constituted a powerful source of discontent that Altschuld had the political savvy to tap. When Herskovitz was hired in 1965, district officials ("typically") assigned her to teach at Coventry school, the elementary building farthest away from her home, even though she had requested assignments closer to her home so that she could go there at lunchtime to say hello to her young children. As she was settling in at Coventry, the principal casually informed her that "his" teachers joined the Teachers Association. It was almost as if he saw the association, Herskovitz marveled, as an arm of the administration.

The elementary teacher eventually discovered the reasons for the principal's sanctioning of a labor union. Association members never saw a written contract—instead they were simply told what wages and benefits they would be receiving—and issues dealing with working conditions seemed to be beyond the association's ken. Looking for someone to champion her need for a decent salary, Herskovitz finally decided to talk with Local 795's newly elected president, Glenn Altschuld, and came away committed to helping him get the AFT unit elected as the teachers' collective bargaining agent. Here was a union leader who shared her outrage with the indignities of an elementary teacher's life, such as not having any free time to go to the bathroom during those weeks when it was one's turn to supervise recess.

Little did Herskovitz suspect that Altschuld placed the blame for the teachers' lack of clout squarely on their own shoulders. (At the time he was courting the votes of the elementary schools' staffs he had been careful not to voice his opinion openly.) In private conversations, however, he often observed that there were two kinds of teachers: "women and men who zipped their pants on the side." In other words, the teaching profession was dominated by women, who thought of themselves as "second-classers and second-wagers." If these self-defeating attitudes had begun to disappear by the time the union president retired in 1990, it was because of labor leaders such as himself, Altschuld believed, who "yelled at teachers to be professional and man the picket lines."

8. These scare tactics had, on the other hand, horrified strike captain Frank Walter. Fearing for the safety of all involved, Walter ordered the strikers to set up their picket line the next day at the rear of the high school. Walter's hopes of avoiding a repeat of the dangerous confrontation between muscle and metal were dashed when the vans, having been rerouted by the administration for similar reasons, showed up early the next morning at the back gates. Walter later heard through the grapevine that district officials were convinced that he had intentionally repositioned his pickets after being alerted to the change in itinerary by a well-placed spy.

9. Even his friends liked to tell a story that illustrated a certain amount of rigidity on

Quail's part. It seemed that Quail came to work in Cleveland Heights completely by accident, after he wandered by mistake into a room in which the school district was recruiting promising education majors at the University of Chicago, where he was a student. Needing a means of transporting himself to his new job in Ohio, he went to a car dealer, bought the first vehicle he saw on the lot (or so the story went) and drove it straight to Cleveland Heights. After locating the high school, Quail continued driving down the street until he saw an apartment building, where he stopped his car, went inside, and rented a suite. He had lived in the same apartment, the story concluded, since his arrival in 1966.

Chapter 8. A Strategic Retreat

1. John I. Goodlad, who directed an intensive study of American schools in the early 1980s as dean of the graduate school of education of the University of California at Los Angeles, was among the leading proponents of restructuring high schools into smaller "schools." "If positive relations with teachers are related to student satisfaction . . . and corrective feedback is related to student achievement, then it becomes imperative to seek school conditions likely to maximize both," Goodlad argued in *A Place Called School: Prospects for the Future,* an influential blueprint for reform based on Goodlad's and his associates' observation of one thousand classrooms in junior and senior high schools across the country, as well as exhaustive surveys of teachers, students, and parents. "The never-ending movement of students and teachers from class to class appears not conducive to teachers and students getting to know one another, let alone to their establishing a stable, mutually supportive relationship. Indeed, it would appear to foster . . . casualness and neutrality."

The concept of schools within a school also spoke to the concerns of a group of African-American scholars who in 1989 had described their fears and hopes for the education of black youth in a thoughtful essay entitled *Visions of a Better Way: A Black Appraisal of Public Schooling.* "Recent reports have largely ignored . . . the centrality of *human relationships in education,*" stated Dr. Sara Lawrence Lightfoot, a professor at Harvard University's Graduate School of Education, who wrote the report on behalf of the Committee on Policy for Racial Justice. "Testing and tracking are obvious topics of discussion; the lack of reinforcing relationships in the learning experiences of black children is equally at issue. Neither teaching nor learning is a purely mechanical process. Few children are motivated to inquire into the wonders of the world around them if they are not aided by a warm and caring relationship with another human being."

2. Burkett, for his part, had been looking for a nontraditionalist whose first priority would not be to "protect the books." In recasting the job of high school librarian into a teaching position, Fran Walter proved his instincts about her to be right. Instead of spending their days cataloging books and admonishing noisy students to be quiet, Walter and Barbara Reynolds Schmunk, the other full-time librarian hired by Burkett, made a practice of consulting with teachers about the content of their courses and then pulling together books and reference materials that they thought would be helpful. They also regularly advised students conducting research projects on the existence of

pertinent information, invited teachers to bring their students to the library for lectures on research techniques, and frequented the school's computer labs, offering word-processing instruction to both students and teachers alike.

Chapter 9. Intramural Rivalry

1. In attributing the squeeze on district finances solely to exorbitant teachers' salaries, Moskowitz reduced a complicated problem to its most simplistic terms. True, wages constituted about 85 percent of the school system's budget. But when contract negotiations began in August 1988, the average salary earned by Cleveland Heights teachers ranked only seventeenth highest of thirty-one districts in Cuyahoga County. At the conclusion of the first year of operation under the stringent new contract negotiated by the Moskowitz administration, Cleveland Heights had sunk to twenty-fifth highest, a ranking less than conducive to the system's avowed goal of recruiting the best teachers available.

Just as pertinent in considering the problem was the fact that, like mature, inner-ring suburbs throughout the country, Cleveland Heights and University Heights had no large tracts of unused land for new industrial, commercial, or even residential development. For this reason the two suburbs had comparatively low property tax bases (in this case, the fifth lowest of the county's thirty-one school districts).

The landlocked nature of Cleveland Heights and University Heights made the public schools overly dependent on the residents' willingness to tax themselves at an increasingly higher rate in order to cover ever rising expenses. (During the decade preceding the 1988 contract negotiations, the school's budget nearly doubled, growing from $21.1 million to $40.9 million.) On the whole, the community had risen to the challenge: the district boasted one of Ohio's highest property tax rates.

Yet the district was unable to capture most of the new revenues arising from increases in its voted millage and from growth in the value of existing property, thanks to the passage in 1986 of Ohio House Bill 920. A tax-relief measure, House Bill 920 froze the income that a public school district could derive from each of its voted mills at the dollar amount yielded in the year the millage was passed. At the same time, the state department of education continued to subtract 2 percent of a district's total assessed property valuation as a charge-off from its basic-aid package to the school, a calculation that had the effect of a double whammy in that it assumed that school districts earned more tax revenues (due to inflationary growth in property values) than they were actually able to collect under the provisions of House Bill 920.

As if that situation were not bad enough, the department of education also built into its calculations of each district's basic-aid package a "cost-of-doing-business" factor capped at a percentage far less than the disparity between teachers' salaries in urban and rural areas.

Due to these inequities, the Cleveland Heights–University Heights schools were able to afford an expenditure of only $5,347 per pupil in 1988–89, a per-pupil expenditure equivalent to that spent by the hard-pressed Cleveland public schools. On the other hand, more affluent counterparts in the adjoining suburbs of Shaker Heights and Beachwood were able to muster $7,574 and $11,089, respectively, per student.

Some reformers have pointed to this built-in disparity in the financial resources of property-poor and property-rich school districts—a problem affecting the quality of public education in all fifty states—as reason to switch to a system based on federal redistribution of funds. Overburdened homeowners in Michigan adopted another tack in 1994. They voted to begin using sales and other taxes, rather than levies against property, to pay for the operation of the state's public schools.

2. An additional $2 million was needed to cover the increase in salaries in the first year of the new contract alone.

3. "Clueless" was his favorite description for central-office administrators, such as a certain department head who, Burkett liked to claim, had been on the job for two years without setting foot in the high school or even calling him on the phone. The high school principal freely admitted to having no use for most central-office types, which was why, Moskowitz had informed him more than once, they stayed away from the high school.

4. Even as simple a task as the preparation of the high school's annual handbook of course descriptions became a point of contention between the two administrators. The trouble began when the assistant superintendent learned about Burkett's practice of allowing his various academic departments to establish teachers' schedules. Concerned that this attempt at site-based management might adversely affect the student-teacher ratio that the central office tried to maintain systemwide in order to prevent overstaffing, Gearity reminded Burkett that the board of education must approve the offering of any high school course for which fewer than eighteen students had preenrolled.

Burkett saw the matter differently: If the high school's foreign language department, for example, wanted to offer a course in Russian, knowing that only a small number of students would sign up to take it, the department should be allowed to make that determination, provided that all the other teachers in the department were willing to pick up the slack by increasing the sizes of their classes.

In Burkett's view, the fact that he submitted a list of the high school's undersized classes to the board for approval *after* they had been scheduled was a technicality, and a procedure that had never before been questioned. Gearity might have shared Burkett's relaxed attitude had she possessed more experience in dealing with the board, but, as a newcomer to central administration who needed to prove herself capable of handling a "man's" job, she felt compelled to bring to the superintendent's attention this example of insubordination.

As a result, Moskowitz called Burkett and Frank Walter into his office and chewed them out in Gearity's presence. Burkett interpreted the reprimand as primarily a show of moral support for the assistant superintendent, who at the time was "taking punches" for Moskowitz as the superintendent's surrogate in contract negotiations with the union.

Chapter 10. Hearts and Minds

1. This fateful decision was made at the May 1989 retreat, when, after describing the troubled state of race relations at Heights High as the "elephant in the living room," Cas McBride inquired how the group should deal with the school's unhealthy social climate.

"I'm going to jump out the window," Hugh Burkett said. "It's so depressing."

"It's not going to heal until you lance it and let out the pus," McBride counseled.

"Are we a broad-based enough group to talk about this?" Burkett asked, referring to the absence of African Americans in the project's inner circle.

"If we *were* broad-based, we wouldn't be talking about this," Bill Thomas observed. There was a tacit agreement between black and white teachers not to ruffle the appearance of civility they maintained toward one another.

"I would leave this stuff alone," cautioned Steve Young. "The staff is more likely to respond to practical proposals. If we deal with changing things like school structure and governance and curriculum, then the climate will automatically change."

"Don't you think there would be some excitement to deal with these issues?" Fran Walter countered. "Wouldn't people get a rush out of being able to say, as first step, that school climate is a problem? If somebody were to ask *me*, *I* would say that lack of communication and fear are our biggest problems."

In the end it was Young's pragmatism rather than Walter's passion that carried the day. With so many other problems to resolve, the Model School Project leaders decided to forgo an attempt to address the knotty issue of race relations directly.

2. A study conducted a few years later by the College Board in New York City, creators of the Scholastic Aptitude Test, discovered that minority students who mastered algebra and geometry in high school succeeded in college at almost the same rate as whites.

3. Wessels's Accelerated Math Support Project, which began during the summer of 1991, was targeted at black seventh graders who had not voluntarily signed up to take Algebra I in the eighth grade. In its first year the program offered ninety students willing to change their minds a place in a four-week summer institute that combined intensive math instruction with individual tutoring and morale-building activities. These services, which Wessels had deemed necessary to the students' success in Algebra I (along with continued monitoring during the postinstitute school year), were provided by a youthful, all-black faculty made up of several recent graduates of Heights High School who were majoring in math in college and some of Wessels's own advanced-math students.

Wessels found additional outside funding to repeat the institute the following three summers. As a result, black enrollment in algebra classes at Heights had noticeably increased by the fall of 1994, signaling the beginning of a bloodless revolution. In fact, Wessels's success in quietly raising expectations about the academic potential of African-American students promised to be the most important legacy of the Model School Project.

Chapter 11. Hidden Agendas

1. For example, Steve Young had recently been declared "Brownnose of the Year," a title bestowed upon the group member deemed to have cooperated with the administration in the most egregious way. Young won for his leadership of the Model School Project.

2. Moskowitz usually remarked about the study teams' slow progress, a show of im-

patience designed to get Burkett's goat, some observers felt. The superintendent seemed to have forgotten that his original project leader appointee had not worked out. (During an interview with me conducted two years later, Moskowitz would distance himself even further from Allan Wolf's appointment, claiming that "Irwin" Wolf had been Burkett's choice for project manager.)

The teachers' seeming lack of vision and their proclivity to tinker also troubled the superintendent. Too often education reform consisted of trying to make existing programs better, Moskowitz counseled the project leaders, adding that he expected a model high school to look very different from the current institution. Give me some glitz, he urged, referring to such futuristic innovations as the satellite transmission of university courses that he envisioned as one of the hallmarks of a model school.

Moskowitz's preoccupation with technological gadgetry—which Burkett attributed to continuous pressure on the superintendent from the powers-that-be to find the magic ingredients that would prevent the remaining Caucasian students' flight from the system—contrasted sharply with the fiscal conservatism of his assistant superintendent, revealed in her only telling remark. Setting the tone of her future administration, Gearity warned the coordinators not to allow the teachers to design a Cadillac of a model school when the district could afford to pay only for a Chevrolet.

3. Local 795 members still remembered the times Walter spoke extemporaneously from the floor at union rallies during the 1983 contract negotiations and strike. On one occasion after Walter had concluded a particularly stirring speech, Glenn Altschuld turned to the steward standing next to him and commented dryly, "Who made him king?" At that moment the steward realized that Altschuld would either nurture Walter or rid himself of Walter as a union leader.

4. Such strictures may have prevented the abuse of administrative power, but they could also hamstring the operation of the schools. If a legitimate need for a fifteenth faculty meeting arose during the school year, a principal could schedule it, but he could not demand that anyone attend. Their sense of professionalism would no doubt prompt many faculty members to show up voluntarily, but it was not hard to see how some teachers could interpret the contract as a blueprint that spelled out exactly what people could and could not get away with.

Especially in times of greater than usual union-management tension some teachers felt justified in doing only the minimum work required. For example, the contract specified that the teachers' day began at 8:15 A.M. and ended seven and one-half hours later. Unlike other professionals such as lawyers or doctors, whose long hours conferred certain bragging rights, Heights teachers almost to a person groused about the fact that they had to take papers home to grade at night. One member of the faculty carried clock-watching to extremes. At any monthly faculty meeting that ran late, this teacher could be counted on to stand up at exactly 3:45, the end of the teachers' contractual day, and walk out the door, unabashedly abandoning the proceedings in midsentence.

5. MacDonald first ran for steward in the mid-1970s (upon returning to the school system after serving in Vietnam) because he wanted to challenge what he perceived to be the union's undemocratic tendencies. Once elected, he began attending meetings of the executive board (consisting of the union's officers and the stewards from each of the system's schools), where he confirmed his impression that one person wielded most of the power in determining Local 795 policy and strategy: Glenn Altschuld. There were a

couple of practices that MacDonald found especially disturbing, such as the president's tactic of quashing debate with the call for a voice vote that invariably produced a "unanimous" decision in Altschuld's favor. MacDonald began automatically objecting to every voice vote, which required the president to proceed to a roll-call vote, until an official tally became a matter of course.

The practice of awarding the chairs of standing committees a vote in executive board deliberations also bothered MacDonald because the chairpersons were appointed by the president and could be counted on to vote according to his dictates (or face removal from office). When Altschuld, having apparently decided that he wanted to "nurture" the gadfly MacDonald, asked him to join a five-member committee charged with revising the union's constitution, the steward agreed to serve, but only on the condition that minority opinions be included in the committee's report. (He knew that otherwise he would be outvoted and unheard.)

The concession allowed MacDonald to present a variety of reforms, such as a provision that stripped the president of his block of votes. The operation of Local 795 was by the late 1980s much more democratic, in MacDonald's view, although he admitted that his wife saw it differently. She liked to kid him, saying that the only thing that had really changed was his status as a union outsider.

Chapter 12. A Minor Uprising

1. Although the presence of faculty members at sporting and social events was thought to boost student morale, the teachers' contract did not require attendance at after-school activities; thus, most Heights staff members felt no qualms about shunning these events.

2. For the record, Burkett eventually agreed to a talent show but insisted that it be held in the evening so that parents could also attend. This precaution apparently invalidated the concession in Pace's eyes.

3. The board's statement read, in part:

The frustrating persistency of war in general and the Vietnam-Cambodia-Laos conflict in particular have . . . resulted in serious strains on the fabric of the American democratic system. It has resulted in increasing polarization of opinions and actions by both the young and the adult American populace. . . . We view with gravity the continued stresses within our student body. By the same token, honest questioning, critical analysis and meaningful assent . . . is equally as important. . . . Peaceful protest to achieve meaningful change, in the tradition of Mohandas K. Gandhi and Martin Luther King, Jr., can be an asset to the learning experience just as much as the more traditional methods in the educational process.

At the time Cleveland Heights was on the cusp of sociopolitical change. That the majority of the residents did not yet share the liberal views of the board of education could be surmised from the results of the next presidential election. Democratic peace activist George McGovern did not carry the suburb in 1972. By 1992, however, registered Democrats outnumbered registered Republicans in the suburb three to one.

4. As so often happens with unpopular policy, the authority of the principal to determine the editorial content of the *Black and Gold* was subverted. Unbeknownst to Burkett, the high school's journalism teacher, who acted as the advisor to the student newspaper, decided to sign Aram's editorial policy as a way of indicating his opposition to censorship of the paper.

After Burkett left the district, the journalism teacher seized upon an opportunity to institutionalize the policy that presented itself when Burkett's successor inquired about his right to see articles before they were published in the *Black and Gold*. The journalism teacher later told Bethany Aram that he had informed the new principal that it would not be possible to preview student copy. "We have a written editorial policy," Aram quoted the teacher as explaining, "and we abide by its terms."

Chapter 13. The Question of Exclusion

1. The following excerpt from *Citizens Guide to Children out of School* offers a fuller explanation of how subjectivity can enter into disciplinary decision making. Kaeser states:

> In most cases, the discipline system is activated when an adult receives a complaint or witnesses a student misbehaving. Not everyone will react to an incident of misbehavior in the same way. Despite a set of rules, each staff person decides what behavior is inappropriate and worthy of intervention, and what type of intervention is appropriate. For a system to be completely consistent there must be agreement among all teachers and staff about what behavior is inappropriate, what it looks like when it happens, and what to do about it when it is found. There is rarely this type of agreement. . . . Thus, much of the apparent discrimination in serious forms of punishment, such as suspensions, stems from the subjective nature of the process which leaves space for overt and subtle cultural conflicts, personality conflicts, and other personal biases to enter into disciplinary actions. Discrimination can occur. In fact, differential treatment of minorities may be the result of biases by a few teachers in the school building.
>
> The [national] data on suspension by race and reason support this view. . . . There is little variation by race for offenses widely agreed to be serious examples of misconduct. The differential rates stem from those rule violations where there is less agreement among educators that the behavior is serious enough to warrant exclusion (e.g., smoking), less agreement that exclusion is appropriate (e.g., truancy), or where the violation is unclear (e.g., defy authority, disrespectful) and therefore extremely susceptible to subjective decision making. It is in these grey areas that rates of suspension vary most by race.

2. In addition, some members of the task force believed that the board of education itself never seriously examined the dozens upon dozens of recommendations contained in SCP's two annual reports.

The district had been a reluctant sponsor of the school-improvement project in the first place, as the idea had not originated internally. Normally a whiz at public relations—

indeed, certain observers thought he had been *too* successful in limiting public discussion of the educational problems that had accompanied the district's integration—superintendent Al Abramovitz had found no graceful way to diffuse growing support for a community-led strategic planning process. The offer of outside assistance was made especially hard to turn down because it had been accompanied by the strong prospect of project underwriting from the Cleveland Foundation.

Although SCP leaders understood intellectually that the district might not relish being told what to do by outsiders, they were nonetheless crushed when board members praised their voluminous reports as a job well done, but otherwise ignored them. Abramovitz's successor, Irv Moskowitz, had been similarly noncommittal about his plans for implementing SCP's recommendations.

3. Local 795's protest preceded by several years the entry of AFT's national leadership into the debate over the question of whether school safety and order takes precedence over students' rights. In the mid-1990s the national teachers' union began to push for widespread acceptance of the concept of zero tolerance of students who behave violently or bring weapons to school. Indeed, AFT national president Albert Shanker went so far as to call for federal legislation permitting schools to remove from class disruptive students who make learning difficult or impossible for their peers.

4. As part of this agreement, former high school steward Lou Salvator was also released from the Penalty Box and returned to Heights High.

Chapter 14. The Silent Majority

1. The political shenanigans surrounding the appointment of Weigand's ally to the board the August before the elections only added to the mood of displeasure with the school's elected leadership. When the board position opened in mid-July, the remaining members had two options. If they appointed a replacement by early August, the appointee would be required by state law to run for election in November. Much to the consternation of the citizenry, the board decided to take the full thirty days allowed such deliberations. Only Judith Glickson had opposed the maneuver that denied voters the opportunity to select the person who would fill the unexpired two-year term.

Although the other board members attempted to justify their action—Weigand, for example, explained to reporters that it would have been irresponsible to rush such an important decision—the appointment was regarded throughout the community as a calculated move on the part of a board faction to consolidate its power over the district. Even the *Sun Press,* the normally bland suburban newspaper, denounced the action as "pure political arrogance."

Residents of a certain age may have been reminded of an earlier era in the suburb's history when the local Republican Party had successfully employed a similar tactic to perpetuate its control over city council for decades. The Republicans' ploy (which also allowed them to dominate city hall, since the mayor of Cleveland Heights is named to that position by his fellow city councilors) was transparently political. Whenever a Republican city councilor decided that the time had come to resign, he waited to do so until midterm, so that his colleagues could appoint a successor. By the time the appointee needed to run for election, he had a leg up in terms of name recognition and other campaign resources.

2. The catalytic incident took place, according to Allen, one summer evening in 1970. At twilight, several carloads of white youths pulled into the parking lot of the newly integrated Cleveland Heights YMCA where Allen worked. A group of young men in their late teens and early twenties disembarked, wearing khakis, boots, and swastikas and carrying baseball bats and metal posts. The youths rushed into the Y and began pushing around members of the staff. "We aren't going to have any more niggers around here," one of them threatened.

Somehow the staff managed to disarm the intruders and call the police, who cordoned off the street. Much to Allen's surprise and dismay, when the police entered the building, they returned the bats and poles to the youths and allowed them to leave. Not even trespassing charges were filed, she claimed. "For all you know they could have been on their way to a ball game," Allen remembered one of the police officers told her in attempting to explain why the young men had been dismissed without so much as a scolding.

Allen had lived in Cleveland Heights since 1964. When she and her husband first moved into their new home on Lee Road a few blocks from the high school, stink bombs and debris were regularly thrown into the front yard. Her children were chased from a nearby public swimming pool by taunts that "niggers were not welcome." (Allen explained to her kids that they were not niggers, dried their tears, and marched them back to the pool, where she loudly announced that her children would be coming there to swim every day, maybe up to two or three times a day, adding that she was sure that there would be no further objections to their patronage.)

A fearless woman, Allen had lost count of the times that she had stayed up all night to guard her home, looking apprehensively out the front window whenever a car roared past, especially if its occupants were screaming insults. But it was not until the Y was invaded that she had understood how little the powers-that-be in Cleveland Heights could be counted on to take part in finding a solution to racial harassment. If they were ever to ensure equitable treatment of their children, black parents must organize. In this realization lay the seeds of CICR.

3. Had the Model School Project participants been challenged to look beyond the implicit stereotype of blacks as shiftless for the real causes of parental apathy, they might have glimpsed the role that some observers believed white prejudice played. The insensitivity of whites discouraged African Americans from taking part in school-related activities, or so David Sweet, a white founder of Heights Committee for Educational Leadership, had concluded after experiencing difficulties in recruiting black members for the organization. Why seek out opportunities to be offended?

Black activist Doris Allen agreed with this premise. Most white liberals were unaware that even to champion the cause of integrated education was to rub some African Americans the wrong way. When whites espoused the concept of integration, they were invariably referring to a situation in which blacks were in the minority. As far as Allen was concerned, this was tantamount to saying that blacks benefited from being in the company of their superiors.

4. Only in hindsight would it become clear that the enthusiasm for reform exhibited by the district's most affluent parents did not translate into support for one of the Model School Project's key proposals: the recommendation that ability grouping be abolished as inequitable. Indeed, believing the practice to be of benefit to their children, this constituency would later rally to its defense.

5. A ward-by-ward analysis of the balloting shows that the vote, predictably, split along racial and religious lines. Glickson, who received the second largest number of votes, owed her victory to her first-place finish in University Heights and her strong showing among Orthodox Jewish voters in Cleveland Heights. Klein, the top vote getter, outpolled his fellow contenders among Orthodox Jews in Cleveland Heights and had a strong showing in University Heights. Because of his presence on the reform slate he also did well among both blacks and affluent whites in Cleveland Heights. Bullock, who finished third, outperformed all other contenders in the predominately black wards of Cleveland Heights, while also doing well in the suburb's most affluent (and largely white) neighborhoods and among Orthodox Jews, where his respectable showing could be traced in part to his affiliation with Stu Klein.

Cleveland Heights also has a considerable number of Catholic voters, a presence dating back to the nineteenth century, when a prosperous local farmer imported immigrants from Italy to work his vineyards. After the turn of the century, the enclave of Italian Americans increased geometrically when several hundred Italian workers were brought in to build sewers and water lines for the quickly growing village. But the large number of Catholic ethnics in the Heights area did not finally help slate candidate Victor Leanza, an Italian-American psychologist who formerly taught special education at Heights High. Leanza finished sixth.

Chapter 15. A Failure to Communicate

1. Klein's were not the only questions being raised about the coordinators' leadership. Phyllis Fowlkes, the former chairperson of the race relations study team, had passed along to the group a critical remark she heard at a Model School Project–hosted luncheon for the Heights High faculty the previous month. (Held on a day when there were no afternoon classes because of final exams, the luncheon kicked off the election of super-retreat representatives. Those teachers who had attended a retreat were asked to stay after lunch to vote. The coordinators also used the occasion to brief the faculty on the project's next steps, including their plan to address various community groups.)

After lunch Fowlkes approached McBride and Young, who were in the cafeteria recording the election results. Turning to McBride, she reported that someone at lunch had questioned the coordinators' ability to sell the Model School Project in the African-American community. The questioner doubted whether black parents would feel comfortable sharing their true feelings about the restructuring project with whites.

Then Fowlkes, who had been defeated in her bid to become a super-retreat representative, turned to Young, mentioning her own doubts about how well he had been received by the classes he visited on the project's behalf. Black males, she informed him, responded well only to people who could walk the walk and talk the talk.

"I almost asked why they wouldn't respond to someone genuine," McBride later recalled. Instead she merely thanked the social studies teacher for her comments. After Fowlkes left, the two coordinators decided that she was "crazy." It was hard for them not to take her remarks personally, but, in doing so, they overlooked the warning implicit in her comments: that certain members of the black faculty felt as if they had no role in the Heights High School reform plan.

Chapter 16. Masters of a Slow Death

1. In an earlier era the Jewish community also had to fight the board of education to win official recognition of major Jewish holidays. Al Abramovitz remembered that when he began teaching at Heights High in the mid-1950s, school was scheduled to be in session on Yom Kippur whenever the Day of Atonement fell during the week. When Abramovitz finally grew tired of having to work on the holiest of Jewish holidays, he informed the assistant superintendent of personnel of his intention to take the day off. She noted that no other Jewish teachers were doing so. "I can't speak for them," Abramovitz retorted, amazed at the gall of the woman.

In the end it was decided that, since the physics teacher was doing such a good job, district officials would look the other way if he called in sick. Jewish students were not afforded even this minimal consideration. Not only were they not allowed to make up work when they missed school for religious reasons, but certain teachers (or so it seemed to Abramovitz) always scheduled tests on the Jewish holidays.

Although Hebrew was introduced at the high school as a foreign language course option in the 1950s, other changes came slowly, according to Abramovitz. When Jewish civic leaders approached Miramar to request that important school activities not be scheduled on major Jewish holidays, the then-superintendent made excuses for the lapse by pleading ignorance of their dates. Undaunted, the Jewish community published a calendar pinpointing the dates of major Jewish holidays several years into the future and presented it to the superintendent.

By the 1960s school officials had begun to be more accommodating of the needs of the sizable number of Jewish students and teachers in the district. For example, it was made known that elementary-age Jewish children did not have to attend Christmas pageants and that Jewish high school students would be allowed to make up work missed for religious reasons. In the 1970s a literature of the Holocaust course was piloted at the high school, and Yom Kippur became an official school holiday districtwide. However, Abramovitz suspected that the latter development may have been prompted as much by the difficulty of finding substitutes for all the Jewish teachers who took sick leave on the Day of Atonement as by an increase in sensitivity.

2. While Lott's presence on the board of education was brief (she served only one full term), it gave much-needed credibility to efforts to recruit minority educators. During her tenure, the district hired such key personnel as central-office administrative assistant Larry Peacock, who went on to become Moskowitz's director of staff development. Lott died in 1983.

3. First, Gearity mailed a survey to every family in the district with elementary-age children, asking parents to state which of six options for the magnet's academic theme they preferred. She also created an advisory committee consisting of two parents

affiliated with each of the system's elementary schools to review the developing plans for the Belvoir magnet, whose special emphasis was to be the provision of individualized instruction. The final details of the new program were then presented to the public at evening meetings held in each of the system's elementary schools.

4. The community's peaceful acceptance of desegregation seemed all the more remarkable to those insiders who recognized that some University Heights residents' commitment to the public school system had weakened. School board member Harvey Feinberg became aware of this trend when two other University Heights residents then sitting on the board of education invited him to meet privately with them shortly after he was first elected in 1973. The subject his colleagues wished to discuss was their city's possible secession from the school district. Unlike Cleveland Heights, University Heights had remained nearly all white, and Feinberg suspected that the talk of secession was motivated by the desire to escape the problems that had accompanied the school system's integration. Not sharing such sentiments, the new school board member declined to join ranks with the dissidents.

Dissatisfaction with the existing educational arrangement resurfaced in University Heights in the mid-1980s, when the board of education announced its decision to close the last remaining neighborhood elementary school in the western part of the suburb as part of a cost-saving reorganization plan. In response, a small group of disgruntled University Heights parents (whose numbers now included Harvey Feinberg) began a Save Our Schools crusade. Save Our Schools (SOS) filed a lawsuit seeking a court injunction against the closing of Northwood elementary school, and the City of University Heights soon became a coplaintiff. When the suit failed, SOS began a whispering campaign against a proposed school tax levy that was on the ballot in 1985. The levy passed, even though a narrow majority in University Heights voted against it.

The Save Our Schools revolt helped to launch the political career of Judith Glickson, the organization's treasurer, who was elected to the board of education that year. It may also have played a role in ending the long career of superintendent Al Abramovitz, the author of the unpopular reorganization plan. Displeased that the board had dragged its feet on renewing his contract for three months while the controversy raged on, then offered him only a token raise, Abramovitz announced his resignation midway through the 1985 levy campaign.

Abramovitz's abrupt departure after thirty years of service to the district paved the way for the hiring of Irv Moskowitz, who would have to contend with the fact the school district could no longer count on the previously reliable support of the residents of University Heights. In three of five subsequent elections in which property or income tax levies in support of the public schools were on the ballot, the majority of voters in University Heights pulled the "no" lever. In each case the levy went down to defeat.

Chapter 17. The Walkout

1. In the end no one involved in the Taylor Road altercation was expelled. However, the suspensions of the youths were upheld.

2. Ironically, King herself had contributed to the unrest. The rumor about Black

History Month's cancellation started when she ordered student-made posters advertising the event removed from the hallways as unworthy because they were amateurishly executed.

3. When they reflected on the events of February 15th, Burkett and Walter did indeed finger King as the ringleader of the walkout. They also concluded that King had possessed an ulterior motive for egging on the students—namely, that she was hoping the unrest would prompt the high school's African-American faculty to rise up against the Burkett administration, with whom she had been wrangling over the duties she was to perform as student activities advisor.

Chapter 18. Management by Crisis

1. Having come to prominence as a black community leader in the aftermath of the 1990 walkout, Evans would subsequently be appointed to fill a vacant seat on the Cleveland Heights city council in 1993.

2. The tenth grader and his cousin were convicted in August 1990 of murdering Stallworth-Bey. Each received a sentence of fifteen years to life. In a letter to the suburban newspaper published the following October, the tenth grader's mother stated that everyone in Cleveland Heights shared some of the blame for the misfortune that had befallen her family and the Stallworth-Beys. "Our black children are destroying each other," she wrote. "Why does it take a tragedy for [problems] to come out in the open? . . . Everyone wants to speak out and find an alternative afterwards when they know the problem was there all the time and ignored and denied it."

3. By summertime the Community Steering Council had organized a free softball league to provide the suburb's idle youth with a wholesome recreational alternative to gang membership. The softball program would eventually be taken over by the city recreation department, freeing the committee to redefine itself as an advocate for needed youth services. Although the Community Steering Council went on to inspire the creation of new drop-in programs and summer camps during its second year of operation, it failed to have an impact on the gang problem, in the estimation of its cochair. The community's most intractable youth had simply not availed themselves of the special programming, and council members had no clear answers to the puzzling question of how to reach them.

4. Among the changes made were the addition of an explicit prohibition against gang membership; the specification of which types of offenses would automatically be reported to police; and the inclusion of *excused* (as well as unexcused) absences in the tally of missed classes that automatically resulted in a student's failing a course. The language governing school jurisdiction was left virtually unchanged, except for the clarification that the district's ability to regulate the behavior of students who were en route from class did not extend beyond "the first destination." Previously, the policy stated that a student could be disciplined for misconduct "occurring on school property, at school-sponsored activities on or off school property, while en route to and from school and/or while under the jurisdiction of school personnel."

5. "The Cleveland Heights–University Heights School System cannot be deemed to be a racist system," the commission's report stated, "nor does there appear to be any

segment of the school hierarchy or populace that feels free to discriminate against others, or to condone such acts. This does not mean that individual acts of discrimination do not occur, or have not occurred. There is, however, no evidence that any such isolated wrongful acts were committed willfully as school policy nor have they been accepted by peers or supervisors as proper conduct."

6. "Once referred, students receive equal penalties for like offenses," the Office for Civil Rights report elaborated. "Further, race was not found to be a basis for the District's decisions in suspension and expulsion hearings. However, at the high school level, the evidence shows that black students are disproportionately referred for subjective offenses based on improper racial considerations. Interviews with students, teachers and administrators support the inference that staff members apply inconsistent and arbitrary criteria which result in formal disciplinary action being taken against black students."

OCR's examination of the kinds of offenses for which Heights High students were suspended in 1989–90 yielded the only compelling empirical evidence of the racial bias that the report alleged. OCR investigators first divided the district's list of twenty-six misdeeds punishable by suspension into two categories: subjective and objective. Fighting, for example, was deemed to be a subjective offense because "the teacher would have to decide whether students are engaging in an actual fight or in a 'scuffle' or 'horseplay.'" Cutting class and unauthorized leave from campus were deemed to be objective offenses since neither involved a teacher's judgment. After categorizing the listed offenses, OCR investigators then calculated the rates at which black and white students were referred for each category of misdeed.

"Data show that the disciplinary rates of black students are significantly higher than nonminority students in subjective offenses," OCR investigators determined. "OCR found that of all referrals for the subjective offenses of fighting, disruption, and disorderly conduct, 85 percent were referrals of black students and only 15 percent were referrals of white students. In the objective categories of cutting class, leaving school grounds, and miscellaneous offenses, referrals for black students were at the rate of 63.6 percent, which is within 2 percent of the total percentage of black students at the school (61.7 percent).

"If black students account for 63.6 percent of the referrals for objective offenses, then under a nondiscriminatory application of referrals," the OCR report concluded, "black students would be expected to account for approximately the same percentage of referrals for subjective offenses. As this is not the case, and as administrators have suggested that staff judgment causes more referrals of black students, OCR finds that different standards are applied to black students' behavior."

Chapter 19. Deadly Decisions

1. At the end of the 1989–90 school year, Altschuld did go on the record in opposition to the 25-to-1 student-teacher ratio proposed as the outside limit for schools within a school. In an open letter to the Model School coordinators the union president stated his preference for boosting, rather than lowering, the average class size in the district. Accepted educational research indicated that student achievement was positively corre-

lated to a student-teacher ratio of 15 to 1 or less. If Altschuld had his druthers, however, classes in the Cleveland Heights schools would average 30.4 students each. He added in the letter that he would even be willing to consider a 38 to 1 student-teacher ratio, as this would free up enough monies to give teachers a 20 percent raise.

How understaffing in the classroom would affect the quality of education provided was not a subject Altschuld addressed. Instead he chastised his Model School colleagues for spreading heretical notions. "If this school district wants a 25 to 1 ratio, let the voters choose such," Altschuld wrote, "but I see no reason why we, the teachers should continue subsidizing [lower class sizes] and am upset that . . . Model Schools promote[s] continued subsidizing by us, the teachers."

2. The community's response to the workshop proved to be even more offhanded. At the last minute the coordinators had decided to add several evening sessions to the workshop so that the public could attend, counting on the suburban newspaper to publish the dates that residents were invited to the high school to review the Model School Project's proposals. The evening sessions were intended as a substitute for the formal presentations that the coordinators had once hoped to make to community groups. Yet, had they recalled the attendance problems that plagued Heights High's annual open house, they might have anticipated that a secondhand invitation to attend a seemingly arcane educational program at the high school would produce a chorus of ho hums. Sure enough, not a single parent or resident took the time to wander over to the high school and familiarize himself with the Model School Project during the specially scheduled evening hours.

3. Altschuld's peremptory attitude toward those colleagues who disagreed with his opposition to the principal selection plan provided a glimpse of the manner in which he ruled Local 795. In a memo announcing that a forum would be held after school to discuss the issue, Altschuld instructed his critics in the proper way to express their dissent. "Statements must be succinct, to the point, and—not take all day," the union president declared. "Therefore, be prepared, or don't speak. The speakers must address issues, not personalities. We are not, I repeat not, interested in emotional tirades."

4. More than two-thirds of the 114 survey respondents liked the idea of schools within a school, and 43 percent supported the concept of a core curriculum. A similar percentage agreed with the statement that, except for the provision of advanced placement courses, the practice of ability grouping should be eliminated.

5. As the coordinators envisioned it, the super-retreat representatives would carry detailed explanations about the proposed model school framework back to their retreat groups. In turn the members of the retreat groups would convey their questions and concerns to the planning team via their representatives. Meeting twice a month, the planning team would work with the coordinators on adjusting the model school framework until it was acceptable to the retreat groups. Two new advisory councils—one consisting of students and one of parents and community representatives—would be fit into this "recycling" process, which the organizational development consultant had suggested would produce the desired consensus.

The coordinators further proposed that, as consensus was achieved on each component of the framework, the planning team would request that the High School Steering Committee, consisting of all building stewards and administrators, approve the creation of a faculty task force to design the proposed program in its entirety. After conducting the necessary library research and making site visits to public schools experimenting with similar innovations, the task force would present its recommendations to the planning team, which would "recycle" them through the retreat groups and advisory councils until consensus had been reached. Then the design would go to the High School Steering Committee for approval or modification.

By the time a proposal to create a new program had reached this stage, it would carry considerable clout, which would expand geometrically each time it cleared a successive level of authority. The plan called for program proposals to go to the District Steering Committee for approval or modification after receiving the imprimatur of the High School Steering Committee. If a program survived the scrutiny of the superintendent, other district-level administrators, and the top union officials who made up the DSC, the superintendent would then recommend its implementation to the board of education.

Epilogue

1. The November 1993 board elections saw whites regain the majority.

2. This was the explanation that the police chief offered Phyllis Evans, the cochair of the school district's Commission on Excellence and Equity, when she called him to ask why her teenage son had been ticketed for jaywalking. However, the police chief responded to my written request for an interview by turning the matter over to a subordinate.

3. National Honor Society eligibility statistics released around the same time confirmed the school's continuing problem with student achievement, albeit from a slightly different angle. To be eligible for NHS membership at Heights, a junior or senior needed to maintain at least a 3.5 grade point average. In 1993 only one hundred upperclass students qualified for honor society membership. Of this select group of B+ or better pupils, ten were African Americans.

Appendix

1. The retreats were held throughout the 1989–90 school year on the following dates: May 19–22, August 11–14, September 29–October 2, October 27–30, November 15–17, December 5 and 6, December 8–11, and February 20.

Source Notes

Unless otherwise indicated below, the comments, thoughts, attitudes, beliefs, and opinions attributed to a person named in the text were expressed by the person during a formal interview with the author, expressed by the person in a casual conversation of which the author made a written record, or expressed by the person at a meeting or event observed by the author.

Actions said to have been taken by a person in the text were either avowed by the person in the presence of the author or observed by the author, unless otherwise noted.

Characterizations in the text of the general attitudes of the high school administration, the faculty and its various factions, and the student body are the author's own. Descriptions of general school policy and practices are based on the author's observation and interviewing.

Events described in the text as taking place between the spring of 1988 and the summer of 1991 (particularly Model School Project meetings, retreats, and related activities) were observed by the author. Events that have been reconstructed from news accounts and/or interviews with the participants will be noted.

In the notes, abbreviations will stand for the following frequently cited sources:

BG—*The Black and Gold,* Heights High School's student newspaper

CP—*The Cleveland Press*

PD—*The (Cleveland) Plain Dealer*

MSP—Author's copies of Model School Project internal documents: worksheets, memoranda, announcements, and reports

SCP1—School Consensus Project, "First Year Report"

SCP2—School Consensus Project, "Second Year Report"

SP—*The Sun Press,* a weekly newspaper covering the Cleveland suburbs of Cleveland Heights, University Heights, and Shaker Heights

Preface

ix. KOZOL QUOTED: Charles, Nick. "The Division in American Schools." *PD,* 29 Apr. 1992.

ix. DOZEN REFORM NETWORKS: Walters, Laurel Sharper. "'Breaking the Mold' of Education." *Christian Science Monitor,* 20 July 1992.

ix. NEW AMERICAN SCHOOLS DEVELOPMENT CORPORATION: Walters, Laurel Sharper. "'Breaking the Mold' of Education." *Christian Science Monitor,* 20 July 1992.

ix. NATIONAL ALLIANCE FOR RESTRUCTURING EDUCATION: Olson, Lynn. "Beyond Model Schools." *Education Week,* 8 Feb. 1995.

xi. "REMARKABLE HUMAN ASSORTMENT": Simon, Scott. "Cleveland Heights High School: Integration Success." *Weekend Edition,* National Public Radio, 22 Oct. 1994.

Mise-en-Scène

1. HISTORY OF HEIGHTS AREA: Hannibal interview.
1–2. HISTORY OF SUBURB AND HIGH SCHOOL: Harris and Robinson; Hellwig; and Jones. Extant copies of the high school yearbook dating back to 1908 were also consulted.
2. PHONE BOOTH JOKE: Hruby interview.
2. PRODUCTION OF DOCTORAL DEGREES: "Study Shows Alumni Tops in Ohio." *BG,* 17 Jan. 1964.
3. 1980 ENROLLMENT STATISTICS: "Annual Report 1980–81," Cleveland Heights–University Heights School District.
3. NOTE 1: "Racial Isolation Grows at School." *PD,* 28 Feb. 1994.
4. RACE/CLASS RELIABLE PREDICTORS OF ONE'S QUALITY OF EDUCATION: Cremin, 265.

Chapter 1. A Simple Remodeling Job

8. NOBEL PRIZE-WINNING GRADUATE: Watkins, Steve. "Twenty Heights High Graduates Inducted into First Hall of Fame." *BG,* 19 May 1981.
9. INTERNATIONAL BACCALAUREATE PROGRAM: Chisolm, Adrienne. "Heights May Join Baccalaureate Program." *BG,* 26 Nov. 1986.
9. ALL-AMERICA CITY AWARDS: Jindra, Christine J. "All-America Again." *PD,* 13 Apr. 1978.
10. POVERTY STATISTICS: *Poverty Indicators,* 23.
10. PAST AND PRESENT GRADUATION RATES: Goodman, Steve. "College—Not for Everyone." *BG,* 21 Nov. 1976; "Report of the NCA Evaluation Team Visitation of Cleveland Heights High School." North Central Association of Secondary Schools and Colleges, May 1986, 12.
10. BLACKS OVERREPRESENTED AMONG THOSE FAILING: SCP1, 81; Burkett interview, 16–17 Mar. 1991; SCP2, 67.
11. "'HAVES' AND 'HAVE-NOTS'": Moskowitz, Irv, and Hugh Burkett. "A High School Planning Grant." Submitted to the Cleveland Foundation by the Cleveland Heights–University Heights School District, Dec. 1987, 1.
11. ACADEMIC FAILINGS OF NATION'S YOUTH: *Nation at Risk,* 9.

11. 1950 NATIONAL GRADUATION RATE: Goodlad, *Place,* 12.

11. 1980 NATIONAL GRADUATION RATE: Cremin, 664–65.

12. RACIAL MAKEUP OF FUTURE WORKFORCE: Hodgkinson, Harold L. *All One System: Demographics of Education, Kindergarten through Graduate School.* Institute for Educational Leadership, n.d., 7.

12. "TRADITION-SHATTERING REFORM": Weinraub, Bernard. "Bush and Governors Set Education Goals." *New York Times,* 29 Sept. 1989.

12. NATIONAL CALL FOR SCHOOL RESTRUCTURING: Fiske, Edward B. "Paying Attention to the Schools Is National Mission Now." *New York Times,* 1 Oct. 1989.

12. NOTE 2: Lane, Mary Beth. "Goals 2000: Plan to Help Education or to Control It?" *PD,* 19 Mar. 1995.

14. "PROFESSION EQUAL TO THE TASK": *Nation Prepared,* 2.

14. RARITY OF SITE-BASED MANAGEMENT: Viadero, Debra. "Site-Based Management Found to Require More Sweeping Changes Than Anticipated." *Education Week,* 19 June 1991.

Chapter 2. A New Principle

16–22. PRINCIPAL'S FIRST DAYS/DISCOVERIES: Burkett interviews, 15 June 1990 and 16–17 Mar. 1991.

17, 23– BURKETT'S BIO: Burkett interviews, 14 Sept. 1989, 15 June 1990, and
24. 16–17 Mar. 1991.

18. STRICT DISCIPLINE OF AN EARLIER ERA: Budin interview; Kessler interview; Willen interview.

18. NOTE 1: EXISTENCE OF ANTI-WAR GROUPS—Abramovitz interviews; Barnett, Barbara. "Student Activist Unit Banned in Heights Schools." *CP,* 6 Apr. 1970; Kay, Leslie. "Severance Meets Tax Challenge with Tale of Woe." *PD,* 18 July 1971.

18. LACK OF DISCIPLINE DURING 1960S: Hellstern interview; McBride interview, 24 July 1991; Thomas interview, 11 June 1991.

18. DISCIPLINARY MEASURES OF PRINCIPAL'S PREDECESSOR: Ferrato interview.

18–19. ACTIVITIES IN LOT 5: Burkett interview, 16–17 Mar. 1991; Frank Walter interview, 13 Mar. 1991.

19. ALTSCHULD'S BIO: Altschuld interview; Kincaid, Sue. "Tough Teacher Heads Union in Heights." *CP,* 11 Jan. 1980.

20. SHANKER'S SUPPORT OF REFORM: Shanker, Albert. Address, opening session. AFT School Restructuring Academy, East Lansing, Mich., 7–11 Aug. 1989.

20. AFFILIATES' FAILURE TO HEED SHANKER: Toch, 149.

20. TEACHER'S SALARY STATISTICS: Herkner, M. W. "The Day the Teachers Skipped School." Report of the administrative director of research. Cleveland Heights–University Heights School District, Jan. 1968; Altschuld, Glenn. "Salary Offer Continued." *Bargaining Table,* Nov. 1988.

20. NOTE 2: "MIGHT MADE RIGHT"—Herskovitz interview.

21. UNION PRESIDENT QUOTED: Salvator interview.

22. ERA OF OPEN RACIAL HOSTILITY: To track the changing social climate at Heights High (among other issues), the author reviewed every issue of the *Black and Gold* published since the 1960s.

22. INCIDENT WITH BAG OF FLOUR: Ferrato interview.

22. NOTE 3: Michelson, Ben. "Den's Future Brightens." *BG*, 30 Jan. 1976; "Club Holds Hopes for Den." Editorial. *BG*, 27 Feb. 1976.

22. RACIAL MAKEUP OF SPORTS TEAMS: Eleanor Trawick. "Race Relations at Heights High Show Progress over Last Decade." *BG*, 13 June 1983.

23. NEAR-UNIVERSALITY OF ABILITY GROUPING: Oakes, 3.

24. EDMONDS'S RESEARCH: Fredericksen, John, and Ronald Edmonds. "Identification of Instructionally Effective and Ineffective Schools." Manuscript, n.d., 28–31.

24. NOTE 5: Cremin, 265–67.

24. NOTE 6: Edmonds, *Discussion of Effective Schooling*, 35.

24. CLIMATE IN AN EFFECTIVE SCHOOL: Edmonds, *Discussion of Effective Schooling*, 32.

24. "NO TEST OF PUBLIC INSTRUCTION": *Discussion of Effective Schooling*, 16.

25. READING SCORES: "Heights Has New Reading Program." *BG*, 25 Oct. 1984.

26. VIEWS ON TEACHER'S APPOINTMENT AS ADMINISTRATOR: Burkett interview, 16–17 Mar. 1991; Frank Walter interview, 13 Mar. 1991; Salvator interview.

Chapter 3. Discipline First

28. BURKETT'S LOOKS INFLUENCED HIS HIRING: Baron interview.

28–40. DESCRIPTION OF DISCIPLINE PROBLEMS AND BURKETT'S DISCIPLINARY INITIATIVES: Burkett interview, 16–17 Mar. 1991; Frank Walter interview, 13 Mar. 1991; *BG*, 1984–89; Walter, Frank. Farewell speech to Burkett. Cleveland Heights High School, 15 June 1990.

28–29. KUNJUFU'S VISITS: Frank Walter interview, 13 Mar. 1991; Lisa Romanoff. "Dr. Kunjufu Returns by Popular Demand." *BG*, 25 Feb. 1985.

29. NOTE 1: Kunjufu, 16–17, 40–41.

29. KING'S VISIT: Burkett interview, 16–17 Mar. 1991; Schuyler, Gwen, and Naomi Finkelstein. "Student Motivator Speaks at Heights." *BG*, 16 May 1985.

29. EUPHORIC AFTERMATH OF ASSEMBLY: Dooley interview.

29–30. STATEWIDE ATTENDANCE RANKING: Kaeser, *Citizens Guide*, 8.

30. SCHEDULING PROBLEMS: Frank Walter interview, 14 May 1991.

30. LIBRARY NETWORK: Ziegler, Kristin. "Heights First in Nation to Join Library Network." *BG*, 20 Apr. 1987.

31. COMPLAINTS ABOUT PRINCIPAL'S LOW PROFILE: Friedman, Laura. "Letter to the Editor." *BG*, 25 Oct. 1984.

31. "LUNCH WITH THE PRINCIPAL": "Lunching with Burkett." *BG*, 14 Feb. 1986.

31. COMPUTERIZED ATTENDANCE PROBLEMS AND STUDENT COMMENTARY ON THEM: Trawick, Matt. "Computerized Attendance: What Next?" *BG*, 29 Mar. 1985.

31. TWO THOUSAND WITHDRAWALS: Torgerson, Kirstin. "Burkett Gives Views for '86." *BG*, 23 Oct. 1985.

31–32. REVISIONS TO DISCIPLINARY RULES: SCP1, Appendix G, 3.

32. VIOLENT ASSAULTS: Jordan, George E. "Heights High Tries Tougher Penalties to Stem Violence." *PD*, 21 Apr. 1985.

32. "LET THERE BE NO MISTAKE": SCP1, Appendix G, 3.

32. "ANGER AND HOSTILITY": Trawick, Matt. "New Rules Create Hostility." *BG*, 16 May 1985.

32–33. WHY EMERGENCY REMOVAL INSTITUTED: "In-School Fighting Down." *BG*, 2 May 1986.

33. KNIFE-WIELDING STUDENT: "Two Monitors Wounded." *BG*, 21 Mar. 1986.

33. NEW EXPULSION POLICY ANNOUNCED: SCP1, 99.

33. INTERGROUP RIVALRIES CAUSE OF VIOLENCE: Weber, Laura. "Staff, Administrators Discuss Unchartered Groups." *BG*, 22 Dec. 1989.

33. CHARACTERIZATIONS OF B.A.T. FRATERNITY: Abramovitz interview, 9 May 1991; Burkett interview, 16–17 Mar. 1991.

33. ORIGINS OF THE BROTHERS: Frank Walter interview, 13 Mar. 1991; Hicks, Desiree F. "Group Banned from Awarding Scholarships." *PD*, 31 May 1989.

33. ORIGINS OF HOME BOYS AND SPREAD OF BLACK GANGS AT HEIGHTS HIGH: Frank Walter interview, 13 Mar. 1991 and 14 May 1991; Mixon interview.

33. HOME BOYS' INDUCTION RITUAL: James Heard interview.

34. FRATERNITY "DEATH WARRANTS" AND THEIR CONSEQUENCE: "Heights Frats Hang Symbol of Defeat." *PD*, 26 Feb. 1953; "Heights High Secret Groups Call It Quits." *CP*, 26 Feb. 1953.

34. NON-CHARTERED ORGANIZATION COUNCIL: "Rules Established for Non-Chartered Clubs." *BG*, 14 Feb. 1986.

34. COUNCIL DISBANDED: Frank Walter interviews, 13 Mar. 1991 and 14 May 1991; Laura Hubbert. "Non-Chartered Clubs Banned." *BG*, 8 June 1987.

34. NEED FOR COMMUNITY ANTIGANG COALITION: SCP1, 98; Burkett interview, 16–17 Mar. 1991.

34. INVITATION TO NATIONAL SCHOOL SAFETY CENTER: Burkett interview, 16–17 Mar. 1991; SCP1, 105.

34–35. JOINT BOARDS' MEETING WITH MOSKOWITZ AND ITS OUT-
COME: Weigand interview.

35. EXPANSION OF SECURITY STAFF: Petretich, Peter. "Layoff of Monitors Lowers Security Level." *BG*, 17 Oct. 1986.

35. LARGEST SECURITY STAFF IN AREA: SCP1, 99.

35. NEW SECURITY CHIEF AND HIS INITIATIVES: Caswell, Chris.
"Security: 'We Mean Business!'" *BG*, 23 Oct. 1985.

35. NOTE 3: Toch, 237.

35. UP AND DOWN STAIRCASES: "Timely Tidbits Spark Memories." *BG*,
21 Nov. 1976.

35. SHORTAGES DUE TO INFLUX OF NINTH GRADERS: "Burkett
Sets Heights Goals." *BG*, 11 June 1986.

35. OFFICIAL DROPOUT RATE: SCP2, 69.

35–36. STUDENTS TAKE MORE THAN FOUR YEARS TO GRADUATE:
MSP, "Ninth Grade Summer Institute Program Description." Summer
Institute Task Force, n.d., 3.

36. SUSPENSION RATE SAME SINCE 1970S: "Student Disciplinary Action Data." Reports for the 1978–79, 1983–84, 1986–87, and 1988–89
school years. Department of Pupil Services, Cleveland Heights–University
Heights Board of Education.

36. EXPULSIONS FIGURES RISE UNDER BURKETT: "Student Disciplinary Action Data." Report for the 1986–87 school year. Department of
Pupil Services, Cleveland Heights–University Heights Board of Education.

36. SUPERINTENDENT QUOTED: Frank Walter interview, 14 May 1991.

36. BLACKS TWICE AS LIKELY TO BE SUSPENDED: "Study Says Blacks
More Apt to Be Suspended by School." *PD*, 12 Dec. 1988.

36. NOTE 4: "Student Disciplinary Action Data." Report for the 1986–87
school year. Department of Pupil Services, Cleveland Heights–University
Heights Board of Education.

36. PHONE SURVEY RESULTS: SCP1, 24.

36. LACK OF DISCIPLINE A CONTINUING NATIONAL CONCERN:
Shanker, Albert. "Discipline in Our Schools." *New York Times*, 12 May
1991.

36–37. DISCIPLINARY INNOVATIONS: SCP2, 93; SCP1, 103–4; Burkett
interview, 16–17 Mar. 1991.

37. NOTE 6: Ferrato interview.

37. NOTE 7: "Student Disciplinary Action Data." Report for the 1988–89
school year. Department of Pupil Services, Cleveland Heights–University
Heights Board of Education.

37. BURKETT'S CHILDHOOD INJURY: Burkett interviews, 27 June 1989
and 16–17 Mar. 1991.

37–38. TROUBLE AT SPORTING EVENTS: Banks, Sandy. "Heights Police
Chief Holds That Line on Move to Bring Back Night Football." *CP*, 25
July 1979; "Pupil Is Slain after Dance at Heights High." *PD*, 23 Feb. 1976.

38. POLICE IMPRESSED BY PRINCIPAL'S HANDS-ON APPROACH

TO DISCIPLINE: Author's 15 July 1991 interview with two Cleveland Heights police officers who requested anonymity.

38. NOTE 8: Myers, Ken. "Ghosts in Black and White." *Cleveland Edition*, 29 Mar. 1990; Hinman, Reed. "Three Teachers Charge Police Misconduct." *CP*, 29 Jan. 1975.

38. PRINCIPAL WELCOMES POLICE ON CAMPUS: Frank Walter interview, 14 May 1991.

38–39. EXAMPLES OF POLICE-SCHOOL INFORMATION-SHARING: Frank Walter interview, 14 May 1991.

39. DISCIPLINARY INITIATIVES SHOW MODEST PAYOFF: "Grades and Attendance Up, Closed Campus Attributed." *BG*, 11 June 1986.

39. STEWARD QUESTIONS IMPROVEMENTS: "Has Truancy Really Decreased?" *BG*, 2 May 1986.

39. PRINCIPAL'S RESPONSE: "Grades and Attendance Up, Closed Campus Attributed." *BG*, 11 June 1986.

40. "TO THINK": Walter, Frank. Farewell speech to Burkett. Cleveland Heights High School, 15 June 1990.

Chapter 4. Time for Reflection

42. RACIAL COMPOSITION OF STANDARD CLASSES: SCP1, Appendix F, 5.

42–43. DISTRICT'S POSITION ON ABILITY GROUPING: This discussion is founded on the author's examination of a file in the office of Heights High's assistant principal of curriculum containing dozens of memoranda and other board-level documents on the topic dating from the late 1980s back to the late 1950s.

43. BOARD APPROVAL OF ABILITY GROUPING: Policy 6130, "Policy Notebook," Cleveland Heights–University Heights Board of Education.

43. POSITION OF INTERNAL CURRICULUM COMMITTEE AND URBAN LEAGUE: SCP1, Appendix F, 2; Burns, Diann. "Hts. Schools Accused of Segregating Pupil Ranks." *PD*, 17 Aug. 1980.

43. "DUAL INSTRUCTIONAL SYSTEM": *Educational Tracking*, viii.

43. SUPERINTENDENT'S RESPONSE: Kincaid, Sue. "Heights School Board Reviews Ability Grouping Procedure." *CP*, 11 Sept. 1980.

43. NOTE 1: ABRAMOVITZ'S ROLE IN ADOPTION OF ABILITY GROUPING—Abramovitz interview, 9 May 1991. FORMATION OF GROUPING TASK FORCE AND ITS RECOMMENDATIONS— Shtull interview; assistant principal's file on grouping. CONCLUSION OF DISSERTATION—Abramovitz, Albert Joseph. "A Framework for Analyzing Citizen Lay Committees and Its Application to the Cleveland Heights–University Heights School District for the Period 1955–1975."

Diss. Case Western Reserve University, 1977. PERCEPTION OF SYSTEM'S DECLINE IN QUALITY RELATED TO ITS CHANGING DEMOGRAPHICS—Boyle interview; Lewis interview; McKinney interview; Oliver interview; Sweet interview. REASONS FOR LACK OF CHANGE IN GROUPING PRACTICES—SCP1, 80–81. BLACK PARENTS' PERCEPTION OF THE GUIDANCE DEPARTMENT— Bullock interview; McKinney interview. ACHIEVEMENT CENTERS CLOSED—Roszak, Debbie. "Budget Cuts Close Achievement Centers." *BG,* 21 Oct. 1987.

43. SUBCOMMITTEE REPORT CITED: SCP1, 85.

43. ISSUE OF ABILITY GROUPING TOO EMOTIONAL TO HANDLE: McKinney interview; Oliver interview.

43. BOARD ASKED TO REEXAMINE ITS POSITION: SCP2, 4.

43. SUPERINTENDENT'S WRITTEN PROMISE: SCP2, Appendix A, 2.

43. FATE OF HIGH SCHOOL COMMITTEE STUDYING GROUPING: McBride interview, 24 July 1991; assistant principal's file on grouping.

43. PARENTS' SUPPORT OF ABILITY GROUPING: SCP1, 75.

44. STATISTICS ON AND ANALYSIS OF THE CAUSES OF WHITE FLIGHT; RESPONSE TO SURVEY QUESTION ABOUT WHITE FLIGHT: SCP1, 110–11; SCP2, Appendix C, 10.

44. NOTE 2: Ziegler, Kristin. "AP May Come to CHHS." *BG,* 10 Nov. 1986.

45. STANDARD STUDENTS' SHARE OF FAILING GRADES: SCP2, 67.

45. CAUSES OF FAILING GRADES: SCP2, 69.

45. NEWCOMERS LARGELY RESPONSIBLE FOR DISCIPLINARY PROBLEMS: Burkett interview, 27 July 1988.

45–46. FINDINGS OF NINTH-GRADE SURVEY: Moskowitz interview, 26 Sept. 1991.

46. BLACK TEACHERS' SUSPICIONS: Watson, Mary Cole. Memorandum to the African-American staff of Cleveland Heights High School, 18 Dec. 1990. This memo summarizes the concerns expressed by black teachers at a private meeting the previous day.

47. TEACHERS PROTEST REPAINTING: "Burkett Stops Painting." *BG,* 23 Feb. 1987.

47. MULTIMILLION-DOLLAR DEFICIT: "Annual Report 1986–87," Cleveland Heights–University Heights School District.

48. TEACHER-ORIENTED PRINCIPAL: Salvator interview.

48. REINSTITUTION OF POSITION OF DEPARTMENT CHAIRPERSON: Frank Walter interview, 13 Mar. 1991.

48. WHY POSITION ABOLISHED: McBride interview, 24 July 1991; Steve Young interview, 25 Mar. 1991.

48. POWERS OF DEPARTMENT LIAISONS: Frank Walter interview, 13 Mar. 1991.

48. PREVIOUS PROCEDURE REGARDING USE OF SCANTRON FORM: Burkett interview, 16–17 Mar. 1991.

49. STEWARDS' EXPECTATIONS OF HIGH SCHOOL ADMINISTRATION: Frank Walter interview, 13 Mar. 1991.

49–50. STEWARDS' VIEW OF THEIR MANAGEMENT RESPONSIBILI-
TIES: Quail interview, 3 May 1991.

50. AMOUNT OF FOUNDATION GRANTS: "1988 Annual Report,"
Cleveland Foundation; "1989 Annual Report," Cleveland Foundation.

51. LENGTH OF CONTRACTUAL DAY: "Contract between Cleveland
Heights–University Heights Board of Education and Cleveland Heights
Teachers Union," 10 Apr. 1989, 38–39.

51. PURPOSE OF GRANT MONIES: Moskowitz, Irv, and Hugh Burkett.
"A High School Planning Grant." Submitted to the Cleveland Foundation
by the Cleveland Heights–University Heights School District, Dec. 1987,
2–3.

Chapter 5. The Dilemma of Leadership

54. PROPOSAL TO REDUCE TEACHING LOAD OF ENGLISH
TEACHERS AND FACULTY REACTION: Comments made by Hugh
Burkett and teacher Bill Thomas at the 19–22 May 1989 Model School
Project retreat.

55. HOW TEACHER AND SUPERINTENDENT BECAME FRIENDS:
Wolf interview, 19 Sept. 1991.

55. SUPERINTENDENT'S FRIENDSHIP WITH ISLER: Wolf interview,
19 Sept. 1991.

55–56. WOLF TOLD HE WAS NOT FIRST CHOICE: Wolf interview, 1 Apr.
1991.

57. PROJECT TIMETABLE: "Planning Grant," 5–6.

59. NOTE 2: Price interview.

Chapter 6. Less Is More

62. PRINCIPAL'S ADVOCACY OF SIZER: Wolf interview, 19 Sept. 1991.

62. NOTE 1: Toch, Thomas, and Matthew Cooper. "Lessons from the
Trenches." *U.S. News and World Report,* 26 Feb. 1990; "Rewarded by
Annenberg in the Bronx." *New York Times,* 22 Dec. 1993; Powell, Farrar,
and Cohen, 5–6.

63. SIZER CITED: *Horace's Compromise,* 131.

63–64. MODEL SCHOOL ADVISORY COMMITTEE: "Planning Grant," 4.

64. CENTRAL-OFFICE RESENTMENT: Peacock interview, 14 Aug. 1991.

65. PRINCIPAL'S GUIDING PRINCIPLES: MSP, "Memorandum to the
Model School Steering Committe [*sic*] and Team Leaders," 11 Nov. 1988.

66. NOTE 4: "Course Description Scheduling Guide." 1987–88 handbook.
Cleveland Heights High School; Burkett interview, 16–17 Mar. 1991.

66. CURRICULUM STUDY TEAM QUOTED: MSP, "Mission Statements/Guiding Principles," ca. Dec. 1988.

68. RACE RELATIONS STUDY TEAM QUOTED: MSP, "Mission Statements/Guiding Principles," ca. Dec. 1988.

68. "COMBAT RACISM BY RECOGNIZING IT": MSP, "Mission Statements/Guiding Principles," ca. Dec. 1988.

68. FOWLKES'S BIO: Fowlkes interview, 27 Sept. 1988.

69. BLACK TEACHERS SNUBBED BY WHITE STUDENTS/PARENTS: Comments made by teachers Phyllis Fowlkes, Margie Harper, and Beverly Simmons at 27 Sept. 1988 meeting of race relations study team.

70. RACE RELATIONS STUDY TEAM QUOTED: MSP, "Mission Statements/Guiding Principles," ca. Dec. 1988.

71. PERCENTAGE OF BLACK STAFF AT HIGH SCHOOL: SCP2, 53.

71. BLACK STAFF ACTIVISTS REQUEST MEETING WITH PRINCIPAL: Burkett interview, 16–17 Mar. 1991; Price interview; Simmons interview.

71–72. PRINCIPAL'S PIGHEADEDNESS: Price interview.

Chapter 7. Solidarity Forever

74. PROJECT MANAGER APPROACHES UNION: Wolf interview, 19 Sept. 1991.

74. CUSICK'S WARNING: Wolf interview, 19 Sept. 1991.

74. NOTE 1: Frolik, Joe. "Rochester Schools' Teamwork Sets Pace." *PD,* 27 May 1990; Peterson, Brian. "How School Based Management Is Faring in Miami." Letter to the editor. *Education Week,* 12 June 1991.

74. UNION PRESIDENT CLAIMS SUPERINTENDENT/PRINCIPAL USING PROJECT MANAGER: Wolf interview, 1 Aug. 1988.

74. UNION PRESIDENT'S POSITION ON VOLUNTEER WORK: Altschuld, Glenn. "The President's Position: Invariable and Almost Invariable." Memorandum to the executive board of the Cleveland Heights Teachers Union, 23 Apr. 1990.

75. UNION PRESIDENT GIVES HIS BLESSING: Wolf interview, 1 Aug. 1988.

75. UNION PRESIDENT'S ADVICE TO PROJECT MANAGER: Wolf interview, 1 Aug. 1988.

75. STEWARDS' JOB DESCRIPTION: "Building Steward Handbook," Cleveland Heights Teachers Union, n.d., 8.

76. CONTROVERSY SURROUNDING INCIDENT INVOLVING STUDENT WHO THREATENED TEACHER: Esch interview; Salvator interview.

76. "KID KILLERS": Esch interview; Salvator interview.

76. NOTE 2: "Hts. Teachers' Strike Hinges on Board Vote." *PD,* 11 Apr.

1975; "Discipline Policy Adoption Averts Hts. School Strike." *PD,* 13 Apr. 1975.

76. REASON FOR TARDY ROOM'S CLOSING: Salvator interview.

76. THREATENED JOB ACTION: Esch interview; Salvator interview.

76. OUTCOME OF THREAT: Esch interview.

77. WHY SOME BLACK TEACHERS OPPOSED SCHEDULING CHANGE: Burkett interview, 16–17 Mar. 1991.

77. WHY SCIENCE TEACHERS OPPOSED SCHEDULING CHANGE: Burkett interview, 16–17 Mar. 1991; Frank Walter interview, 13 Mar. 1991; Quail interview, 8 Mar. 1991.

77–78. ADMINISTRATION'S PLEASURE AT ADJUSTING UNEQUAL WORKLOADS: Frank Walter interview, 13 Mar. 1991.

78. WHY PRINCIPAL OPPOSED STUDY HALLS: Salvator interview.

78. STEWARDS' VIEW OF SCHEDULING TALKS: Esch interview.

78. FEELINGS OF BETRAYAL: Esch interview; Salvator interview.

78. SUPERINTENDENT URGED PRINCIPAL TO PRESENT PLANS: Esch interview.

78. PRESSURE TO CUT STAFF: Burkett interview, 16–17 Mar. 1991.

78. LABOR COMPLAINTS: Altschuld, Glenn. Memorandum to members of the Cleveland Heights Teachers Union, 7 Sept. 1989.

78–79. PLANNED JOB ACTION: Esch interview; Salvator interview.

79. FACULTY OBJECTIONS TO JOB ACTION: Frank Walter interview, 13 Mar. 1991.

79. SUCCESS OF JOB ACTION: Esch interview.

79. WRITTEN REPRIMANDS: Altschuld, Glenn. Memorandum to members of the Cleveland Heights Teachers Union, 22 Sept. 1989.

79. THIRD LABOR COMPLAINT AND DISTRICT'S COUNTER-CHARGE: Bragg, Marsha Lynn. "Finding Favors Teachers in Class Period Dispute." *SP,* 5 Oct. 1989.

79. "PENALTY BOX": Salvator interview.

79–80. PRINCIPAL BLAMED FOR STEWARD'S TRANSFER: Salvator interview.

80. EXAMPLE OF SUPERINTENDENT'S COMPETITIVENESS: Tribble interview.

80. PETITION OPPOSING TRANSFER: Salvator interview.

80. CHIEF STEWARD'S SYMPATHETIC COMMENTS: Salvator interview.

80. MADELINE HUNTER ANNOUNCEMENT: Burkett, Hugh. Letter to the Cleveland Heights High School faculty, 11 July 1988.

80. UNION PRESIDENT'S OPPOSITION TO HUNTER INVITATION: Altschuld, Glenn. "Voluntary and Compensated: Some History." Letter to members of the Cleveland Heights Teachers Union, 22 Aug. 1988.

80. UNION PRESIDENT'S VIEW OF PROFESSIONAL DEVELOPMENT: Altschuld, Glenn. "Voluntary and Compensated: Some History." Letter to members of the Cleveland Heights Teachers Union, 22 Aug. 1988.

81. "GREW FANGS": Wolf interview, 1 Aug. 1988.
81. PRINCIPAL'S THREAT TO INCREASE FREQUENCY OF EVALU-ATIONS: Quail interview, 8 Mar. 1991. "*LIVING* WITH TEACHERS": Wolf interview, 1 Aug. 1988.
81. INADEQUATE NUMBER OF ADMINISTRATORS: Quail interview, 8 Mar. 1991.
82. AFT'S MODEST MEMBERSHIP ROSTER IN 1960S: Herskovitz interview; Quail interview, 3 May 1991.
82. AFT'S POSITION ON STRIKES: Herskovitz interview; Quail interview, 3 May 1991.
82. NEA NEGOTIATORS' PROMOTIONS TO ADMINISTRATIVE JOBS: Warner interview.
82. FAILURE OF LEVY PAVES WAY FOR ASCENDANCY OF LOCAL 795: "Heights Teachers Chose Union as Bargaining Agent." *PD,* 11 June 1971.
82–83. STEWARD'S CLASS GRIEVANCE: Burkett interview, 16–17 Mar. 1991.
83. HOW PRINCIPAL VIEWED STEWARD'S MILITANCY: Wolf interview, 3 Aug. 1988.
83–84. PRINCIPAL SAYS HE WILL STOP MEETING WITH STEWARDS: Wolf interview, 1 Aug. 1988.
84. ABRUPT DEPARTURE OF PRINCIPAL/ASSISTANT PRINCIPAL: Quail interview, 8 Mar. 1991.
84. CONDITION ATTACHED TO RESUMPTION OF MEETINGS: Frank Walter interview, 13 Mar. 1991.
84. STEWARDS POLL FACULTY: Burkett interview, 16–17 Mar. 1991.
84. HSSC FORMED: Burkett interview, 16–17 Mar. 1991.
84. SUPERINTENDENT/UNION PRESIDENT RELUCTANT TO PARTICIPATE IN DSC: MacDonald interview, 4 June 1991; Sweet interview.
84. "DUPLICITY": Altschuld, Glenn, and Tom Schmida. Handwritten memorandum to the executive board of the Cleveland Heights Teachers Union, 30 June 1989.
84. IDEA FOR DSC: SCP1, 58.

Chapter 8. A Strategic Retreat

90. STUDENT LIFE STUDY TEAM QUOTED: MSP, "Mission Statements/Guiding Principles," ca. Dec. 1988.
90. STUDENT LIFE TEAM LEADER QUOTED: MSP, "Interim Report," ca. Apr. 1989.
90. FAMILY RELATIONS STUDY TEAM QUOTED: MSP, "Interim Report," ca. Apr. 1989.
90. HIGH EXPECTATIONS STUDY TEAM QUOTED: MSP, "Interim Report," ca. Apr. 1989.

91. SUMMARY OF RACE RELATIONS STUDY TEAM RECOMMEN-
DATIONS: MSP, "Interim Report," ca. Apr. 1989.

93. NOTE 1: Goodlad, *Place,* 112; Committee on Policy for Racial Justice, 3.

96. SCHEDULE DISCUSSED IN SIZER NEWSLETTER: "Scheduling the
Essential School." *Horace,* May 1989.

9. Intramural Rivalry

103. AVERAGE TENURE OF BIG-CITY SUPERINTENDENTS: "Schools
Scramble to Fill Superintendent Vacancies." *PD,* 8 Dec. 1990.

103. WHY SUPERINTENDENT RESIGNED: Fine interview.

103. NUMBER OF STUDENTS WHO FAILED NINTH GRADE: "The
Conflict over Taylor Academy." Editorial. *PD,* 20 July 1987.

104. NOTE 1: PERCENTAGE OF BUDGET DUE TO WAGES—"1988 Lay
Finance Committee Report," Cleveland Heights–University Heights
School District, 7 Nov. 1988, 1. RANKING OF SALARIES IN DIS-
TRICT—Ohio Department of Education. BUDGET DOUBLED—
"Annual Report 1977–78," Cleveland Heights–University Heights School
District; "Annual Report 1987–88," Cleveland Heights–University Heights
School District. AMONG HIGHEST PROPERTY TAX RATES IN
STATE—Geneva interview; Resseger interview. DISCUSSION OF
IMPACT OF STATE LAWS/POLICY ON SCHOOL DISTRICTS—
"White Paper on Phantom Revenue." Cleveland Heights: Coalition for
School Funding Reform, June 1991. 1988–89 PER PUPIL EXPENDI-
TURES—Ohio Department of Education. MICHIGAN'S NEW
SCHOOL FINANCING ARRANGEMENT—Celis, William. "Michi-
gan Votes for Revolution in Financing Its Public Schools." *New York Times,*
17 Mar. 1994.

104. TERMS OF 1985 CONTRACT: "1987 Lay Finance Committee Report," Cleveland Heights–University Heights School District, 3 Aug.
1987, i.

104. UNION PRESIDENT'S PRAISE OF CONTRACT: "Board/Teachers
Reach Agreement." *BG,* 14 Feb. 1986.

104. SOME BOARD MEMBERS TURN AGAINST UNION: Weigand
interview.

104. NOTE 2: "1987 Lay Finance Committee Report," Cleveland Heights–
University Heights School District, 3 Aug. 1987, i.

104. NEW LAW FIRM HIRED: Bragg, Marsha Lynn. "Union Board Advises
Teachers to Reject Offer." *SP,* 10 Nov. 1988.

104–5. UNION PRESIDENT ON SUPERINTENDENT: Altschuld, Glenn.
"The Stone Wall." *Bargaining Table,* Nov. 1988.

105. SUPERINTENDENT'S RESPONSE: Moskowitz, Irv. Letter to the
teaching staff of the Cleveland Heights–University Heights School District,
3 Nov. 1988.

105. GAS FUMES AND A MATCH: MacDonald interview, 10 July 1991.

105. "THAT MAN IS EVIL": Comments made on a not-for-attribution basis by a former Cleveland Heights–University Heights School District administrator on 9 May 1991.

105. SUPERINTENDENT INTENDS TO DESTROY UNION: Wolf interview, 19 Sept. 1991.

106. SUBSTITUTE TEACHERS ON CALL: Moskowitz, Irv. Letter mailed to parents or guardians of students in the Cleveland Heights–University Heights School District, 4 Jan. 1988.

106. CYNICAL CALCULATION: Abramovitz interviews; Frank Walter interview, 13 Mar. 1991.

106. UNION PRESIDENT'S OBJECTION TO ART GRANT: Wilkinson, Robert. "School Art Program Stifled by Dispute." *SP*, 1 Dec. 1977.

106. OBSERVATION ABOUT SUPERINTENDENT'S PERSONALITY: Herskovitz interview.

106. UNION PRESIDENT ON HIS TRANSFER: Altschuld, Glenn. Letter to the members of the Cleveland Heights Teachers Union, 28 Apr. 1989.

107. GEARITY'S BIO: Gearity interview, 27 Mar. 1991.

108. PRINCIPAL'S ATTITUDE TOWARD FEMALE SUPERIORS: Frank Walter interview, 13 Mar. 1991.

108. SUPERINTENDENT'S PRAISE OF GEARITY'S ABILITIES AS PRINCIPAL: Kaeser interview.

108. FIRST BLACK FEMALE MAYOR: Hicks, Desiree F. "Boyd Takes Reins with Friends' Help." *PD*, 9 Jan. 1992.

109. NOTE 4: Burkett interviews, 27 July 1988 and 16–17 Mar. 1991.

109. ACTING SUPERINTENDENT OFFERS ASSISTANT SUPERIN-TENDENCY TO ASSISTANT PRINCIPAL: Frank Walter interview, 13 Mar. 1991.

109. WHY ASSISTANT PRINCIPAL DECLINES: Fran Walter interview, 10 July 1991.

109. ACTING SUPERINTENDENT EXPLAINS WHY PRINCIPAL PASSED OVER: Burkett interview, 27 June 1989.

109–10. "FIGHTS/INTIMIDATION/HAZING": Burkett, Hugh. Letter to the members of the Cleveland Heights–University Heights Board of Education, 1 June 1989.

110. BOARD PRESIDENT ARRANGES FOR BROTHERS TO SPEAK: Aram, Beth. "Burkett and B.O.E. Disagree over Brothers Award." *BG*, 9 June 1989.

110. REPRESENTATIVE OF BROTHERS EXPLAINS CLUB'S PUR-POSE: Hicks, Desiree F. "Group Banned from Awarding Scholarships." *PD*, 31 May 1989.

110. BOARD MEMBER'S SUGGESTED COMPROMISE: Hicks, Desiree F. "Principal Turns Board Critic." *PD*, 2 June 1989.

110. VOTE ON COMPROMISE: Hicks, Desiree F. "Brothers, Sisters Can Present Awards." *PD*, 1 June 1989.

111. "OUT OF LINE": Hicks, Desiree F. "Principal Turns Board Critic." *PD*, 2 June 1989.

111. *PLAIN DEALER* CHASTISES BOARD: "An Exception outside the Rule." Editorial. *PD,* 13 June 1989.

111. PRINCIPAL INTENDED TO EMBARRASS BOARD: Fine interview.

112. "GET BURKETT": Burkett interview, 14 Sept. 1989.

112. WHY PRINCIPAL DECIDES NOT TO SEEK SUPERINTEN-DENCY: Fran Walter interview, 2 Aug. 1989.

Chapter 10. Hearts and Minds

115–16. ACTIVITIES OF STUDENTS IN A MODEL SCHOOL: MSP, "Report," 5 June 1989.

116. FOWLKES'S COMPLAINTS: Comments made by Fran Walter and Steve Young at 13 June 1989 coordinators' meeting.

124. NOTE 2: Woessner, Robert. "Equity 2000: A Summation of Successful Strategies." *USA Today,* 18 Mar. 1992.

129. NOTE 3: "Cleveland Heights–University Heights Accelerated Math Support Project." Grant proposal submitted to BP America Foundation, Mar. 1991, n.p.

130. COMPONENTS OF DESIRED SCHOOL CULTURE: MSP, "August Retreat Final Report," 5 Dec. 1989.

Chapter 11. Hidden Agendas

133. NEW SCHOOL'S UNCONVENTIONAL COURSES: 1978 *Cauldron,* Cleveland Heights High School yearbook, 31.

133. PASS-FAIL OPTION AND OPPORTUNITY TO TEACH: "New School Concepts: Aid to Entire School." *BG,* 29 Oct. 1973.

133. HOW NEW SCHOOLERS WERE VIEWED: Frank Walter interview, 23 Feb. 1991.

133. NEW SCHOOLERS GIVEN SAY IN GOVERNANCE: 1978 *Cauldron,* Cleveland Heights High School yearbook, 31.

136. INTERIM SUPERINTENDENT NOT AN IDEA PERSON: Bullock interview; Kaeser interview; Weigand interview.

137. NOTE 3: Salvator interview; Herskovitz interview.

137. FOURTEEN FACULTY MEETINGS PER YEAR: "Contract between Cleveland Heights–University Heights Board of Education and Cleveland Heights Teachers Union," 10 Apr. 1989, 39.

137. UNION ALLOTTED TIME AT FACULTY MEETINGS: "Contract between Cleveland Heights–University Heights Board of Education and Cleveland Heights Teachers Union," 10 Apr. 1989, 40.

Chapter 12. A Minor Uprising

144. BOYCOTT LEADER REJOICES: Weber, Laura. "Students Unite, Boycott Cafeteria." *BG*, 12 Oct. 1989.

144. RESULTS OF STUDENT ATTITUDES SURVEY: "Effective School Battery Interpretive Summary: Cleveland Heights High School Psychosocial Climate—Student Reports." Psychological Assessment Resources, Inc., Dec. 1989.

145. UNCHARTERED GROUPS PROVIDE BOYCOTT LEADERSHIP: Bragg, Marsha Lynn. "Student Groups Leading School Lunch Boycott." *SP*, 27 Sept. 1989.

148. MODEL SCHOOL DISRUPTIVE OF STUDENTS' EDUCATION: Pollock interview.

150. OUTCOME OF EGGING INCIDENT: "School Head Honors Judge's Slap." *PD*, 1 Dec. 1953.

150. VICTIMS OF HYSTERIA: Weidenthal, Bud. "Vandals' Parents Bitter at Penalty." *CP*, 1 Dec. 1953.

151. STUDENTS TUTOR OR REGISTER VOTERS: Abramovitz interview, 9 May 1991.

151. CONSERVATIVE STUDENTS IN MAJORITY: Budin interview.

151. FLAG-RAISING INCIDENT: Abramovitz interview, 9 May 1991.

151. NEW STUDENT FREEDOMS IN SECOND HALF OF 1960S: "Principal Myslenski Resigns, Recalls Educational Innovations." *BG*, 7 Feb. 1969; "Happening at Heights," *PD*, 21 Nov. 1969.

151–52. WHY PRINCIPAL RETIRED: Abramovitz interview, 21 May 1991.

152. DRESS CODE LIBERALIZATION AND ITS AFTERMATH: "Heights Wants Boys to Wear the Trousers." *PD*, 30 Jan. 1969.

152. "NO POLICEMAN": Barnett, Barbara. "O'Toole Arrives at Heights High." *CP*, 30 July 1969.

152. CIVIL RIGHTS POLICY APPROVED: Barnett, Barbara. "Student Activist Unit Banned in Heights Schools." *CP*, 6 Apr. 1970.

152. SMC CONTROVERSY: Barnett, Barbara. "Student Activist Unit Banned in Heights Schools." *CP*, 6 Apr. 1970.

152–53. SMC ATTORNEY'S ARGUMENT: "Heights Board Mum on Peace Group Ban." *CP*, 12 May 1970.

153. BOARD UPHOLDS FREEDOM OF SPEECH AND ASSEMBLY: Almond, Peter. "Heights Board Backs Right to Dissent." *CP*, 9 June 1970.

153. NOTE 3: BOARD STATEMENT QUOTED—Almond, Peter. "Heights Board Backs Right to Dissent." *CP*, 9 June 1970. CHANGES IN PARTY ALLEGIANCE—Boyle interview.

153. MICKEY SPROUTS GENITALIA: Burkett interview, 16–17 Mar. 1991.

153. MICKEY REAPPEARS: "Mickey Is Back." Photo caption. *BG*, 21 Oct. 1987.

154. EDITORS' DESCRIPTION OF STUDENT PAPER: Masthead. *BG*, 4 Oct. 1974.

154. PROPOSED EDITORIAL POLICY: Author's copy of Sept. 1989 draft.

154. EDITORIAL POLICY REWRITTEN SEVERAL TIMES: Aram interview.

154. PRINCIPAL REFUSES TO APPROVE POLICY: Aram interview.

154. ARAM'S GUEST COLUMN: Aram, Beth. "A Youthful World's Fight against Ignorance, Apathy." Column. *SP,* 1 Mar. 1990.

155. LIBRARIAN ASKS FOR *BG* STORY: Aram interview.

Chapter 13. The Question of Exclusion

158. BLACK-ON-WHITE ASSAULTS AND THEIR AFTERMATH: Author's copy of an unpublished news story written for *BG* by Beth Aram; report made by high school steward Ed Esch at 18 Oct. 1989 faculty meeting.

159. ARAM'S CONFESSION: Aram interview.

159. PRINCIPAL CENSORS STUDENT NEWSPAPER STORY: Aram interview; comments made by Cas McBride and Fran Walter at 16 Oct. 1989 coordinators' meeting.

160. PROTEST FAILS TO PREVENT TAYLOR'S OPENING: Hicks, Desiree F. "Taylor Academy Passes the Test in Its First Year." *PD,* 19 June 1988.

160. MILITANT PARENTS OFFER ADVOCACY SERVICES: Madison interview.

160. SUPERINTENDENT OVERRULES FOUR EXPULSIONS: Altschuld, Glenn. Memorandum to the members of the Cleveland Heights Teachers Union, 25 Oct. 1989.

162. NATURE OF CICR INVESTIGATION: Lott interview.

162. CICR'S ANNUAL MEETING WITH SUPERINTENDENT: Abramovitz interview, 21 May 1991; Lott interview.

162. DISPARITY IN DISTRICT'S BLACK AND WHITE SUSPENSION RATES: Kaeser, *Citizens Guide,* 27.

162. KAESER CITED: *Citizens Guide,* 27.

162. NOTE 1: Kaeser, *Citizens Guide,* 19.

163. "ORDERLY SCHOOLS": SCP "Excellence and Equity," 5.

163. SCP'S REQUEST FOR COMMUNITY FORUMS: Kaeser interview.

163. WHY SCP REQUEST DENIED: Kaeser interview.

163–64. SUPERINTENDENT'S MEETING ON SUSPENSION RATES: Gearity interview, 21 July 1992.

164. TEACHER ASSAULTED: Altschuld, Glenn. Memorandum to the members of the Cleveland Heights Teachers Union, 25 Oct. 1989.

164. NATURE OF ASSAULT: Hodakievic interview.

164. WHY DISTRICT DECLINED TO EXPEL STUDENT: MacDonald interview, 11 June 1991; Frank Walter interview, 14 May 1991.

165. NOTE 3: Eskey, Kenneth. "Students Who Won't Behave a Plague for Big City Schools." *PD,* 29 Jan. 1995.

165. "LIGHTNING STRUCK": MacDonald, Dan. "Update." Memorandum to the teachers of Cleveland Heights High School, 23 Oct. 1989.

165. POOR RESPONSE TO CALL FOR JOB ACTION: MacDonald interview, 10 July 1991.

165. UNION FILES FOUR DISCIPLINARY GRIEVANCES: Altschuld, Glenn. Memorandum to the members of the Cleveland Heights Teachers Union, 25 Oct. 1989.

165. COMPLAINT ABOUT INADEQUATE DOCUMENTATION: MacDonald interviews, 11 June 1991 and 10 July 1991.

166. MIRAMAR'S PERSPECTIVE: MacDonald interview, 11 June 1991.

166. PRINCIPAL POUNDS FIST AND SHOUTS: MacDonald interview, 10 July 1991.

166. UNION PRESIDENT APPOINTED TECHNICAL COMPLIANCE OFFICER: *Union News.* AFT Local 795 newsletter. Jan. 1990.

166. "FUN": Altschuld interview.

166. NEW SUPERINTENDENT SEEKS RAPPROCHEMENT WITH UNION: Altschuld, Glenn, and Tom Schmida. Handwritten memorandum to the executive board of the Cleveland Heights Teachers Union, 30 June 1989.

166. SUPERINTENDENT REINSTATES REGULAR MEETING WITH UNION LEADERSHIP: Altschuld, Glenn, and Tom Schmida. Handwritten memorandum to the executive board of the Cleveland Heights Teachers Union, 30 June 1989.

167. "A MORE PREDICTABLE PERSONALITY": Altschuld, Glenn. "Seventeen Eventful Months: Part 2 of 3." Memorandum to the members of the Cleveland Heights Teachers Union, 12 Jan. 1990.

167. OUTCOME OF REOPENED CONTRACT NEGOTIATIONS: Altschuld, Glenn. "Seventeen Eventful Months: Part 2 of 3." Memorandum to the members of the Cleveland Heights Teachers Union, 12 Jan. 1990.

167. "A NEW BEGINNING": Altschuld, Glenn. Memorandum to the members of the Cleveland Heights Teachers Union, 25 Oct. 1989.

167–68. LABOR RULING: Bragg, Marsha Lynn. "Finding Favors Teachers in Class Dispute." *SP,* 5 Oct. 1989.

168. COMPENSATION LIKELY: Altschuld interview; MacDonald interview, 23 July 1992.

168. UNION/BOARD RESPONSE TO LABOR RULING: Bragg, Marsha Lynn. "Finding Favors Teachers in Class Dispute." *SP,* 5 Oct. 1989.

168. "BROWBEATEN/VINDICATED": Altschuld, Glenn. Memorandum to the members of the Cleveland Heights Teachers Union, 26 Sept. 1989.

168. TOLL ON PRINCIPAL: Burkett interview, 29 Oct. 1989.

Chapter 14. The Silent Majority

172. ONLY SUPERINTENDENT ASKED TO APPROVE WINSTON'S HIRING: Burkett interview, 16–17 Mar. 1991.

172. HIGH SCHOOL ADMINISTRATION CANNOT PUBLISH NEWS-PAPER: Burkett interview, 16–17 Mar. 1991; Winston interview, 10 Oct. 1990.

172–73. SUPERINTENDENT'S COUNTEROFFER: Winston interview, 10 Oct. 1990.

173. SLATE'S CAMPAIGN PROMISE: "Elect Leanza/Bullock/Klein." Flyer. Committee to Elect Leanza, Bullock, and Klein, Cleveland Heights, ca. Fall 1989.

173. "NO MORE STRIKES": Glickson, Judith. Campaign letter to the residents of Cleveland Heights and University Heights. Mailed by the Committee to Re-Elect Judith Glickson, Cleveland Heights, ca. Fall 1989.

173. BOARD MEMBER SUSPECTED OF LEAKS: Bragg, Marsha Lynn. "Policy Changes Will Greet New Board Members." SP, 21 Dec. 1989.

173–74. ONLY BOARD MEMBER TO OBJECT TO 1988–89 CONTRACT OFFER: Hicks, Desiree F. "Heights Hears Bottom Line on Teacher Pay." PD, 19 Jan. 1989.

174. NOTE 1: BOARD'S ACTIONS AND EXPLANATIONS—Bragg, Marsha Lynn. "School Board Will Pick Coughlin Replacement." SP, 20 July 1989. SP QUOTED—"Reasons Don't Wash." Editorial. SP, 27 July 1989. SIMILAR TACTIC USED IN AN EARLIER ERA—Boyle interview.

174. BOARD MEMBER'S INITIAL ENDORSEMENT BY UNION: Frank Walter interview, 23 Feb. 1991.

174–75. DOUBTS ABOUT BOARD MEMBER'S UNION LOYALTIES: Rose interview, 2 Aug. 1991.

175. "HARDENING OF INTELLECTUAL ARTERIES": Sweet interview.

175. BOARD MEMBER'S NEGATIVE ATTITUDE: Kaeser interview.

175. HCEL'S ORIGINS AND GOALS: Kaeser interview; Oliver interview; Sweet interview.

175. SLATE PROMISES NATIONAL SEARCH: Fran Walter interview, 10 July 1991.

176. REA'S POLITICAL GOALS: Rose interview, 2 Aug. 1991.

176. NUMBER OF PROSPECTIVE CANDIDATES EXAMINED: Bragg, Marsha Lynn. "Seventeen Interviewed in Organization's Search." SP, 3 Aug. 1989.

176. SLATE PICKED: Bragg, Marsha Lynn. "Community Groups Pick School Board Hopefuls." SP, 3 Aug. 1989.

176. CICR'S INITIAL GOAL: Allen interview.

178. HCP COFFEES: Luke Isler interview.

178. HCP'S RECRUITMENT PROBLEMS: Luke Isler interview.

179. LEADERSHIP VACUUM AT HCP PRESENTS OPPORTUNITY: Luke Isler interview.

179. HCP PRESIDENT BLASTS TAYLOR: Luke Isler interview.

179. HCP PRESIDENT OUSTED: Breckenridge, Tom. "Taylor School Critic Refuses to Leave Post." PD, 18 Sept. 1987.

179. PROTEST BLOCKS MANDATORY ENROLLMENT AT TAYLOR:

Madison interview; Breckenridge, Tom. "Keep Academy Shut, NAACP
Tells State." *PD*, 3 Sept. 1987.

179. DISTRICT SEEKS HCP'S COUNSEL: Luke Isler interview.

181. WHY HCP PREFERRED TEMPERATE APPROACH: Evans interview.

Chapter 15. A Failure to Communicate

186. NEW BOARD MEMBERS ELECT PRESIDENT: Bragg, Marsha Lynn.
"BOE, New President Seeking Harmony." *SP*, 11 Jan. 1990.

186. WHY BOARD PRESIDENT NOT ENDORSED BY HCEL: Kaeser
interview; Rose interview, 2 Aug. 1991.

186–87. BOARD PRESIDENT'S ARGUMENTS AGAINST NATIONAL
SEARCH: Bragg, Marsha Lynn. "New Leader at the Helm." *SP*, 15 Feb.
1990.

187. "CHUMPS": Kaeser interview.

190. CHIEF UNION STEWARD EXPRESSES SUPPORT FOR MODEL
SCHOOL PROJECT: *Union News*. AFT Local 795 newsletter. Jan. 1990.

Chapter 16. Masters of a Slow Death

192. NUMBER OF BLACK FAMILIES MOVING INTO CLEVELAND
HEIGHTS EACH YEAR: Griffith, Gary. "A Shadow at Evening: New
Neighbors in Cleveland Heights." *Cleveland Magazine*, Jan. 1973.

192. VIOLENCE ENCOUNTERED BY NEWCOMERS: Allen interview.

192–93. ARSON/BOMBINGS: Griffith, Gary. "A Shadow at Evening: New
Neighbors in Cleveland Heights." *Cleveland Magazine*, Jan. 1973; Gunning
interview; Storey interview.

193. IMPETUS FOR TASK FORCE: Weiner, Rick. "Offers Five-Point Plan
on Human Relations." *CP*, 8 July 1964.

193. TASK FORCE RECOMMENDATIONS: Ingram, Bill. "Human Rela-
tions Rumors Bring Crowd to Meeting." *CP*, 15 Nov. 1966; "Heights
Schools Racial Plan Criticized, Praised." *PD*, 15 Nov. 1966; "Heights
School Board Passes New Policy on Human Relations." *PD*, 13 Dec. 1966.

193. RESPONSE TO RECOMMENDATIONS: Ingram, Bill. "Petitions
against Rights Plan Set for Head of School Board." *CP*, 13 Dec. 1966.

193. "GENERALLY REPRESENTATIVE": "Heights School Board Passes
New Policy on Human Relations. *PD*, 13 Dec. 1966.

193. OPPOSITION TO AGGRESSIVE MINORITY RECRUITMENT
PROGRAM: Ingram, Bill. "Human Relations Rumors Bring Crowd to
Meeting." *CP*, 15 Nov. 1966.

194. "BILL OF GOODS": Friedman interview.

194. BOARD RESPONSE: "Board Turns to the People for Help in Rights
Policy." *CP*, 13 Dec. 1966.

194. TASK FORCE COCHAIR'S PROGRESS REPORT: Minutes of a

meeting of the board of trustees of Plan of Action by Citizens in Education (PACE), Jewish Community Federation, Cleveland, 11 Jan. 1966.

194. PERCENTAGE OF BLACK TEACHING STAFF DISTRICTWIDE: "Answer Black Student Needs." Editorial. *PD*, 12 June 1974.

194. ORIGINS AND OUTCOME OF BLACK PARENT PATROLS: Lott interview.

195. FIGHTING BY BLACK STUDENTS JUSTIFIED: Lott interview.

195. "BENIGN ADMINISTRATIVE NEGLECT": "Answer Black Student Needs." Editorial. *PD*, 12 June 1974.

195. ADMINISTRATION UNRESPONSIVE TO BLACK PARENTS' REQUESTS: "Black Parents Claim Heights Schools Biased." *CP*, 11 June 1974; Lott interview.

195. CICR TAKES COMPLAINTS PUBLIC: "Blacks Protest against Heights School Policies." *PD*, 11 June 1974.

195. CICR'S DEMANDS: Hatton, Katherine L. "Black Students' Needs Are Aired at Special Heights School Meeting." *PD*, 18 June 1974; Hatton, Katherine L. "Hts. Board Turns Down Black Group Demands." *PD*, 16 July 1974.

195. BAD REPUTATION OF GUIDANCE DEPARTMENT: Lott interview.

195. BOARD'S RESPONSE: Hatton, Katherine L. "Hts. Board Turns Down Black Group Demands." *PD*, 16 July 1974.

195. "QUALITY QUOTA": Hatton, Katherine L. "Hts. Board Turns Down Black Group Demands." *PD*, 16 July 1974.

195–96. CICR MEMBERS FELT AS IF THEY HAD BEEN STONEWALLED: Allen interview; Lott interview.

196. CICR PRESS STATEMENT: "Probe of Heights Schools Is Asked by Parents." *PD*, 11 Oct. 1974.

196. JUSTICE DEPARTMENT MEDIATOR INTERVENES: Hatton, Katherine L. "Justice Official Enters Heights Fray." *PD*, n.d.

196. TERMS OF WRITTEN AGREEMENT: "Heights Minority Hiring to Reach 15%." *CP*, 3 Apr. 1975.

196. SUPERINTENDENT'S CLAIMS ABOUT DIFFICULTIES OF RE-CRUITING MINORITIES: Lott interview.

196. PERCENTAGE OF BLACK PROFESSIONAL STAFF DISTRICT-WIDE: "Heights Schools Pledge 20% Minority Employment." *CP*, 20 Jan. 1981.

197. NOTE 2: LOTT'S TENURE GAVE CREDIBILITY TO MINORITY RECRUITMENT EFFORT—Feinberg interview.

197. FIRST BLACK WOMAN EVER TO SERVE IN AN ELECTIVE CA-PACITY: "Bernice Lott Does Lots." *PD*, 5 Oct. 1976.

197. LOTT'S ROLE IN ENCOURAGING VOLUNTARY DESEGREGA-TION: Baron interview; Feinberg interview.

197. PERCENTAGE OF MINORITY STUDENTS AT BELVOIR AND BOULEVARD: Hatch, J. Stephen. "Heights Residents Seem Split over School Integration Plans." *PD*, 27 May 1977; "Money Is Factor in Heights Hearing." *CP*, 1 June 1977.

197. BOARD'S FEAR OF FEDERAL CONTROL: "Are Heights Schools under the Gun?" *CP*, 2 June 1977; Baron interview.

197. DESEGREGATION COMMITTEE CREATED: Sartin, V. David. "Hts. Panel to Have Thirty for Racial Study." *PD*, 16 Dec. 1976.

197–98. SHOTGUN FIRED: Funk, John. "Gun Fired at School Official's Home." *CP*, 20 Dec. 1977; Baron interview.

198. COST OF PROPOSED DESEGREGATION PLANS: Wilkinson, Robert. "Money Is Key as Board Nears Desegregation Move." *SP*, 9 June 1977.

198. RESPONSE OF BLACK COMMUNITY: Simoneau interview.

198. RESPONSE OF WHITE PARENTS: Funk, John. "Heights Integration Meeting Is Spirited." *CP*, 26 May 1977.

198. BOARD TABLES PLANS: Wilkinson, Robert. "Hasty Schools Decision Ruled Out." *SP*, 10 June 1977.

198. SUPERINTENDENT'S PREDECESSOR FIRED: Baron interview.

198. SUPERINTENDENT'S COMPROMISE PLAN: Wilkinson, Robert. "Schools Unveil Conversion Plan." *SP*, 20 Apr. 1978; Abramovitz interviews.

198. STUDENTS TO BE BUSED ARE PRIMARILY BLACK: Wilkinson, Robert. "Schools Redistricting Plan Set for '79–'80." *SP*, 31 Aug. 1978; Simoneau interview.

198–99. SITES OF MAGNET PROGRAMS: Weidenthal, Bud. "Heights to Expand Magnet School Program." *CP*, 28 Mar. 1979.

199. GEARITY'S RESEARCH ON MAGNETS: Wilkinson, Robert. "Parents to Be Polled about Magnet School." *SP*, 16 Feb. 1978.

199. NOTE 3: Gearity interview, 27 Mar. 1991.

199. SOME BELVOIR PARENTS CHOSE TO LEAVE DISTRICT: Gearity interview, 11 July 1991.

199. BELVOIR MAGNET'S INITIAL ENROLLMENT: Gearity interview, 11 July 1991.

199. NOTE 4: REORGANIZATION PLAN—Abramovitz, Albert. "The Preservation of Excellence . . . through the '80s and Beyond." A Report to the Cleveland Heights–University Heights Board of Education. 11 June 1984. SAVE OUR SCHOOL CAMPAIGN AND ITS AFTERMATH—Gabe, Catherine. "Parents Sue to Halt Closing of Two Heights Schools." *PD*, 27 Dec. 1984; "University Hts. Tries to Join School-Closing Suit." *PD*, 24 Jan. 1985; Jordan, George E. "Board, University Hts. Split on School Use." *PD*, 17 July 1985; Loughlin, Sean. "School Closings a Side Issue in Heights Vote." *PD*, 25 Aug. 1985. ABRAMOVITZ'S RESIGNATION—Abramovitz interview, 9 May 1991.

199. MINORITY ENROLLMENT AT BELVOIR AND BOULEVARD BY LATE 1980S: "Minority Data." Second quarter 1988–89 report. Department of Pupil Services, Cleveland Heights–University Heights Board of Education.

199. PARENTS SHOULD HAVE FINAL SAY: Gearity interview, 21 July 1992.

199. NEW SUPERINTENDENT'S DESIRED ATTRIBUTES: Bragg, Marsha Lynn. "New Leader at Helm." *SP*, 15 Feb. 1990.

200. GEARITY CREDITS GLICKSON WITH HER PROMOTION: Bragg, Marsha Lynn. "Heights District Loses Its 'Champion of Students.'" *SP*, 31 Dec. 1992.

200. SUPERINTENDENT'S STARTING SALARY: Hicks, Desiree F. "New School Chief Praised as Pillar of Stability, Continuity." *PD*, 15 Feb. 1990.

200. NEW BOARD MEMBERS MAKE VOTE UNANIMOUS: Boyle interview; Kaeser interview; Sweet interview.

201. "SAVED MONEY AMOUNT": Altschuld, Glenn. Memorandum to the executive board of the Cleveland Heights Teachers Union, 8 Nov. 1989.

201. GLICKSON QUOTED: Bragg, Marsha Lynn. "New Leader at the Helm." *SP*, 15 Feb. 1990.

201. WEIGAND QUOTED: Bragg, Marsha Lynn. "New Leader at the Helm." *SP*, 15 Feb. 1990.

Chapter 17. The Walkout

205. GREATEST NUMBER OF A'S SINCE 1981: Burkett interview, 16–17 Mar. 1991.

205. HIGH SCHOOL'S GRADE POINT AVERAGE: Mlynek, Lawrence S. "Grade Distribution for First Semester." Memorandum to the administrators of Heights High School, 13 Feb. 1990.

205. PRINCIPAL'S DEPARTURE FOR THE BEST: Burkett interview, 16–17 Mar. 1991.

205. PROTESTERS ALLEGE POLICE CONSPIRACY: Bragg, Marsha Lynn. "Parents, Students Protest Policies." *SP*, 22 Feb. 1990.

205. ORIGINS OF WALKOUT: Nita Heard interview; Madison interview.

205–7. DESCRIPTION OF OFF-CAMPUS ASSAULTS: 22 Oct. 1991 interview with Cleveland Heights police sergeant Arthur Lichtinger.

206. BOARD POLICY MANDATES SHARING INFORMATION WITH POLICE: Policy 1500, "Policy Notebook," Cleveland Heights–University Heights Board of Education.

206. PRINCIPAL'S RESPONSE TO ASSAULTS: Burkett interview, 16–17 Mar. 1991; Forman interview; James Heard interview.

206. COURTYARD FIGHT: Burkett interview, 16–17 Mar. 1991; Franklin interview.

207. CHARGES FILED AGAINST HOME BOYS: Lichtinger interview.

207. CHARGES STEMMING FROM STREET FIGHT: Lichtinger interview.

207. YOUNG WOMAN QUESTIONED AT SCENE: Hicks, Desiree F. "Officials Vow to Probe Concerns." *PD*, 25 Feb. 1990.

207. BOARD POLICY GOVERNING MISCONDUCT AWAY FROM SCHOOL: "Rights and Responsibilities of Students." Policy 5133

brochure. Department of Pupil Services, Cleveland Heights–University
Heights School District, revised 11 July 1988, 8.

207. PRINCIPAL DECLINES TO SUSPEND STUDENTS: Forman interview.

207. HIGH SCHOOL ADMINISTRATION CANNOT SERVE AS UNOF-
FICIAL POLICE: Mixon interview.

208. PARENTS PROTEST THEIR CHILDREN'S INNOCENCE: Bragg,
Marsha Lynn. "Parents, Students Protest Policies." *SP*, 22 Feb. 1990; Hicks,
Desiree F. "Officials Vow to Probe Concerns." *PD*, 25 Feb. 1990.

209. WHY PARENTS TOOK COMPLAINTS TO SUPERINTENDENT:
Nita Heard interview.

209. SUPERINTENDENT'S MEETING WITH PARENTS: Hicks, Desiree
F. "School Chief Says Parents Stalled to Mobilize Rally." *PD*, 22 Feb. 1990.

209. SUPERINTENDENT'S REASSURANCES: Nita Heard interview.

209. NOTE 1: Nita Heard interview; Madison interview.

209. STATEMENT ON FLYER: Pollak, Debbie. "Parents Protest Discipline
Policy." *BG*, 23 Feb. 1990.

209–10. SUPERINTENDENT'S PHONE CALL TO HIGH SCHOOL: Frank
Walter interview, 14 May 1991; Jean King interview.

210. MAINTENANCE CREW'S ARRIVAL: Frank Walter interview, 14 May
1991.

210. SUPERINTENDENT REFUSES TO LEAVE: Burkett interview, 16–17
May 1991.

210. SUPERINTENDENT IGNORES PRINCIPAL'S ADVICE: Burkett
interview, 16–17 May 1991.

210. SUPERINTENDENT ALLOWS PROTESTERS TO ENTER
SCHOOL GROUNDS: Burkett interview, 16–17 May 1991.

210. "A MORE POSITIVE ATMOSPHERE": Bragg, Marsha Lynn. "Parents,
Students Protest Policies." *SP*, 22 Feb. 1990.

210. "NEW POWERS-THAT-BE": Bragg, Marsha Lynn. "Parents, Students
Protest Policies." *SP*, 22 Feb. 1990.

211. CLARK'S BIO: Freedman, 359–60.

211. SEVERAL HUNDRED STUDENTS CONGREGATE INSIDE: Frank
Walter interview, 14 May 1991.

211. RUMORS FUEL CROWD'S SIZE: "Myth vs. Fact." *BG*, 23 Feb. 1990.

211. ACTIVITIES OF SUMMAS: Yarrow interview.

211. ADMINISTRATORS MOVE STUDENTS TO SOCIAL ROOM:
Frank Walter interview, 14 May 1991.

211. MESSAGES ON PLACARDS: Photograph accompanying 22 Feb. 1990
SP coverage of the walkout.

212. "ONE FOR ALL AND ALL FOR ONE": Travis, Brennan. "Students
Rally, Walk Out of Classes." *BG*, 23 Feb. 1990.

212. MOST STUDENTS WALK OUT OF SOCIAL ROOM: McLin interview.

212. RESPONSE OF CITY SPOKESPERSON: Madison interview.

213. MADISON'S SUMMARY OF PARENTS' DEMANDS: Bragg, Marsha Lynn. "Parents, Students Protest Policies." *SP,* 22 Feb. 1990.

213. SUPERINTENDENT'S ARRIVAL/ACTIONS AT CITY HALL: Burkett interview, 16–17 Mar. 1991.

213. STUDENTS DEMAND AUDIENCE WITH PRINCIPAL: Frank Walter interview, 14 May 1991.

213. STUDENTS' COMPLAINTS/DEMANDS: Burkett interview, 16–17 Mar. 1991; Hicks, Desiree F. "Officials, Pupils Meet to Discuss Concerns." *PD,* 17 Feb. 1990.

214. SUPERINTENDENT'S ACTIONS AT SIT-IN: Burkett interview, 16–17 Mar. 1991.

214–15. OCR DECIDES TO INVESTIGATE: Bragg, Marsha Lynn. "CH-UH Subject of Racial Bias Investigation." *SP,* 17 May 1990.

215. BLACK POLITICAL ESTABLISHMENT DECLINES TO INTERVENE: Ali-Bey interview; Madison interview; Prentiss interview.

215. MESSAGE TO STUDENTS BY STATE BOARD OF EDUCATION MEMBER: Prentiss interview.

215. NOT ALL BLACK PARENTS BELIEVED SCHOOL SYSTEM GUILTY OF RACIAL DISCRIMINATION: Evans interview.

215–16. FORMATION AND OUTCOME OF "QUALITY OF LIFE" TEAM: Frank Walter interview, 14 May 1991.

Chapter 18. Management by Crisis

221. SOME BLACK PARENTS EMBARRASSED BY MADISON'S POWER PLAY: Nita Heard interview.

221–22. TEACHER QUOTED: Hicks, Desiree F. "Dispute Mars Meeting on Racism." *PD,* 25 Feb. 1990.

222. "WORSE THAN I THOUGHT": Hicks, Desiree F. "Dispute Mars Meeting on Racism." *PD,* 25 Feb. 1990.

222. CITY'S RESPONSE TO MEDIA COVERAGE: "A Question of Equal Treatment in Cleveland Heights." Letter to the editor. *PD,* 5 Mar. 1990.

222. "DEATH OF CLEVELAND HEIGHTS": Comment made to the author by Robert A. Greene at 21 Feb. 1990 Cleveland Heights–University Heights School District press conference.

222. BOARD PRESIDENT QUOTED: Hicks, Desiree F. "Officials, Pupils Meet to Discuss Concerns." *PD,* 17 Feb. 1990.

222–23. NO CREDIBLE DEFENSE: Comments made to the author by Robert A. Greene at 21 Feb. 1990 Cleveland Heights–University Heights School District press conference.

224. TEACHER ASKS FOR BLACK LEADERSHIP OF MODEL SCHOOL PROJECT: Author's copy of a prepared statement read by Mary Cole Watson at 9 Mar. 1990 meeting of Heights Alliance of Black School Educa-

tors and central-office administrators of the Cleveland Heights–University Heights School District.

224. "RECOVERING RACISTS": Watson interview, 16 May 1991.

224. NOTE 1: Hoke, Wendy Ann. "Veteran Activist Is Newest Heights Council Member." *SP*, 4 Feb. 1993.

225. INCIDENTS LEADING UP TO STALLWORTH-BEY'S MURDER: 21 Aug. 1991 interview with University Heights police detective James Williams; Hicks, Desiree F. "Heights Boy Killed in Gang Shooting." *PD*, 6 Mar. 1990; Jacobs, Dan. "Teen Dies in Gang Shooting." *SP*, 8 Mar. 1990.

225. NOTE 2: CONVICTIONS—Hicks, Desiree F. "Two Teens Convicted in Drive-by Shooting." *PD*, 7 July 1990. LETTER—Newsom, Sandra. "Community Should Share Blame in Gang Shooting." Letter to the editor. *SP*, 11 Oct. 1990.

226. MAYOR QUOTED: Hicks, Desiree F., and Michael A. Hobbs. "Boy's Killing May Bring Gang Issue to a Head." *PD*, 7 Mar. 1990.

226. POLICE CHIEF QUOTED: Hicks, Desiree F., and Michael A. Hobbs. "Boy's Killing May Bring Gang Issue to a Head." *PD*, 7 Mar. 1990.

226. MOTHER'S PLEA: Shepard, Paul. "'Tomorrow Is Not Guaranteed.'" *PD*, 10 Mar. 1990.

226. "RUNNING AMOK": Hobbs, Michael A., and Desiree F. Hicks. "Parents Pledge Crackdown." *PD*, 8 Mar. 1990.

226. "NIP IN THE BUD": Hobbs, Michael A., and Desiree F. Hicks. "Parents Pledge Crackdown." *PD*, 8 Mar. 1990.

227. BOARD PRESIDENT QUOTED: Hicks, Desiree F., and Michael A. Hobbs. "Boy's Killing May Bring Gang Issue to a Head." *PD*, 7 Mar. 1990.

227. NOTE 3: Oliver interview.

227. CITY GANGS "RIPE" FOR RECRUITMENT BY LARGER CRIMINAL ORGANIZATIONS: Hicks, Desiree F. "Gang Recruitment Step Called a Real Danger." *PD*, 14 Dec. 1990.

227. DISCIPLINARY POLICY STRENGTHENED: Hicks, Desiree F. "Revised Policy Spells out Students' Responsibilities." *PD*, 19 Dec. 1990; Bragg, Marsha Lynn. "Intense Deliberation Ends in Revised Code of Conduct." *SP*, 27 Dec. 1990; Rajki, Eva. "Students' Rights and Responsibilities Redefined." *BG*, 18 Apr. 1991.

227. NOTE 4: "Rights and Responsibilities of Students." Statement of board of education policy 5133. Cleveland Heights–University Heights School District, revised 17 Dec. 1990.

227. NOTE 5: Heights Commission on Excellence and Equity, 23.

228. OCR FINDS RACIAL BIAS: Mines, Kenneth A. Letter to the superintendent of the Cleveland Heights–University Heights School District from the Region 5 director of the Office for Civil Rights of the U.S. Department of Education, n.d.

228. NOTE 6: Mines, Kenneth A. Letter to the superintendent of the Cleveland Heights–University Heights School District from the Region 5 director of the Office for Civil Rights of the U.S. Department of Education, n.d., 8.

228. DISTRICT IN VIOLATION OF CIVIL RIGHTS ACT OF 1964: Bragg, Marsha Lynn. "District Citing Follows Probe." *SP,* 23 May 1991.

228. DISTRICT AGREES TO ENFORCE "RACE NEUTRALITY": Hicks, Desiree F. "Heights System Showed Bias in Discipline, Report Says." *PD,* 18 May 1991.

228. UNION'S CRITICISM OF OCR REPORT: Schmida, Tom. "OCR Report." Letter to the members of the Cleveland Heights Teachers Union, 21 May 1991.

Chapter 19. Deadly Decisions

233. UPDATE ANNOUNCES PRINCIPAL SELECTION PLAN: MSP, "The Model School Project," 1 Mar. 1990.

235. NOTE 1: Altschuld, Glenn. "Open Letter." Memorandum to the Model School Project coordinators, 7 June 1990.

236. SUPERINTENDENT BACKS AWAY FROM PLAN: Gearity, Lauree. Memorandum to the members of the Heights High School staff, 27 Mar. 1990.

236. CLEVER MANAGEMENT TRAP: Comments made by Altschuld at 5 Apr. 1990 after-school meeting held to answer the faculty's questions about the union's opposition to the principal selection plan.

236. NOTE 3: Altschuld, Glenn. Memorandum to the faculty of Heights High School, 30 Mar. 1990.

239. NOTE 4: MSP, "Survey Results," 11 June 1990.

241–42. SIGNIFICANCE OF ASSISTANT PRINCIPAL'S BEING PASSED OVER: Evans interview; Kaeser interview.

242–43. DISTRICT'S PUBLISHED MISSION STATEMENT: "Annual Report 1990–91," Cleveland Heights–University Heights School District.

243. ACTIVISTS DECIDE TO APPOINT FOUR COORDINATORS: Carol King interview.

244. ACTIVISTS PREPARED TO COMPROMISE: Carol King interview.

244. SUPERINTENDENT SYMPATHIZES WITH ACTIVISTS' CONCERNS: Carol King interview.

244–45. MODEL SCHOOL PROJECT'S LACK OF PROGRESS REFLECTS POORLY ON FOUNDATION/DISTRICT: Daniels interview, 2 July 1990.

Epilogue

247–48. OUTCOME OF RESTRUCTURING EFFORTS ELSEWHERE: Elsberg, Ted. "In Our Opinion." Advertisement. *Education Week,* 3 Apr. 1991; Shanker, Albert. "Just Whose Opinion Was It Anyway?" Advertisement. *Education Week,* 29 May 1991; Peterson, Brian. "How School-Based

Management Is Faring in Miami." Letter to the editor. *Education Week,* 12 June 1991; Chira, Susan. "Rochester: An Uneasy Symbol of School Reform." *New York Times,* 10 Apr. 1991; Bradley, Ann. "Rochester Union, District Reach New Agreement." *Education Week,* 24 Apr. 1991; Bradley, Ann. "On Third Try, School Board and Teachers Agree on Two-Year Contract in Rochester." *Education Week,* 1 May 1991.

252. PRINCIPAL QUOTED: Bragg, Marsha Lynn. "New Heights Head Man Has Sights Set High." *SP,* 30 Aug. 1990.

252. "WALK ON WATER": Bragg, Marsha Lynn. "Superintendent Upbeat over Administrative Additions." *SP,* 21 June 1990.

252. COST AND EXTENT OF LOBBY RENOVATION: Barnett, Desmond. "Hallway Closed to Finish Renovations." *BG,* 18 Apr. 1991.

252. "ROTTEN": Shaddow interview, 26 Mar. 1991.

252. PRINCIPAL QUOTED ON ACADEMIC SUCCESS: Bragg, Marsha Lynn. "New Heights Head Man Has Sights Set High." *SP,* 30 Aug. 1990.

253. RETURN TO TRADITIONAL STRUCTURES: McBride interview, 28 Apr. 1992.

253. ONLY 20 PERCENT OF STUDENTS SERVED: Price interview.

253. "JUST LIKE HIS HAIR": Wolf interview, 19 Sept. 1991.

254. ASSISTANT PRINCIPAL CITED: Walter, Francis. Memorandum to the faculty of Heights High School, 19 Nov. 1990.

254. GANG PROBLEMS NONEXISTENT: Hicks, Desiree F. "'Ubiquitous' Principal Hailed for Positive Changes." *PD,* 25 Nov. 1990.

255. FORMER BOARD MEMBER QUOTED: Hathaway, Marlene. "Problems Demand Collective Attention." *SP,* 20 May 1993.

255. "STRAIGHT TALK": Shaddow, Charles M. "Making School the Place to Be." Letter to the editor. *PD,* 9 Feb. 1992.

255. SUSPENSIONS TEMPORARILY DECREASE: Mitchell, Tim. "In-School Detention." First semester 1989–90 report of the number, length, and causes of in-school detentions and suspensions, n.d., n.p.; Mitchell, Tim. "In-School Detention." First semester 1990–91 report of the number, length, and causes of in-school detentions and suspensions, n.d., n.p.

256. SHADDOW'S SUSPENSIONS SURPASS BURKETT'S: "Monitoring Report." Submitted to the Office for Civil Rights of the U.S. Department of Education by the Cleveland Heights–University Heights School District, Feb. 1992, G1.

256. THOSE SUSPENDED DISPROPORTIONATELY BLACK: "Monitoring Report." Submitted to the Office for Civil Rights of the U.S. Department of Education by the Cleveland Heights–University Heights School District, Feb. 1992, G1.

256. STANDARD STUDENTS ACCOUNT FOR GREATEST NUMBER OF THOSE REFERRED: "Monitoring Report." Submitted to the Office for Civil Rights of the U.S. Department of Education by the Cleveland Heights–University Heights School District, Feb. 1992, 18.

257. SUMMER INSTITUTE ENROLLMENT: Gearity interview, 21 July 1992.

258. REASON FOR GRIEVANCE AGAINST SCHOOL WITHIN A
     SCHOOL: Comments made by Gearity at 18 Feb. 1992 meeting with
     Steve Young and Mike Shaddow.
258. ULTERIOR MOTIVE FOR GRIEVANCE: Comments made by Lauree
     Gearity at 18 Feb. 1992 meeting with Steve Young and Mike Shaddow;
     comments made by Steve Young and union representative Stephen
     Titchenal at 24 Feb. 1992 Model School Planning Team meeting; Schmida
     interview.
259. SPEED OF CONTRACT NEGOTIATIONS: Bragg, Marsha Lynn.
     "Teachers Quick to OK New Pact." *SP*, 19 Dec. 1991.
259. SUPERINTENDENT COMMENDED: "Channels." Staff newsletter.
     Cleveland Heights–University Heights School District, Dec. 1991.
259. 1993–94 DEFICIT: Bragg, Marsha Lynn. "It's Official: Levy Set for 8.9
     Mills." *SP*, 12 Aug. 1993.
259. "TREMENDOUS FINANCIAL JEOPARDY": Bragg, Marsha Lynn.
     "It's Official: Levy Set for 8.9 Mills." *SP*, 12 Aug. 1993.
259. WHY SOME WHITES ALIENATED: Drexler, Michael. "Heights
     Schools Debate Grouping by Ability." *PD*, 29 Apr. 1992; Bragg, Marsha
     Lynn. "Grouping Decision Must Reflect Work That Went into It." Col-
     umn. *SP*, 29 Apr. 1993; Pollock interview.
259–60. RECOMMENDATION OF LAY COMMITTEE ON GROUPING:
     Bragg, Marsha Lynn. "Committee Recommends Grouping Change." *SP*,
     11 Feb. 1993.
260. SUPERINTENDENT MODIFIES PROPOSED GROUPING PLAN:
     "Board Unveils Four-Level Plan." *SP*, 6 May 1993.
260. GROUPING IN MIDDLE SCHOOLS RETAINED: "Heights Board
     Rejects Grouping Plan." *PD*, 22 Mar. 1994.
260. COMPLAINT FILED WITH OCR: Hicks, Desiree F. "Heights Schools
     Face Bias Probe." *PD*, 8 June 1994.
260. RESULTS OF FIRST PROFICIENCY TEST: Rutti, Ronald. "Test
     Scores Indicate Schools Have Math Problems to Solve." *PD*, 30 Jan. 1991;
     Bragg, Marsha Lynn. "School Leaders Give Mixed Grades to State Test."
     SP, 7 Feb. 1991.
261. "CAUSE FOR PANIC": MSP, "Proposal of the School-within-a-School
     Task Force," n.d., n.p.
262. RESULTS OF 1992 PROFICIENCY TEST: Theiss, Evelyn, and Desiree
     F. Hicks. "Math Figures Aren't Good." *PD*, 11 Feb. 1993.
262. NOTE 3: Bragg, Marsha Lynn. "Subjectivity, Confidentiality among NHS
     Questions." *SP*, 11 Feb. 1993.

Afterword

264. SIZE OF AMERICA'S HIGH SCHOOLS: Toch, 237.
265. CLARK CITED: *Dark Ghetto*, 112.

Bibliography

Author's Interviews

Administrators and Supervisory Personnel

Albert Abramovitz (9 May 1991, 21 May 1991); Patrick Bernardo (1 Aug. 1991); Hugh Burkett (27 July 1988, 4 Aug. 1988, 7 Sept. 1988, 24 Oct. 1988, 26 Oct. 1988, 15 Feb. 1989, 27 June 1989, 14 Sept. 1989, 29 Oct. 1989, 9 Mar. 1990, 14 June 1990, 15 June 1990, 28 June 1990, 16–17 Mar. 1991); Michael Ferrato (30 July 1991); Jeffrey Forman (24 May 1991); Lauree Gearity (27 Mar. 1991, 11 July 1991, 21 July 1992); Timothy Mitchell (6 May 1991); Clarence Mixon (31 May 1991); Irving Moskowitz (27 July 1988, 26 Sept. 1991); Larry Peacock (9 Aug. 1991, 14 Aug. 1991); Michael Shaddow (9 Jan. 1991, 26 Mar. 1991); Janet Tribble (22 Feb. 1991); Frank Walter (23 Feb. 1991, 13 Mar. 1991, 14 May 1991)

Teachers and Guidance Counselors

Ann Austin (27 Feb. 1991); Delores Ballard (14 Mar. 1991); Patricia Benedict (2 May 1991); JoAnne Broadbooks (12 Mar. 1991); James Blaine (6 Dec. 1990); Janet Cosner (14 Mar. 1991); Phyllis Fowlkes (27 Sept. 1988, 27 Feb. 1991); Joseph Geiger (26 Feb. 1991); Sam Guarino (11 Apr. 1991); Margie Harper (1 May 1991); Virginia Hellstern (14 Feb. 1991); Kerry Hodakievic (30 Apr. 1991); Henry Hudson (1 Mar. 1991); Carol King (7 June 1991); Jean King (5 June 1991); Gregg Krause (21 Mar. 1991); Jeanne Lee (5 Mar. 1991); Reva Leizman (20 Feb. 1991, 30 Apr. 1991); Cathleen McBride (24 July 1991, 28 Apr. 1992); Fred Mills (19 Feb. 1991); David Muthersbaugh (13 Mar. 1991); Kaye Price (22 Aug. 1991); Eugene Rackoff (4 Mar. 1991); Cal Rose (24 Feb. 1990, 28 Feb. 1991, 2 Aug. 1991, 14 April 1992); Carol Shiles (21 Feb. 1991, 10 May 1991); Rita Shtull (7 Aug. 1991); Beverly Simmons (22 May 1991); David Smith (24 Feb. 1990, 3 June 1991); Willie Smith (29 May 1991); John Stephens (13 Mar. 1991); Sylvia Stewart (24 May 1991); William Tarter (15 Mar. 1991); William Thomas (16 Feb. 1990, 11 June 1991); Fran Walter (2 Aug. 1989, 10 July 1991); Mary Watson (22 Mar. 1991, 16 May 1991, 25 July 1991); Mark Wessels (1 Mar. 1991); Allan Wolf (1 Aug. 1988, 3 Aug. 1988, 24 Oct. 1988, 11 Jan. 1989, 1 Apr. 1991, 19 Sept. 1991); Steven Young (25 Mar. 1991, 15 June 1992)

Board of Education

Russell Baron (13 July 1991); Steve Bullock (1 June 1994); Harvey Feinberg (10 Sept. 1991); Phillip Fine (20 Sept. 1991); E. D. Friedman (17 July 1991); Stuart Klein (25 May 1994); Maureen Weigand (19 May 1994)

Union and Association Representatives

Glenn Altschuld (29 July 1992); Ed Esch (13 June 1991); Frances Herskovitz (7 Aug. 1991); Daniel MacDonald (30 Nov. 1990, 3 May 1991, 4 June 1991, 11 June 1991, 10 July 1991, 23 July 1992); Robert Quail (8 Mar. 1991, 3 May 1991); Louis Salvator (18 July 1991); Tom Schmida (26 Aug. 1992); Ray Warner (20 Aug. 1991)

Students and Graduates

Bethany Aram (27 Aug. 1991); Marsha Lynn Bragg (18 Jan. 1991); David Budin (6 May 1991); Lucia DeLeon Colizoli (31 July 1991); Miguel Cora (14 May 1991); Benjamin Dooley (1 Apr. 1991); Lloyd Franklin (16 May 1991); James Heard (24 May 1991); Frank Hruby (25 Feb. 1991); Martin Kessler (21 Dec. 1990); Traci McLin (13 Sept. 1991); Cordell Pace (16 May 1991, 28 May 1991); Brooke Tierney (20 May 1991); Dion Walton (23 May 1991, 29 May 1991); Carol Willen (7 Dec. 1990); Ben Yarrow (16 Mar. 1991)

Parents and Community Leaders

Omar Ali-Bey (7 Sept. 1991); Doris Allen (18 July 1991); Donald Barclay (11 Sept. 1991); John J. Boyle (25 July 1991); Lana Cowell (17 Sept. 1991); Phyllis Evans (16 July 1991); Jayne Geneva (23 Sept. 1991); David Gunning (24 July 1991); Nita Heard (8 Aug. 1991); Luke Isler (16 July 1991); Saul Isler (9 July 1991); Susan Kaeser (17 July 1991); Robert L. Lewis (23 Sept. 1991); Lacy Lott (11 July 1991); Barbara Madison (19 Sept. 1991); Edward McKinney (24 Sept. 1991); Louisa Oliver (21 Aug. 1991); Marian Pledger (21 Aug. 1991); Martha Pollock (16 July 1992); Jan Resseger (23 Sept. 1991); Robert Simoneau (11 July 1991); Pat Solomon (14 Aug. 1991); Robert D. Storey (24 July 1991); David Sweet (30 July 1991); Hyla Winston (10 Oct. 1990, 3 Dec. 1990)

Government, Police, and Philanthropic Officials

Joyce Daniels (2 July 1990, 25 Mar. 1991); Arthur Lichtinger (22 Oct. 1991); C. J. Prentiss (17 Sept. 1991); Linda Schmidt (23 July 1991); Michael L. Walker (23 July 1991); James Williams (21 Aug. 1991); Victor Young (16 June 1988)

Miscellaneous

Howard Berger (9 Aug. 1991); Joseph Hannibal (16 Aug. 1991); Judah Rubenstein (17 July 1991); Ann Schorr (19 July 1991)

Books

Boyer, Ernest L. *High School: A Report on Secondary Education in America.* New York: Harper & Row, 1983.

Clark, Kenneth B. *Dark Ghetto: Dilemmas of Social Power.* New York: Harper & Row, 1965.

Conant, James Bryant. *The American High School Today: A First Report to Interested Citizens.* New York: McGraw-Hill, 1959.

Cremin, Lawrence A. *American Education: The Metropolitan Experience, 1876–1980.* New York: Harper & Row, 1988.

Cusick, Philip A. *The Egalitarian Ideal and the American High School: Studies of Three Schools.* New York: Longman, 1983.

Fantini, Mario, Marilyn Gittell, and Richard Magat. *Community Control and the Urban School.* New York: Praeger, 1970.

Freedman, Samuel G. *Small Victories: The Real World of a Teacher, Her Students, and Their High School.* New York: Harper & Row, 1990.

Glasser, William. *The Quality School: Managing Students without Coercion.* New York: Harper & Row, 1990.

Goodlad, John I. *The Dynamics of Educational Change: Toward Responsive Schools.* New York: McGraw-Hill, 1975.

———. *A Place Called School: Prospects for the Future.* New York: McGraw-Hill, 1984.

Harris, Mary Emma, and Ruth Mills Robinson. *The Proud Heritage of Cleveland Heights, Ohio.* Cleveland: Howard Allen, n.d.

Hirsch, E. D., Jr. *Cultural Literacy: What Every American Needs to Know.* Boston: Houghton Mifflin, 1987.

Holt, John. *How Children Fail.* New York: Delacorte/Seymour Lawrence, 1982.

Jones, Suzanne Ringler, ed. *In Our Day: Cleveland Heights, Its People, Its Places, Its Past.* Cleveland Heights: Heights Community Congress, ca. 1982.

Kidder, Tracy. *Among Schoolchildren.* Boston: Houghton Mifflin, 1989.

Kozol, Jonathan. *Death at an Early Age: The Destruction of the Hearts and Minds of Negro Children in the Boston Public Schools.* New York: New American Library, 1967.

———. *Savage Inequalities: Children in America's Schools.* New York: Crown, 1991.

Kunjufu, Jawanza. *Countering the Conspiracy to Destroy Black Boys, Volume II.* Chicago: African American Images, 1986.

Lagemann, Ellen Condliffe. *The Politics of Knowledge: The Carnegie Corporation, Philanthropy and Public Policy.* Middletown, Conn.: Wesleyan Univ. Press, 1989.

Lightfoot, Sara Lawrence. *The Good High School: Portraits of Character and Culture.* New York: Basic Books, 1983.

Lortie, Dan C. *Schoolteacher: A Sociological Study.* Chicago: Univ. of Chicago Press, 1975.

Maeroff, Gene I. *The Empowerment of Teachers: Overcoming the Crisis of Confidence.* New York: Teachers College Press, 1988.

Meyer, Adolphe E. *An Educational History of the Western World.* New York: McGraw-Hill, 1965.

Oakes, Jeannie. *Keeping Track: How Schools Structure Inequality.* New Haven: Yale Univ. Press, 1985.

Powell, Arthur G., Eleanor Farrar, and David K. Cohen. *The Shopping Mall High School: Winners and Losers in the Educational Marketplace.* Boston: Houghton Mifflin, 1985.

Ravitch, Diane. *The Troubled Crusade: American Education 1945–1980.* New York: Basic Books, 1983.

Rogers, David. *110 Livingston Street: Politics and Bureaucracy in the New York City Schools.* New York: Random House, 1968.

Sarason, Seymour B. *The Culture of the School and the Problem of Change.* Boston: Allyn and Bacon, 1982.

———. *The Predictable Failure of Education Reform: Can We Change Course before It's Too Late?* San Francisco: Jossey-Bass, 1991.

Schlecty, Phillip C. *Schools for the Twenty-first Century: Leadership Imperatives for Educational Reform.* San Francisco: Jossey-Bass, 1990.

Selden, David. *The Teacher Rebellion.* Washington, D.C.: Howard Univ. Press, 1985.

Silberman, Charles E. *Crisis in the Classroom: The Remaking of American Education.* New York: Random House, 1970.

Sizer, Theodore R. *Horace's Compromise: The Dilemma of the American High School.* Boston: Houghton Mifflin, 1984.

———. *Horace's School: Redesigning the American High School.* Boston: Houghton Mifflin, 1992.

Steele, Shelby. *The Content of Our Character: A New Vision of Race in America.* New York: St. Martin's, 1990.

Toch, Thomas. *In the Name of Excellence: The Struggle to Reform the Nation's Schools, Why It's Failing, and What Should Be Done.* New York: Oxford Univ. Press, 1991.

Reports

Committee on Policy for Racial Justice. *Visions of a Better Way: A Black Appraisal of Public Schooling.* Washington, D.C.: Joint Center for Political Studies Press, 1989.

Edmonds, Ronald. *A Discussion of the Literature and Issues Related to Effective Schooling.* St. Louis: CEMREL, Inc., 1979.

Educational Tracking: The System's Response to Black Migration. Urban League of Greater Cleveland, 1980.

Heights Commission on Excellence and Equity in Education. "Report." Submitted to the Cleveland Heights–University Heights Board of Education, 4 Feb. 1991.

Hellwig, Clay. "More about 'The Proud Heritage.'" Pamphlet. Cleveland, 1980.

Kaeser, Susan C. *Citizens Guide to Children Out of School.* Cleveland: Citizens' Council for Ohio Schools, 1984.

National Center for Effective Schools. *A Conversation between James Comer and Ronald Edmonds: Fundamentals of Effective School Improvement.* Dubuque, Iowa: Kendall/Hunt, 1989.

A Nation at Risk: The Imperative for Educational Reform. National Commission on Excellence in Education, 1983.

A Nation Prepared: Teachers for the Twenty-first Century. Task Force on Teachers as a Profession, Carnegie Forum on Education and the Economy, Carnegie Corporation of New York, May 1986.

Poverty Indicators: Trends 1970–1990, Cuyahoga County, Ohio. Council for Economic Opportunities in Greater Cleveland, 1990.

School Consensus Project. "First Year Report of the Task Force." Submitted to the Cleveland Heights–University Heights Board of Education, Heights Community Congress, and Heights Interfaith Council, Oct. 1986.

———. "Second Year Report of the Task Force." Submitted to the Cleveland Heights–University Heights Board of Education, Heights Community Congress, and Heights Interfaith Council, June 1987.

———. "Excellence and Equity: A Report to the Community." Oct. 1987.

Index

Urban Life and Urban Landscape Series
Zane L. Miller and Henry D. Shapiro,
General Editors

The series examines the history of urban life and the development of the urban landscape through works that place social, economic, and political issues in the intellectual and cultural context of their times.